GROUPS IN CONTEXT

GROUPS IN CONTEXT

A New Perspective on Group Dynamics

Jonathon Gillette and
Marion McCollom,
Editors

ADDISON-WESLEY PUBLISHING COMPANY, INC.
Reading, Massachusetts   Menlo Park, California   New York
Don Mills, California   Wokingham, England   Amsterdam   Bonn
Sydney   Singapore   Tokyo   Madrid   San Juan

Library of Congress Cataloging-in-Publication Data

Groups in context : a new perspective on group dynamics / Jonathon
   Gillette and Marion McCollom, editors.
      p.   cm.
   Includes bibliographical references.
   ISBN 0-201-09504-1
   1. Small groups.   I. Gillette, Jonathon.   II. McCollom, Marion.
   HM133.G758   1990
   302.3'4—dc20   89-29191

Copyright © 1990 by Addison-Wesley Publishing Company, Inc.

Cover design by Amy MacGregor
Text design by Carson Design, Manchester, MA
Set in 10-pt. Trump Mediaeval by ITC

ABCDEFGHIJ–MA–9543210
First printing, March 1990

ACKNOWLEDGMENTS

As editors of this volume, we give our acknowledgments primarily to our contributors—our teachers, students, and colleagues—for their work in creating the community from which we draw personal and professional support. We want in particular to recognize Clay Alderfer and David Berg for their labor of love in designing and developing a tradition of experiential education at Yale; indirectly, through the programs they shaped, and directly, through their teaching, they have enriched our own and others' lives.

In addition, there are others who, though not represented in this volume, have played key roles in supporting us. For Marion, these people include her colleagues at Boston University, who are committed to bridging theory and practice, who provide mentoring and friendship, who set high standards, and who enjoy their work. The Organizational Behavior Department there has proved to be a fertile ground to develop skills, try new ideas, and nurture a professional identity.

For Jack, students and clients over the years have enriched the learning process by being both demanding and willing to engage their experiences with emerging theories. His wife, Joanie's, daily work experiences have also provided a reminder of the enormous complexities of human behavior. This has been an important lesson that the value of a theory lies in its practical application.

Finally, this section would be incomplete if we did not acknowledge each other. A working partnership that really "works" is rare and valuable; over the years, we have learned to respect each other, disagree with each other, and listen to each other. Working together in the field, as well as in print, has been deeply rewarding.

Jonathon Gillette   Marion McCollom
New Haven, CT   Boston, MA

February, 1990

CONTENTS

CONTRIBUTORS

Clayton P. Alderfer, Ph.D., is professor of organizational behavior at the Yale School of Management, where he has served as associate dean for professional studies and director of graduate studies in organizational behavior for the Graduate School of Arts and Sciences. A winner of awards for research and author of several books and more than sixty articles on human needs, group and intergroup relations, personality and leadership, race relations, and organizational diagnosis, he is editor of the *Journal of Applied Behavioral Science.*

David N. Berg, Ph.D., is a professor in the practice of clinical methods at Yale. His professional interests are in group and intergroup relations, clinical research methods, and the dynamics of collaboration.

Jonathon Gillette, Ph.D., is currently an independent consultant specializing in public school restructuring. The interaction of theory and practice are a central part of his consultation. Dr. Gillette received his doctorate in organizational behavior from Yale University.

Edward B. Klein, Ph.D., is professor, Department of Psychology, University of Cincinnati; faculty member, Cincinnati Psychoanalytic Institute; board member, A. K. Rice Institute; and coauthor of *Seasons of a Man's Life.* Dr. Klein's interest in groups, social systems, and adult development are reflected in teaching, research, consultation, clinical work, and his chapter in this volume.

James Krantz, Ph.D., is assistant professor at the Yale School of Organization and Management. His research interests include organizational design and its impact upon collaboration, the unconscious background to work and organization, and the changing character of professional practice in postindustrial society. Professor Krantz received his doctorate in social systems sciences from the Wharton School of the University of Pennsylvania.

Vicki Van Steenberg LaFarge, Ph.D., is an assistant professor of management at Bentley College, where she teaches courses in organizational behavior and group dynamics. Her recent research includes a study of termination issues for employees leaving their jobs.

Mark Leach is a consultant and researcher specializing in group and intergroup relations, organizational diagnosis and change, and multiorganization collaboration. As an associate at the Institute for Development Research, he works with managers of social change and third-world economic development organizations. Also a consultant with the Kaleel Jamison Consulting Group, Mr. Leach holds an M.P.P.M. degree from the Yale School of Organization and Management and is a doctoral candidate at Boston University in organizational behavior.

Marion McCollom, Ph.D., is assistant professor of organizational behavior at the Boston University School of Management. She teaches and consults in the areas of group dynamics and conflict and change processes in organizations. Her research focuses on organizational subcultures, on the function of organizational narratives, and on family-business relationships in family firms.

Kenwyn K. Smith, Ph.D., is a member of the Organizational Behavior Group at the Wharton School of the University of Pennsylvania. His research interests are group dynamics, organizational diagnosis and change, and social epistemology. His two most recent books, both with David Berg, are *Paradoxes of Group Life* and *The Self and Social Inquiry*.

David A. Thomas, Ph.D., is assistant professor of management at the Wharton School of the University of Pennsylvania. He conducts research on intergroup relations and organizational change. Dr. Thomas is also involved in the application of group dynamics and systems theory in action research with organizations.

Leroy Wells, Jr., Ph.D., is associate professor of business and public administration at Howard University. Dr. Wells writes on unconscious processes in groups. He is an associate of the Washington Baltimore Center of the A. K. Rice Institute and a member of the National Training Laboratory Institute.

GROUPS IN
CONTEXT

Introduction

The Emergence of a New
Experiential Tradition

MARION McCOLLOM AND
JONATHON GILLETTE

This book attempts to reclaim the relevance and vitality of small group analysis by integrating it into, instead of separating it from, general theories about organizational processes and management practices. Our goal is to provide a framework, both conceptual and methodological, for those who work with and teach about groups. In short, we want to establish a bridge between theory (in the small group, intergroup, and organizational areas) and practice.

This book is rooted in the theoretical and applied work on groups that has been ongoing over the last fifteen years at the Yale School of Organization and Management (SOM). Field research and consulting projects on group and intergroup relations in organizations, and courses on group dynamics and organizational diagnosis, have led to the creation of a rich interpretive frame of analysis. Small-group processes are understood by looking not just at the group itself but also at issues and influences in the larger organizational context. In this volume, we attempt to capture and share the resulting learnings about groups, their dynamics, and the ways one can intervene to change them.

The perspective we describe developed in part within an experientially based course on group dynamics, taught within the management curriculum at the Yale SOM (see Van Steenberg and Gillette, 1984, for a description of the course). The course has provided an opportunity for faculty members and graduate students to explore how group processes unfold and how they are influenced by the institutional context of the group.

Most of the contributors to this book draw their data from experiential groups like those created in the Yale group dynamics course, although some rely as well on groups formed in conferences, consultation projects, or training work. The theoretical content of group dynamics instruction, the influence of context on groups courses, and the consultant experience in working with such groups constitute the core material of the book. However, the authors provide more than specialized advice for small-group instructors; they contribute significant new theoretical perspectives to the field, important insights into group process, and new applications of group theory, useful to all practitioners who work with groups.

ORIENTATION TO THE TRADITION

In order to explain the "perspective" presented here, we need to acquaint readers with the type of group examined in these chapters ("experiential") and to explain the relationship of the new perspective to two prominent schools of experiential group training. An experiential group is charged with learning about group processes; members accomplish this task by examining their own group's dynamics as they unfold in real time (in the "here-and-now"). Typically, these groups are facilitated by one or two consultants, or "trainers." Experiential group instruction is used as a learning or training technique in undergraduate and graduate school curricula, in management training programs, and in organizational intervention projects.

Experiential learning groups may be clearly distinguished from other self-analytic groups in their purpose and in the way they are conducted. They focus primarily on developing members' understanding of group-level processes and of their own behavior in groups. They are not therapy groups, in which the focus is on individual intrapsychic growth and recovery (Frank, 1964), or encounter groups, in which the purpose is to allow members to experiment with the direct expression of their feelings (O'Day, 1974).

Two organizations have been particularly influential in the development of experiential group instruction. The National Training Laboratories (NTL) in 1951 began a program of experiential learning in T-(Training) groups, in which the focus was on developing interpersonal skills and understanding change processes (Benne, 1964). NTL courses continue to emphasize interpersonal communication, individual role-taking in the group, and perceptions of self and others in the group. The objectives of the instruction are personal growth, interpersonal competence, and behavioral change.

The A. K. Rice Institute (an American offshoot of the British Tavistock Institute) has run experiential group relations conferences since 1965. The conferences focus on small group dynamics but also on intergroup relationships within the larger institution (the conference) (Rioch, 1975). The A. K. Rice conferences offer little or no didactic content and focus primarily on authority relations between conference staff and members. Members are given the opportunity to apply conference learning to their outside organizational roles.

The perspective we present here draws on both the NTL and A. K. Rice traditions, although it is focused less on the individual and on interpersonal relationships than is the former and is more didactic than the latter. Three features identify and differentiate this "new tradition":

- the tradition is located within, and reflective of, the multidisciplinary field of organizational behavior;
- the tradition is anchored in open systems and psychodynamic theory but offers a distinctive synthesis of academic perspectives;
- practitioners in the tradition rely on theory to inform method, and vice versa.

In addition, we recognize the influence of our own activities on groups and other human systems and use our own experience as data about the dynamics of these systems (see Berg and Smith, 1985, defining "clinical" methods for social research and practice).

We will explore these three points in more depth, as they create the threads that link the variety of perspectives and topics contained in the chapters that follow.

The Disciplinary Perspective of Organizational Behavior

Organizational behavior (OB) is an interdisciplinary field that brings together clinical, social, and industrial psychology; sociology; anthropology; management theory; and other disciplines. It is distinguished from other fields primarily by its concern with human systems at multiple levels—individual, group, and organizational—and by its application to the workplace. OB writers describing groups, for example, acknowledge the individual group member's experience, the group process and output, and the environmental context of the group all as important components of group theory.

The OB perspective on small groups is thus different from that of either sociology or psychology (Katz and Kahn, 1978). In the formulation of Olmsted and Hare (1978), sociology has sought to examine the external aspects of group life, while psychology has looked into the internal terrain of groups. Thus sociologists see "societies as (composed of) groups" while psychologists see "groups as societies" (Olmsted and Hare, 1978, p. 16).

The difference between these two views, and the distinct perspective of OB, are sharply reflected in definitions of "group" that have been employed by each discipline. The sociologist Albion Small offered the following definition in 1905: "The term 'group' serves as a convenient sociological designation for any number of people, larger or smaller, between whom such relations are discovered that they must be thought of together" (Small, 1905, p. 495).

This definition reflects the sociologist's interest in the societal roles of groups. Olmsted and Hare (1978) presented a fuller definition that reflects the psychologist's view: "A group may be defined as a plurality of individuals who are in contact with one another, who take one another into account, and who are aware of some significant commonality" (p. 21).

Here the attention is more internally focused; what is lost is the sense of any interaction with nonmembers. A definition utilized in OB gives a more complete sense of both the internal and external terrain of a group. From Alderfer (1984):

> A human group is a collection of individuals (1) who have significantly interdependent relations with each other, (2) who perceive themselves as a group, reliably distinguishing members from nonmembers, (3) whose group identity is recognized by nonmembers, (4) who, as group members acting alone or in concert, have significantly interdependent relations with other groups, and (5) whose roles in the group are therefore a function of expectations from themselves, from other group members, and from non-group members (p. 39).

A group is defined here by individual members' experience, by the relationships among members, and by members' relations with nonmembers. The "new tradition" we describe here requires maintaining a complex view of the simultaneous influences on group dynamics created at different levels of the social system in which the group exists.

The Theoretical Framework

This new perspective of understanding and teaching about groups is built on several familiar theoretical foundations. The first conceptual model is provided by the application of open systems theory to social structures such as groups and organizations (Katz and Kahn, 1978; Homans, 1950; Likert, 1967). Groups, for instance, are seen as comprising interrelated subsystems and as open to environmental influence (Morgan, 1986). (The application of this theory to groups and organizations is spelled out in more detail in Chapter 2.) The model provides explanations of the structural relationships among group members, the processes behind group dynamics, and the influence upon a group of its organizational setting.

The second central theoretical model is psychodynamic theory, in which unconscious processes are assumed to drive many aspects of human behavior. Although Freud, Jung, and others wrote about unconscious processes in larger collectives, the psychodynamic model derives from theories at the individual (really, intrapsychic) level. The idea that individual behavior in groups is motivated by internal unconscious thoughts and emotions provides an explanatory framework for how individual group members perceive themselves and others and for how they behave.

Over the last forty years, these two theoretical traditions have been synthesized into a third, which may be labeled loosely as the "group dynamics" literature. Within this area, with some exceptions, writers have tended to focus on either organizational or group-level processes. The organization school is represented in the work of key Tavistock Institute and A. K. Rice thinkers (Rice, 1963; Menzies, 1975; Jaques, 1974). These writers describe the unconscious processes that characterize human experience in social systems. "Rational" processes in organizations—hierarchical structures, task performance, and managerial decision-making, for example—are seen as serving emotional functions, including defending organization members against anxiety. Writers in this tradition focus on the concept of boundaries as the key linkage between systems and psychodynamic theories (see, for example, Miller and Rice, 1967).

The researchers focusing primarily on groups come from a variety of backgrounds: group psychotherapy (Bion, 1959; Whitaker and Lieberman, 1964); academic social science research and teaching (Bales, 1950; Slater, 1967; Mann, 1967); and management consultation and training (Bennis and Shepard, 1974; Bradford, Gibb, and Benne, 1964). These writers have focused on how unconscious processes drive behavior in groups and how group dynamics unfold over time. Group context is relatively deemphasized in this research.

Borrowing from both schools, the perspective presented here sees a group as a distinct phenomenon whose characteristics are created by the shared unconscious and conscious experiences of members as well as by the context of the group. Thus the primary level of analysis is the group, and models of group-level phenomena are theoretical cornerstones (see Wells, 1980, and Smith and Berg, 1987, for example). However, the context of the group is understood to be a major influence on group process; group behavior, therefore, is interpreted based on a thorough understanding of the multiple environments in which group members are acting (Alderfer, 1977, illustrates this type of analysis).

The theoretical theme that runs through this book is that small group dynamics are distinct processes that interact with individual members' emotions and personalities, with the dynamics of the larger systems in which the group is embedded, and also with the specific task of the group. This approach clearly distinguishes the chapters in this volume from other streams of work on groups. A group is not seen primarily as the intersection of individual members' experience nor predominantly as a microcosm of a larger system.

The implication of this approach is that interpretations of group behavior utilize individual and contextual data but begin and end at the group level. For example, an individual's personality may lead her to take a predictable role in groups; however, the key group-level question is, why is the group using this person in this way at this time? Similarly, men and women will bring their historical antagonisms into groups, but the principal diagnostic question is why, right now, in this group, are these men and women fighting one another?

Bridging Theory and Practice

The goal of practitioners working with this perspective is to bring a sophisticated theory of group dynamics to our work. Specific instructional and consultation methods vary, depending on the purpose of the work: for example, to generate individual learning, to enhance group effectiveness, or to facilitate organizational change. However, the perspective is reflected in an iterative linkage between group theory and professional practice, in which each is used continually to inform the other. (See Alderfer's diagram of the theory-social technology-data cycle in Chapter 9.)

In addition, this approach requires that the practitioner's own presence and activities become a part of the analysis. Given the simultaneous influence of multiple levels of the system (from systems theory) and the inherent contradictions and confusions created by the mix of conscious and unconscious intents in human behavior (from psychodynamic theory), effective instruction or intervention is difficult to achieve. The powerful forces that lock group members into unproductive behaviors easily capture those working with a group. The challenge is to acknowledge the complex dynamics of the system *and the practitioner's own involvement in those dynamics* without losing sight of the goals of the work. Practitioners must conceptualize the impact of their work on the group and its context, and understand the impact of these systems on themselves and their work.

HISTORY OF THE BOOK PROJECT

This book has been for both of us a project to establish our own distinct professional perspectives while acknowledging our debt to and our membership in the Yale tradition. After leaving the Ph.D. program in organizational behavior, we have followed different paths. Jack is an organizational consultant, working alone or with others, specializing in educational systems. From 1984 to 1989, he taught the group dynamics course at the Yale SOM. Marion has taken an academic route; she is a faculty member in the department of organizational behavior at the Boston University School of Management. Her energy is directed toward teaching and research, although she also maintains a consulting practice.

We initially conceived of the book as an opportunity to record and disseminate the perspective of our graduate training. While we were in the doctoral program at Yale, learnings about small group theory and practice were passed among faculty members and students as a result of working relationships within courses or consultation work or research projects. However, key concepts and models often remained unwritten or appeared in informal lecture notes that literally were handed from one teaching assistant to the next each year. Occasionally, fragments of the tradition appeared within the written work of individual faculty members and students. We decided to make sure that what for us was an extremely valuable oral tradition was recorded as a whole and preserved.

To achieve this end, we invited the participation of others who had been a part of this tradition. The contributors as a group share the commonalities and diversity of the editorial pair. All were students and/or faculty members within the organizational behavior program at Yale. Like the editors, most stand profesionally on one side or the other of the theory-practice bridge, but all are committed to maintaining a presence in both worlds. Some are primarily academics who have applied theory to practice; others are consultants who draw on theory to inform their work. Most have years of experience in the classroom and/or the world of consultation.

Looking at the group of contributors from a generational perspective, it is possible to identify at least four generations of teacher-student relationships. Despite the history of hierarchical relationships (or perhaps because of it, as ideas have flowed from student to teacher, as well as vice versa), the contributors now function primarily as colleagues and as members of a larger community.

Changes in this community created new meaning for the project after it was underway. First, the editors realized that neither we nor the contributors were interested in simply preserving the past. Each of us continues to push ahead in our work with groups. What became exciting was the idea of soliciting the work of contributors who were familiar with the tradition but who were continuing to develop their individual approaches to theory and practice. The book represents, then, the continuing evolution of a tradition, not some rarefied "knowledge" developed ten or twenty years ago and passed along intact.

Second, although we understood the book as a termination project—that is, as a way for us to come to terms with leaving a system to which we were deeply attached—we did not know the full extent to which this would be true. The appointment of a new dean at the Yale SOM in 1988 led to the termination of all junior organizational behavior faculty contracts, to the elimination of small group courses within the management curriculum, and to the dismantlement of the OB doctoral program. Thus, although the tradition will continue at other institutions through the work of these contributors and others, the system that fostered its evolution will have ceased to exist by 1990.

The termination of the experiential tradition within organizational behavior at Yale itself points to the importance of this book. The study of group processes, especially on the irrational and unconscious level, is difficult to manage within any institutional context. As both Alderfer and Krantz note in their chapters (and as Jaques, Menzies, and others might predict), acknowledging the inherent confusion and uncertainty of human experience in organizations is threatening to institutional needs for order and certainty. In addition, a program that explores the limits of its own understanding can easily find itself undermined in the volatile political environment of academia. Ironically, the irrationality displayed in the way the program was dismantled underlines the importance of continued research and practice in the field.

THE STRUCTURE OF THE BOOK

The structure and contents of this book reflect our objective of bridging theory and practice within the same volume. The three sections of the book discuss the basic theoretical content of group dynamics instruction, the influence of organizational context on experiential group learning, and the experience of the consultant working with an experiential group.

In the first section, the authors offer important contributions to the literature on small groups. Some chapters contain new theory; others offer reviews of or new perspectives on existing small group theory. To facilitate the application of theory to instructional practice, the topics in this section are arranged so that instruction can track the sequence of developmental stages in the learning group (that is, moving from formation to termination).

Gillette's chapter introduces a *method* of learning about groups, laying out a framework for how group experience can be translated into learning. Next, McCollom integrates theory on boundaries and culture into a discussion of group formation and leadership. We then reprint Wells's ground breaking article explaining the group-level concept of "group-as-a-whole."

New theoretical formulations of central group processes follow: Gillette argues that intimacy in work groups must be framed in the context of multiple levels of influence, and that a major challenge is negotiating openness and disclosure in a way that maintains a line between the individual's public and private self. Next, Berg and Smith summarize their work on paradoxical processes in groups; this perspective represents a fundamental reframing of how groups address and work through key issues. McCollom then reviews and critiques the literature on group development, arguing that stage models do not ask the right questions nor provide convincing answers to improve our understanding of how groups change over time.

Thomas explores the systematic neglect of application work

in group dynamics study and offers thoughts about how application topics can be integrated into the curriculum.

In the final chapter of Section One, Van Steenberg LaFarge applies her research on termination in organizations to develop a framework for analyzing termination processes in small groups.

In the second section, "Creating a Context for Group Learning," the contributors explore the impact of institutional context on group process and output. Looking at learning groups in various environments, they examine how setting influences group dynamics and discuss the implications of this understanding for course design. Alderfer identifies the necessary conditions for teaching experiential groups, describing the social and institutional influences on his work with one course at Yale. Krantz illustrates the complexities of learning contexts in a comparison of classroom and conference settings. The impact of the consultant's identity on the nature and outcome of group consultation, given events in the larger system, is addressed by Klein.

Section Three offers a framework for understanding the group consultation process, as contributors describe their views of and experience with the dilemmas of group training. Alderfer provides an overview of the issues of authority and leadership for experiential training staffs: the capacities required to do the work, the demands of the task, and the roles and styles that group consultants often adopt. Smith's chapter articulates a sophisticated set of guidelines for group consultants in using the "self" as an instrument in group work. Finally, Leach and Berg present reciprocal views of the supervision relationship in a group training setting, Leach analyzing his experience of authorization as a consultant trainee and Berg reflecting on his experience as a supervisor.

We hope that this volume will make a contribution to the understanding of small groups in three ways: in developing theory, in enhancing practice, and in illuminating application. We have striven to reflect an integrated and comprehensive theoretical perspective on small groups: we have included theory about a variety of dimensions of group life and we have looked at groups in *context*. This should give academics and other social science practitioners the opportunity to reexamine the validity of small group models, as they fit (or don't fit) with individual- and organization-level theory.

The focus on theory should also help improve practice with small groups. We argue that practitioners need to consider theory carefully, in order to explore and criticize the often unarticulated assumptions that drive their decisions about how they work. In addition, the second and third sections of the book—on the context of group learning and the experience of consulting—should serve as a resource for practitioners facing the difficult dilemmas posed by groups. Our hope is that the book will both enhance competence in group training as well as establish an agenda for areas in which more work is needed.

Finally, we want to reinforce the relevance of research on and practice with small groups by focusing in this volume on the application of this work to organizational life. Explanations of human experience in organizations are incomplete if they do not include group-level analysis. Group membership has a profound effect on the behaviors and attitudes of managers and workers; understanding group process is crucial to the development of valid diagnoses of organizational dynamics and of successful intervention strategies. This new perspective on group dynamics should result in clearer insight into managerial and organizational dilemmas.

ADVANCING THE GROUP DYNAMICS THEORY

Chapter 1

Toward a Practice of Learning

JONATHON GILLETTE

INTRODUCTION

The scene is a hospital staff meeting. It is fifteen minutes after the starting time, and still the members have not turned their attention to the work at hand. The hospital administrator looks to the chief medical resident to get things started, but she is busy in conversation with one of the staff nurses about a patient treatment. After another five minutes have passed, the administrator attempts to pull the group together. As he starts, he feels a gnawing insecurity growing that he is not going to be able to get the group to accomplish what needs doing in the forty-five minutes left. Sure enough, side issues, personal bickering, and drifting attention all lead to an incomplete discussion. As the administrator tries to schedule a follow-up meeting, half the members leave, including the chief resident, complaining that they are late for other work. The administrator feels defeated.

This scenario is unfortunately all too familiar to anyone who has worked in a group setting. While group work can be exciting and energizing, it can also generate frustration, anger, and even a sense of hopelessness. I can recall many times when I am left, at the end of a group meeting, shaking my head and wondering what in the world has just been going on. Despite many years of training, I can still be dumbfounded by the complexity of group processes.

How can an individual begin to address such complexity? How in the case above can the administrator get the group to work more effectively? One avenue is to try to learn more about the basic dynamics of the group. The assumption is that what you eventually do to manage or even just participate in a work group is affected by your understanding of the situation. Further, the more informed the understanding, the more effective the action. The more the administrator can learn about what is influencing the members of the hospital staff *during that meeting,* the more effective he will be as a manager and as a group member.

But what does learning in such an on-line situation involve? Is it really possible to understand the group in the middle of the pressure of immediate events? While experience can be a great teacher, what exactly is it that is learned? What about all the theories and concepts about groups learned at graduate school? How do they fit in?

This chapter examines how you can develop an approach to learning about groups when there is a significant on-line experiential context. This approach is titled a "practice of learning," where practice means a *method* of action or working. Such a practice is developed from experiences, from examination of theories, and from efforts to bring theory and experience together.

The practice of learning can be understood in a conceptual *structure* that takes into account four specific types of learning contexts. An on-line context consists of the time when the learner is involved directly in the work group dynamics, as, for example, the administrator is in the events portrayed at the beginning of the chapter. An off-line context is when the learner is not meeting with the group but is either at work elsewhere in the organization or off from work. The two additional contexts are the transitions from on to off and from off to on. Each context presents different opportunities for learning and demands a different set of skills.

The practice of learning is also developmental. That is, learners move from being novice learners toward expertise as they become familiar with the method and gain greater command over the skills. This development requires more than the passage of time; it requires that the learner practice the "practice." Iterative moments of pulling together theory and experience, on-line and off-line, create the foundation for growth.

This framework was originally developed from my experience as a teacher in two particular school settings, a management school and a nursing school, and is informed by the various small group and organization theories I use to make sense of the world. Management students applied the practice to studying small group dynamics, while the nursing students applied the practice to studying their organizational work placements. Although both settings were schools, both shared four important elements.

First, each class had a significant experiential component. In the management class, weekly self-study groups engaged in the primary task of learning about small group dynamics as they emerged in the here and now. In the nursing school class, each of the students worked up to twenty hours a week in a health-care organization. The learning, then, presumed a member role in some working group. The goal was to deal with what it meant to be working and learning simultaneously.

Second, each class was in a university setting: that is, it was embedded in a larger context. In essence, each was a working group within a larger working institution. Thus, the students' perspective was created by their membership in both the larger system and the small group.

Third, students found a great deal of support for certain kinds of skills and activities in the larger system and less support for other kinds of skills and activities. Cognitive and conceptual work, in the two classes I taught, were valued over emotional work.

Finally, while the courses did have a definite beginning and an end, members moved from the course work group to the larger environment and back again. The experience was contained neither physically nor temporally.

In sum, the practice of learning emerges from the perspective of a group member, from simultaneous small group and organizational membership, and from the passage of time. Since this particular learning model was derived from my experience with two experientially based classes, another course or training design might call for a different learning process. My hope is that readers can use the outline of this model to understand how to develop a practice of learning in other settings. To return to the hospital administrator, my hope is that he, by reading this chapter, could build an approach to learning that would enable him to deal with the work group more effectively.

THE PRACTICE OF LEARNING IN GROUPS

There are a number of theorists who have examined experiential learning (Kolb, 1984; Schon, 1983; Benner, 1984). Much of their work seeks to bridge the gap that traditionally has existed between theory and experience; schools teach theory, while life on the job provides the experiences. Schon (1983) and Benner (1984) have pointed out how highly skilled professionals utilize both theory and experience *in their practice.* In describing how nurses move from novice to expert, Benner writes, "As the nurse gains experience, clinical knowledge, that is a hybrid between naive practical knowledge and unrefined theoretical knowledge, develops" (p. 8).

Some of these same theorists have proposed models or steps in the learning process. Kolb points to a cycle that moves from concrete experience to reflective observation to abstract conceptualization to active experimentation. Schon proposes a similar cycle that moves from experience to reflection and back. These models provide an important starting place for understanding a practice of learning, but they are limited. They do not address how one can manage simultaneous group and organizational memberships nor how learning relates to the crossing of temporal boundaries around the group.

Central to the model presented here is the delineation of "on-line" and "off-line" time periods. On-line consists of the times when the working group is in formal session. During that time the group members are engaged collectively in the here-and-now dynamics. Off-line consists of times when the group is not in formal session, but the members are still within the larger organization. While this may seem like an obvious division, what is not obvious is that the conditions and processes of learning in each situation are qualitatively different. Further, on-line and off-line dynamics influence each other in very specific ways, and different opportunities emerge for members as they pass from on-line to off-line and vice versa. Developing a practice of learning involves recognizing different activities in each time phase and requires a sensitivity to their interaction. The four stages of the cycle—on-line, transition to off-line, off-line, and transition to on-line—are examined below.

On-Line

The on-line stage is often described as the most involving and overwhelming time period. Members comment, "I got caught up with the process and found it hard to even remember what happened, much less whether I learned anything." On the other hand, on-line time is the opportunity to engage the process directly. Developing a practice of learning in this stage requires the integration of three skills: the ability *to experience,* to be in, to be open to the forces at work within the group; the ability *to reflect,* to step out, to generate a process of critical judgments; the ability *to manage these two states,* to be able to judge how to balance the two.

Experience. The ability to experience consists of attending to and being open to both feelings and thoughts. Being open requires emotional and intellectual energy. Emotionally, it is difficult to be open in unstructured, often chaotic, situations. The degree of uncertainty and intensity often found in experiential groups generates tremendous forces for safety and certainty. Complexities are often only partially engaged as members shrink back from the realization that they have no idea what is going on. It takes energy to retain the contradictions and ambiguities that are present in every moment of group life.

In addition, staying open requires not only emotional energy but courage. As Smith and Berg (1987) note, "It demands courage to fully *belong* to a group, to struggle with forming an identity through involvement with others. . . . To trust enough to self-disclose, when the available signs suggest the instability of the social contexts in which we find ourselves, requires courage."

Being open also requires intellectual energy. What we know and think about our own reactions to group pressures can give guidance that increases perceptiveness. If I am aware that I tend to absorb a group's fight feelings, I can work to notice how and when signals are being sent my way. New levels of complexity can be experienced as well as understood as the intellectual and emotional parts of the self work to widen the range of one's openness to the experiences of the group. It is a partnership—not the intellectual control of feelings, but one where what you feel and know is a result of the thinking and feeling self.

The fact that the setting of my courses is an academic institution, one where intellectual ability has been rewarded, often makes for an imbalance between intellectual and emotional energy. Given the choice, most graduate students are able to generate a great deal of intellectual energy, often to the detriment of emotional energy. Thus, the intellectual energy must often be spent in an effort to prevent defenses from emotional engagement. In essence, powerful intellectual drives, harnessed to the task of learning from the experience, need to work to get out of the way so that the events in the group can be engaged fully.

What, then, is the nature of this openness? Is it to sit in a group and act like a sponge, soaking up all that is around you? To a certain extent the answer is yes—it is important to listen, to attend, and to soak up the atmosphere. This is the opportunity to *gather information* about what is being both thought and felt in the group. But open engagement has its costs. Experiences can be overwhelming and can undermine cognitive abilities. There can be so much information available that one enters a form of sensory overload. Eventually it is important to know how much can be taken in and to manage that openness by also being able to close up and withdraw.

Reflection. The ability to reflect consists of being able to step out of an experience and generate, through the increased distance, a different perspective on that experience. It is not a flight from self but a dialogue with self. I often imagine it as the generation of an internal dialogue, between a temporarily created new "me" and the "me" who is filled with the experiences. It is a sort of internal debriefing process.

Schon (1983) calls this process "reflection-in-action." His concept is drawn from observing how architects and other professionals generate solutions in their day-to-day work. He notes:

> When a practitioner reflects in and on his practice, the possible objects of his reflection are as varied as the kinds of phenomena before him and the systems of knowing-in-practice which he brings to them. He may reflect on the tacit norms and appreciations which underlie a judgment, or on the strategies and theories implicit in a pattern of behavior. He may reflect on the feeling for a situation which has led him to adopt a particular course of action, on the way in which he has framed the problem he has tried to solve, or the role he has constructed for himself within the larger institutional context (p. 62).

It is important to underscore three elements mentioned by Schon. The first is that emotions as well as thoughts are part of the reflective process. The idea is neither to ignore nor to wallow in the emotions. The goal is to affirm their relevance by tying them, through intellectual efforts, to an understanding of the dynamics at work in the group. Again, this requires a partnership of intellect and emotion—a joining to make a complete reflective process. Second, the reflection seeks to uncover assumptions or, as Schon says, "tacit norms." It is precisely the unspoken, unchallenged assumptions that lay the foundations for Bion's theory of unconscious processes in groups. It is there that important insights can emerge.

Finally, Schon points to the importance of reflection as a way to understand "framing." Framing is the technique of setting up an analysis, of setting out the criteria for evaluating which questions are most important and which are tangential. As groups are enormously complex, uncertain, highly ambiguous, and relatively unstable, the framing process becomes extraordinarily important. Framing precedes the identification of problems, so that what might be a problem in one framework is relatively unimportant in another. Too often reflection assumes a frame and moves quickly to identifying problems. This can mean that enormous amounts of energy are spent on problems that are not in fact important.

From an open systems perspective, levels of analysis provide an analytic frame that allows members to focus on a specific set of questions rather than on everything at once. If the frame is the interpersonal level, for example, then actions and solutions will be directed at particular individuals in the group and the nature of their relationship. But if the level of analysis is the group as a whole, then actions and solutions will be aimed at all the members.

Framing, while clearly analytical and based on past experiences, is also creative. Often our analysis is blocked by a failure of imagination; we lack the vision to capture the phenomena we see and experience. One way of generating creative frames is the development of what Schon (1979) calls a "generative metaphor." He argues that metaphors themselves are powerful framing devices and new metaphors alter how we think of the new situation as well as how we think of the metaphor's original setting. Because group settings are such rich experiences, metaphors are often present in the interactions themselves. They have the ability to bring together disparate and conflicting data into a coherent picture.

Judgment: Managing experience and reflection. Thus, on-line learning requires both experience and reflection. The third of the three skills is the ability to manage the two states. When do you move toward experience and when toward reflection? The time boundary of the group experience is *not* the dividing line. That is, on-line time is not just experiencing and off-line time is not just reflection. In on-line periods, an individual moves back and forth between experience and reflection while the group is working. This demands judgment, as reflection pulls one out—in a sense shuts down temporarily the experiencing—and experiencing makes reflection difficult. Experiencing and reflection are more an alternating state than a simultaneous process. A judgment has to be continuously made based on an assessment of which state is most likely to generate a deeper understanding at that moment.

It is helpful to think of the two states as existing on a continuum of proximity to the events in the group, a continuum that members move along throughout the life of the group.

| "Closeness" ← — — — — — — — — — — → "Distance" |
Experience	Reflection
openness	defendedness
gathering information	challenging assumptions/framing

The closer you get to the activities of the group, the greater the openness and the stronger the state of experiencing become. The greater the distance taken from the events, the greater the defendedness and the stronger the state of reflection become. At the "experience" end of the continuum the reflective component is overwhelmed and thus insight achieved may feel magical or intuitive. At the "reflection" end, insight can feel intellectualized or divorced from reality.

The third skill of judgment, of managing one's place on the continuum, is in itself influenced by both the context of the group and the dynamics within the group. The context can skew the range in which the group may move on the closeness-distance continuum. In an organizationally based training session, a group might not go as far toward the "closeness" end of the scale as in a freestanding conference training session. The dynamics within the group can also influence individual movement on the continuum. It is possible, for example, that a group could covertly divide the work of emotion and thinking and could drive one member to take on the thinking work while another would take on the emotional work. Each member might enact his or her role with a great deal of support from other members. Both would find their ability to move from thinking to feeling extremely difficult.

Thus, a final part of the skill of judgment is monitoring the pressures that drive you one way or the other. It is possible early on in the life of a group to discover how you manage these two states, and this insight can serve as an important entry into learning.

Testing. An essential companion to openness and reflection is testing what it is you are experiencing and how you understand those experiences through reflection. I use "testing" in this case not in the tradition of a social science paradigm, where there are hypothesized effects and manipulatable variables. I intend it more as a process described by Schon (1983) as testing *in transaction:* testing/sharing as an attempt to shape the situation but in conversation with it, and with a further openness to be shaped by the process. Part of what makes testing so essential is the importance of figuring out whether and to what extent what you are experiencing within the self is being experienced by others in the group. After all, a group is a collection of individuals; if members are silent or withhold their experiences, group understanding and learning are complicated. Interaction is the major avenue to information.

One specific way of testing is to follow the simple concept of moving toward anxiety. That is, when seeking further confirmation or disconfirmation, it is better to move toward the disturbing phenomenon than away from it. The assumption is that the source of the anxiety is precisely the phenomenon that needs understanding. And yet, to find the source, a member must be open to discovering the disturbance and capable of engaging and exploring it.

If we return to the opening hospital staff meeting, it is entirely possible that the behavior is influenced by everyone's desire to prevent a fight between the administrator and the medical resident. Thus they all engage in "flight" behaviors and move away from that fear. Alternatively, a member might have raised the fearful issue directly. If the anxiety level increased, it would indicate that the issue did contain anxiety. Exploration could lead to either a resolution or further evidence of the strength of the anxiety. Either way, important learnings could be gained.

Transition: On-Line to Off-Line

Originally I conceived of the practice of learning as containing only two time contexts, on-line and off-line. But a number of recent studies have confirmed the importance of transitions as important periods in and of themselves. In architecture, for example, designers such as Frank Lloyd Wright paid special attention to the passage from one place to another. In many of his buildings, the dramatic effect of large rooms is amplified by the narrowness of halls that lead into the large space. Recent marketing studies of commuters have influenced the specific types of radio shows for those in transition to work (strong comedy) versus shows during the drive-time home (angry talk shows). Thus, paying attention to the transitions in group temporal boundaries can enhance the learning process.

The dynamics of a working group do not stop when a meeting breaks up. Its influence lingers. When a working session ends, its forces continue inside and between members. While a member gains greater distance from the events of that day, he or she does not escape the grip of those events. Further, members do not leave the embedded institution, where they may have a host of other overlapping working and/or social interactions.

The bottom line is that members always "carry the group" with them. Emotional reactions are the most obvious examples of this carrying. It isn't any easier to forget your anger just because the formal session has ended. In fact, it is this very awareness of carrying that often inhibits group behavior. There is an awareness that whatever gets started in the group can and will export itself into outside working relationships.

Members also carry the group intellectually. The frames gained through reflection are left in place and postgroup ruminations rely heavily on those final frames. Members often become more convinced of their interpretations and learning as the emotional and intellectual loose ends get tied up through Monday morning quarterbacking.

An example of how powerful the dynamics are off-line can be found in student papers. In my courses, the written assignment is to examine theory and to apply it to the events of the experiential sessions. Students are aware of the need to step back and challenge assumptions and in general are able to produce insightful comments. But, more often than not, their role in the ongoing group has a direct influence on how they write and what they say. The angry group member writes a scathing criticism of the teacher's theory. The silent member shares very little data. The social-emotional leader comments on how good members are to each other. And on and on. It is not that the analysis rendered is wrong. It is that the influence of the group experience is carried into the very core of members' critical thinking processes.

The transition to off-line also means a reentry into the dynamics of the larger setting. Members often look forward to this in the hopes that they can have more "regular" interactions with other individuals in the group. While "carrying the group" in essence eliminates that possibility, it does not preclude larger institutional forces from entering each member. For example, if the course itself is under attack in the larger institution, members may spend out-of-class time defending it. This may have a direct effect on how critical of the course they are able to be when entering the process of analysis.

Understanding that there is an important ongoing dynamic in a group off-line is one of the most important steps on the way to a practice of learning. The implications are clear. Off-line is not an escape, and thus there must be processes designed to work with the continuing, unfolding process of the group. Further, the actual transition from on- to off-line is an important key to understanding. The goal is to attend to the transition process. Are there sudden shifts in mood or tone? Are there stable elements? What events remain particularly vivid in the student's memory? What is it that the student finds him- or herself doing when seeking to leave the event? How and in what ways does the student find his or her perspective shifting?

Off-Line

Off-line time provides important opportunities for extending learning about the dynamics of the working group. But it is essential to do more than simply continue reflection. The distance and time made available by being off-line allow for a qualitatively different process to be engaged. If reflection was a form of dialogue with self, then off-line *analysis* is a form of dialogue with self *about* self.

Traditional social science analysis treats the analyst as if he or she stood outside the human equation. A practice of learning does the exact opposite. It assumes that everyone is a part of the dynamic under examination. Thus, this kind of analysis both incorporates traditional forms of rigorous testing and also places the self as an object of that scrutiny. Under this approach, the analysis is enriched rather than ruined through the incorporation of the analyst's self (Berg and Smith, 1985). But such an incorporation raises the importance of following a process of rigorous testing and of placing one's own thoughts, feelings, and behavior under scrutiny.

Rigorous testing. An analysis, as opposed to a reflection, must contain elements of what I term rigorous testing. This is really a shorthand way of stating that interpretations and findings gain credibility to the extent to which the analyst can demonstrate that he or she has used a logical process to generate findings and has attempted to challenge those results. Guidance for such an analytic process can be found in Erikson's (1958) concept of "disciplined subjectivity." He builds on the therapeutic tradition where the theory itself includes the relationship between the analyst and patient. Concepts such as transference and countertransference are cornerstones of that tradition. In this tradition the analyst works with her or his own subjective responses as a part of the analysis, yet at the same time subjects those responses to challenge and criticism.

But what exactly does it mean to take on a practice of disciplined subjectivity? Edelson (1985) provides a response in his assertion that two phases of scientific inquiry, *discovery* and *justification*, are unaffected by moving to a subjective interpretive frame. Discovery involves the formulation of hypotheses or guesses as to what is influencing behavior. It is the point at which the investigator sets the frame of reference for the analysis: for example, what is the domain to be studied, what makes up that domain, and what are the important things to look at in that domain. The hospital administrator may decide that the problem resides in the chief medical director and that her personality is the important factor. However "subjective" this hypothesis may be, it is no less valuable than any other hypothesis prior to testing.

Justification is "taking a skeptical or critical attitude toward causal explanations and subjecting them to rigorous empirical tests" (Edelson, 1985, p. 77). It is the process of backing up your assertions. Hackman (1985), in an article about discovering his own clinical voice, lists three tests or conditions, based on "core scholarly values," that he feels must be a part of any rigorous analysis. He outlines them as

1. trustworthy, verifiable data as a basis for interpretation,
2. a means of assessing the meaning of those data that are accessible to other scholars,
3. sound logic of inference in drawing conclusions from data.

This means that hypotheses need to be backed by data that are available to others. The data can be either some observed event or an experience shared by the person doing the analysis, but in either case, the data need to be explicit. Further, the analytic process must follow basic tenets of logic—there are no magical jumps from phenomenon to analysis. Sometimes this is extremely difficult, especially if the insights arrive before "analysis." But that insight is valid only if, even in retrospect, it can be articulated and explicated.

Central to all these steps is a willingness to disconfirm an analysis. The richness of data available in a working group opens up the possibility of simply collecting confirming data. Systematic review, however, might discover that the confirming data are substantially outweighed by disconfirming data. The analyst must be willing to reframe, to test, and to reframe further her or his understandings.

Self as object in analysis. If one's self is involved in the process of analysis then the self must be included as an object of analysis. This is the dialogue *about* self. This is not an easy or simple process. It depends on the analyst's ability, first of all, to know the self. What kinds of bias do you carry? What types of data do you usually notice? How have past experiences with some of the members shaped your predilections? Increased self-awareness increases the ability to look during analysis for the data that are likely to be missed or ignored.

In addition, the analyst must be able to "own" the feelings and thoughts experienced while in the group. The commitment to work with all available data must include one's own reactions and actions. But often members feel badly about their behavior or about statements made during an on-line session and flee from examining these experiences during analysis. This is especially true in academic settings, where students, trained to be critical examiners of the behavior of others, are extremely hard on themselves. This harsh judgmental quality makes it difficult to reengage the data from the group. It is not a pleasant experience to listen to yourself on tape or to review notes of a situation you are embarrassed about. But this "owning" is essential for the analysis to be complete.

Once the data are owned, and everyone, including the analyst, is a part of the picture, central assumptions can be challenged and argued through the disciplined analysis. For example, John's statement in the group made me convinced he was manipulating the other members. I was really angry. How do I understand my anger? Was I threatened by my own loss of influence? Were there legitimate reasons for his behavior? Is there another way of framing our conflict? Are there specific data to support an alternative explanation to manipulation? In the end, the analysis may still be that John is manipulative, but the descriptive context and understanding of that manipulation should be significantly richer.

The question then arises as to how much analysis is enough. What guides are there to help distinguish good analysis from bad? To some extent, traditional criteria of evaluation are still applicable. Analytic papers in an academic class, for example, can be graded in terms of validity (did data presented support the hypothesis?), organization (do the ideas flow in some logical and coherent order?), conceptual or intellectual clarity (are there concepts or theories that are applied correctly?), or even creativity (are new patterns discerned?).

The subjective aspect of the analysis, however, requires some additional criteria, criteria that look directly at how the self was treated. One possible measure has been proposed by Simmons (1985). She proposes "empathy as a validity test." She felt that an in-depth analysis brought with it an ability to " 'be with' the other in a way that allowed for full empathy." It was then that she was able to be certain that she had worked through her own initial reactions. In examining the start-up of a new public service organization she wrote,

> Only after riding this emotional roller-coaster several times was I able to integrate my own feelings about county and state into an intergroup framework that allowed me to take account of both perspectives on the struggle: I could understand how county and state people justified their own feelings and how they came to despise the other group, without judging one perspective to be "right." I wrote in my journal, "I've gone back and forth so much with emotional identifications so many times that I now feel very sympathetic to just about everyone. I think I've got it" (p. 297).

Thus, a complete analysis should display both an acknowledgment of initial reactions—"owning"—and a sense of insight into the behavior of others. This in no way implies an acceptance of everyone's behavior. Rather, it implies a sense of understanding about their behavior.

Gillette (1985) points to an additional step—looking for patterns over time. He argues that phenomena cannot be fully understood or analyzed by simply focusing on the here and now. The passage of time can reveal large movements that are buried in the nitty-gritty of the moment-by-moment experiences in the group. Major shifts rarely emerge suddenly and completely. Rather, they evolve as root forces become spent and other root processes gear up.

It takes time for a context of interpretation to develop and it takes time for deeply rooted patterns to emerge. But, perhaps most important, time changes the position of the analyst to the group, and it is during those shifts that understandings about past interpretations can emerge. In some ways, you only know where you are after you have been there.

The final results look more like ethnographic studies than traditional social science hypothesis testing. Borrowing from the tradition of semiotic anthropology in particular, the purpose of their analysis is not so much to find "truth" as to reduce puzzlement. An event or set of behaviors that doesn't make sense is framed in a way that brings coherence and understanding, not so much to allow *predictions* as to allow *anticipation*. It is valid if it significantly reduces the possible range of future patterns, not because it is able to predict a singular pattern.

There is still the traditional value of using theory in its most basic sense. That is, theory is the process of connecting together seemingly disparate events into a pattern that makes sense. New theories connect events across concepts that were previously seen as mutually exclusive. For example, quantum mechanics progressed when it linked the concepts of the atom as having both a defined shape and no defined shape. Accepting this paradox opened up vast new ways of learning. In a practice of learning, theory has exactly this role—to connect and thereby to explain.

In sum, the practice of learning off-line consists of engaging an analysis of rigorous testing. It demands that there be a commitment to look at all the phenomena, including the self, afresh; to push at preconceptions; to search for alternative explanations; to look across time boundaries; and to utilize theory. It provides an opportunity for what Friedlander (1975) has termed "reconstructive learning":

> In reconstructive learning the organization questions its premises, purposes, values. For individuals these are represented in one's goals, principles, life-style, beliefs. . . . Reconstructive learning calls for in-

depth confrontation of old patterns and the development of radically different ones. It suggests the construction of new goals, policies, norms, styles rather than the simple modification of the old (p. 76).

Off-Line to On-Line

If "carrying the group experience" is the important process in the transition from on-line to off-line, then "carrying analysis" is the central process in the transition from off- to on-line. Three elements of this process stand out: the need to retain both humility and courage about the analysis, the need to recognize that full analysis is a reciprocal process, and the awareness that different analytic frames will import different pressures for behavior back into the working group.

Humility. The first element reflects a tendency that often follows rigorous analysis. The analyst, having invested considerable effort, returns to a work group with "the truth," and then spends additional effort convincing others that they are wrong and that he or she is correct. Additional disconfirming data in the here and now are ignored as the dynamic shifts to a contest of power and will. When the analysis includes one's own self, the defenses against seeing the weakness in the analysis are unusually strong.

As a counter to this tendency, it is important to recognize the tentativeness of any analysis. While disciplined subjectivity can generate meaningful insights into a group's behavior, it should also reinforce a sense of humility. It is inevitably a flawed process. One's own unconscious is always at work and is by definition out of awareness yet not out of influence. Thus, despite every best effort, the process of analysis itself is influenced by processes that are unobserved.

Thus, a touch of humility is essential, along with a willingness to be open for correction and criticism. Yet is is equally important not to fall into the opposite trap of self-doubt. The purpose of analysis is to make interpretations, and to take a stand, for it is only in interaction between analysis and experience that learning, individual and collective, can move forward. Again, courage is essential—to act on the basis of what you know and experience and not to be filled up with uncertainty and hesitation. Over time, it is possible to develop the ability to hold or contain greater uncertainty and ambiguity *and still act.*

Reciprocity. Humility, then, can facilitate working toward the recognition that each individual perspective in the working group is likely to capture only a part of the whole story. It follows that in-depth diagnosis requires a form of reciprocal exchange between members, with each sharing and building on the others' analysis. Conflicting interpretations, while often experienced as a contest for who is right and who is wrong, are often the vehicle for altering the overall frame of interpretation and for discovering new dynamics that had previously been unseen. But this requires a commitment to reciprocity.

In essence, reciprocity is based on a member perspective where the goal is not an understanding *of* events but an understanding *with* events. Interpretations, as well as individual experiences, are a product of the collective process, and as such need to be shared and tested by the collective.

Interpretation drives action. Finally, pressures for action are generated from analysis, and different kinds of analysis can lead to pressures for different kinds of action. For example, if the analyst concludes that the dominant dynamic is intergroup competition between men and women, he or she is likely to frame new behaviors in those terms and may take a seat in a way that breaks up an emergent male-female seating pattern. If the analyst interprets events using an individual-level frame, he or she might blame one person for group dilemmas and try to exclude that member from the group. Or if an individual discovers through analysis that he is acting as the rebel for the group, he may attempt to shift his behavior by remaining quiet and by resisting opportunities to express rebelliousness.

What is essential to remember is that analytic process is not a passive exercise done and left in the past. It is carried into the group and as such becomes a part of the fabric of the dynamic process. The cycle begins again, with members experiencing/reflecting, carrying the group away with them, generating an analysis, and importing an altered frame back into the group.

THE PRACTICE OF LEARNING AS A DEVELOPMENTAL PROCESS

The development of a practice of learning takes time and, most of all, takes practice. It is a complex process and demands a high level of skill. In the beginning, one is a novice and, as pointed out by Benner (1984), the passage from novice to expert is discontinuous. That is, the novice acts differently from the expert even though the process involved—in this case a practice of learning—is the same for each. The novice begins without experience and must fall back on the outlined step-by-step procedures. Until the process is internalized, each piece of the process must be approached separately. The novice often loses the larger picture as he or she gets caught up in the details. As in learning any new process, such as riding a bike or acquiring a new language, the early steps require attending to *all* the details. But with experience, the details are incorporated and thus more room is left for examining the whole process. A person fluent in another language would, in fact, be slowed down if forced to think about all the structures of nouns and verbs.

The expert, then, has both internalized the process and has the benefit of past experiences. As Schon (1983) states in his description of a complex problem being approached by an expert practitioner: "It is our capacity to see unfamiliar situations as familiar ones, and to do in the former as we have done in the latter, that enables us to bring our past experience to bear on the unique case. It is our capacity to see-as and to do-as that allows us to have a feel for problems that do not fit existing rules" (p. 139).

Thus, a practice of learning is based on bringing together theories that are learned and experiences that are had and, through repeated efforts, developing expertise in integrating the two. It can't happen the first time. Expertise is based on having worked at it. The goal is to end up with what Benner calls "clinical knowledge," which she defines as "a hybrid between naive practical knowledge and unrefined theoretical knowledge" (p. 8).

CONCLUSION

Working toward a practice of learning in experiential groups involves examining both on-line and off-line experiences. At each time period, distinct and different processes can be enacted. Through repeated cycles of experiencing and reflecting, carrying out, analyzing, and carrying back in, a learner can both develop skills and a deeper understanding of the dynamics involved. All the steps demand a willingness to own, acknowledge, and work with one's experiences, thoughts, and feelings: all of them—the good, the bad, and the ugly. It is in some ways the ultimate "throwing oneself into the work."

Where then, does this leave the hospital administrator and the medical group portrayed at the beginning of this chapter? Through his membership experiences, he has access to information both about the group and about his own responses. Off-line, he can begin the process of analyzing the group and his responses and, at the next meeting, can import his learning back into the group. Since interventions are always based on analysis, a more complete analytic process, one that leads to examining all the data, one that takes advantage of all four learning contexts, increases the probability that he can lead the group more effectively. "Effective" managerial behavior then emerges not from simply following a generic management "cookbook" but from engaging a complex and demanding learning process to understand the dynamics of a specific group in a particular context.

Chapter 2

Group Formation: Boundaries, Leadership, and Culture

MARION McCOLLOM

Poor David Baker. In the Harvard Business School case "Acton-Burnett, Inc." (Gabarro, 1983), David is enlisted by his bosses to do an impossible job. In a prototypically melodramatic case backdrop, Baker, a recent M.B.A. working in a profitable metallurgy company, has been assigned the leadership of a newly created, cross-functional task force charged with explaining (finding the party responsible for?) the company's recent financial setback. Everything goes wrong, of course: Baker allows a more senior member to set the agenda of the first meeting, the group splinters into noncommunicating subgroups, he avoids supervising one member because of a previous conflict, and intense interdepartmental rivalry seeps into the group as members suppress or exploit information damaging to one functional unit. The case ends with David poised on the brink of disaster after group dynamics have sabotaged a key presentation of the task force's work. Students are asked to evaluate Baker's leadership style and to prescribe retrospective remedies.

The handout used to supplement this case is called "Managing a Task Force" (Ware, 1977). This rational document lays out in detail what steps a manager must take to assert and maintain control of a group: set out the goals of the group, determine who should be on the task force, contact members before the first meeting, define working procedures in the group, schedule regular group meetings, set and enforce deadlines for intermediate products, and communicate information among task force members.

There are legitimate reasons why an M.B.A. student aspiring to task force leadership should think about what it takes to get the work done in that kind of group. Groups, by definition (see, for example, Alderfer, 1983; Cartwright and Zander, 1960), have a task or goal that requires the interdependent effort of individuals. Turquet (1974) argues that the survival of a group depends on the identification and accomplishment of what Rice (1963) calls its "primary task": "Failure in these matters inevitably leads to the dismemberment of the group, and hence to its final dissolution" (p. 350). Thus, it seems reasonable to assume that Baker's group fell apart because he and they did not find a successful approach to the task.

What this argument obscures, however, is why Baker's group members did what they did. Group theory suggests that groups serve both psychological functions for individual members as well as formal organizational functions (Schein, 1980). Members attend both to task accomplishment and to building and maintaining the group, to insure that the group meets their needs. Bales (1958) argued that group leadership must be exercised in both the task and the socio-emotional arenas.

The author of "Managing a Task Force" says very little, however, about the interior experience of the individuals on Baker's task force. The maintenance, or "process," side of group management is left out (Luft, 1970; Eddy, 1985). And, more specifically, he does not explore the particular needs that people have as members of new groups: what they are likely to feel on entering a new group and why, and how they behave in the start-up stage to protect their psychological well-being (Schein, 1969).

Finally, the main message of "Managing a Task Force" for Baker-type group leaders is "assert control," an individual-level prescription. Leadership research suggests, however, that there is no single effective leadership style (Schein, 1980). The effectiveness of group leaders depends on their ability to understand and represent the group as a whole: in dealing with organizational demands, in assessing the developmental stage of the group, and in balancing the group's task and maintenance needs. Unless they are moved toward this group-level understanding, aspiring group leaders will skip down the primrose path as innocently as David Baker did, wondering why they cannot "assert control."

In this chapter, I will explore group formation, focusing ultimately on the process issues that should concern leaders of new groups. I will use systems theory, particularly the concept of boundaries, to provide a framework for understanding what happens when a group forms. I will then summarize the literature describing the individual's emotional experience in joining a group. Finally, I will link group formation to the creation of group culture, exploring the circumstances under which a collection of individuals transforms itself into a cohesive, functioning work unit.

This approach is not meant to argue against the importance of task leadership. Rather, it is an effort to focus attention on the more irrational processes that often sabotage the efforts of group leaders. The processes underlying early events in a group's life influence to a great degree the eventual cohesiveness of the team and members' ability to work together effectively.

BOUNDARIES

To describe a theoretical model of the formation process for groups in general and for Baker's task force in particular, I begin with open systems theory as a base. Key to the discussion is the concept of *boundaries.*

Miller and Rice (1975) and Alderfer (1976a) have provided groundbreaking applications of open systems theory to human organizations and groups, paying particular attention to system boundaries. According to their formulations, human systems, like other living systems (think of the cell), maintain vitality by importing material across a boundary, transforming that material into life-sustaining products, and exporting some of the products of this transaction back across the boundary to the environment. The boundary of an open system (the analogy of the cell wall will help here) serves several functions: it separates what is inside the system from what is outside, it provides a structure for the system, and it regulates the system's transactions with the environment.

Human systems, like other open systems, are composed of subunits in interdependent relationship with one another (Alderfer, 1976a). Organizations can be conceptualized as groups structured in overlapping hierarchies, smaller systems embedded in numerous larger ones (Alderfer and Smith, 1982). Contained within the boundaries of a group like Baker's task force are the boundaries around individual members and the boundaries defining subgroups of the larger group (task subgroups, for instance). Overlapping the task force boundaries are the boundaries of organization groups, like functional departments, that have representatives on the task force.

Stability and growth in an open system are dependent on the internal relationships among these various bounded subunits of a system; also critical is the relationship of the system to its external environment (Alderfer, 1976a). Boundaries are permeable to a greater or lesser degree, permitting more or less interaction with the environment. The vitality of the system depends in large measure on the "fit" between the permeability of the boundary and the need of the system to receive resources from the environment. Too little permeability can starve the system of the resources it needs to thrive; too much can overwhelm and sometimes poison the system.

For some systems (the cell, for instance), the boundary is palpable and its functions apparent. When we speak of a group, the term *boundary* is an abstraction, referring to both observable and subjective measures that people use to distinguish members of a group from outsiders. However, group boundaries also vary in permeability. Some groups are shut off from their environment, unable to incorporate information and resources from other groups ("overbounded" in Alderfer's, 1976b, terminology). In contrast, "underbounded" groups, like David Baker's task force, have boundaries so permeable that information "leaks" out and the group cannot organize its activities. The concept of boundary permeability plays a key role in understanding group formation.

"Observable" group boundaries, according to Alderfer (1976a), are the physical, spatial, and temporal divisions that differentiate a group from other groups. A group sitting in a circle or meeting around a table creates a physical boundary that describes the group. Nonmembers often sit outside the boundary, or at least must ask permission to enter the space that identifies group membership. Sometimes groups "own" rooms or areas of a room; architectural divisions of space (walls, doors, partitions) represent group boundaries that nonmembers are reluctant to cross even when group members are not present. The permeability of these observable group boundaries can be assessed by how difficult or easy it is for nonmembers to enter the group space.

Groups are also bounded by time. While some, like the family, are defined by their members' life spans (and beyond), others exist only for a limited duration (like the task force, for instance, or an experiential learning group). Temporal boundaries are also marked by the beginning and ending times of group meetings, or the time period during which one can actually see the group gathered as a collectivity. In this case, permeability is reflected in how readily the group adheres to its agreed-upon meeting times and how easily the group is distracted to nontask activities during its meetings. We can see the Acton-Burnett task force as temporally underbounded because Baker could not get all its members together at the same time for a meeting.

"Subjective" group boundaries are known more commonly as psychological boundaries. They can be defined as the "psychosocial basis of group structure" (Hartman and Gibbard, 1974, p. 155) or, more simply, as the group's understanding of who belongs to the group and who doesn't (Redlich and Astrachan, 1975). In a group in which psychological boundaries are undefined (that is, too permeable), group members may feel they do not want to be in the group or sometimes are not even sure whether they are in the group or not. While formal group membership status may be quickly determined, psychological membership takes time to develop.

Group formation is the process by which a group develops psychological boundaries, so that members achieve a sense of belonging to and identifying with the group and enact this membership in their interactions with each other and with nonmembers of the group (see Alderfer's, 1983, definition of "group"). The process involves the gradual establishment of a group boundary from the point at which it (and the group) does not exist to the point at which all members of the group experience commitment, to greater or lesser degrees, to membership in the group. At this hypothetical point, we can say that a group has "formed."

One conclusion that can be drawn from the Acton-Burnett case is that task force members never experienced membership in that group; the disintegration of the work resulted from the group's undefined psychological boundaries. For individuals on the task force, psychological membership in departmental groups was much stronger than their identification with the task force. Their commitment to the tasks of their functional units overwhelmed their loyalty to the work of Baker's group.

To move beyond an abstract model of group formation, we need to understand how individuals experience membership in a new group. Agreement on task definition and working procedures, as called for by the "Managing a Task Force" author, can certainly help members understand rationally what membership in a group will require. However, there are critical emotional and unconscious questions that will remain unanswered if task remains the sole focus. We need to consider what it takes for members of a new group to truly "join" that group. What are the processes by which group members "test" their membership in interaction and decide if they want to join?

THE INDIVIDUAL EXPERIENCE OF GROUP FORMATION

Examining our own experiences in groups, we can understand why a sense of belonging does not emerge immediately when people enter a new group. One reason is that individuals in this situation typically experience unpleasant emotions. Many writers in the group and organizations literature have named anxiety as the primary emotion associated with entry into a new group or system (see, for example, Louis, 1980; Hartman and Gibbard, 1974). The anxiety arises from multiple sources, some of them conscious and some of them unconscious.

In general, anxiety is evoked by the uncertainty that is built into the undertaking. In the creation of a new group, prospective group members, by definition, do not know what membership in the group will mean, because the group does not exist. Formation requires them to "join" without knowing what they are joining (Smith and Berg, 1987).

Despite the human need to "belong," to feel membership in groups (Ross, 1989), and despite the opportunities created for individuals by group membership, joining a group is not without cost. To function, groups require resources—time, energy, information— most of which are supplied by members. Groups require members to play intellectually and emotionally demanding roles. Group membership also means the reduction of personal autonomy (Gibbard, Hartman, and Mann, 1974a), and it may mean joining with others whose values or goals are antithetical to one's own.

Ultimately, a group can threaten or damage members—for example, a group in which there is perpetual conflict, or a group that scapegoats individuals. In the case of the task force, a group that was brought together by senior management to "point the finger" at those responsible for the company's recent losses, membership could be highly rewarding or extremely dangerous, depending on the outcome of the investigation and on the motives of the managers who asked that the work be done.

Considering the risks and rewards of group membership, it is not surprising that people approach groups with profound ambivalence and anxiety (Smith and Berg, 1987). Because one does not know in advance what the group will be, one entertains a dual worry: if one joins, one may wind up a member of a group that one doesn't want to be in; if one does not join, one may be rejected by a group that one wants to be in.

The individual's rational ambivalence during group formation (that is, his justifiable concern about what group membership may mean) reflects the deeper unconscious anxiety that all individuals carry about joining groups. To explain the source of this anxiety, Wells (see Chapter 3) and others have tapped the work of Melanie Klein on individual psychodynamics. This work posits that individuals experience emotional regression in groups (Whitman, 1964), because group membership recalls the anxieties of childhood. Members must be willing to cope with this anxiety in the formation process.

To summarize the aspects of the theory that are relevant for this discussion: Klein (1984) argues that all newborns experience fusion with the mother, a state in which they do not know the difference between what is "self" and what is "other." In a typical developmental pattern, babies over time differentiate themselves from the mother: that is, they develop an individual psychological boundary and a separate sense of self.

The application of Klein's theory to groups rests on the idea that a new group is "boundaryless," as yet unformed and undifferentiated from its environment. Writers have argued that adults experience a new group as an amorphous entity, the undifferentiated "mother" of infant experience (Gibbard, Hartman, and Mann, 1974b). This provokes what Schein (1985) calls the "core conflict" of group membership; each member wants to be absorbed into the group, to lose individual identity, and at the same time to remain independent from the group.

Diamond and Allcorn (1987) express the experience as follows:

> The central dilemma for the individual in the work group rests in his or her ability to maintain individuality (personal identity and self-esteem) and group membership (a sense of belongingness and affiliation) without becoming overly distressed. The existence of regression and related primitive defenses in groups . . . arise [sic] to ward off anxiety provoked by perceived annihilation in membership on the one hand and separation and loss of affiliation on the other (p. 526).

In other words, every individual has experienced a developmental struggle from fusion to individuation, which is characterized by a strong fear of being overwhelmed or annihilated. Encountering a new group, because we foresee an emotional merger with a powerful and "unknown" entity that reminds us of the "mother" we experienced in infancy, we face these dual fears anew. We may be swallowed up in the group, or we may be rejected.

The anxiety experienced by Baker's task force members is therefore likely to be significant; theoretically, each will have a powerful individual intrapsychic reaction to membership in the new group. In addition, each has perfectly rational reasons to believe that joining the task force may be professionally hazardous. The environment is politically charged, their departments' reputations are in question, and they have been cast in a finger-pointing role. The question is, under what circumstances could they identify with the task force in a way that allowed a psychological boundary to form?

THE PROCESS OF GROUP FORMATION

Smith and Berg (1987), in writing about the paradoxes of group life (see Chapter 5), describe a set of hopes accompanying the fears experienced at the beginning of groups. Groups can rob members of autonomy, but can also provide identity and security. In addition, groups can foster self-expression and growth. At the individual level, we hope (again, in a regressed emotional state) that the groups we join will restore the happy but lost conditions of infancy, satisfying every need and still allowing individuation. So, while anxiety is propelling new group members away from joining, hope is moving them toward accepting membership in the group, or toward group formation.

Group formation requires that group members understand and accept what membership in the group will mean, at both cognitive and emotional levels. "Managing a Task Force" advises leaders to achieve this acceptance in advance: work out operating procedures, set deadlines, clarify the goals of the work before the group meets. These activities can, in fact, be helpful in moving a group toward accomplishment of its task. However, in very basic ways, acceptance of membership cannot be achieved before the group members come together. Until the group meets, members will not know at an emotional level what membership will mean for them. This testing takes place in the early face-to-face processes by which group norms are negotiated (Schein, 1985).

In addition to being exclusively task-focused, "Managing a Task Force" conveys the message that the leader can control the norms (and ultimately the culture) of a group: again, the individual-level bias. However, the amount of influence a formal leader can exercise over group norms depends to a great degree on the amount of informal influence he or she can wield in the group (Eddy, 1985). Powerful leaders can shape group norms significantly; leaders who do not wield informal power must struggle to establish their authority. To understand the dynamics of leadership during the formation process, we need to define "norms" and "culture" and then explore how these phenomena emerge in new groups during the process of group formation.

Norms are the usually tacit "rules" of behavior that govern a group: who can do what when (Katz and Kahn, 1978). Culture is a set of beliefs and values, along with the patterns of language, behavior and symbols that express those beliefs and values, that provide identity and framework of meaning for people in a group (McCollom, 1987). Norms, then, are a behavioral subset of culture and are grounded in a complicated cultural system of beliefs and assumptions about relationships within the group and between the group and the outside environment.

How are the norms of David Baker's task force likely to be established? The process occurs in two stages, and is activated when individual first encounters group (Schein, 1969). The first stage is expectation: before the group meets, each member develops expectations about how the group will operate and about what membership will mean. The second step is interaction: people test their expectations against what really happens in the first group meeting.

If Baker had spoken with task force members in advance of the first meeting, their expectations would have been based, in part, on what Baker had said about his plans for the group. However, individual expectations about group membership are formed by a variety of powerful factors; in this case, individuals would be influenced by wider systemic norms for task force operation, the reputation of this particular project, the members' experience in similar groups either at Acton-Burnett or previously, and each individual's feelings about and experience with other members of the task force.

Group members bring these mostly unarticulated expectations to the first meeting. Here begins the usually tacit negotiation that takes place when a group gets together for the first time. Each member will behave according to his or her expectations of what is appropriate, and the dynamics of the group—content and process—will determine whose expectations will rule. (See Schein, 1985, chapter 7, for a discussion of how personality differences come into play at this stage.) People may discuss some topics directly—for instance, how to approach the task or when to meet next—but the crucial "conversation" is in the group process: who listens to whom, whose ideas are accepted, how much influence each member wields.

Norms form as some behaviors are accepted by the group and

others rejected. Individuals test their expectations and watch the group's response (for example, expectations that Baker would be a weak leader may have been confirmed when he did not offer a clear agenda for the first meeting). Where expectations are not shared, the group can erupt in conflict or become "stuck" (Baker's group could not move past one member's idiosyncratic idea of the group's task). Where expectations are shared, "rules" are likely to emerge quickly (seniority became the basis for authority in Baker's group when a senior member stepped in to suggest a strategy for approaching the work).

At an unconscious level, individuals are "testing" the emotional environment of the new group in this norm-building behavior: how dangerous is it? Will it meet my needs? Who will I be in this group? Who is influential and what will his or her influence mean for me? Will the group accept me? (Schein, 1985; Eddy, 1985). In this testing process, the deeper patterns of beliefs and values that will form the culture begin to be established: that is, the group will reveal itself to be a place in which frank discussion is valued or in which honesty can be dangerous.

Typically, group members' expectations derive from their prior experience in the organization. The group formation process, or the establishment of a group boundary, differentiates the group from the rest of the system. As norms develop, the group establishes group-specific patterns of belief about the task, about individual roles in the group, and about the group's relationship to the wider organization. These patterns of behavior (norms) and belief form the group culture. This does not mean that group members think and act alike; it means that the group develops characteristic patterns of relations. For example, two subgroups may always disagree, or the leader's attempts to establish control may usually be undermined, or the group may consistently portray itself as under siege by the outside environment.

The character of the culture determines to a large extent whether group members are able to overcome their anxiety about membership; if they feel included, influential, and accepted (Schein, 1985), they will "join" the group and formation will be accomplished. If they feel unsafe or powerless, they are likely to stay disengaged. This means not just that formation will be inhibited; it means that the group will be more vulnerable to the larger system because its boundaries will remain too permeable.

In order to analyze group and organizational cultures, writers have identified broad categories of cultural activity (for example, McCollom, 1987). Within the culture of the client organization for that research, I identified seven themes—authority, caretaking, communication, conflict, intimacy, security, and work. That is, there were distinct patterns of behavior and belief associated with these themes. These categories are similar to the variables Hall (1973) calls "primary message systems"—universal human concerns that are rooted in biological activity but that reflect the culture of a human system—and to the categories of group process activities listed by Eddy (1985).

The charater of a group's culture can be described utilizing these themes: how are authority relations handled? How does communication occur? What attitudes and behaviors prevail regarding intimacy among group members? For example, Baker's group very quickly established a pattern of conflict avoidance, perhaps in response to the danger of their situation (three members had to evaluate their bosses in order to accomplish the task). By breaking into subgroups at the first meeting, rather than working as a group to thrash out different opinions about the task, they sowed the seeds of a culture in which conflict was suppressed. As is typical of this pattern of conflict management, the group eventually exploded. Baker himself was influential in the creation and maintenance of this pattern, as he chose not to confront the renegade member of his group, with whom he had personally conflictual relations.

In this case, then, the culture of the group reinforced the belief that membership was dangerous. As a consequence, the boundary around the task force remained undefined; members retained their primary emotional affiliations with functional groups and collectively sabotaged their own work. Even though they performed duties as task force members, they did not fully accept "membership" in that group.

LEADERSHIP AND GROUP FORMATION

With this understanding of group formation, we can approach the question of leadership in the group and offer some advice to David Baker. Clearly, the leader of a task force would like to control the norms and to create a culture that is cohesive and effective. However, the emotional aspects of group formation are not within his or her power to control by fiat.

The central task of leadership on the process side of life in a new group, following from the argument so far, is to help manage the anxiety of group formation and to strive toward the creation of a well-defined (but not impermeable) group boundary. The more dangerous the group's environment, the clearer the boundary will need to be to allow members to feel included, influential, and accepted. This means the leader must understand the rational and unconscious fears new members carry and attempt to address those worries. Clarifying goals and setting procedures in advance will help members feel more certain about what group membership will mean; new members will have questions about how the group's task will be accomplished. However, members also need to see the leader's behavior in the group as they test their expectations in the norm-building process; to join, they need to feel that the group will be a safe and productive place.

The identity of the leader, given the context in which the group must work, is crucial to the successful accomplishment of this work, however. A powerful leader who holds formal authority in the system can be sure that his or her behavior will exert strong influence on the norms of the group. By being careful to include all members, by explicitly addressing issues that are likely to cause anxiety, and by encouraging the expression of different opinions, a strong formal leader can move the group toward formation by encouraging the creation of a culture that members can work in. This kind of leader behavior is desired by members, who rely on the leader to clarify uncertainty and reduce their anxiety (the "dependency" dynamics described by Wilfred Bion; see Rioch, 1975).

In a hostile environment, such as the one facing Baker's task force, the leader's job is more difficult. She or he must work toward a group culture that is highly differentiated from, and to a certain degree protected from, the culture of the larger system. The leader's skills and authority are thus subjected to intense scrutiny, as members assure themselves that the leader can operate effectively in this boundary-preserving role (Gibbard, Hartman, and Mann, 1974c). If group members can identify with and establish trust in the leader (Turquet, 1974), they can begin to take the risks necessary to establish trust with other group members (Smith and Berg, 1987).

If the formal leader of the group has little influence in the wider system, however, the dynamics of formation can be quite different. Members of Baker's task force probably felt, justifiably, that Baker did not have the experience or clout in the company to protect group members from penalization for their participation in this group. In their dependency, they naturally looked to more senior members of the group for signals about how the group might operate "safely." Lacking formal authority to run the group, these members might also have felt uncertain about what the group should do, but might also respond (as the senior member of Baker's group did) to the group's need for direction. Thus, the natural search to reduce anxiety led the group to reject Baker's leadership. As he did not act to reclaim his central role and to win the trust of group members, the group lacked the ingredients essential to establishing a well-defined psychological boundary. Trust among group members and commitment to the task were never established.

Attempts by a leader in Baker's position to exercise control autocratically during group formation are likely to heighten rather than diminish anxiety if, in fact, he or she does not have the skills or authority to protect the group from the larger system. It will not work for Baker to inflate his authority in representing his role to the group; group members will rely on multiple sources of data to draw their conclusions about his adequacy as a leader. However, he could work to clarify for group members (and for himself) the real scope of his authority. For example, he could bring senior management into the first meeting of the group to establish support for the group's activities and for his formal role.

Baker could also acknowledge the skills of senior members of the group without yielding his authority. If he builds collaborative relationships with them—works to understand their concerns and communicates his expectations for the group—their collective influence during the norm-building process can support group formation. One-on-one meetings with all group members before the first group meeting could also help him understand and address individual expectations and concerns. Simply meeting face-to-face with the leader can help new members manage their anxiety about what membership in the group will mean. Finally, Baker could work hard, starting with his own behavior, to establish a group culture that promotes frank discussion rather than conflict suppression.

The politics of the broader environment may undermine these activities, in which case the leader must do the best he or she can to influence norm-building and establish a modicum of trust in the group. Sometimes less experienced leaders are brash and/or charismatic enough to overcome members' anxieties and rally the group around them. However, if the leader cannot achieve the support of those in more powerful positions, the outcome is more likely to follow the script of Acton-Burnett; the anxiety of group formation is never adequately addressed, a fragmented or destructive culture is created, and the group either falls apart or explodes.

CONCLUSION

There is pressure in management education to give students the tools to guarantee that they can emerge professionally unscathed from demanding organizational dilemmas. This leads to an emphasis on task accomplishment and a lack of attention to the social and emotional dimensions of life in organizations. If good management is equated with individual prowess, students will discount the value of a group-level perspective that is based on solid analysis but also on empathy and introspection. Even with the focus on work groups that has been incorporated into most M.B.A. curricula, the pedagogy is aimed at the individual. No wonder we hear complaints about the immaturity of recent M.B.A.'s.

Teaching M.B.A.'s or anyone else to manage group formation by exerting strong control of the task process alone is courting disaster. Effective work in groups requires that managers understand the powerful emotional and unconscious processes that drive individual behavior in collective situations. Most of the time, these processes will catch and spin the leader with a force equal to or greater than the force exerted by the leader on individual members. Learning to "read the spin" and simultaneously manage the formation process are the art and science of the experienced group leader.

Managers (present and future) can take important lessons from David Baker's experience: (1) group leaders need to pay close attention to process issues as well as to task accomplishment; (2) leaders must utilize group-level models in preparing strategies for leadership and managing problems that arise in groups; and (3) negotiating group formation, a crucial and fragile period in group life, requires leaders to attend carefully to their own behavior, as well as to the dynamics of the larger system.

No one, not even David Baker at his best, can be guaranteed success in this venture, especially if the organization's culture effectively prevents trust from being established among group members. In that case, as in Acton-Burnett, the group leader needs to go back to his bosses and negotiate for a project redefinition that allows the work to be accomplished. Success will come only when the emotional dynamics of group formation can be addressed, group psychological boundaries can be defined, and a relatively cohesive and productive group culture can emerge.

Chapter 3

The Group as a Whole: A Systemic Socioanalytic Perspective on Interpersonal and Group Relations

LEROY WELLS, JR.

INTRODUCTION

This chapter presents concepts that are central to understanding interpersonal processes and group relations in an organizational context. Emphasis is placed on interpreting interpersonal relations from the group level using what may be labeled a systemic socioanalytic perspective. Several case studies are used to examine interpersonal relations from the systemic socioanalytic perspective. Heuristics are delineated that help agents of organizational change to better understand, interpret, and intervene in interpersonal and group relations.

AIMS AND PRINCIPLES

The present theoretical framework for understanding group and organizational processes has been heavily influenced by work of writers from the Tavistock Centre for Human Relations in London. These scholars have greatly influenced the author's conceptual development and largely account for the biases that color his understanding of group and organizational phenomena.

The systemic socioanalytic perspective for understanding organizational processes integrates:

1. Current thinking regarding the application of open systems theory to group and organizational behavior (Alderfer, 1976b; Baker, 1973; Reed et al., 1978; Wells, 1978b; Singer et al., 1975; Astrachan, 1970);

2. Concepts associated with Kleinian psychoanalysis (Klein, 1932, 1955; Klein and Riviere, 1964; Jaques, 1955);

3. Principles articulated by the psychoanalytic group psychology tradition (Bion, 1961; Gibbard, Hartman, and Mann, 1974d; Gibbard, 1975; Colman and Bexton, 1975).

Through the integration of these perspectives and their concepts, a more cogent framework is formed from which the complexity of interpersonal processes can more readily be discerned.

Traditional experimental and social psychological views of interpersonal relations represented by Cartwright and Zander (1968), Thibaut and Kelly (1959), Krech et al. (1962), Newcomb (1961), and Lott and Lott (1965) are eschewed in this discussion.[1] This does not suggest that traditional social psychological perspectives are not useful in understanding interpersonal relations, but that the perspective utilized here is novel for *most* applied behavioral scientists. The aim of this chapter is to provide another vantage point from which organizational processes can be understood.

On the other hand, work from the psychoanalytic group tradition (Gibbard, 1975; Bion, 1961) is often written in a form that is alien and meaningless to the reader who is untrained in psychoanalytic concepts and concomitant jargon. Thus, the contribution that psychoanalytic group concepts can make to a better understanding of group processes goes unrecognized or is diminished. This chapter is an attempt to present psychoanalytically derived concepts in a schema that is helpful for organizational diagnosticians who are not familiar with the analytic tradition.

ORGANIZATIONAL PROCESSES

Organizational processes refer to actual working activities, formal and informal relations, and psychosocial phenomena that occur among individuals and groups in organizations. Groups and organizations are considered open living systems that exchange energy, material, and information with the environment (Miller and Rice,

---

[1]An excellent discussion on interpersonal relations from the traditional social psychological perspective can be found in Albanese (1975, pp. 525–38).

1969; Alderfer, 1976b; Baker, 1973). They are vehicles through which a variety of goals can be pursued.

Alderfer (1977a), using an open systems perspective, defines a human group as

> a collection of individuals 1) who have significantly interdependent relations with each other; 2) who perceive themselves as a group by reliably distinguishing members from non-members; 3) whose group identity is recognized by non-members; 4) who have differentiated roles in the group as a function of expectations from themselves, other members and non-group members; and 5) who as group members acting alone or in concert have significantly interdependent relations with other groups (p. 230).

Moreover, Singer et al. (1975) and Alderfer (1976) have described three levels of group processes. These perspectives provide the theoretical background for further discussion of group and organizational processes.

Wells (1978b) has described (extending the Singer et al. (1975), Alderfer (1976a), and Astrachan (1970) models) five levels of organizational processes. They are: (1) intrapersonal, (2) interpersonal, (3) group-level (group as a whole), (4) intergroup, and (5) interorganizational (see Figure 1).

1. *Intrapersonal processes* in an organizational context refer to the co-actor's relatedness to him- or herself. Analysis of *intrapersonal* processes focuses on the personality characteristics, character traits, mode of ego defense, ego ideal, and various need levels of the co-actors. In short, an intrapersonal analysis assumes that the behavior emerges from the internal life or from within the co-actor (Astrachan, 1970).

Personnel departments and assessment centers typically evaluate behavior of their employees or clients from an intrapersonal perspective. Personnel departments usually use a battery of psychological tests (MPPI, TAT, IQ, Stanford-Binet) to evaluate aspects of their employees' personalities. Little attention is paid to processes that occur outside or between individuals. Emphasis is placed on the employee's personality, knowledge, and skills.

Additionally, gestalt therapy and personal growth groups focus on and use the intrapersonal level of analysis as the foundation of their work (Perls, 1970; Yalom, 1970; Weir and Weir, 1978).

2. *Interpersonal processes* refer to *member-to-member* relations. The focus is on the quality and type of relationships that exist between co-actors. Emphasis is placed on communication patterns,

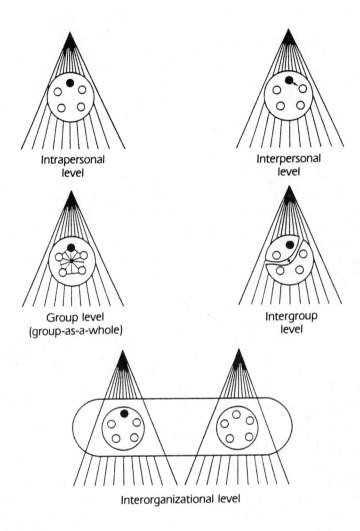

Figure 1. *Five Levels of Organizational Processes*

information flow, level of conflict and trust, and relating styles of co-actors (Astrachan, 1970; Argyris, 1962). Interpersonal processes examine how well or poorly individuals relate to their peers, subordinates, and supervisors. Emphasis is placed on how well individuals listen and establish meaningful and viable alliances.

The T-group examines interpersonal processes and focuses on increasing participants' level of social relating skills and interpersonal competence (Argyris, 1962).

3. *Group-level processes* refer to the behavior of the group as

a social system and the co-actor's relatedness to that system. The focus is on the group-as-a-whole (suprapersonal) (Bion, 1961; Gibbard, 1975; Rioch, 1970).

The unit of analysis is the *group* as a system. Groups can be considered more or less the sum total of their parts. Hence, group members are considered interdependent subsystems co-acting and interacting together via the group's life mentality. Group-level analysis assumes that when a co-actor acts, he or she is acting not only on his or her own behalf, but on behalf of the group or parts of the group. Co-actor behavior from a group-level perspective cannot be simply examined by assuming that the motivation and genesis of the co-actor is merely a function of his or her idiosyncrasies. It must be viewed as a synthesis of and interaction with the *group's* life and mentality. Simply stated, the co-actor is seen as a vehicle through which the group expresses its life. (An in-depth discussion of group-level phenomena follows.)

Tavistock small study groups use the group-as-a-whole as the unit of analysis (Rice, 1965; Klein and Astrachan, 1971). Miller and Rice (1967) also use group-level analysis for work redesign strategies and autonomous work groups.

4. *Intergroup processes* refer, in part, to relations among various groups or subgroups. The intergroup processes derive from the group memberships that co-actors carry with them into groups and their behavior toward other groups. The basis for intergroup relations can develop from hierarchical and task position, sex, race, age, ethnic identities, and ideological differences (Alderfer, 1977). Intergroup relations: (1) determine in part how we treat and are treated by others, (2) profoundly color our perception of the world, and (3) play a critical role in determining how co-actors form their personal sense of reality (Smith, 1977). Experiential simulations are sometimes used to study intergroup phenomena (Wells, 1978c; Oshry, 1978).

5. *Interorganizational processes* refer to relationships that exist between organizations and their environment and concern the set of organizations that make demands of, or have impact upon, the focal organization (Evan, 1966). Interorganizational analysis focuses on the ecotone and the causal texture of the environment (Emery and Trist, 1973a).

Each of the five levels described above refers to behavioral systems conceptually different from, but not unrelated to or without connection to, one another. Analysis of organizational processes at these levels moves toward a comprehensive view of individual and group dynamics.

Since behavior is multidetermined, organizational processes can be examined and understood in terms of any or all of these levels. Organizational processes are analogous to a radio broadcasting band. If one tunes into 107.5 FM, this does not mean that 96.0 is not broadcasting, but rather that one has just amplified a particular station. Thus, if one focuses on interpersonal processes, it does not mean that group-level processes are not occurring, but only that one has selected a particular level of organizational process for attention. For the purposes of this chapter, group-level phenomena are elucidated. In other words, group-level processes are amplified.

THE GROUP-AS-A-WHOLE (GROUP LEVEL) AS A UNIT OF ANALYSIS

Using a group-level perspective, a group is conceptualized as being more *and* less than the sum total of the individual co-actors (members) and their intrapsychic dynamics. Group life exists above and below that of individual group members, and the group has a life of its own distinct from but related to the dynamics of the co-actors who compose the group membership.

Groups are living systems and group members are interdependent co-actors (subsystems) whose interactions form a *gestalt.* That gestalt is the élan vital of the group, and becomes the object of study from the group-level perspective.

In this connection, Bion (1961) has postulated that a group's mentality[2] exists beyond that of the individual group members. He suggests that the group's mentality connects (bonds) group members by an unconscious tacit agreement. Gibbard (1975) suggests that the group's mentality is best understood as "a process of unconscious collusion . . . 'a machinery of intercommunication' . . . which is at

---

[2]Bion's concept of group mentality and the concept of the group's élan vital (its quintessence, its existential core) are related in a very fundamental way. They both assert that there is a phenomenon that exists above or below that of individual group members. These concepts postulate that a group life exists distinct from the individual group members. Yet Bion's group mentality and its conceptual cousin, basic assumption group, are helpful but often confusing (Sherwood, 1964). (For an excellent review of Bionic theory, see Gibbard, 1975.) In their present conceptual form they leave too many unresolved and knotty theoretical issues that cloud rather than clarify.

For conceptual simplicity, I will refrain from their use here. I will offer an alternative heuristic concept (projective identification motif) by which to understand the group-as-a-whole phenomenon.

once a characteristic of groups and a reflection of the individual's ability or even his propensity to express drives and feelings covertly, unconsciously, and anonymously" (p. 7).

At this point it would be helpful to consider the following series of questions:

1. Of what substance is the group's élan vital made?

2. Using the group as the unit of analysis, why are co-actors considered interdependent? And, why are all of their behaviors conceptualized as mere manifestations and representations of the group's existential core?

3. Do individuals have ultimate control over determining what they say, think, and do in groups?

These questions are only a sampling of the myriad that could be raised. The material below attempts to answer them and describes the theory upon which a group-level analysis using a systemic socioanalytic perspective is founded.

GROUP-AS-MOTHER

Competent individuals often behave as though they were deskilled, nonrational, or lobotomized. When brought together in a group to perform tasks, capable human beings often lose their problem-solving facilities, become emotionally segregated, and blame others for their failure. Their behavior in these instances is marked by an infantile, regressed quality.

Groups and group members can behave in effective problem-solving ways, yet all groups regress at some point in their life. It is the group's *regression* to which this chapter addresses itself.

Bion (1961), Gibbard (1975), and Scheidlinger (1964) assert that the central issue for individuals, when joining or participating in groups, is the tension generated by the unconscious fear of being engulfed, obliterated by the group (fused with) at one extreme and becoming a person-in-isolation (estranged/separated) from the group at the other extreme. Both extremes are severely undesirable. This tension creates strong ambivalent (love/hate) feelings toward the group situation. The individual is conceptualized as possessing conflicting feelings about the same object (that is, the group situation) simultaneously. Moreover, these strong ambivalent feelings unconsciously return the adults to their infant roots.

An infant, too, struggles with ambivalence. On the one hand, he seeks to be engulfed and fused with his mother, while on the other he seeks to become separated from her. Indeed, for the infant's survival both options are undesirable ends. Given this tension, the infant has strong ambivalent feelings about the mother. In a word, infants have both conflicting love/hate feelings about the same object—the mother. The infant's struggles with the mother and the individual struggles with the group are parallel. Bion (1961) states that the group-as-a-whole "approximates too closely in the minds of individuals comprising it very primitive fantasies about the contents of the mother's body." In short, the group represents the *primal mother* for the individual.

This tension and ambivalence experienced by the infant and the individual-in-group create an unbearable psychological state of affairs. There is a need to resolve these ambivalent feelings, thus relieving the frustration about the same object—for the infant it is the mother, for the individual-in-group the group.

Object-relations theory suggests (Klein, 1946; Mahler, 1972) that an infant initially is unable to make a distinction between what is inside the self and what is outside the self. Thus, the infant has no "ego" to differentiate self from the world; he or she experiences self as the world, and to him or her everything *is* self. Concomitantly, the infant experiences self as omnipotent. This omnipotence is reinforced by continuous meeting of the neonate's needs. As time passes, the infant matures and some needs are gradually frustrated. Greatly troubled by the frustration, the infant develops a strategy to cope with this condition by projecting "good" and "bad" feelings onto outside objects. Rice (1965) suggests:

> So far as it excites him and gratifies him, it is a "good object" which he loves and on which he lavishes his care; so far as it frustrates or hurts him, it is a "bad object" which he hates and on which he vents his rage. In his struggle to deal with these contradictory attributes he splits objects into good and bad, which represent their satisfying and frustrating aspects. (p. 11).

What complicates matters more is that the infant learns that the same object (typically mother) sometimes satisfies and sometimes frustrates—hence the same object is both good and bad. Yet, the infant wants to lavish the good object and wants to destroy (eschew) the bad object.

This condition creates a major problem for the infant—to take in the good object (mother), the infant also takes in what is bad—thus threatening to destroy what he wants most to preserve, i.e., good

object. In this confusing state of affairs the infant is unable to cope
with simultaneously conflicting feelings about the same object—then
splits off the bad parts into others (p. 11).

The infant both loves and hates object/mother. Unable to cope
with the overwhelming ambivalent feelings, the infant uses splitting
and projective identification to maintain psychological equilibrium
and to cope with life-threatening anxiety generated by having both
bad and good in the same object. Often the infant's solution to this
ambivalence is to have a good Mummy and bad Daddy. As infants
progress, their solution then becomes good parents–bad strangers.
Infants always act to maintain an *autistic preambivalent state*. They
seek an autistic state akin to intrauterine life.

Splitting is a primitive psychological mechanism used where
individuals disown parts of self that are undesirable. *Projective identification* is a psychological mechanism by which individuals unconsciously identify with an object (person, event, attitude) by
externalizing (projecting) split (disowned) parts of themselves.

Melanie Klein (1946) introduced the term *projective identification* to indicate a process by which parts of the self are split off
and projected into an external object or part object (Malin and Grotstein, 1966). Hanna Segal (1964), a colleague of Klein, remarks: "Projective identification is the result of the projection of parts of the
self into an object. It may result in the object being perceived as
having acquired the characteristics of the projected part of the self,
but it can also result in the self becoming identified with the object
of its projection."

Jaques (1955) suggests that adults in institutional and group
settings often use infantile coping strategies—for example, projective identification—to cope with overwhelming ambivalent feelings
generated in the course of social relations. Illustrating the concept
of projective identification, he states:

> The soldiers who take their leader for their ego ideal, are in effect
> projectively identifying with him or putting part of themselves into
> him. It is this common or shared projective identification which en-
> ables the soldiers to identify with each other. In the extreme form of
> projective identification of this kind, the followers become totally
> dependent on the leader because each has given up a part of himself
> to the leader (p. 482).

He goes on to cite Freud's (1959) case of how Assyrian soldiers
became totally confused and acted as though they were brain-
damaged. They retreated in confusion upon hearing that their leader,
Holofernes, had had his head cut off by Judith. For not only had the

commonly shared external object (the figurehead) binding them all together been lost, but the leader had also lost his head. Thus, every soldier had lost his head because each was inside the leader via projective identification.

Groups (families, work groups, classrooms, experiential learning laboratories) elicit strong ambivalent feelings in their members. Groups both nurture and scold. Groups are needed, yet resented, by individuals. Groups are experienced as both bad and good simultaneously. Groups create feelings of bliss and despair. Groups, like mothers, create strong, conflicting ambivalent feelings of love and hate.

Gibbard (1975) aptly states: "The natural psychological habitat of man is the group. Man's adaptation to that habitat is imperfect, a state of affairs which is reflected in his chronic ambivalence towards groups. Group membership is psychologically essential and yet a source of increasing discomfort" (p. 33).

Bion (1961) declares: "The individual is a group animal at war not simply with the group, but with himself for being a group animal and with those aspects of his personality that constitute his 'groupishness' " (p. 131).

Ambivalence is central for infant-mother relations and for the individual-in-group relationship. Groups create the same range of feelings that is created in the infant-mother relationship. Moreover, both infants in relation to mothers and individuals in relation to groups use projective identification and splitting to cope with overwhelming tension and ambivalence. Hence, the concept of group-as-mother is established.

It is the *group-as-mother* paradigm that underlies the group-level analysis. The interplay between projective and introjective

Individual's (infant) relationship with mother	Individual's relationship with group

—Struggles with fusing/joining and separating/becoming independent

—Experiences nurturance and frustration

—Experiences strong ambivalent feelings

—Experiences both love and hate

—Elicits defense mechanisms of splitting and projective identification to cope with anxiety identification[3] and splitting that brings group members together is being analyzed in the group-as-a-whole approach. Moreover, it is the dynamic unconscious pattern or matrix shared by the group members that provides the substance of the group's élan vital. Thus, individual group members are considered connected to each other by an unconscious or preconscious tacit alliance.

This unconscious (tacit) alliance allows each member to use other members as objects to express split parts of him- or herself. The unconscious alliance and concomitant motif begins when the group members experience tension and ambivalence created by the struggle between engulfment or enstrangement by the group. This struggle unconsciously returns the adults to their infant roots— therefore to the infant-mother dyad, concomitant dynamics, and coping strategies used by the infant: for example, projective identification.

Group-level analysis is an important perspective in understanding group and interpersonal relations. The integration of system theory and Kleinian concepts provides a helpful vantage point from which organizational processes can be discerned. Projective identification, role differentiation, and scapegoating are common manifestations of these dynamics.

PROJECTIVE IDENTIFICATION, ROLE DIFFERENTIATION, AND SCAPEGOATING IN GROUPS

Projective identification, role differentiation, and scapegoating in groups are defined and discussed in detail in this section. The premise is that excessive projective identification leads to rigid role differentiation, which ultimately can cause scapegoating (a special and destructive form of role differentiation) in groups. Particular attention is given to analyzing interpersonal (member-to-member) relations in groups from a socioanalytic perspective. Understanding these concepts and their relationships is central to the "systemic socioanalytic" approach.

---

[3]Introjective identification is a psychological defense by which the individual identifies with an external object by taking the object into him- or herself.

Projective Identification

The term *projective identification* was first proposed by Melanie Klein (1946) to describe a psychological process by which individuals project split parts of self into an external object. Zinner (1976) states:

> Projective identification is an activity of the ego that modifies perception of the object and, in reciprocal fashion, alters the image of the self. These conjoined changes in perception influence and may, in fact, govern behavior of the self toward the object. Thus, projective identification provides an important conceptual bridge between an individual and an interpersonal psychology, since our awareness of the mechanism permits us to understand specific interaction among persons in terms of specific dynamic conflict occurring within individuals.

Thus, projective identification provides us with a way to understand the psychosocial matrix that exists between individuals and groups.

Klein (1946) further defines projective identification as "a combination of splitting off parts of the self and projecting them onto another person." In her later work (Klein, 1959), she describes projective identification as the "feeling of identification with other people because one has attributed qualities or attributes of one's own to them."

As indicated earlier, projective identification is a coping mechanism—a defense—that infants use to manage anxiety and ambivalence that is generated in relation to the mother for being both a good (nurturing) and a bad (frustrating) object. Wanting only the good-nurturing object, the infant splits off bad parts and projects these out to others (nonmother). Hence, projective identification is the primary psychological defense mechanism employed by infants to cope with life-threatening bad objects. Projective identification entails some distortion of reality. It simplifies one's emotional life: for example, making mother into an "all good" object.

Zinner (1976), Jaffe (1968), and Malin and Grotstein (1966) all remark that projective identification is closely related to Anna Freud's description of Edward Bibring's concept of "altruistic surrender." Anna Freud (1946) describes altruistic surrender as when the "self finds a proxy in the outside world to serve as a repository for the self's own wishes," where the self can experience vicarious gratification of the projected impulse. There is an implicit willingness by the object to collude in providing vicarious gratification for the subject.

Malin and Grotstein (1966) suggest that projection cannot occur without identification with the object upon which the projection is thrown. They assert:

> When we start with the projection it is necessary that there be some process of identification or internalization in general, or else we can never be aware of the projection. That is, what is projected would be lost like a satellite rocketed out of the gravitational pull of the Earth. Eventually, all contact with the satellite will be lost. Although the satellite has left Earth, it must remain under the influence of Earth's gravitational pull in order for it to maintain some contact with Earth. A projection of itself seems meaningless unless the individual can retain some contact with what is projected. That contact is a type of internalization, or, loosely, an identification (p. 27).

In short, a projection has an object with which the individual must identify, often unconsciously. The individual identifies with the object through projection. Projection implies an identification.

In further refinement, Zinner (1976) describes four ways in which projective identification operates within interpersonal and group relations. He states:

> (1) the subject perceives the object as if the object contained elements of the subject's personality; (2) the subject can evoke behavior or feelings in the object that conform with the subject's perceptions; (3) the subject can experience vicariously the activity and feelings of the object; and (4) participants in close relationship are often in collusion with one another to sustain mutual projection: that is, to support one another's defensive operations and to provide experiences through which the other can participate vicariously (p. 285).

Zinner (1976) further states: "For projective identification to function effectively as a defense, the true nature of the relationship between the self and its projected part must remain unconscious" (p. 295–6).

Projective identification not only functions as a defense, but it is also the psychodynamic basis upon which individuals are able to empathize with another. Projecting parts of the self onto the other, then identifying with the other allows the person to feel with the other. Yet, excessive identification seeks an autistic, preambivalent state—akin to the life of the neonate.

Laughlin (1970) describes the King David reaction, which is closely related to excessive projective identification. The King David reaction is based upon the biblical character King David and the Little Ewe Lamb parable (2 Sam. 11–12). Briefly, King David has lain with Bathsheba, the wife of his general Uriah, while Uriah was off at battle. Bathsheba conceived and sent word to David, saying, "I am with child." David then sent for Uriah from battle, hoping that he would lie with Bathsheba. Uriah, a committed general, would not lie with Bathsheba because his men could not rest and eat well. Uriah slept at the king's door, refusing to go home. David then sent Uriah back to the front lines so that he might be killed. Uriah was indeed killed. Then the prophet Nathan is sent to David.

> . . . And he came unto him, and said unto him,
> There were two men in one city; the one rich, and the other poor.
> The rich man had exceeding many flocks and herds:
> But the poor man had nothing, save one little ewe lamb, which he had bought and nourished up: and it grew up together with him, and with his children; it did eat of his own meat, and drank of his own cup, and lay in his bosom, and was unto him as a daughter.
> And there came a traveller unto the rich man, and he spared to take of his own flock and of his own herd, to dress for the wayfaring man that was come unto him; but took the poor man's lamb, and dressed it for the man that was come to him.
> And David's anger was greatly kindled against the man; and he said to Nathan, As the Lord liveth, the man that has done this thing shall surely die:
> And he shall restore the lamb fourfold, because he did this thing, and because he had no pity.
> And Nathan said to David, Thou art the man. . . .

David reacted with great contempt for the rich, selfish man. Clearly, he was reacting to a consciously unrecognized and disowned aspect of himself. Nathan poignantly points to this fact with "Thou art the man."

The King David reaction is operative when individuals respond to others with excessively positive or negative feelings, and evaluate them accordingly. The King David reaction often emerges from scant real data about the other. Powerful unconscious identification occurs with the other through projection of either approved or disapproved aspects of the self. The subject recognizes a part of self in the object.

Laughlin (1970) defines the King David reaction as

> a complex intrapsychic defensive operation involving the cooperation and mutual interaction of repression, projection and identification; it is usually supported in some measure by rationalization and at times related to denial. . . . Through this reaction consciously unrecognized and disowned elements of the self-appraisal which were often ordinarily present to some extent in the other person are also further ascribed to him through projection—and reacted to accordingly. This

process has evoked the otherwise unexplained feelings which are experienced toward the other person. The King David reaction may be negative or positive (p. 238).

As human beings we have a tendency to act in self-serving ways. We eschew parts of ourselves that make us uncomfortable, but readily see those parts in others. Projective identification in general and the King David reaction in particular are useful concepts that increase our understanding of interpersonal relations and group behavior.

Zinner (1976) and Greenspan and Mannis (1974) cogently describe how projective identification operates in the marital relationship. Zinner and Shapiro (1972) articulate how projective identification affects families and their adolescents. Malin and Grotstein (1966) discuss the ramifications of projective identification in therapeutic relationships. Bion (1955, 1956) and Rosenfeld (1952, 1954) use the concept of projective identification to understand and treat psychosis.

Scheidlinger (1964, 1968), Gibbard (1975), and Bion (1961) postulate that adults employ projective identification to cope with the "threat of losing one's personal identity in groups." In using the group-as-mother, individuals employ projective identification and splitting to defend against primitive anxiety and ambivalence that threaten the person's sense of self. Additionally, these writers assert that group members act as proxies in which to deposit disowned (split) parts of themselves. Hence, each group member can become a receptacle for the projected parts of their cohorts. Each group member is likely to elicit a particular kind of projection and is thus symbolized in unique ways. This process of symbolization differentiates group members and thrusts them into specialized roles within the group. Role differentiation results from splitting, projective identification (that is, unconscious alliance), and symbolization among group members.

In essence, each member is called upon to assume role(s) (given how they are symbolized) that provide a service to the group. These differentiated roles divide and distribute expressive, cognitive, instrumental, mythical, and reparative elements within the group. Fundamentally, roles in groups, in part, serve to manage anxiety, defend against deindividualization or estrangement, structure the group's élan vital, and get work done.

Hence, each group member performs important functions on behalf of the group. In this regard all services and functions (that is, roles) performed in groups are interdependent. This individual role behavior must always be analyzed in the context of the constellation of roles distributed in the group. In short, individual role behavior is *embedded* in the field of other roles. *All* roles serve meaningful and purposeful functions in groups.

Projective Identification Motif in Groups

The group's projective identification is the precursor for symbolization and role differentiation. The *projective identification motif* refers to the unconscious (tacit) alliance that forms among group members. It describes how individuals are connected to co-members—often in consciously unrecognized ways. Through projective identification, group members are connected to each other by passion, indifference, silence, contempt, respect, love, guilt, hate, or in other ways. The patterning of projective identification *bonds* group members together.

Myriad and recurrent patterns of projective identification occur within small groups. Task, technological and environmental demands, and constraints interacting upon group members' valence bonds, together with members' willingness to assume roles (although often unconsciously), determine various patterns that emerge in the groups.

The patterning of projective identification in groups is also dependent upon individual group members' *valence bonds*. Individual group members elicit, introject, and collude with particular kinds of projections ascribed to them. The group member's valence bonds, or tendency to respond to certain types of projections and to adopt special roles, are analogous to the propensity that elements have to combine as in a chemical reaction (Bion, 1961). By definition, projective identification between individuals (subject and object) involves unconscious collusion. This *collusion* is based on a person's valence bonds and his or her relation to the group.

Valency, or the propensity to collude, introject, and respond to projections by others, is dependent upon (1) the individual's object relations (that is, how the individual relates to himself and to the outside world)—his or her psychological set; (2) the individual's identity based on demographic characteristics (for example, socioeconomic status, race, ethnicity, age, and gender) and stereotypic attributions (that is, projections, symbolizations, and imagoes) ascribed to these demographic characteristics by others. (For example, women are typically affective, men are cognitive and rational; blacks are hypersexual, whites are nonsexual. See Kovel, 1970.)

These attributions ascribed to a particular demographic identity group make a significant contribution to the valence of the individual. Hence, valency is determined by the person's object re-lations and attributions ascribed to his or her identity group. Indeed, a person's object relations should involve how he or she responds to skin color, gender, age, sex. Yet it has not been extensively dis-cussed in the literature how sociological characteristics affect psy-chological operations. Stated simply, the propensity to collude, introject, and respond to projections from others and to adopt roles in groups is dependent upon an individual's personal and group iden-tity. This definition of valency includes an individual's psycholog-ical and sociological identity. For example, in a mixed-gender group men typically attribute affective-emotional qualities to women. Women are expected to play caretaking and maintenance roles in groups. Similarly, women often ascribe rational and cognitive qual-ities to men. Men are expected to play task-oriented aggressive roles. Through projective identification men and women maintain these affective/cognitive, caretaking/rational splits among and within themselves. Although progress is being made on redefining tradi-tional sex role behavior, the collusive system of projective identi-fication among males and females makes it difficult for them to experience themselves as having both affective and cognitive qual-ities. Indeed, it is difficult to be a *whole* person in this culture.

If a white male executive in banking were to be affectively expressive, it is highly probable that he would be limited in ad-vancement or eventually dismissed. To be affectively expressive violates norms governing the behavior of banking executives. White males (in particular), through projective identification, carry the bur-den of being simply rational, nonemotional creatures. Given the high correlation between Type A personality and executives, their sup-pressed affects have health consequences that often result in fatal coronary disease (Jenkins, 1971; Caplan and Jones, 1975).

The excessive use of projective identification to manage inter-personal relations and group situations becomes a major problem and interferes with group effectiveness. For example, Janis's (1972) analysis of the Kennedy cabinet and Bay of Pigs clearly indicates how excessive projective identification was used to keep individuals in highly rigid roles. Age and social status dictated that undersecre-taries should not speak in cabinet meetings unless they were asked questions by senior cabinet members. A collusive system developed between junior and senior cabinet members that maintained highly rigid roles. It allowed each member to split off parts of himself (the uncertain parts) in each of the others. The "logic" of this projective identification is this:

If senior cabinet members believe that they are most knowl-edgeable, the most experienced and possess most insight regarding national security, they then can split the parts of themselves that may doubt their omniscience, and project their doubts onto the junior cabinet members. Junior cabinet members are then perceived as less knowledgeable and competent. This allows the senior cabinet members to keep the illusion of superior competence in understanding national security matters. In short, senior cabinet members manage to reduce their anxiety by splitting then projecting the doubting parts off in the junior members.

In juxtaposition, junior cabinet members projected their competent parts on the senior members. If the junior members project their competent parts onto the senior members, it allows them to avoid responsibility for taking a definitive stance about national security policies. The junior members could hide behind their lower status. Indeed, senior members were more than willing to have the junior members defer to their greater wisdom. In short, junior members treated senior members like they had *all* the competence. The senior members colluded with this illusion.

Hence, senior and junior members, by excessive use of projective identification, developed a collusive system of illusions and rigid roles that prevented effective problem-solving behavior.

The cabinet's behavior in handling the Bay of Pigs incident illustrates how projective identification in groups operates: (1) to protect individuals from threats to their identity (ego-ideal), (2) to maintain highly rigid roles, and (3) to maintain a collusive system. It also demonstrates how valency, in this case based on social status and age, can contribute to role behavior in groups.

Effective problem-solving and decision-making in groups are related to projective identification that develops among group members. This is a recurrent motif that emerges in groups that hinders or facilitates task accomplishment. Excessive projective identification among group members is more likely to lead to task ineffectiveness, rigid role differentiation, and destructive scapegoating.

Role Differentiation in Groups

Role differentiation results from the projective identification and symbolization that emerge in groups. Role differentiation is the vehicle by which group members manage their conflicts, ambivalence, and task(s). Gibbard (1974) states:

> Role differentiation . . . is in part a defensive and restitutive effort; and the cost of such differentiation, to the individual and the group, is that splitting, projection and compartmentalization all entail some distortion and simplification of emotional life.

Any specialization limits the individual's range of possibilities—a limitation often compounded by group pressures which seduce or lock the individual into roles that do not meet his emotional requirements. Scapegoating is only the most dramatic manifestation of the group's tendency to exploit the individual. To some degree all group membership is contingent on a conscious or unconscious contract which obligates the individual to sacrifice or suppress some aspect of himself in order to express or develop others. Thus, the individual often finds that groups do not permit him to "be himself" (p. 250).

Role differentiation also serves an adaptive function for the group. Gibbard (1974) asserts further:

Rather than becoming flooded with conflict, the group can make use of individuals (or dyads or subgroups) to circumscribe, localize and isolate conflicts. Through projective identification, a group is divided into actors and audience. Members are recruited to dramatize the central conflicts of the collectivity, and other members are able to participate vicariously in this dramatization (p. 251).

Thus, role differentiation can serve both defensive and adaptive functions that are intended to protect individuals from anxiety and ambivalence. Roles provide vehicles that bridge and anchor the group. Individuals use roles to find psychological security, often by depositing and exchanging unwanted parts. The matrix of these transactions and their meanings change during the group's life.

Roles are interdependent and distribute the group's élan vital. The distribution produces a variety of actors with different scripts. These actors play their "parts" in service of the group's plot. The group's drama creates myriad "parts" for individuals to assume. Each member has a "part" in unfolding the group's drama. Hence, an array of roles emerges in groups based on projective identification (for example, hero, seducer, silent member, loved object, combatant, scapegoat, pariah, taskmaster, clown, politician, oppressor, victim, patient, conciliator, incompetent, counterdependent, uninvolved, protector). These roles emerge from the group's plot (that is, unconscious relationships and aims of the group) and the valency of the members to assume particular "parts."

To understand a role in groups we must examine how it is *embedded* in the context of other roles. Embedded role analysis is critical to the socioanalytic approach. The following vignette describes a classroom situation and how roles are embedded and interdependent.

Dave B. had been acting out; he was consistently trying the patience of the teacher, Ms. T. She was finding Dave's behavior quite unbearable. She inferred that Dave had poor impulse control, inadequate parental guidance, and poor analytical skills. She essentially used an intrapersonal analysis to understand Dave's behavior. The conclusion of her analysis was that Dave needed to be put into a special class for emotionally disturbed children. She then made this recommendation to the principal. Dave was sent to the special class.

On the day of Dave's departure from class, Clay, another student in class, began to ask a series of questions of the teacher, spoke when others were speaking, and became "disruptive." His behavior resembled Dave's behavior. Using an intrapersonal analysis again, the teacher concluded that Clay had "problems" similar to Dave's. Hence, Clay was finally put into the special class.

As this was occurring, the other class members often giggled; first at Dave, then at Clay. As the teacher would scold the boys, the class would sit back smiling—not at Dave or Clay, but rather at Ms. T. The class seemed to have an investment in seeing Ms. T. upset and troubled. It also allowed the class task to be abandoned. Clay's and Dave's classmates appeared well behaved and attentive. They seemed to have an agreement to act "as if" they were good little children, and let two of their members express their discontent with task and contempt toward the teacher.

Additionally, on the day Clay was transferred, John began to behave in a similar way—to play Dave's and Clay's part. The plot continues.

This illustration shows the power of group-level processes. Ms. T. thought that the problem with the classroom was within the characterological structure of the students. She assumed that if she could get rid of the "troublemakers" things would go quite smoothly. She failed to understand, however, that these students were expressing concerns on behalf of the group. They were only vehicles through which the group expressed its contempt and rage not only for the task but also for the teacher.

It was mentioned that we have ambivalent feelings about authority figures and groups—we both love and hate them simultaneously. However, it is difficult to have conflicting feelings about the same object; hence, we split off our negative feelings into others. Yet, through projective identification we identify with the person who is expressing negative affect by projecting our disowned negative parts. This enables us (audience) to act "as if" all of the contempt, rage, and discontent exist in the other (actor) (Gibbard, 1975). Here is the origin of scapegoating.

We see this phenomenon in work groups and organizations where an individual is symbolized as incompetent or ineffective. Typically, his or her associates secretly discuss the incompetence or the anxiety level of the individual. They act "as if" this person is the only one who is incompetent or has feelings of anxiety. There seems to be a tacit agreement among them to localize the incompetence into this particular person. The manager of the unit evaluates the individual similarly. The person is then put on probation, transferred, or dismissed. The manager in this situation acts "as if" the problems of his unit exist at the intrapersonal level: that is, within the individual. The manager does not examine the context in which the "incompetent" worker occurred. He or she does not examine why the group has allowed this person to become incompetent. Moreover, he or she does not ask how it serves the unit to *have* this particular person incompetent. It could serve the unit in several ways. It allows the other members to split off their feelings of incompetence (bad parts) into this member, and at the same time, through projective identification, identify with the person's incompetence (because this incompetence is also a part of the member's internal world that he has disowned and externally projected). Hence, the incompetence seen in this particular member represents the projected bad parts of the other group members. Moreover, the projected bad parts are to be destroyed; thus, there seems to be an investment in seeing that this member carry incompetence, hoping that it will vanish. Yet we know that it does not solve the problem.

After this person is put on probation, transferred, or dismissed, another person may be asked to carry the incompetence on behalf of the unit. In short, if a unit allows one of its group members to carry all of the anxiety or feelings of incompetence, the person will indeed go crazy or get dismissed. Implicit in this conceptual framework is the interdependence of roles.

Role differentiation is, indeed, an imperfect solution for managing the group's problem. This can be seen in the prior illustration. What often results from role differentiation is a compartmentalization of key members who are flooded with anxiety. Winter (1974) describes Redl's (1942) concept of *group psychological role suction* where "under certain conditions a specific group situation seems to have an amazing power to 'suck' individuals into performing certain tasks, even though they may not have been strongly inclined in that direction; these are tasks which are important for the comfort, or which respond to the motivational or organizational needs of the group" (p. 83).

The group's psychological role suction is a powerful force in the group to keep members in their roles—even if they are not consciously willing to play them. For example, it is rare that a person consciously volunteers to play the scapegoat role. This, however, does not suggest that there is not a collusion to take the role. The scapegoat role appears to be ubiquitous and perhaps the most costly and destructive to the group and individuals. This is not to say that other roles are not important, but rather that scapegoating in a group should receive more examination. The following section describes scapegoating in detail.

In sum, role differentiation is essentially a way that individuals cope with the group situation. The emergence of roles serves defensive and adaptive functions. Changing role differentiation is a manifestation of the group's changing pattern of projective identification.

Scapegoating in Groups

Scapegoating is a special and destructive form of role differentiation, particularly in the context of work groups. The origin of scapegoating has its roots in myths and rituals of mankind. It emerges from the religious ritual of sacrifice and totemistic practices (Jaffe, 1968; Lieberman et al., 1973).

The ritual of scapegoating is found in the Book of Leviticus 16:1-34. Scapegoating was practiced by the early Hebrew tribes to atone for their transgressions against their God. Leviticus 16, verses 7-10, states:

> (7) And he should take the two goats, and present them before the Lord at the door of the tabernacle of the congregation.
> (8) And Aaron shall cast lots upon the two goats; one lot for the Lord, and the other lot for the scapegoat.
> (9) And Aaron shall bring the goat upon which the Lord's lot fell, and offer him for a sin offering.
> (10) But the goat, on which the lot fell to be scapegoat, shall be presented alive before the Lord, to make atonement with him, and to let him go for a scapegoat into the wilderness.

The scapegoat represented sins of the tribes that must be separated from themselves and sent into the wilderness. The tribe could project and exorcise their sins through the scapegoat. This act of exorcising the sin (bad parts) on the head of the scapegoat is a mechanism used to cope with their ambivalent relationship to their deity and group. Jaffe (1968) states:

> In the process of atonement and purification, the ritual involves, among other things, the disposition of two goats. One is killed and the blood sprinkled upon the arkcover and then upon the altar . . . it is burnt to make smoke. . . .

The ritual proceeds to dispose of the second goat, which is the "scape-goat." *The entire removal of the sin and guilt of the community is symbolized by placing these upon the head of the goat who is then sent away, bearing all of the inequities, into the wilderness or "land which is cut off" (to prevent the animal's return).*

When later it was no longer possible to send the goat to a place whence it could not return to inhabited parts, the practice became one of casting the animal down a precipice (p. 667) (author's italics).

Groups often search for the scapegoat to represent and repent for their badness (that is, anxiety, weakness, sins, et cetera). The scapegoat role provides the group with an imperfect solution to its felt badness: for example, incompetence, anxiety, racism, or conflict. By projective identification group members deposit their unwanted parts (their guilt, rage, contempt) in another, then proceed to drive the other into the wilderness or into death.

As the Hebrew children used the scapegoat to atone for their sins and to eliminate their guilt, the group uses the scapegoat to cope with its anxiety and badness. Groups create scapegoats to hide every person's self-contempt, self-doubt, weakness, and destruc-tiveness. Miller (1974) states:

Scapegoating is a stereotyped example in groups where shared patterns of denial are focused by the process of projective identification on one member. That member is asked and often agrees to express all of the given undesirable attitudes for the group (p. 12).

The *search* for a scapegoat or scapegoats typically begins after the group experiences aggression or frustration. Unconsciously the group members' thought may be: "Someone is responsible for my anxiety." This begins the group's search-and-destroy mission.

Typically, people with different demographic characteristics, expressive personalities, and valency for patient or martyr roles be-come excellent candidates for scapegoating. Groups may even locate a dyad or triad to deposit their denied feelings and then behave in ways to isolate or render them crazy.

Using a scapegoat is an easy (albeit infantile) psychological solution for anxiety and unwanted parts. Excessive projective iden-tification allows group mmbers to deposit all unwanted parts in the scapegoat at the expense of the scapegoat. The scapegoat allows other group members to maintain their self-righteous autistic imagoes. This is why the scapegoat must be separated and sent away; the group cannot stand to look at or face itself seen in the scapegoat. Hence, group members deny any responsibility for making a scape-goat or having any characteristics of the scapegoat.

This cycle of search, isolate, destroy, and denial creates group casualties: to fill a person up with the group's anxiety (psychotic feelings); isolate these feelings in the person as if he or she is the only one who is feeling crazy; exorcise the person from the group; and then deny any responsibility for making a person into a scape-goat is a subtle and dangerous operation. Scapegoating has taken its toll of human life, destroying work groups, organizations, and fam-ilies (Lieberman et al., 1973).

Excessive projective identification and rigid role differentiation lead to scapegoating. Role reversal, maintenance discussion, and/or interventions in the group's projective identification motif can alter the scapegoating phenomenon.

Comprehending the complexity of the scapegoating phenom-enon is essential to the systemic socioanalytic approach. Increasing the awareness of group members may abate the group's tendency to scapegoat. There are indeed other ways groups can cope with their anxiety and frustration.

DIAGNOSTIC HEURISTICS

The group-as-a-whole framework provides a basis for diagnos-ing organizational behavior. A variety of heuristics will be given and then applied to a concrete case.

Diagnostic Strategies of the Socioanalytic Approach[4]

1. Make an initial analysis of the group's processes, using all psychological levels of organizational processes (that is, intrapersonal, interpersonal, group-level, intergroup level, interorganizational).

2. Develop alternative and competing hypotheses about what is occurring in the group situation.

3. Give greater emphasis to interpersonal, group-level, and intergroup processes than to intrapersonal processes. The diagnostician should give individuals in conflict the benefit of the doubt that the reason for the "problems" is not solely dependent on their intrapsychic condition. Too often intrapersonal analyses are made. This often prematurely indicts/blames individuals for an organizational problem. Intrapersonal analysis is quite costly for the individual's life and career and for the organization in terms of turnover. Hence, only make intrapersonal attribution about organizational problems when all of the other process levels have been fully explored.

4. When analyzing organizational processes from a group-level perspective, the diagnostician must raise these questions about the group under examination: (a) What does this conflict represent on behalf of the group-as-a-whole? (b) What does the conflict symbolize for the group? (c) What feelings (via projective identification) are being put in these co-actors? (d) Do they express the anxiety, incompetence, or hope on behalf of the group? (e) How does it serve the group to have these co-actors take their specialized roles?

5. The diagnostician must examine him- or herself by stepping back and using the "observing ego" to check the "experiencing ego" or the internal experience of being with the client group. The diagnostician aims to use him- or herself and his or her experiences as a barometer to understand the group's processes.

6. The diagnostician must examine ways he or she may be using projective identification to cope with the consulting role. Projective identification can be abated by working on *owning and living with* ambivalence and concomitant anxiety. This reduces the need to split off internal bad/good feelings.

7. Gather data on the group's unconscious alliances by listen-

---

[4]It is assumed that a diagnostician has been called to consult to a work group where a personality problem exists between Mr. or Ms. X or Mr. or Ms. Y. These heuristics and concomitant discussion will by no means prepare the reader to use the socioanalytic approach. They rather highlight major aspects of the approach.

ing to group themes, the tone of the discussion. Attempt to link and compare the content of the discussion to the "here-and-now" group concerns.

8. Diagnosticians must ask themselves what feelings are being put into them. If the diagnostician feels anxious, hopeless, et cetera, at some levels, the group feels the same and has unconsciously asked the consultant to carry the feelings. At the same time, if the diagnostician feels powerful, competent, "able to leap tall buildings at a single bound," the group via projective identification may be acting "as if" they are incompetent, deskilled infants in need of protection. To collude with the group's wishes confirms that they are infants (which they actually resent), thus creating a more problematic situation.

With the preceding heuristics in mind, the diagnostician can begin to formulate interventions focused at the group level. Interventions are aimed at the group-as-a-whole. They should be interpretative or demonstrative in nature. Comments should be offered about what the group is doing to the individuals who are the identified problems.

The data used to formulate these interventions should always be presented. The use of the "because clause" (Turquet, 1974) is extremely helpful when intervening at the group level. The because clause is a hypothesis about the reason for the group's behavior and how the co-actors express aspects of the group's élan vital.

The diagnostician should discuss the conceptual perspective that he or she uses to examine group processes. It should be stated that individual behavior in groups is assumed to represent the group-as-a-whole. Hence, when a person acts, he or she acts not only on his or her own behalf, but on behalf of the group's life.

Members typically challenge the group-as-a-whole concept. In Western society group members like to see themselves as acting always under their own initiatives. This attitude may represent individualistic norms of the Western world. To adopt a group-level perspective about individual behavior in the group violates the narcissistic striving of the group members. They are frightened by the possibility that they may be controlled by some force other than themselves. To take the group-level perspective elicits anger and fear in group members. They experience the group-level perspective in itself as a narcissistic blow. It challenges their vanity. Hence, resistance against interventions rapidly grows. A working through of the group's response to the intervention is critical. The diagnostician can request the group to step back and examine the moments when the intervention was made and offer comments about the difficulty in understanding the notion that we exist as interdependent co-actors connected by a covert and unconscious relationship.

The diagnostician should only aim to reduce the pressure on the individuals (that is, alter the group's projective identification motif) who represent the identified problem. The diagnostician may consult with the individuals separately to discuss how the group may be using them as a repository.

A series of interventions used to reduce the pressure on and conflict between Ms. A. and Mr. K. follows as an illustration of the socioanalytic approach.

A Case Illustration[5]

A five-day experiential learning laboratory for drug treatment counselors about the treatment and rehabilitation of minority (colored) substance abusers was offered in a large northeastern metropolitan city. During this workshop conflict and hostility developed between two participants: Ms. A., a black woman, and Mr. K., an anglo man. Fifteen participants (eight anglos, five blacks, and two hispanics) comprised the workshop, three blacks the staff. The dean of the laboratory was a black man.

The conflict between Ms. A. and Mr. K. escalated as the laboratory progressed. In large group sessions they often interrupted and disagreed with one another. While these combatants engaged in their seemingly interpersonal problem, the other group members sat as a silent audience, watching with great interest. The *content* of their disagreement focused on the validity of the material presented by the staff (that is, black authority). For example:

> Mr. K. (angrily): These theories do not represent my experience. I don't really know if there are any real differences between black and white clients. A lot of these theories are mere abstractions and bullshit!

> Ms. A. (to Mr. K.): They are real to me. If you don't like it, or it is not consistent with your experience, you can get out—leave. You don't need to help anybody anyway—except your damn self!

Ms. A. always defended the validity of the material. Mr. K. always raised questions about the validity of the material. It was "as if" a discussion regarding the relative merits or deficiencies of the material presented could not occur without erupting into a conflict. Moreover, when Ms. A. and Mr. K. discussed to the point where

[5]The author's role was that of the dean in this case.

they might agree, a member of the group would say: "You really don't listen to each other." (Other members would nod their heads in agreement.) This would act to rekindle the conflict between Ms. A. and Mr. K. They would accuse each other of not listening and the cycle continued, their conflict roles reinforced.

In spite of their promotion of the conflict between Ms. A. and Mr. K. by remaining silently attentive during the interchanges and introducing inflammatory material whenever the two would approach agreement, the other group members were not at all grateful for the services of Ms. A. and Mr. K. on their behalf. On the contrary, they complained, both inside and outside the sessions, that Ms. A. and Mr. K. were "too aggressive," "took up too much air time," and that they were "tired of listening to them."

From an intrapersonal perspective, it would appear that Ms. A. and Mr. K. have personality problems: for example, they each lack impulse control, are excessively insecure and competitive, or just "crazy." The problem lies *within* Ms. A. and Mr. K. To resolve these "intrapersonal problems," individual psychotherapy is recommended.

From an interpersonal perspective, the behaviors of Ms. A. and Mr. K. suggest that their respective communication styles are incongruent, and that they lack interpersonal competence. The problem lies *between* only Ms. A. and Mr. K. To resolve these interpersonal problems, a "training" (T) group experience is recommended.

Using the systemic socioanalytic approach (that is, group-as-a-whole method of analysis), it would appear that Ms. A. and Mr. K. are involved in a conflict in which the other group members are intensely interested. Moreover, it also seemed that the participants had a stake in the conflict between Ms. A. and Mr. K. The other group members, through projective identification, forced Ms. A. and Mr. K. to confront issues for them that were perceived as difficult and anxiety-laden. Once the opposing positions were assumed, they were scapegoated.

By using Ms. A. and Mr. K. as receptacles, the group can simultaneously express its frustration and feel contempt for the dyad. To assume that the problem lies only within Ms. A. or Mr. K., or only between Ms. A. and Mr. K., would be erroneous. Zinner (1976) would say the dyad acted as a "proxy" in the world (outside the self) that served as a repository for the other group members' wishes.

Moreover, it appears "as if" Ms. A. and Mr. K. represented opposite aspects of the ambivalence that the member group had toward the staff group. The group acted out its ambivalence through the dyad—one black, the other white. It is not coincidental that Ms. A., the black woman, expressed the positive side of the ambivalence, and Mr. K., an anglo male, expressed the negative side. The group members wanted to simplify their lives; they wanted things clear—in "black-and-white" terms.

Through projective identification the group used the dyad to resolve strong, conflicting feelings. It was "as if" Ms. A. was in support of the staff without reservation and Mr. K. was against the staff without reservation. In reality, it was more likely that Ms. A. had some reservations about the content of the course and the training staff and Mr. K. had some positive feelings about the course content and the training staff. Yet it was very difficult for either Ms. A. or Mr. K. to have appropriately mixed feelings about the course and training staff.

Under the influence of the group's motif of projective identification, the dyad could not "break out" of their roles without help from other members. They were involved in Redl's (1959) group psychological role suction. The influence of the group's projective identification pattern is revealed in the group members' interest in the pair fighting. They had an unconscious alliance with each other to maintain the pair. At a fantasy level for the group, perhaps, Ms. A. and Mr. K. would come together and produce the *answer* (messiah) to the difficulty in learning by experience and resolve the racial conflicts, but, most of all, they would reduce the overwhelming anxiety generated by participating in this temporary educational enterprise.

This is quite a dangerous situation for the dyads who become the repository for split-off parts of the group. In extreme form, group members in these roles are scapegoated, used, driven crazy, and exorcised from the group or organization. Without a group-level analysis we could assume that the problem lies within the individuals involved. Yet the group projective identification motif reveals that there are forces working to fill up Ms. A. and Mr. K. with negative affect and conflict. It is, indeed, this process that drives individuals psychotic in group and organizational contexts.

Through the use of projective identification, group members (the audience) experience vicarious gratifications of their projected impulses as expressed by the conflict in the black-white dyad. Using Ms. A. and Mr. K. to express conflict allowed the release of the group's frustration and anxiety. It also allowed the other group members (audience) to withdraw and stay aloof, as though they had no investment nor internal tension about participating in the laboratory. Projective identification allowed the audience to take an unconscious voyeuristic attitude toward the interaction between Ms. A. and Mr. K. This unconscious voyeuristic posture assumed by the group members provided a vehicle through which they could split off their bad parts and put them into Ms. A. and Mr. K. Splitting and externalizing the bad parts (that is, anxiety-producing parts) is a defensive maneuver to achieve the preambivalent, autistic state of a neonate.

Yet, what of the implicit collusion by Ms. A. and Mr. K. to express the group's frustration and anxiety? It appeared that Ms. A. was predisposed for strong identification with the staff's competence. She wanted to protect the staff from the anger, contempt, and competition of the group. Through the use of projective identification she could positively identify with the black staff. This, therefore, made it more difficult to experience consciously her own competitive, envious, angry, and contemptuous feelings—unconsciously Ms. A. thought the staff would be destroyed by her badness.

The interaction between Ms. A. and her predisposition or valence toward identifying with the staff[6] and the group members' symbolization of and attribution to her sociological characteristics (that is, black female) extended her identification with the staff to include the function of protecting them. Dumas (1975) suggests that in social systems tremendous pressure is exerted on black women to perform "nanny" or protective, caretaking roles. Hence, at some level, Ms. A. was available to protect the staff. Yet the protection of the staff put extreme pressure on her (on leaving the workshop, Ms. A. and Mr. K. both complained of headaches and fatigue). From an individual point of view, under the influence of the group's projective identification Ms. A.'s *valence bonds* were exaggerated or extended so that it became psychologically uncomfortable and anxiety-provoking for her. She became swept up in the influence of the group's projective identification, which allowed her to take on scapegoat functions concomitantly with Mr. K.

Mr. K., an anglo male, was also predisposed to collude in the group's projective identification. Mr. K. reported that he worked in an all-black organization with a black male director. Hence, he had several concerns. First, he had a sincere desire to work with people of color, and he viewed himself as a sensitive, committed individual

---

[6]Nobles (1974, 1976) suggests that Afro-Americans have maintained their African connection, or "Africanity," despite the assertions made by white "scholars." This Africanity is clearly seen in the black extended family system (Nobles, 1976; Hayles, 1978).

The oneness of being and survival of the tribe are the principles upon which Africanity is based. Thus, in the ontology of Afrocentric people throughout the black diaspora, there is an existential view that all black people are of the "same being," of the same "vital life force" that connects them as one. As an analog, the spider's web represents the relationships in Africa and throughout the black diaspora, as Ms. A.'s identification with the staff, in part, represents Africanity. There seemed to be an implicit existential connection between Ms. A. and the black staff. Her identification with the staff was facilitated by her being-black-in-the-world.

who championed social causes. However, he had ambivalence about having a subordinate role working with black people. At work, he was apparently unaware of his negative feeling about working in an all-black organization in his subordinate and minority status. In the laboratory, he projectively identified with other anglos whom he perceived as uninterested in social causes and racist.

In this laboratory situation, Mr. K.'s ambivalence toward his minority working status was triggered by working with an all-black staff who had no "real world"[7] authority to affect his employment. Hence, he had a valence, given his ambivalence toward his work situation, to come under the influence of the group's projective identification.

He colluded with the group's wishes to compete with and challenge the staff. He also expressed the group's fantasy that the staff really might be incompetent, and that the only reason they were hired was because of affirmative action plans, or "that they were just running a 'good game' without having any skills to teach anything." The former attitude represented the covert attitudes of the anglo participants, the latter black participants' covert attitudes. Mr. K.'s expressions of admiration and trust for the staff (the other side of his ambivalence) could not be expressed under the influence of the group's projective identification. He developed psychosomatic complaints during the week under the stress of acting as the repository for the negative feeling toward the staff and being scapegoated for it. Yet, like Ms. A.'s, Mr. K.'s *valence bonds* were stretched so that he got swept up in his *role* and became a candidate for scapegoating.

This case study and interpretation provide an illustration of how projective identification, role differentiation, and the psychological needs of scapegoating are used in a group setting. A discussion on intervening in interpersonal relations from a systemic socioanalytic perspective follows.

Interventions

On the third day of the laboratory, the staff decided that conflict between Ms. A. and Mr. K. had escalated and begun to have a negative impact on the progress of the course. It was thought that the conflict between Ms. A. and Mr. K. should be openly discussed in the large group session.

---

[7]"Real world" authority meaning that, as trainers, the staff had no relationship with his work organization.

During the large group session the dean offered the following comments: "It seems to me that the group has allowed Ms. A. and Mr. K. to express mixed feelings and reactions to the relevance of the course content or the competence of the staff that exist inside each and everyone here. Surely, it is much easier to let Ms. A. and Mr. K. carry and express each side of the conflicting feelings about the staff on behalf of everyone here."

In response to the dean's comment, a member replied: "This is Ms. A.'s and Mr. K.'s conflict—it's their trip. I don't have anything to do with it."

The dean then offered this comment: "Indeed, it would be a simple solution to live under the pretense that the conflict is just Ms. A.'s and Mr. K.'s. Surely, they are willing actors who allow themselves to be used in this way. It seems that Ms. A. represents the part of each member that may want to protect the staff. Mr. K. represents the part of everyone that may question the content of the course and the staff's competence. It's quite easy to have Ms. A. and Mr. K. simply resolve the group's internal ambivalence."

This intervention[8] had several purposes: (1) to articulate how the group was using Ms. A. and Mr. K. to reduce other group members' internal conflict and tension; (2) to illustrate how Ms. A. and Mr. K. colluded with the group's wishes—implicitly suggesting that they should stop the collusion; (3) to uncover "tacit alliances" that existed among the members. Making explicit by surfacing the group's tacit alliance (the group's projective identification motif) through the intervention renders this particular form of group alliance inoperative. Tacit group alliances can operate only when they are indeed unconscious or covert.

Interventions from a group-level perspective are often resisted and resented by the group members. They experience the intervention, as Tarachow (1963) suggests, as a "double deprivation." Firstly, the intervention uncovers the unconscious alliance that exists among the group members, which they experience as being "found out" or "caught." Secondly, there is an implicit statement that staff in this case will not collude with how the group is relating to and using each other. In short, they must change their behavior toward one another and themselves.

The group's wish to have the conflicting feelings and tension bottled up in two of its members is challenged by the intervention. The *wish* (or the hope) that putting the feelings into Ms. A. and Mr.

---

[8]The group-as-a-whole approach had been discussed with the group members earlier. Hence, the group was familiar with the concepts of projective identification and splitting. If a group is unfamiliar with these concepts, they should be given a lecturette.

K. can resolve complex feelings and painful anxiety is extinguished.

The message to the group members is that each of them must *own* the parts of themselves that are split off into others via projective identification. The intervention invites each member to tolerate his or her ambivalence and anxiety. The intervention requests the members to refrain from using others to carry and express unwanted split parts. The intervention asks members to abandon their neonate coping strategy (that is, projective identification) to manage the feelings generated by the laboratory experience. The intervention robs the group of its infantile wishes.

The members often respond defensively and with denial to these interventions. To illustrate, a member commented in response to the dean's interventions: "I don't know what you are talking about. I think the course is OK. I am just waiting to see how you [staff] are going to tie it together. But I feel all right."

Another group member commented: "Well, I have a number of questions about what has been going on here. Yet Mr. K. seemed to have raised them for me. I really didn't want to seem like a smart-ass always asking questions. I might get misinterpreted because I'm white."

A black member commented: "I find the theories presented helpful. Yet there are questions I don't ask because I think the white members here will use them to criticize you [staff]. So I just keep things to myself and ask you about them after the sessions are over."

There seemed to be an underlying fear that prevented members from bringing their whole person into the laboratory. It appeared that they needed to keep some of their thoughts and feelings out of the workshop. There seemed a need to "put a lid on things." Fantasies of violence and conflict were uppermost in members' minds. Kovel (1970) suggests that even discussing race relations in America elicits primitive and violent fantasies. Hence, there was a concern that things might get out of hand—someone might get hurt. An easy solution to the underlying anxiety was for Ms. A. and Mr. K. to carry and hopefully resolve the conflict on behalf of the group by scapegoating the black/white dyad—if the group could fill up Ms. A. and Mr. K. with affect and cast them off to atone for the badness (bad feelings) in each member.

In the attempted scapegoating of Ms. A. and Mr. K., the staff interfered with this solution by making an intervention from the group level. The group members could no longer ignore how they were using each other and how destructively and violently they were behaving.

In response to the members' comments, the dean made this intervention: "Denied feelings seek expression. We often split off our feelings and put them into others. Yet that really does not resolve the feelings; they only get repressed, waiting with greater magnitude for expression.

"To deny the truth increases its force a thousandfold. To deny feelings increases them beyond endurance.

"It seems, then, the major question for this group is: 'Can people bring their *whole* selves into the experience of the laboratory—both positive and negative feelings, emotion and intellect?' "

A white member responded: "I feel I can't let all of my thoughts out. Things might happen. Conflict, confusion, and hostility may erupt. I don't want to be called a fuckin' racist!"

Other members nodded in silent agreement. Then a black group member remarked: "I feel I can't raise questions or say very much because everyone may get into a conflict. I hate confusion and conflict. I'd rather avoid it. And you [the dean] don't help matters either!"

A comment from a latino member followed: "The conflict in this group is between anglo and black people. I'm just here to learn. I don't say much because I can see both sides of the issue. I have my own special issues. They are not black or anglo; so, I'll let you all fight. But, I feel that the issues of latino clients were not addressed. There aren't any latinos on staff! And, seemingly, nothing can be done about it. So, I'll sit back, and let all of this bullshit go on—crazy Americans!"

After these members had responded to the dean's intervention, other group members shared their feelings about the course and each other. As discussion among the group members became more open, exploration of the group's fantasies and fears occurred.

The intervention changed the motif of projective identification among the group members. It robbed the group of its unconscious alliances and thus freed group members to form other types of alliances that were less destructive. Consequently, the group's investment in using Ms. A. and Mr. K. to express the conflict abated. They were released from their conflict roles. Their candidacy for scapegoats was relinquished.

To test whether the conflict was interpersonal in nature, the staff asked if Ms. A. and Mr. K. wanted to have a third-party (Walton, 1969) consultation to help them resolve their "interpersonal problem." There was little interest in this solution by Ms. A. or Mr. K. In subsequent sessions, conflict between them ceased. Other group members became more active and gave feedback. Negative *and* positive feelings were shared.

Critical and positive evaluations were offered. Even greater openness emerged as the session progressed. Group members seemed more able to take responsibility for their feelings (both negative and positive) and for their learning.

At the end of the workshop, Ms. A. and Mr. K. did not necessarily adore each other. But they were not engaged in conflict or scapegoated. Indeed, both had learned a lot about how groups can use individuals and how one can collude. Moreover, they became acutely aware that when one *acts* in a group, the acts may not be the function of one's own intrapersonal conditions, but rather that of the group. Groups can make individuals behave in certain and prescribed ways. Perhaps Ms. A. and Mr. K. learned more than other members by being in the entrails of the group.

In evaluating the laboratory, members commented:

> Feelings *can* be put *in* you!
>
> A person often uses and is used by other group members to act in a certain way—to assume a particular role.
>
> I don't want to believe that groups can control my behavior.
>
> When I came here I thought all of that psychoanalytic stuff was bullshit. It really might have some relevance; I have to reconsider.
>
> I have more to learn; all has not sunk in yet.
>
> This was a hard experience. I learned a lot about myself—and the treatment of minorities.

Interventions from a systemic socioanalytic perspective can provide meaningful learning for organization members. They can teach group members that they are all responsible, in part, for what happens in their work group. Often by tacit agreement, through silence and collusion, we determine what people say or how they act in groups and organizations. We can and do fill others with our split, projected parts. Moreover, socioanalytic intervention may teach us that we *are* what we have disdain and contempt for. We are indeed, in part, all of those undesirable traits and behaviors we see in others. Group-level interventions help us to be more emphatic with those whom we would like to kill off. We all, at times, act like King David, author of the Psalms.

The underlying intent of the socioanalytic approach is to increase individuals' and groups' understanding of their covert dynamics. It is hoped that individuals exposed to the socioanalytic approach will be more task-effective and humane to each other. Increased consciousness enables individuals to become more competent managers and better leaders and followers. It may also reduce the amount of human wreckage and pathos that occurs in groups and organizations at alarming rates.

Simply stated, the socioanalytic intervention and approach helps individuals understand that we must take individual and collective responsibility for what happens in groups. We are not solipsists, unaffected by others, nor individuals in isolation, but rather connected and driven by collective ties. We are indeed group creatures. The wise poet John Donne (ed. Hayward, 1949) eloquently describes our "groupishness" and man's identity:

> Who bends not his ear to any bell which upon any occasion rings, but who can remove it from that bell which is passing a piece of himself out of this world?
> No man is an island, entire of itself; every man is a piece of the continent, a part of the main. . . .
> Any man's death diminishes me, because I am involved in mankind, and therefore never send to know for whom the bell tolls; it tolls for thee (from *Devotion XVII*).

SUMMARY AND CONCLUSIONS

This chapter delineates the theoretical and diagnostic aspects of the systemic socioanalytic approach. A number of concepts have been defined and applied to several case illustrations. This is only an introduction to the developing approach, and raises more questions than it answers. Many of the concepts presented here hopefully have heuristic value for scholars and practitioners.

The group-as-a-whole phenomenon is important, but little recognized in determining quality of life in social systems. Phenomena often defined as personality problems or personal incompetence may in reality be a manifestation of the group's struggle with its anxiety and tension. Indeed, the group-as-a-whole concept is intellectually challenging and appears to violate Western notions of individual uniqueness and autonomy. Nevertheless, it can explain a large portion of variance in individual behavior within groups. The group-as-a-whole approach also makes it clear that members of Homo sapiens are connected by their "groupishness," regardless of their contempt for that idea.

Chapter 4

Intimacy in Work Groups: Looking from the Inside Out

JONATHON GILLETTE

INTRODUCTION

A basic premise of most group literature is that the nature of the relationships between and among members plays a major role in determining the way a group operates. Group process influences group output. It follows, therefore, that intense connections between members would be an important area of exploration. Indeed, conflict, leadership struggles, power dynamics, and political alliances are all recognized areas of study. But when the intense connections concern powerful emotions such as intimacy, affection, love, or sexuality, the amount and depth of research drop dramtically.

It is not hard to understand the reasons for this avoidance. These emotions are extremely difficult to work with in a group setting. They raise concerns about vulnerability and exploitation. They embarrass and thrill simultaneously. At the most basic level, it is the part of ourselves we are most reluctant to put into the work, yet our senses tell us over and over that much of that part of us is already working.

Teaching and/or training a group to examine these feelings is in itself a risky venture. The topic generates enormous reactive powers. Simply mentioning intimacy creates expectations that it will appear and criticism that it is being artificially produced. If the teaching or training context is like many university and corporate settings where these issues are ignored and feared throughout the system, examination generates distorting images and denigrating labels about the work. Group courses often are seen as unscientific and as nothing more than "group grope."

The theoretical work that has been done on intimacy in work

groups has been at best unclear and at worst misleading. The problem begins in a failure to outline clearly just what is intimacy. The idea of intimacy, borrowed primarily from interpersonal theory, has been primarily applied to group settings to describe cohesive and/ or affectionate behavior among members. The exact terms vary: Schutz (1958) uses "affection"; Dunphy (1968) uses "concern for affection"; Kaplan (1974) uses "intimacy"; Bennis and Shepard (1956) use "member orientation toward intimacy"; Shambaugh (1978) uses "psychological closeness"; Smith and Berg (1987) use "intimacy." Each researcher sees groups as potentially moving toward more intimate relationships as the group develops.

The definition of "group intimacy" is never clearly spelled out, but must be inferred from the behavioral descriptions. For some— for example, Bennis and Shepard (1956)—group intimacy relates to the increase in member-to-member affection or an increase in the collective amount of positive feeling: intimacy *within* a group. For others—for example, Smith and Berg (1987)—the phenomenon encompasses the group as a whole, so that group intimacy involves the individual-group relationship: intimacy *with* a group.

The groups under study are almost exclusively self-study groups and, as a result, the dominant theoretical frame does not incorporate the influences of the task and the larger contextual environment. Stripped of these connections, the approach to intimacy becomes misleading and divorced from the realities of organizational life. The notion that groups develop or mature toward greater and greater disclosure and intimacy—and indeed that individuals who fail to go along potentially retard developmental progress—is not only overly simplistic, but quite frankly dangerous in many work contexts.

Self-study groups are an effective way of uncovering basic processes of interaction. But the actual behaviors—such as increasing levels of self-disclosure—need to be seen as products of that work group, working in a specific context, on a specific task (see also Chapter 6). When the topic of study is as volatile as intimacy, the larger contextual elements must be integrated into the analysis if generalization is to be achieved.

The purpose of this chapter is to recapture the importance and relevance of examining intimacy in work groups by setting out a frame of understanding that incorporates multiple levels of influence. The first section puts forth a definition of intimacy based on the work of interpersonal and ego psychologists. The second section then examines the influence of group, organizational, and societal processes on intimate relations. The third section outlines how the various levels of influence can combine and conflict and suggests both implications and consequences of the combined analysis. Work groups are central arenas for both our connections to one another and our professional accomplishments. The challenge is ultimately to develop ways of managing self and others in complex work settings as we strive simultaneously to connect and excel.

As an aside, the writing of this chapter has itself been a case study in the very influences described here. I have felt the tension of being identified with the topic, and have scanned my academic environment for potential reactions. The work on this chapter has also set off an internal struggle as I confronted my own internal resolutions about intimacy and my relations with others. It was impossible not to have a lot of my self in this work, and I hesitated for a long time. Yet to not examine the topic, when the purpose of this book is to understand behavior in groups, is to collude with the forces that make the work difficult and to continue to ignore what we have all experienced as powerful forces. To state that working groups are not influenced by individuals' fantasies or wishes for intimate connections is simply wrong. These pulls finally pushed me onward—task and work are powerful persuaders. Thus, I invite readers to reflect on their own reactions to this chapter as an additional way of exploring the topic.

TOWARD A DEFINITION OF INTIMACY

Defining the term intimacy is tricky business. Many writers before me have tried. But the concept of intimacy, like love or laughter, has a slippery and amorphous quality to it. If you were to look up a definition—and I did—you would find numerous variations. One, Davis (1973), built an entire book as a definition. Part of the variance occurs in that each definition is, in fact, the summary statement of a particular theoretical perspective. In addition, certain definitions tended to highlight a particular aspect of intimacy.

The definition presented here attempts to lay out intimacy as a complex construct with numerous elements. It is based primarily on the theoretical work of Sullivan and Erikson, as their work is heavily referenced by group theorists.

Elements of Intimacy

Intimacy is a basic human need. The foundation for this element of intimacy comes from the work of Harry Stack Sullivan. Sullivan is a major figure in the development of the psychiatry of interpersonal relations. He emphasized the importance of viewing the individual in the context of relationships and, in seeing the two-way process of interaction, of seeing each "involved as a portion of an interpersonal field, rather than as a specific entity, in processes which effect or are affected by the field" (Sullivan, 1953, p. xii). One of his key concepts was the study of "dynamisms," which are "relatively enduring patterns of energy transformation which recurrently characterize the interpersonal relations" (p. xiv). These patterns are developed in early life and carried into the present. These patterns themselves are influenced by what Sullivan sees as three basic needs: the need for personal security, for freedom from anxiety; the need for intimacy, for collaboration with at least one other person; and the need for lustful satisfaction, genitally driven.

Thus, for Sullivan, intimacy is a basic part of the individual psyche, part of the basic motivating forces of life. Individuals are drawn into contact with each other in order to meet basic needs. Loneliness is the other end of the continuum, "the exceedingly unpleasant and driving experience connected with an inadequate discharge of the need for human intimacy, for interpersonal intimacy" (p. 290). Frieda Fromm-Reichmann (1959), who writes about loneliness, follows up Sullivan's concepts by stating, "The longing for interpersonal intimacy stays with every human being from infancy throughout life; and there is no human being who is not threatened by its loss" (p. 4).

If we accept this perspective, then we imagine that people have a need and a longing for intimate connections, and that they carry these needs and longings into every interpersonal setting, where they either lie latent and unconscious or become conscious.

Intimacy involves our innermost self. The term *intimacy* seeks to differentiate a particular kind of interpersonal relationship, one that is stronger or more powerful than friend or acquaintance. The Merriam-Webster dictionary defines "intimate" as "very private or closely personal; pertaining to the innermost or essential nature" (Webster, 1983). If we conceive of an individual as having multiple layers of self, each one inside another, an intimate relationship would involve the innermost layers. Other, more distant, relationships would involve more outside layers, aspects of the self that are generally shared or available to others.

Intimate relationships involve disclosure and receptivity. A number of theorists (Davis, 1973; Shadish, 1984) define intimacy by focusing on what they term intimate behaviors. Chief among those behaviors is the process of disclosure, the spontaneous expression of self. This involves an opening up of areas that are usually defended and demonstrates a trust with the other that the vulnerability in the sharing will not be abused. Equally important, but underemphasized in the current literature, is the role of listening or receiving by the other. It is a form of being present and open to the disclosure in a way that affirms the exchange. It is entirely possible that the recipient never says a word yet is involved in an intimate exchange.

Intimacy involves a sharing of one's whole self. The process of opening up assumes that the relationship moves toward greater involvement of the self until ultimately, in intimate relationships, the whole self is shared. Sullivan (1953) defines intimacy as "that type of situation involving two people which permits validation of all components of personal worth. Validation of personal worth requires a type of relationship which I call collaboration, by which I mean clearly formulated adjustments of one's behavior to the expressed needs of the other person in the pursuit of increasingly identical—that is, more and more nearly mutual—satisfactions, and in the maintenance of increasingly similar security operations" (p. 246).

What does this definition mean and what does it imply? To begin with, all components of the person are validated: the good, the bad, and the ugly. The validation comes not as a blank check but as a mutual process of adjustment, of moving from an individual course to a more mutual dance, each becoming increasingly a part of defining the dyad as a unit. This is not unbounded acceptance nor is it just an exchange of needs but a sharing of the whole self that incorporates restraint and obligation.

Intimate relationships involve commitment. Intimate relationships are differentiated from casual relationships by many theorists on the dimension of commitment. Indeed, Erikson (1950) defines intimacy as "the capacity to commit to concrete affiliations and partnerships and to develop the ethical strength to abide by such commitments even though they call for significant sacrifices and compromises" (p. 263). The willingness to stay in a relationship through tough times generates a form of deep trust that feeds intimacy.

Numerous experiences are thus a form of requirement for intimacy, a necessary but not sufficient foundation. These experiences make up the history of interaction and demonstrate the pattern of commitment. These experiences may be compressed—as in a weekend encounter group—or spread out. In either case, later experiences will qualitatively differ from earlier experiences.

Intimacy requires a developed sense of self. This element is based on the work of Erikson and his developmental theory. In his presentation of his eight stages of man, Erikson (1950) took a view that at each stage a set of basic issues were at work within the individual. And, depending on the resolution of those issues, personality formation took on indelible qualities, not only at that time and age, but as a foundation that affected all subsequent struggles.

The sixth stage of development Erikson titled "Intimacy versus Isolation." This stage is based on successful navigation of the previous stage where identity was established. Erikson notes:

> The strength acquired at any stage is tested by the necessity to transcend it in such a way that the individual can take chances in the next stage with what was most vulnerably precious in the previous one. Thus, the young adult, emerging from the search for and the insistence on identity, is eager and willing to fuse his identity with that of others. He is ready for intimacy . . . (p. 263).

Erikson's definition, therefore, implies the prior development of identity, the "result and test of firm self-delineation" (p. 265). It involves opening up and sharing, a process that requires a clear sense of what is inside and what is outside one's own personal boundaries.

Recent theory has begun to question whether the pattern described by Erikson is accurate for women's development. Gilligan (1982) pays particular attention to the issue of intimacy versus isolation:

> The sequential ordering of identity and intimacy in the transition from adolescence to adulthood better fits the development of men than it does the development of women. Power and separation secure the man in an identity achieved through work, but they leave him at a distance from others. . . . Given this distance, intimacy becomes the critical experience that brings the self back into connection with others. . . . Women define their identity through relationships of intimacy and care (p. 163).
>
> The critical experience [for women] then becomes not intimacy but choice, creating an encounter with self that clarifies the under-

standing of responsibility and truth. . . . For both, the transition to adulthood is the same conflict—integrity and care—but the approach is from different directions (p. 164).

The entire process of individuation—the balancing of separation and connection—described as different for men and women by Gilligan, has important implications for the development of intimate relationships. Different experiences may facilitate the development of self and thus the development of intimacy for men as opposed to women. The question of choice is pivotal, as the next element explains futher.

Intimacy requires some control over the boundaries of the self. If the self is conceived as a bounded area that differentiates what is inside from what is outside, then some form of control over opening up and closing down is essential for intimate relationships. Weiss (1987) begins with Erikson's premise "without access to a secure sense of individual privacy, only pseudointimacy is possible" (p. 119). Weiss goes on to discuss the sharing process as deeply connected to the process of intimacy and to the maintenance of the individual boundary. "Not all disclosure is intended to, or is likely to, assist in the development of intimacy. In addition, disclosure alone will never result in intimacy" (p. 120). This can lead to the breakdown of the individual boundary or identity and thus eliminate the foundation for intimacy. Secure privacy is essential.

Brown (1979) makes the same point in an interesting way. He talks of intimacy as a dance of courtship that vacillates from closeness to distance. He goes on to state, "The prerequisite for 'letting someone in' is the certain knowledge that one can 'keep them out' and if need be, 'throw them out' if they prove ungracious. Thus the best playgrounds have fences, and a secure gate, which can open and close at will and lock, if necessary" (p. 12).

Sexuality is a related but separate construct. One of the most confusing aspects of studying intimacy is the blurred line between sexuality and intimacy. Some theorists such as Slater (1967) deal exclusively with sexuality, yet the behaviors described fall into the category of intimate behaviors. Other theorists (for example, Hearn and Parkin, 1987) criticize those who use the term *intimacy* as attempting to strip it of its powerful sexual component.

I find it most useful to see sexuality as a related but separate construct. Sullivan's outline of needs presented above is a useful guide. He states that both intimacy and sexuality—his term is *lustful satisfaction*—are different. He argues:

There is, so far as I know, no necessarily close relationship between lust, as an integrating tendency, and the need for intimacy, which we have previously discussed, except that they both characterize people at a certain stage in development. The two are strikingly distinct. In fact, making much sense of the complexities and difficulties which are experienced in adolescence and subsequent phases of life, depends, in considerable measure, on the clarity with which one distinguishes three needs, which are often very intricately combined and at the same time contradictory. These are the needs for personal security—that is, for freedom from anxiety; for intimacy—that is, for collaboration with at least one other person; and the need for lustful satisfaction, which is connected with genital activity in pursuit of the orgasm" (1963, p. 264).

The distinction is important, for the three elements can overlap or they can collide. Certain forms of sexual interaction can damage both one's sense of self and the possibilities for intimacy. Key to development, for Sullivan, is the integration of each of these elements so that intimacy is enhanced, along with one's sense of self, through sexuality.

Taken together, these eight elements give us markers that are useful in making distinctions among different kinds of relationships—of which intimate relationships are a specific subset. It then becomes possible to examine group interaction and determine the presence or absence of intimate interactions.

It also becomes possible to examine the impact of joining a working group, or an organization, or taking on a task, or developing in our society, on the elements of intimacy themselves: that is, to examine how, for example, the dynamic requirements of group membership interact with members' sense of self or their control over their own boundaries. As a result, it will be possible to see new complexities and to expand a perspective that was originally based on interpersonal theory by taking into account additional dimensions of influence.

INTIMACY AND MULTIPLE LEVELS OF ANALYSIS

Intimacy and Group Membership

Joining a group immeasurably complicates life. Various chapters in this book describe aspects of that complexity: the emergent paradoxes, the demands on the self, the process of regression, and the influence of unconscious processes. Given what we know about intimate relationships, how is the drive for intimate contact influenced by a group setting?

Group membership initially unravels a sense of self in relationship. Joining a group to accomplish a task generates an inevitable internal conflict, one that puts pressure on one's own sense of self. The conflict is described by Gibbard, Hartman, and Mann (1974):

> The basic antagonism is between the individual's commitment to himself—to his own needs, beliefs, and ambitions—and his yearning for psychological submersion in a group, for an obliteration of those qualities that make him unique and thus distinct and separate from others. Submersion brings a measure of security and a sense of connectedness and belonging, but it undermines individual autonomy, obstructs the attainment of any goal which is not shared, and may in other respects demand a sacrifice of individual wishes to those of the group (p. 177).

This antagonism takes place under conditions of high uncertainty as the nature of the group and the nature of self required for membership are initially unknown. Both individual and group boundaries are unclear (see Chapter 2).

This process of increased boundary uncertainty conflicts directly with the element of intimacy that requires clear boundaries as a prerequisite for intimacy. Thus movement toward intimate relationships in a group can only take place through a process whereby individuals regain a sense of their individual boundaries in relationship with others. This process often stirs up members' earlier resolutions of identity and intimacy and can at times give group interactions an adolescent flavor. However, movement toward group resolution is not a simple reenactment of individual issues. The process must take place in a multitude of relationships, varying degrees of closeness, and a particular orientation toward the group as a whole.

Group membership can lead to questions of control over self boundaries. As group members become aware of group level processes in general, and unconscious processes in particular, the question of individual autonomy is raised. Winter (1974) describes a phenomenon known as "role suction," whereby the process of splitting and projection around race pulled three quite different black men to act "unlike themselves" in the group. Bion (1961) describes a process that involves one of the most intimate parts of ourselves—our affection for one another. His concept is "pairing." Bion sees pairing as one of the basic assumption modes that work groups potentially enter. Here, an intense connection is forged between two individuals by the group, in order to work out some aspect that has been afflicting group life. As Rioch (1975) describes it:

> Two people get together on behalf of the group to carry out the task of pairing and creation. The sex of the two people is immaterial. They are by no means necessarily a man and a woman. But whoever they are, the basic assumption is that when two people get together it is for sexual purposes . . . the group, through the pair, is living in the hope of the creation of a new leader, or a new thought, or something which will bring about new life, will solve old problems and bring Utopia or heaven, or something of the sort (p. 27).

There is often a heightened air of sexuality involved in pairing as the two members find themselves in an intense attachment. The force of the group projections enters each of them and triggers his or her own latent valence toward engaging with the other. Each may experience an intense attraction toward the other, and, since our normal interpretation is on the individual level of analysis, will understand that attraction as a deeply personal response.

Indeed, that attraction may be very personal, but it is also a product of the dynamics of that group. In essence, each of the part of this pair take up a role for the group that involves their most personal selves. Bion's work sheds light on this process and opens up avenues for discovering other sexual or intimate roles. It is possible, for example, for the group to split all its fear of sexual seduction into one member and then isolate and scapegoat or denigrate that member. It is also possible for a group to resolve its conflicts about intimacy by selecting one couple to represent all intimacy.

Taken together, these processes challenge members' conceptions of their own autonomy. In self-study groups, it is commonplace for a discussion to emerge on having free will versus being puppets of the group. This questioning has its effect on intimacy, as control of boundaries is an essential element. It can also lead to complicated scenarios where members sequentially feel intimate and betrayed.

"The Group" becomes an object for intimate relationship. One of the differences between individual interaction and group interaction is the presence of something that goes beyond the sum of the other individuals. Bion (1961) calls this fantasized "group" evidence of the regressed state of group members. "The belief that a group exists, as distinct from an aggregate of individuals, is an essential part of this regression, as are also the characteristics with which the supposed group is endowed by the individual" (p. 11). But even as a fantasy, the group is a powerful and distinct object with which individuals seek to connect. Further evidence is found in Wells's (1980) formulation of the "group-as-mother." Based on object relations theory, the membership is seen as experiencing "the group" as a specific entity, one that stirs up earlier infant-mother struggles.

In either case, it becomes possible to imagine—and one can find confirming descriptions in group transcripts—members experiencing a warm and "intimate" relationship with the group as a whole and not with each individual member.

Group membership raises issues of authority as well as intimacy. Numerous theorists cite member orientation toward authority and toward intimacy as the two major forces at work within a group (see Bennis and Shepard, 1956, in particular). The presence of some members with greater authority influences the way intimacy emerges and is expressed. Slater (1967) takes the position that peer intimacy is initially prevented by the presence of an authority figure. It is only after a revolt that the focus shifts toward member-member interaction:

> One of the most striking of these [realities of revolt]—especially mystifying in its resemblance to Freud's primal horde myth—is a change in the sexual economy of the group. This may best be summarized by saying that the group members decathect the group leader and experience a dramatic heightening of sexual interest in one another (p. 85).

Although Slater refers to sexuality rather than intimacy, his analysis is useful in that it points to the tension between hierarchy and peer interaction. In addition, he demonstrates that the effects can complicate relationships outside the work group as well. (For other theorists who subscribe to an authority-intimacy developmental path, see Chapter 6.)

Different levels of intimacy within a group can generate strong negativity. The view of intimacy at the interpersonal level ends with the couple. In joining a group, it becomes possible to have a couple *inside a group.* This is one form of a larger set of possibilities: that members will have significantly different levels of intimacy with one another.

Kernberg's (1980) work on "couple dynamics" gives some initial insight into the effects of such inequality of affection within a group. He looks at the dynamic interaction between a couple—a pair that is publicly joined—and their surrounding group. His main point is that the presence of a couple within a group is disturbing. The reaction of the group to the couple is profound ambivalence. "The idealization, hope and longing that the couple evokes in the group is balanced by envy, resentment, and a wish to destroy the couple's union" (p. 308). The longing and hope stem from each individual's need for a hope for intimacy. This is in line with other theorists noted above. But Kernberg takes the analysis further by also pointing to negative feelings, especially aggression. Kernberg focuses repeatedly on aggression, partly because he is convinced that "the importance of aggressive components in all intimate human relations is almost totally neglected."

The aggression that is stirred by the group's envy needs to find an outlet. As the boundaries of the group weaken, the more the aggression gets out of control. "In general terms, while the small group needs the couple, the large group tolerates it only within the limits of stereotyped convention, and the mob does not tolerate it at all" (p. 308).

The couple needs the group as a place to deposit aspects of the self and relationship that are disturbing. A couple cut off from a group can turn and implode. Couples that go too far in the public expression of aggression, for example, can end up like the characters of Albee's play *Who's Afraid of Virginia Woolf?*, who tear apart the remnants of their intimacy.

Intimacy and Organizational Membership

Joining a work group takes place in the context of joining an organization. Despite all the volumes of writing about organizations and their contexts, only a small amount of work has been done to examine the influence of intimacy in organizations and even less work on the influence of intimacy in embedded work groups. This dearth of material is one of the elements that make the research on self-study groups and intimacy seem so distant from the real world of organizations.

This is especially disturbing, as there is ample evidence that intimate connections are all over the place in real organizations:

> Enter most organizations and you enter a world of sexuality. In addition to foyers, lifts, corridors, shop floor machinery, filing cabinets, computers, paper work, desks and telephones, there is usually much (else) that can be called "sexuality." This can include a mass of sexual displays, feelings, fantasies, and innuendoes, as part of everyday organizational life, right through to sexual relationships, open or secret, occasional sexual acts, and sexual violations, including rape.

And yet to read the "mountainous" literature on industrial sociology, organizational sociology, organizational theory, management theory, industrial relations and so on, and you would imagine these organizations, so finely analyzed, are inhabited by a breed of strange, asexual eunuch figures. There is in effect a booming silence (Hearn and Parkin, 1987, p. 7).

Hearn and Parkin (1987) are critical of this silence. Their critique is based on their analysis that the organizational context is an extraordinarily important influence on the ways in which intimacy and sexuality, in particular, play themselves out. Their organizational level of analysis stresses the political or power context with which sexuality and other intense connections are inevitably linked. They go on to point out that power is not equally distributed and that this fact has significant and at times destructive consequences. Further, gender-based role assignment exacerbates the tendency for men to use their power against women. To act as if the organizational context were equitable and without these elements is to obscure analysis.

Quinn (1977) has a similar analysis. In her study of romantic relationships in organizations, she found that the visibility and impact of relationships varied depending on the status of the members involved and the culture of the organization: its mores regarding intimate relationships. Here too, the consequences for men and women were not equal, as twice as many women as men lost their jobs.

Thus the organizational context has a strong influence on the way in which members pursue and display intimate relationships, emphasize the importance of power and authority, and set in motion actions and sanctions that are likely to be more harmful to women than men.

Task and intimacy. Task is one particular element of the organizational context. As such, it needs to be examined on its own, for it contains within it the major vehicle for importing the organizational context into the working group. The effect of task on the nature of inside dynamics is discussed in a number of chapters in this book, most notably Chapter 6. What is specifically important here is how task influences intimate relationships.

Theorists from the socio-technical perspective have provided important understandings about task and group process (see Chapter 10). These include not only the nature of the task, but the structure and design of roles within that task. It is a useful heuristic to think of task and role as elements that penetrate an individual self, that cross the individual boundaries of self.

At times it is easy to see the effect of the influence of task on self. Members quickly begin to identify themselves by their role. I am a "teacher" or a "nurse." Those who have experienced working under intensified task conditions, such as in an emergency room or even an important team sport event, know how the force of that task and role can intensify interpersonal relationships. During a teacher strike I was involved in, I got to know and be known more deeply and intensely in three weeks than in the previous three years. I still carry friendships and grudges from that time.

Further, group contexts are increasingly an element of task and role design. One is now very likely to spend a major part of the job working in a group. Often the groups are charged with highly complex tasks and with ambiguous role structures. Task assignment and group task assignment, in particular, initially generate an unraveling or opening up of the individual boundaries. In combination with an internally based task, it is possible to have the work roles drive a form of exchange and contact that would happen only in rare non-work settings. Part of this is evident in the transcripts of self-study groups where the task of exploring interconnections facilitates a form of intense connection.

Thus, task characteristics can both impede intimacy by un-raveling a sense of self and enhance the possibility of intimacy by driving intense interactions. Either way, the organization member experiences both role and personal elements in the exchange with others, a mix that is impossible to separate.

Intimacy and Society

Larger trends, beyond individual organizational settings, have potentially powerful effects on internal group processes. A number of theorists have looked at intimacy at the societal level, and what they have found suggests an important additional level of influence.

Our current societal context is filled with—some might even say obsessed with—personal connectedness. Every type of media outlet examines, designs, and sells images of intimacy. Popular self-help programs promise to fulfill or expand our ability to be intimate. We can even become our own best friend. All of this takes place in a society that some have assessed as having developed in ways that make in-depth relations well-nigh impossible.

Take for example the popular social analysis *Habits of the Heart* by Bellah et al. (1985). They point to changes in society that have led toward a new concept of the individual and, by definition, a new concept of interpersonal relations. This new individualism is highly utilitarian and "therapeutic" in that it is oriented toward the satisfaction of individual needs. Interpersonal intimacy exists in a new and more exchange-bound context:

> Then love becomes no more than an exchange, with no binding rules except the obligation to full and open communication. A relationship should give each partner what he or she needs while it lasts, and if the relationship ends, at least both partners will have received a reasonable return on their investment (p. 108).

Christopher Lasch's *Culture of Narcissism* (1979) has a similar thesis, but he pushes his analysis further. Lasch argues that this new individual can be labeled as narcissistic. This is not the strong "private" individual who is detached from community and society; this is in fact an individual existing with weak boundaries around self as well as living in a society with weak communal boundaries. Further, such a person is incapable of either aloneness or independence.

Richard Sennett, in *The Fall of Public Man* (1977), describes an ideology of intimacy. According to Sennett, interpersonal interactions have been moving increasingly in a direction that blurs the distinction between public and private self. Even casual contacts in modern society have a "confessional" quality in that the individuals are expected to share important aspects of themselves. This sharing with strangers diminishes the power of sharing with specific friends or lovers. In thinking about intimacy in groups, these insights seem particularly significant.

Given these serious doubts that intimacy is even a possibility for modern people, it is not surprising that much of the popular press is so filled with solutions or that even the solutions reflect the issues described above. It is not impossible that the hope for intimacy is a necessary salve to the terror of our isolation.

Thus, the larger societal context fosters a paradoxical combination of greater individualism and weaker boundaries between the public and private self. Relationships of depth and duration become rare and "confessional" contacts commonplace.

INTIMACY VIEWED FROM A COMBINED ANALYSIS

Taken together, the impact on intimacy at these various levels of analysis—group, organizational, societal—point to a variety of potential combinations of forces, some of which would create a synergistic effect, some of which would create crosscurrents within the individual experience of intimacy. Through the synergistic effect, an element that would have only small importance at one level of analysis would become significant through the impact of other levels. A crosscurrent effect, if powerful enough, could lead to internal and external resolutions that could be potentially damaging to individuals and to the work group. Consider the following combinations.

The pressures on the boundaries of self are multiplied. At each level of analysis there are factors that work to unravel or prevent secure self-definition. Indeed, the initial integrity of the boundaries of the self was questioned in the societal analysis. This may mean that the uncertainty present at the start of any work group may be heightened, leading to the potential for rapid movement toward rigid roles and increased splitting within the group (Gibbard, 1974). Such a context would make collective movement toward closer and more intimate—whole—relationships extremely difficult, and would increase the likelihood of pairing and/or aggression toward a couple.

Control over self boundaries is at risk. Both group-level forces and the demands of task undermine control of self boundaries. Individuals must actively assert their "selves" to regain control. This is made more difficult when the individual must submit to authority and authority is entry into another, either literally or figuratively. Control and task systems in organizations are designed to harness individual selves in the service of work. All of these forces place pressure on an individual's control over self-disclosure. This cuts at one of the basic criteria for intimacy, that one must be able to back away and say, "No." Defending one's boundary may seem to interfere with task work or with others' desires to connect or control.

Authority issues and issues of power are multiplied. Most group theorists recognize the importance of authority issues and most posit that intimacy can only develop when authority issues have been addressed and resolved. But a combined analysis questions whether the two issues can ever be separated. Boss-subordinate intimacy, a significant factor insufficiently addressed in the current group literature, illustrates that any intimate interaction is inevitably and unendingly mixed up with organizational role relationships. The personal and the public are not separable. Rather, the issues of authority and intimacy wrap like grapevines around one another.

Further, it becomes impossible to ignore the different consequences for men and women of intimate relationships in organizational contexts. Add to this fact the possibility that women develop intimacy differently, and Bennis and Shepard's overpersonal versus counterpersonal framework begins to take on new complexities. Women may appear to be counterpersonal if they seek to concentrate on the element of choice or autonomy rather than connection. Or they may be pressured into a traditional role that may look like movement toward intimacy but, lacking the element of control, may be ultimately unsatisfactory. In either case, the possibility of scapegoating—identifying women as the barrier to group progress—is great.

Task demands conflict with organizational demands. The very same organizations that design task demands that generate intense connections may be hostile to any expression of those connections. The members of a working group may find that they have to deal with very personal issues while attempting to appear as unfeeling and asexual creatures to the organization. Indeed, it is possible that the organization will be hostile even to the plan to explore the influence of intimacy, much less to its actual expression. (See Alderfer's, 1988, story on teaching a case about Mary Cuningham.)

This crosscurrent places members in the position of both being told to utilize their feelings and having to hide their feelings. It is not difficult to imagine a number of unhappy or unhealthy resolutions of this pressure, including scapegoating and forms of covert acting out.

The basic need to connect conflicts with work group context. The combined analysis points to how problematic it becomes for basic conditions for intimacy to exist. Yet, no matter what the context, individuals still long for intimate connections. If we spend more and more time in intense work settings that are hostile to intimate relationships, what happens to our internal need and drive for connection? To paraphrase Langston Hughes's question of a dream deferred: it is like a raisin in the sun; it dries up or explodes.

One's private self conflicts with one's public self. The invasion
of work into self and the requirement for intense connections into
work make the process of sorting out public versus private areas of
self extraordinarily problematic. At what point is a "private" feeling
of affection or attraction important public information, necessary
for the management of group work? If it is the "product" of a group,
whom does it belong to? And if it is a part of the group work, doesn't
the group need that information to understand its own workings?
Where do you draw the line between an increasingly aggressive task
and group demand versus managing individual boundaries?

CONCLUSION

The drive for intimate connections is a basic part of the dynamics of working groups. But the traditional perspective of group
theorists is inadequate in generating an understanding of groups
working in an organizational context. Rather, a variety of levels of
influence must be examined and their interactions—synergies and
conflicts—taken into account.

What emerges is a perspective that treats intimate relationships
as a complex phenomenon, one that is more cautionary than prescriptive. Individuals enter working groups with deeply held needs
and, indeed, deeply set patterns of expectations that important relationships will emerge. But the individual experience is one that
is internally and externally complex and conflictful.

Clearly, we need to know a lot more about the interaction of
drives for intimacy in organizational and work contexts. But, given
the preceding analysis, the various influences and crosscurrents will
also influence the study process itself. It is likely to be blocked by
the same kinds of resistances that have made progress so slow in
the first place.

The process of investigation is itself highly invasive and crosses
the traditional line drawn between public and private life. Must
feelings of affection, lust, and love also be exposed and harnessed to
serve some task?

Finally, even when the subject is examined and explored, not
all become equally vulnerable or exposed. Lower-power groups, by
definition, have more to lose and, when the topic is intimacy, they
have been and still continue to be women. In fact, the fantasy exists
that sexuality in the workplace exists only because of women, and

there is a persistent tendency to split out to women the issues of sexuality and intimacy. Those denying the dynamics see less and thus have little to say. Those filled up with the issue can hardly avoid it, yet risk more by asking that it be explored.

In sum, we have a difficult struggle on our hands. While we have some elementary directions to go in, the cost of pursuit will in itself be difficult. If we indeed long for intense connections and yet work so hard to deny them, we set ourselves up for frustration. If we continue to carry, unexamined, images of group life that include idealized conditions of intimacy, we will struggle to do justice even to our here-and-now experiences.

Chapter 5

Paradox and Groups

DAVID N. BERG and
KENWYN K. SMITH

In Full Collaboration

Most of us who work with groups in educational, organizational, or therapeutic settings would not be surprised to hear members use words like *ambivalent, contradictory, tense,* and *conflictual* to describe their experience in groups. We might also expect to hear words like *productive, synergistic,* and even *exhilarating,* but we would probably wonder about the description of a group's process that did not include some of both kinds of words. The more we observe groups, the more we are struck by the coexisting opposites that are a seemingly perpetual feature of group life. Simultaneous and opposing emotions, positions, and reactions exist both inside individual group members and inside the group as a whole. And these coexisting opposites are the source of the group's vitality as well as its paralysis.

The term *paradox* describes a particular relationship between opposites. It is, in its simplest form, a statement or state of affairs seemingly contradictory but expressing a truth. A paradox is an assertion that meaning can be found in the framework that links coexisting and conflicting opposites. This is a chapter about paradox and its relevance to our understanding of group dynamics.

THE LITERATURE ON PARADOX IN GROUPS

The explicit discussion of paradox in groups has been limited. Bion's (1961) point of departure for his work on groups was essentially paradoxical: to understand the individual, it is necessary to look from the perspective of the group, and to understand a group, one must look from the position of the individual (Trist, 1985). In his emphasis on the interdependence of the individual and the group, Bion began to articulate the paradoxical relationship between the individual in the group and the group in the individual.

Schermer (1985) points to another instance of paradox in Bion's work. In the fight/flight group, when individual members begin to experience unmanageable intrapersonal tensions, intermember relations become threatened and the possibility of group dissolution becomes "real" unless some way can be found to defend the members from the consequences of these tensions. The group invariably "manages" this circumstance by splitting into subgroups that fight with each other, thereby shifting the group's attention to these warring subgroups. In the process, the individually based paradoxes (that is, internally coexisting but opposing emotions) are expressed at the group level in the behavior of the opposing subgroups.

Benne (1968), in reviewing his experiences with NTL groups, adopted a paradoxical framework for reflecting on the processes alive in T-groups. His thesis was that much would be gained in a group when naturally occurring polarizations could be transformed into paradoxes. Benne pointed out, for example, that the original goal of an experiential group, to study its own internal processes, creates many ambiguities for the unformed group. These ambiguities become so disorienting that members develop a secondary goal—to dispel the anxieties created by the original goal. The primary and secondary goals become embodied in the emergence of the two subgroups, one of which focuses on producing something, presumably in the hope that production will take the anxieties away, while the other remains invested in feeling the intensity of the anxiety created by the goal of self-analysis.

The dilemma for the "producer" subgroup is that they cannot determine what to produce. Hence the "feelers" point out that the producers are *feeling* frustrated by their inability to produce and that it might be better simply to feel this frustration rather than beat on themselves to produce. On the other side, the producers retort that if the feeling subgroup were not so interested in distracting everyone by insisting on feeling everything, then the process of production might be possible and the feelings would then disappear. At this point the group is stuck and members look to the leader (or facilitator) to set them free. Each side believes that if the leader-facilitator would throw his or her weight behind its particular perspective, all would be well. Of course, to do this would only intensify the struggle and trigger each subgroup into another battle over whether the leader-facilitator is doing the right or wrong thing. Paradoxically, suggests Benne (1968), the function of the leader has to be to give support to both sides, thereby escalating the conflict that needed leadership in the first place. In the process, group members are confronted even more strongly with the realization that they alone can work out the issues for which they feel leadership is necessary.

Another of Benne's paradoxes is that members split on the issue of whether the group exists for the individuals or the individuals for the group. This split is manifest in a struggle over group versus self-maintenance. Of course, this bipolar position fades only when members accept their "groupness" *and* when the group accepts the importance of its individual members. Hence, the group gains its solidarity as individuality is legitimated, and individuality is established when the primacy of the group is affirmed.

A third paradoxical example from Benne's review is this: a group is beneficial in that it enables the generation of more alternatives than are possible for individuals alone; however, for a group to choose, it must make judgments. To make these judgments, standards of intermember interactions must be established, but the establishment of these standards depends on judgments. To break out of this cycle a group must be willing to do what seems impossible: make judgments without first establishing standards and setting standards through the process of making judgments. This is a paradox. By making judgments a group creates the standards it needed in order to make the judgments.

Recently, family therapy research has also explored the role of paradox in family systems and in the conduct of family therapy (for example, Selvini Palazzoli, Buscolo, Gecchin and Prata, 1978; Weeks and L'Abate, 1982). In working with the triangulation process (Karpman, 1968) characteristic of family systems, for example, the therapist often has the paradoxical task of exposing the power of the powerless and the powerlessness of the powerful. In families, the rules that govern the relationships among the persecutor, the victim, and the rescuer may not be what they seem and may, in fact, include the opposite.

The discussion of paradox in groups illustrated above has been primarily devoted to a *description* of the opposing elements commonly observed in therapy groups, T-groups, and families. These paradoxical phenomena have been viewed mainly as consequences of other dynamics: basic assumption life, group development, schizophrenic transactions. What follows in this paper is a paradoxical conceptualization of group dynamics, a perspective on group life that places paradox at the center. We begin with a definition of paradox followed by three examples of paradoxical phenomena in groups. We then place groups in a context and examine the implications of a paradoxical view on a group's relationship with its environment. In the concluding section we look at a paradoxical view of group movement.

WHAT IS PARADOX?

In general, paradox can be understood as a process that involves a vicious cycle, based on disconfirmation, that creates self-renunciation. For example, the statements "I am lying" or "This statement is false" create a paradox (Hughes and Brecht, 1975). The essence of paradox may be seen by examining the following two sentences when they are juxtaposed:

> The statement below is true.
> The above statement is false.

Each of these statements taken separately is quite simple. However, when they are put together, paradox is created—a self-referential, self-contradictory vicious cycle that has the quality of an endless hall of mirrors. While the content of each statement remains the same, its meaning is changed by the fact that it has become framed by the other statement (Hofstadter, 1980).

Consider another example: "Rule #1: All rules are made to be broken, including this one." The paradoxical nature of this statement stems in part from the self-contradiction it contains. If the statement were merely an observation, there would be no paradox, but it is a self-proclaimed "rule" and thereby involves the circular contradiction of paradox. Our logic and our feelings seek a way out, but there is no escape unless we rewrite the statement and eliminate or "separate" its parts.

In this example we also notice the "truth" that is being expressed in the juxtaposition of the paradox's contradictory elements.

If we examine the statements, what emerges is that the establishment of rules and the breaking of them are inextricably linked. The notion of breaking a rule is firmly based on the notion of a rule itself, and vice versa. As we examine the role of paradox in groups, this link between contradictory and opposing forces will emerge as a central feature but one that is often overlooked.

In the above examples, if we remain inside the implied frames, we are caught in a spiral of seemingly contradictory forces, trapped between which of the suggested "truths" is "true." A paradoxical view suggests looking from an outside frame (a metaframe) to see how these seemingly contradictory statements make sense while the apparent contradiction is maintained.

In groups, there are many experiences that surface in contradictory forms and generate tensions that are threatening both to individuals and to the group as a whole. The temptation is to concentrate on one side or the other of this tension and thereby lose the perspective that joins the two and exposes the meaning in the paradox. In this chapter we are interested in exploring what group experiences might look like if these contradictory forces were treated as being a natural and central part of the very concept of groupness.

A GUIDING CONCEPTUALIZATION

Our central thesis is that group life is inherently paradoxical. By this we mean that individual members experience the group as being filled with contradictory and opposing emotions, thoughts, and actions that *coexist* inside the group. Group members' struggles to manage the tensions generated by these contradictory and opposing forces create the essential process dynamics of group life.

Membership in groups is simultaneously comforting and discomforting in a number of ways. The power of the collective and the potential strength of the mutual dependencies therein arouse both fears and hopes: fears, for example, that the group will be either overwhelming or isolating and hopes that participation will be both personally and collectively enhancing. As individuals come together to form groups, their differences allow for the simultaneous expression of both hopes and fears. The simultaneous expression of these contradictory reactions actually makes the group a safer place, albeit a place full of opposing forces. The coexistence of these opposing forces is as necessary as it is disquieting, for their presence in the *group* allows *individuals* to participate in spite of the ambivalence they bring to collective endeavors. It is in this sense that paradox is an essential and inherent characteristic of group life.

By stating that group life is inherently paradoxical we do not mean that group life is not inherently other things as well. Just as when we say someone is inherently intelligent, it does not preclude his or her being inherently attractive or inherently athletic. In saying a group is inherently paradoxical we mean that paradox is contained within the very core of the existence and meaning of groups, and that a group's paradoxical nature needs to be understood along with other aspects of groups.

In presenting a paradoxical view we want to emphasize that the contradictory aspects of group life have both experiential and reflective parts to them. Contradictions can exist in both *what* people experience as actually happening to them in the group and *how* these experiences are thought about or "framed." For example, in a group we might experience at some point the necessity of involvement and at some subsequent point we might experience the necessity of detachment. This conflict between two opposing and contradictory injunctions about life in groups is often *experienced* as paradoxical since both are experienced as simultaneous, legitimate, and opposing demands from the group. Once the individual decides to separate them (for example, I will be detached now, involved later) the paradox is eliminated in a way analogous to separating the "true" and "false" statements from each other.

A paradoxical conceptualization of group dynamics has a number of characteristics. First, it focuses on *underlying group processes*, those emotional and psychological processes that exist when one strips away the influence of group tasks. To put it another way, we are concerned with those processes that are themselves shaped by the specific behavioral tasks that bring many groups together but are neither created nor destroyed by the character of these tasks. The rich and thoughtful tradition of research on these underlying group processes (Freud, 1959; Le Bon, 1895; Bion, 1961; Slater, 1966; Bennis and Shepard, 1956; Tuckman, 1965; Schutz, 1958; Whitaker and Lieberman, 1965; Bales, 1970; Gibbard, Hartman, and Mann, 1974d; Colman and Bexton, 1975) provides an intellectual point of departure for this paradoxical conceptualization.

Second, an exploration of this central thesis requires examination of both *unconscious* as well as *conscious dynamics* at both the individual and collective levels. By definition, these dynamics must be inferred from the behavior of individuals and groups, since they are "out of awareness" unless systematically attended to.

Third, in order to understand what happens in groups and why, it is necessary to examine *both internal group and external or intergroup dynamics* (a central theme of this volume). A study of internal dynamics looks at the events, dilemmas, issues, and processes that occur with regularity in most small groups and seeks to identify what they are and why they occur. The study of intergroup dynamics looks at the group as a unit embedded in a larger social context, connected to its surroundings through its members and through its activities with other groups. A paradoxical conceptualization of group processes requires that we look at both internal and external dynamics.

Fourth, our thesis is an attempt to develop a *descriptive conceptualization* that "best fits" what we and others have observed about groups. This work leads us to certain propositions about group behavior and we find that, inevitably, there are prescriptive elements to the emerging theory. What follows is an elaboration and illustration of a paradoxical conceptualization of groups, not an empirical test of its validity.

Finally, implicit in our description of the paradoxical nature of group life is *a theory about how movement or development* occurs. Group development theory seeks to understand the influence of time on the unfolding of behavior in groups (see Chapter 6). Are there phases, stages, or themes that groups pass through or are there repeating cycles in group life? How do groups move from one phase or theme to another, if they do? Is this progress, and against what standard?

GROUP PARADOXES

When we take experiences in groups and examine them through a paradoxical frame, what do we see? To address this, we will explore the contradictory and self-referential dynamics associated with a number of familiar themes in group life. Understanding a paradox requires an appreciation of the contradictions it contains, the roots of these contradictions in both the individual and the group as a whole, the ways these oppositional forces are linked, and the essential elements of groups that are expressed in the relationship between the opposing elements of these contradictions. We illustrate our paradoxical thinking with a discussion of three paradoxes drawn from a collection of twelve described elsewhere (Smith and Berg, 1987). We believe these three are illustrative of the kinds of paradox found in all groups.

The Paradox of Dependency

In the human life cycle, growth involves the development of a good measure of independence. In a sense, our need for independence is actually driven by our needs for dependency. We break away from our families of origin so that we can create families of our own. In the severing and transformation of one set of dependencies, we become free to create new dependencies, upon spouses, upon our own children, upon networks created or chosen by us.

In groups we observe behavior that can be described as dependent, counterdependent, interdependent, and independent. Although the concepts can be defined as nonoverlapping there are strong experiential and epistemological connections among them. For example, a group member's refusal to accept any guidance from the leader may be an expression of independence, while at the same time being a counterdependent denial of the leader's authority, a denial that unwittingly gives the authority more power than would be the case if some dependency were accepted. The individual behaving counterdependently is as much imprisoned by the dynamics of dependency as someone who openly accepts, without question, the leader's guidance.

A group functions only if members are able, at times, to be dependent on each other. The mutual dependency makes the group a group. To deny this dependency, or try to make it into something other than what it is, diminishes the group's capacity to come together as a whole. The metaphor for the paradox of dependency is ecological. For any part of a system to be able to act independently it must accept its dependency on the other parts together with which it makes up a whole.

If we examine group behavior, we find it very noticeable that the times when members seem most troubled by feelings of dependency are when those depended upon are experienced as untrustworthy. When this is the case, the desire to be independent is very strong, for if one is independent it is much less important to trust others, or so it seems. The dilemma is that the independence sought after and created to compensate for the "untrustworthiness" of others makes the need for trust even greater.

The special nature of the paradox of dependency is that to experience independence in collective life, one constantly has to give expression to one's dependent side. For only as reliable dependencies are established is *inter*dependence possible, and it is the creation of collective interdependence that provides the foundation upon which the notion of independence has its meaning. At a group level there is no way for a group to develop a fabric of reliable, interdependent relationships unless its individual members give expression to their dependency even when this may mean depending on (trusting) that which has yet to be proved to be dependable. Only as individuals allow themselves to depend upon others in the group does the group become a dependable entity. This network of interdependencies frees individuals from the kind of independence that is based upon fear and allows them to express an independence of thought and action that is rooted in the underlying stability of the relationships in the group.

The Paradox of Boundaries

One cannot talk about groups without implicitly invoking the concept of boundaries. There are boundaries in groups that explicitly indicate who belongs and who does not. There are boundaries drawn around each of the subgroups that together form the group as a whole. There are boundaries that define the whole. There are boundaries around each of the individuals that make up the membership, and there are boundaries less easily pointed to, though just as real, created by the psychological sense of belonging group members feel and the attitudes that are acceptable or unacceptable to the group.

The concept of group boundary has been important in social science theories of collective behavior since the work of Kurt Lewin (1951) on field theory. He drew on the prevailing thought in military strategy, and so it seems reasonable to suspect that the concept has been around since humankind began to fight with itself. The place where boundary was most meaningfully elaborated as a pivotal concept at the collective level was in general systems theory (Miller, 1978) and at the individual level in the object relations work of the psychoanalytic school (Kernberg, 1980) and the cognitive theories of Piaget (1963). In each tradition, development is understood in terms of the ability to draw boundaries (for example, learning to distinguish between breast and self, me and not-me, et cetera). Once boundaries have been drawn, the possibility of relationship emerges. Without boundary there can be no relationship. For example, as the infant builds a sense of a self distinct from a parenting figure, then and only then can it develop a relationship with that parent. Without boundaries, there is fusion. In this regard, boundaries are at the base of everything in group life. For the group to have a sense of itself as an entity capable of acting as a whole, it must have clear external boundaries. For the group to develop an internal sense of itself, it must be able to see multiple possibilities for the arrangement of its internal parts (individuals and subgroups). This requires the drawing of distinctions between the parts.

The paradox is that boundaries simultaneously make it possible for a group to take actions and at the same time limit those actions by what the boundaries define. For example, when a group's boundaries are drawn such that the group is defined as management, the fulfilling of the management function becomes possible but the option of being labor is taken away.

This paradox of simultaneous possibility and limitation is most evident in the boundary delineation associated with labeling. In human consciousness, the only way for us to think is via the symbols we use to store our experiences of the world. These symbols make it possible to hold sufficiently constant images of experience for us to reflect upon those experiences. Our reflection, though, is not in terms of those actual experiences, but in terms of the symbols we use to store those experiences. If we have labeled an experience a particular way, that is the frame within which we will think about it. To develop thinking beyond the limits defined by the symbol requires us to break the frame, but even then the breaking out is shaped by that which is being broken out of. The deep paradox is that were it not for the symbols, experience could not be stored and would not be an ongoing part of our experience. At the same time, those very symbols constrain the ways we are able to experience both the past and the future.

One of the most critical functions of a group's boundaries is as a metaphoric container of the anxieties carried by individual members as a consequence of their group membership. If members constantly bear the anxiety of group membership alone, then the group will always be an overwhelming place. It is in the group's interest to provide a way for its members to deal with the reactions the group generates in them. The term *container* is a good one because the most visible aspect of the container is its boundary system. In fact, it is the only property the container has. The metaphor of group as container implies that "stuff" will not leak out and that if you lift the lid appropriately you can pour "stuff" into it.

Jaques (1955) argued that much of the desire to structure experiences in groups comes out of both the individual and collective wish to have a defense against anxiety. But the paradoxical rub about "these boundaries that contain" is that they are the very processes (experienced as structures) that create the anxiety in the first place. Individuals import their own individual anxieties into the group, but collective anxieties are coalesced by that which binds the members together (that is, the group's boundaries). In recognizing this, it would be tempting to suggest that if the group's boundaries *create* such problems, then it would be best to draw the boundaries in a different way, or have none at all. But doing this provides no solution, at least not in any absolute sense, for boundlessness brings with it a set of anxieties that have to be contained in some way or other.

Boundaries, then, both constrain and release, restrict and enable, contain anxiety and create anxiety. The ongoing processes of establishing and negotiating boundaries in groups gives rise, simultaneously, to a host of contradictory and opposing reactions. The vitality of a group rests in part on its ability to erect, modify, take down, and reflect on its physical, intellectual, and emotional boundaries.

The Paradox of Regression

When individuals join a group they are approaching something new, experiences that are unfamiliar. They tend to manage the attendant anxieties by resorting to behaviors learned in similar settings during their personal histories. This can be thought of as a transference process, in that the present is being initially treated as though it were the past, to help get to the point of dealing with the present on its own terms. This transferential dynamic involves the individual's return to an earlier mode of operating in order to deal with the present, a dynamic called regression. Paradoxically, individuals eager to be very present in a new situation need to be able to engage in this regression (that is, allow and acknowledge the transferential dynamics) in order to learn what is meaningfully part of the here and now. The paradox of regression is that in order not to *be* in a regressed state one has to be willing to regress.

Individuals joining a group do so as whole and separate entities, but in so doing they are in the process of becoming parts of something larger than themselves. In order to prepare for their "partness" (which is necessary for a whole [the group] to come together as an integrated entity), the individuals have to allow themselves to experience some fragmentation. To join with others around a common task, for example, often requires that "part" of me connects with "part" of someone else. But it is rare when "all" of me connects with "all" of someone else. Thus, connections in a group are most often connections among "parts" of individuals. Allowing oneself to be a set of "parts" rather than an integrated "whole" feels regressive, as if one were returning to a time of less personal integration and wholeness. Such fragmentation, and the attendant loss of wholeness, is invariably threatening and runs counter to many of the developmental struggles that individuals go through. Resisting this process of inner partitioning, while perhaps making it easier for the members, makes it very hard for the group as a whole to do what it must in order to come together as an integrated entity made up of wholesome parts.

When individual members do allow the necessary regression to take place, they are thrown back to those locations in their own individual histories when fragmentation was problematic, often to those experiences in the family of origin when one's sense of self as an individual unit was being established. While such individual regression is taking place, the group as a whole, in order to function with these members constituting its parts, has to work out a collective way to contain the anxieties stirred in its members as they regress in the service of the group's development. Consider, for example, group members who allow themselves to express their fantasies about malevolent authority figures as a way of joining together to understand their treatment of a group leader. This "regressive" work can only be done if the group as a whole is able to create a climate of trust and support, since the primitive and childlike nature of these fantasies may evoke fears of embarrassment, humiliation, or ridicule in the members. When members are willing to regress, they give the group both the time and the chance to become an adequate container of their anxieties, making the group into a potentially safe place in which to be present as a part. This also gives the group the opportunity to build into its foundation a method for drawing together the elements (the individuals) that are no longer demanding that their own original versions of "wholeness" must be maintained. If and when such a foundation can be created, the members are then able to experience their partness (as elements of the whole group) and their wholeness (as a part of that group).

Groups that learn how to deal with the regressive tendencies of their members can create the conditions where individuals will not require such extensive regression in the future. Hence, paradoxically, the group and the individuals who are able to embrace their regressive sides can learn about how to interact in such ways that they don't end up remaining regressed.

GROUPS IN CONTEXT

In examining the paradoxes above, we have treated groups as if they existed in isolation from other groups and a larger social world. This is clearly an oversimplification. The inherent tensions of group life are given meaning, "framed," by a group's experience with its context, particularly its relationships with other groups in its environment. How are a group's internal, paradoxical tensions shaped and influenced by the group's context? It is to this question that we now turn.

What is a group's context? First, the nature of a group's environment is not automatically given. Just as individuals enact aspects of the world around them, so do groups attend to some, but not all, of the information and activity in their environment. Some groups attend to the psychological and political environment of their organizational or cultural environment more than other groups. Second, a group's composition and history as well as the characteristics of the social environment in which it is embedded all affect what aspects of the "context" become important. Third, how a group elects to act within that context can make the context hospitable and sustaining or hostile and adversarial. The context is largely created by the actions of those entities that belong to it, and since a group's world is filled with *inter*actions with other groups, we next examine the ways in which these interactions create frameworks for understanding internal group experience.

When we look at relations among groups, we make four central observations: (1) as a result of groups existing in a world populated by other groups, they tend to be forever banging into each other, each struggling for its own space and its own identity; (2) each group, to maintain that identity, makes attributions about other groups and encourages them to act in ways that support this particular self-definition; (3) the very notion of multiple groups in the same context means there are multiple interests that may not overlap, creating the potential for conflict among the groups; and (4) how groups regulate their interactions creates a system that each group comes to depend on for its ongoing viability.

Research has suggested that conflict among groups is produced by a variety of factors: competition for scarce resources (money, food, land, information) and differences in goals, values, or desires for power and authority. It is also clear that intergroup conflict can be caused by the displacement of internal hostility (the use of other groups as scapegoats) or by a group's need to solidify its identity or leadership structure. Although these "manufactured" causes have been labeled "nonrealistic" sources of intergroup conflict (Coser, 1956), they contribute to the empirical conclusion that conflict dominates relations between groups.

These findings suggest that if any particular group looks outward it will find itself surrounded by groups in conflict. As a result of living in this environment, groups develop internal characteristics that *seem* necessary for survival. In a world of intergroup conflict, high cohesiveness, strong group loyalty, strict rules of leadership and followership, secrecy, and stereotypical responses to members of other groups are all apparently functional for a group's survival. These internal consequences of intergroup conflict are well documented and universal (Levine and Campbell, 1972; Coser, 1956; Alderfer, 1977; Smith, 1982).

In our terms, the effect of this intergroup conflict is to make it virtually impossible for groups to understand their internal struggles using the framework of paradox described here. Paradoxical thinking would require the group's acceptance of thoughts and feelings that might change in traditional posture toward other groups, putting it at a potential disadvantage. As an example, consider the issues of commitment of members to their group. A paradoxical view of the tensions around commitment would involve accepting both committed and noncommitted feelings as natural parts of any group. In fact, the acceptance and examination of these opposite emotions would be viewed as the basis from which the very concept of commitment would derive its meaning. For a group engaged in external conflict (or one in a constant state of preparedness for conflict) to accept or examine the feelings of "weak" commitment within its ranks is experienced as potentially destructive. It serves the interests of the group if these feelings of potential destructiveness can be displaced and relocated in the other group or in a scapegoated member. In a world of intergroup conflict, lack of solidarity undermines the group's ability to hold its own. A nonparadoxical framing of internal tensions ("you are either for us or against us") better fits the "requirements" of the external, conflictual world because it helps create cohesiveness, loyalty, followership, and ethnocentric attitudes.

The dilemma inherent in this way of coping with external tensions is that it fuels the external conflict even further, increasing the necessity for each group to polarize its internal tensions. By displacing certain internal feelings, the external relations actually become more dangerous. In other words, internal polarization reinforces the external conflict, which in turn creates the necessity for stronger internal polarizations. Once this self-perpetuating cycle is set in place, the possibilities of a group switching to a paradoxical frame for understanding its internal dynamics is unlikely. In this way, a group's internal life comes to mirror the processes at the intergroup level, and vice versa.

If a group does manage to develop a perspective on itself and comes to adapt a paradoxical frame on its own internal tensions, it is still in the dilemma of not being able to get a perspective on what it contributes to its intergroup exchanges. Without a paradoxical viewpoint on both its intergroup dynamics and its intragroup dynamics, it is likely to settle on an ethnocentric frame (we are good, they are evil) to explain its conflict with other groups. In other words, it will need paradoxical perspectives at both levels in order to *maintain* a paradoxical viewpoint on its own internal struggles.

Importation and Exportation

There is yet another way in which the internal paradoxes of a group are given meaning or framed by the intergroup relations occurring in its environment. Rice (1969) pointed out that small groups can be thought of in intergroup terms since each individual is also a representative of a number of other groups. A black female, for example, carries her identity group memberships (black and female) into her "work" group activities. Any small group, therefore, is both a collection of individuals and a set of representatives.

The salience of these representational issues depends on the specific combination of group memberships present. For example, when we, two white males, are with other white, male, professional colleagues, our representativeness is more likely to be in terms of age, our respective institutional affiliations, our Jewish and Christian or American and Australian identifications. However, with a group of black women, these representational facets fade while our whiteness and maleness become predominant.

It is important to note that an individual does not necessarily have to *intend* to be a representative to function as one. A black man in an all-white group *is* a representative by virtue of how he is seen, regardless of how he feels about acting as a representative. Similarly, a supervisor in a team meeting represents "higher authority" whether or not he or she intends to do so. In more subtle ways the interaction between two or more individuals always has representational elements to it since consciously or unconsciously we respond to the age, gender, race, authority level, occupation, and so on, of others as well as to their individual characteristics.

Individuals are usually aware of other members' representativeness. They may or may not pay attention to their own representativeness. In addition, group members enter a group with views about the relationships between the groups that are represented (Berg, 1978). For example, in mixed racial groups all members bring with them expectations of how racial dynamics will be expressed. Membership in a group (race, gender, ethnicity) includes a socialization process that specifies the nature of the relationship between one's own group and other groups. Being Jewish, for example, includes an awareness of Jewish-Christian relations, both historically and in the present. On the other hand, being Christian in a predominantly Christian culture is more likely to include awareness of Catholic-Protestant dynamics than Christian-Jewish relations.

The multiple groups that each individual represents in any given small group and the historical relationship of these groups from other settings set the stage for the ways in which a particular group struggles with the paradoxical nature of collective life. The representational characteristics of individuals provide the mechanism by which the group struggles to manage its paradoxical tensions. Through a process of importation, groups use the representational characteristics of their members to provide both structure and process to the inner tensions in group life. Conversely, the multiple memberships of group members mean, in turn, that the structure and process of managing paradoxical tension in groups will be *exported* to other groups.

In our analysis, the ethnocentric frame on intergroup relations is imported into small groups by virtue of the individuals' memberships in other groups that currently and historically use this frame. These individuals also import into the group a process for managing these issues—namely, conflict resolution—since this is the process used to manage the intergroup dynamics in which they are involved. Once the internal group tensions are framed in these ways and the group struggles with compromise and conflict "management," the cycle is complete, since these individuals in turn export, or take back, these frames and "solutions" to their other groups and to the intergroup relationships that are part of the group's environment. In this case an ethnocentric frame, once established, becomes further entrenched with each group experience because individuals repeatedly use their experience in small groups to frame their participation in other groups. All of this becomes possible because of our simultaneous identity as individuals *and* as representatives of multiple groups.

To illustrate these importation and exportation dynamics, let us consider a group of six men and three women who compose a local school board. After a number of months of working together on the routine business of the board, the group found itself confronted with a number of difficult and emotionally powerful issues. As these issues increasingly became the focus of the group's attention, a curious "split" developed in the group, a split that began to threaten the group's ability to work together. The male and female members of the board seemed unable to talk together about the issues involved. From the men's perspective, every discussion "broke down" into an emotional debate in which it was impossible to "stay with the facts" and resolve anything. Privately, some of the men acknowledged to each other that the women could not deal with the issues without getting emotional. From the men's point of view, this was causing the problem. They were hesitant to say this out loud, however, for fear the women would erupt, accusing them of being sexist, which the men insisted was not true.

The three women on the board also recognized the conflict with the men. Their view was that the discussions lacked compassion, empathy, and an understanding of how the deliberations of the group affected people's lives. In addition, they felt that in the board there was a great deal of tension that was not being expressed, making it hard for the issues to be fully and completely discussed.

The result of this "split" was that the board spent a great deal of time searching for "approaches" to issues (*Robert's Rules of Order*, debate formats, subcommittee work) and very little time discussing the issues themselves. Votes came to be taken more and more frequently, and public meetings became a place where each faction demonstrated the validity of its viewpoint, refusing to listen to other perspectives and engaging in very little dialogue with the community at large.

Paradoxical theory would explain the situation in the school board in the following way. Members of the group had thoughts *and* feelings about the issues they faced, but the simultaneous existence of ideas and emotions in a board meeting produced tension. Instead of a paradoxical frame (one that acknowledged the coexistence of seeming opposites), the group members framed the issue as a battle between ideas and emotions, facts and feelings. This frame itself was imported from the group's environment via the membership of each individual in other groups (work, family, and so forth). In addition, the "solution" to the conflict was also imported from the wider social context: men represented the rational, idea-centered side of the group, while women represented the emotional, feeling-centered side. Relations between men and women in the society at large had evolved these roles for the two gender groups. When confronted with a paradoxical tension—that is, the presence of both thoughts and feelings on the board—the group framed the issue in "either/or" terms and then imported a "solution" from the culture by way of its members' identities in a gender group. Gender group relations provided the model for handling the board's paradox. They merely imported the existing approach. The members also exported their "solution" back into the larger environment, since their experience on the board presumably added to their "understanding" of gender relations in general, setting in motion yet another vicious cycle.

"STUCKNESS" AND MOVEMENT

A paradoxical perspective suggests that the origins of both stuckness and movement are rooted in the ways individuals and groups respond to the presence of coexisting opposites. The central dilemma for both individual group members and the group as a whole is how to survive and flourish in a social world defined in large part by the paradoxical contradictions it evokes. Why do groups get stuck and what is meant by the phrase *group movement*? We are primarily concerned not about the temporary stuckness that may be the result of conflict over scarce resources or the existence of conflicting needs or goals, but rather about the repetitive, psychological, and often unconscious tensions that paralyze a group from even doing the work of problem solving on scarce resources or compromising about conflicting needs. We introduce our discussion of group movement with a metaphor, a description of a hypothetical living system that survives and flourishes in a world of coexisting extremes. The metaphor allows us to illustrate some of the characteristics of stuckness and movement in the paradoxical world of group relations.

A Hypothetical Jovian Organism

Imagine a hypothetical living organism on the planet Jupiter (Feinberg and Shapiro, 1980). The atmosphere on Jupiter is composed of layers of different gases, each with a different temperature. Our hypothetical Jovian organism lives in this atmosphere and has adjusted to a life embedded in temperature extremes. It resembles a hot-air balloon. The living organism is the skin of the balloon and is filled with an inert gas. As we first approach it, the organism is living in a hot lower region of Jupiter's atmosphere. As the gas heats up, the balloon rises through this region and passes into a cooler one. At this point the inert gas filling the living skin cools down and the organism descends through the cool region into the hot layer and the process repeats itself. The cycle continues as long as the organism can "feed" upon the energy in the hot region and deposit "waste" in the cold region. Whatever growth and development occurs in the living skin of the balloon is predicated on this perpetual sojourn between the hot and cold regions of its world.

Our hypothetical Jovian organism lives in a world of coexisting opposites, analogous to the world of collective life we have described. Instead of hot and cold regions, group life is filled with coexisting and opposite reactions and emotions: dependency and counterdependency, inclusion and isolation, observation and involvement, creation and destruction. The organism's growth depends on its ability to ascend or descend fully into the two different regions because this immersion provides sustenance (as well as opportunities to get rid of waste) *and* because immersion is the condition that allows the organism to move through one region to another. Since both regions are a part of the organism's world and since the organism's survival depends on its ability to "get into" both regions, the process of full immersion in each region is critically important. Only through descending into the hot region can the organism rise into the cold, and only through fully ascending into the cold region can the inert gas cool down sufficiently to allow the organism to fall back into the hot region. Any attempt to arrest its ascent or descent would cause the organism to become "stuck" and die.

In an analogous way, we can view a group as engaged in a constant ebb-and-flow dynamic that involves the coexistence of numerous "opposites." For example, in many ways each group contains chaos that results from the clashing, turbulent forces generated by individuals coming together. Hence, in addition to providing the group with one of its basic units, each individual contributes to the chaos of the group, its heat. This heat of the group may become so intense that individuals want to distance themselves from that core, where they can "cool off." As that distancing occurs, however, the turbulence becomes diminished, and the group accordingly becomes less "hot" and less threatening than when members are close. Individuals too become "cooler," by virtue of their distance from the group core. Accordingly, members in their "coolness" seek again the collective "warmth" that brought them together and move again toward the core, in turn making that core more dense, turbulent, and hot. And the cycle repeats itself.

We have tried to show that, like the hypothetical Jovian organism, groups too are embedded in a world of coexisting opposites. For groups, this world is partly of their own making, as the members struggle with the contradictory and conflicting reactions to collective life, and partly a legacy of the history and dynamics of the intergroup relations that surround any group. Like the atmosphere of Jupiter, group life is not *either* hot or cold, but rather an environment in which both termperatures exist. It is a paradoxical world of coexisting opposites, created out of the members' need to express the ambivalence associated with membership in a group.

In groups we are often unable to understand the paradoxical tensions, the polarities with which we struggle, until we immerse ourselves in the extremes of which they are made. This immersion is risky and often filled with fear (of being consumed and of being isolated), but, like the Jovian organism, the oscillation between the extremes may be a necessary aspect of the group's survival and growth. In order to discover the framework that links the opposing and contradictory elements in a group, the group must immerse itself in these same elements, but the fact that the framework is not clear at the outset makes the immersion even more risky and fearful. As a result, groups may choose not to immerse themselves in the extremes and may then experience themselves as stuck, unable to move in productive ways.

Stuckness

Since groups evoke contradictory reactions, the expression of these reactions is an important part of the emotional life of a group. But the expression of opposing reactions and feelings can also threaten the group, because members may, understandably, feel that conflicting and apparently mutually exclusive reactions will tear the group apart at worst and stymie any forward progress at best. As the group struggles to "solve this problem" by reconciling the opposing forces or eliminating the contradictions, pressure is created in the opposite direction in order to insure that the full range of contradictory reactions can be expressed. The more the group tries to eliminate contradictions, the greater the pressure to reassert them. A powerful, albeit unconscious, threat to the group is that only one side of group members' reactions to being in the group will be allowed expression. This fear provides a counterpressure against efforts to eliminate or weaken one side or the other of the group's emotional life.

There are a number of ways that groups attempt to eliminate the paradoxical contradictions. Group members may try to compromise the emotions involved by finding a middle ground that makes the contradiction disappear. A compromise such as this seeks to reduce the intensity of the oppositional forces but simultaneously forces out much of the vitality of the group. Compromise creates paralysis because the group must devote its energy to keeping itself in a narrow region of "averages." The group is hemmed in by the intensity of the possibilities. All of us have had the experience of being in a group that could not move because its members knew what they could not explore and were trapped by this knowledge.

Groups also attempt to eliminate the contradictions by pitting the oppositional reactions against each other to see which is "stronger" or more powerful in the group. As it attempts to subjugate one side of the contradiction to the other, the group's process sets in motion forces that reassert the conquered set of emotions or concerns, for no one wants the group to become a place of emotional or psychological domination, since each individual has ambivalent reactions to the experiences of collectives. The process of competition strengthens both the winning and the losing sides and heightens the probability of paralysis precisely at the point that the group appears ready to move on.

Such efforts produce paralysis because they seek to change the inherent character of collective life, a character that reasserts itself because the group's survival depends on its ability to serve as a forum for the expression of both the *opposing* reactions evoked by group membership. Paradoxical tensions in groups can be more or less strong, but they are always the consequence of coexisting opposite reactions in the group. If the reality of groups is paradoxical, then attempts to eliminate the paradox, to separate or split the elements, and to divorce the two opposing forces from their common source will create a reaction to assert the link and to pull the paradox back into the group so that both sides can be expressed. For groups trying to separate the elements of the paradoxical tension or eliminate them altogether, paralysis is an indication of the group's investment in surviving.

If stuckness is often a consequence of attempts to undo or eliminate the paradoxical tensions in groups, movement is the result of living within the paradox. This statement itself may seem paradoxical, since living within paradox would seem to entail endless circularity and frustration. Only by staying within the paradox, immersing oneself in the opposing forces, is it possible to discover the link between them, the framework that gives meaning to the apparent contradictions in the experience. The discovery, emotional and intellectual, of the link provides a release.

Movement

What do we mean by movement? Movement is the exploration of new ground. In the case of the person or group that runs in place or walks in circles, there is motion but no movement. For individuals, motion without movement can be found in the repetitive patterns (often unsatisfying or counterproductive) that involve different settings, circumstances, or people but feel the same because the pattern of responding to these situations is the same. Similarly, groups also develop patterns such that different situations produce a similar emotional response.

From a paradoxical perspective, movement in groups is the result of two major psychological processes occurring within individuals and within the group as a whole. The first of these is the reclaiming of emotions and reactions that have been split off and projected onto other individuals, subgroups, or groups. The second involves immersion in and exploration of the polarities that are part of the group experience.

Reclaiming split-off emotions and reactions is a very difficult undertaking. The process of splitting actually contributes to the creation of opposing forces in groups (Wells, 1980). Through the mechanism of splitting and projection, members of a group can simplify their ambivalent reactions to collective life by placing one "side" of the ambivalence in another person, subgroup, or group and retaining the emotions on the other "side." The opposing forces that were once inside the individual are now inside the group, or those that were once inside the group are now inside the relationship between groups. But the emotional simplification can occur only if the person or group can "lose sight of" the common source of these opposing reactions: that is, the person or the group. Reclaiming split-off emotions refers to the reintegration of the opposing or contradictory reactions. In terms of our discussion of stuckness, this means struggling to acknowledge, when appropriate, the contradictory nature of our individual or collective reactions instead of trying (through splitting and projection, for example) to eliminate this contradiction.

It is important to note that reintegrating the split-off reactions does not translate into resisting the splitting and projective processes as they occur. Often it is impossible to know when these processes are occurring until after one experiences the consequences. The question is not whether the splitting can be avoided but rather if the recognition that splitting is occurring can lead to efforts at reclaiming that which has been split off. In addition, efforts to prevent splitting, if taken to an extreme, may become a way of avoiding the paradoxical tensions at one level, by focusing on the contradictions at another. If, for example, group members are so concerned about splitting and projection that they are unable to create roles in the group (Gibbard, Hartman, and Mann, 1974), they may see only individual ambivalence and never strong and opposing reactions at the group level.

In the case of groups, the extremes themselves may change in character over the life of the group as it struggles with different paradoxical tensions, but the need for the group to immerse itself in the extremes that compose any given paradox remains. This immersion provides the experience necessary to discover the connection or link between the extremes, if one exists. When the group is struggling with a paradoxical tension, the discovery of the link between two apparently contradictory opposites provides a "reframing" of the relationship between the two. This reframing brings with it new ways of "looking at" the conflicts that have formed in the relationship between the two extremes (individuals, subgroups, groups).

CONCLUSION: IMPLICATIONS FOR ACTION

In considering the application of a paradoxical view of group dynamics to the common problems faced by groups and consultants to groups, a number of issues arise. In this final section we discuss some of these issues as a first step in the articulation of a theory of action based on a paradoxical conception of group life.

Attending to the "Fault Lines"

The key to the discovery of the important paradoxical issues alive in a group is paying attention to the "splits" that exist within it. We can think of these splits as occurring along fault lines, or issues that displace two sides from each other. The double meaning of the term *fault* is relevant in that the splits that divide a group are often accompanied by a great deal of blame. By attending to the issues that are surrounded with strong and reciprocal blame, one is likely to discover the processes of splitting and projection, which point to the self-referential contradiction of paradox. Many of these splits turn out to have their roots in common paradoxical tensions and it is through the cumulative attention to and exploration of each of these fault lines that connections and meaning become clearer.

The splits also deserve attention because their presence suggests that both sides, and therefore the group or system as a whole, are likely to experience events and perceive information in terms of the issues dividing them. This makes it difficult for subgroups to see both their similarities and their internal differences. The blame that surrounds these splits makes it even more unlikely that a subgroup will acknowledge its connections to another subgroup. The fault lines represent the ways the group splits the contradictory elements of the dilemmas it faces in an attempt to manage uncertainty and tension. They can provide a consultant or a group member with a starting point from which to explore *backward* to the paradoxical issues that spawned them.

In many cases, attending to the fault lines may require that the consultant or the group move toward the issues or feelings that evoke the most anxiety. Since tension and conflict have formed along these lines, exploring the meaning of these *particular* polarities for the group may involve living with *more* of what most members and most consultants are trying to eliminate or reduce.

Searching for the Link

From a paradoxical perspective, much of the work of helping a group function effectively involves the search for the link between a series of conflicting and apparently contradictory positions and opinions. These links are often hard to see, overwhelmed by the apparent absence of common ground. Like the groups and subgroups involved, a consultant too is often hard pressed to perceive or understand the connections. Instead, he or she is quickly able to perceive the differences and the lines of "fault." Searching for the link is a concrete step aimed at discovering the "frame" that makes sense of the contradictions.

The consultant must be able to begin with the problem at hand but be willing to develop a relationship with the group that allows *both* the consultant and the group to explore the issues fully, to immerse themselves in them in a search for the patterns that *might* connect. Since the "solutions" to the "problems" are often driven by unconscious forces in the group, the links between competing and contradictory solutions, the "sides" along the fault lines, can be drawn only if group members can begin to learn how their actions and reactions are expressions of unconscious as well as conscious wishes and fears. It is the domain "beneath" the problem that includes the potential for discovering the paradoxical link between the problematic but persistent opposing forces in the group.

This search, in the domain beneath the problem, often takes the consultant and the group on a long odyssey that is hardly apparent to either the consultant or the group when they begin. Recurring and deeply felt conflicts are often extremely powerful influences on groups, but the reasons for their influence are more elusive. In a major way, it is often the consultant's *reluctance* to hang on to his or her initial interpretations and his or her decision to continue to explore additional but seemingly unrelated events and emotions that lead to hypotheses about the links between two opposing subgroups.

The Consultant's Temptation

Consultants often face the temptation to adopt the framework used by the group to understand the "problem" and to "solve" it. Confronted with deep and emotional splits within groups, it is tempting to use familiar approaches to conflict resolution (for example, compromise). There is a great temptation to import a nonparadoxical framework and its attendant solutions to the problem of coexisting opposites. The inability of the system to "solve" certain recurring "problems" often leads to the request for consultation in the first place. At a number of points along the way, the choice to resolve one conflict or another may obscure the paradoxical issues driving the conflict. In these instances, a consultant's efforts to resolve the conflict will take him or her away from the important work of exploring the conflicts and of searching for the unconscious links between the opposing sides.

The temptation to enter into a nonparadoxical framework is intensified by pressure from within the consultant as well as from members of the organization. The consultant may find it hard to choose inaction over action, even when his or her judgment suggests that there is important information yet to be found. Since consulting effectiveness is often defined by the *actions* taken there is significant pressure, particularly in the early stages of work with groups, to produce results within the existing framework rather than to explore the effects of the framework itself. To the extent that the consultant gets pulled into the existing framework he or she further entrenches it.

Facilitating Movement

In most cases, work that facilitates group movement involves support for the expression and exploration of strongly held but conflicting thoughts and feelings in the group. When this is possible the group may experience some release from the repetitive, unproductive cycles that become paralyzing. In the instances we know of in which a consultant searched for a way to help the group affirm and legitimate that which was being negated and considered illegitimate, some form of release occurred. When *both* kinds of reactions or opinions can be expressed and tolerated, when opposing forces can coexist, the group is often able to move. Prior to this release, a group's description of its struggles suggests lots of motion and very little movement.

CONCLUSION

In this chapter we have attempted to introduce a paradoxical perspective from which to reflect on the struggles we all encounter in our experiences in groups, as members, leaders, and interventionists. It has been our intention to make more visible those hidden and troublesome group dynamics that become comprehensible when examined from this paradoxical perspective. We believe that many of our solutions to practical problems have been limited by our ways of thinking about groups. Familiar prescriptions for handling conflict and contradiction in groups often merely displace the problems they attempt to solve. A paradoxical view of groups offers a way to think about groups that may open up new possibilities for the way we act in them.

Chapter 6

Reevaluating Group Development: A Critique of the Familiar Models

MARION McCOLLOM

INTRODUCTION

The concept of group development, or at least the idea that groups change over time, has found its way into most small group instructional settings—introductory M.B.A. classes, executive education courses, and specialized management training sessions, as well as more advanced graduate-level curricula on groups. Yet what is most frequently taught to managers today is Tuckman's simple four-stage model developed in 1965. Granted, Tuckman's basic scheme is useful (and catchy); he identifies the major stages of group development as "forming," "storming," "norming," and "performing." However, given its ubiquity, a substantive review of Tuckman's model seems long overdue, at minimum because it does not incorporate the work of the past twenty-five years.

I will argue here that a close reading of Tuckman and other writers in the group development literature necessitates a reevaluation of that research tradition. Specifically, I question the assumptions behind Tuckman's and other familiar models, which I refer to here as "generalized" group development models. These models generalize across setting, size, task, and other variables to identify common stages of development through which all groups pass as they move through their lifespans.

A quick examination of Tuckman's work will reinforce the need for careful reconsideration of generalized group development models. The publication date is arguably not a severe limitation to the model's validity or relevance: many group development "classics" are roughly of the same vintage as Tuckman's article (Bennis, 1964; Dunphy, 1968; Kaplan and Roman, 1963; Mann, Gibbard, and Hartman, 1967; Schutz, 1958; Slater, 1966; Whitaker and Lieberman,

1964). In fact, little new research on group development has been published since the early seventies (Gersick, 1988, and Srivastva and Barrett, 1988, are exceptions). Also, Tuckman (with Jensen) updated the model in 1977 by adding "adjourning" as a fifth group phase.

A more important reason to revisit Tuckman resides in the text of his own 1965 article, in which the model was introduced. The article surveys research on group development dating from the late 1940s to the early 1960s, most of it conducted in therapy groups. In the discussion section, Tuckman suggests that the path of development might vary for the different types of groups in his survey. He also addresses the difficult methodological questions raised by generalizing across the studies he has surveyed. The well-known model is proposed only in the last two pages of the article. It is ironic that the model has survived for twenty-five years, but his careful warnings, and their message about the validity of the model, have been forgotten.

The ambition to create a generalized group development model has not resided solely with Tuckman but has permeated the field. For example, Lacoursier (1980) retraces Tuckman's route, providing an exhaustive and critical review of the research on group development. However, key questions of methodological rigor and conceptual clarity are lost again as he presents his own version of a generalized model. Other group development writers, working from empirical research on groups rather than from literature surveys like those of Tuckman and Lacoursier, have also presented their findings as applicable to all groups (for example, Bennis and Shepard, 1974).

Despite caveats, then, the field has focused on discovering common developmental patterns in all groups. I propose in this chapter to reevaluate generalized group development models with two questions in mind: first, at the most basic level, can we defend the concept of group development? To judge the usefulness of a model, we must first establish the existence and nature of the phenomenon that the model purports to capture. Second, if the concept is defensible, is the generalized group development model with which we are familiar accurate and helpful in describing the phenomenon?

To begin, I have returned to the concept of "development": what have researchers assumed about groups and about change in groups by using that term? I have consulted the work of several major figures in individual developmental psychology—Erik Erikson, Melanie Klein, Lawrence Kohlberg, Dan Levinson, and Jean Piaget—to derive a set of criteria that define "development." The application of these criteria to group development theory reveals a number of theoretical issues shared at both the individual and group levels: for example, how are stages of development defined, how does movement occur from one stage to another, what forces drive development? On the basis of this analysis, I conclude that the concept of group development can be defended (at least to the degree to which individual development is theoretically defensible).

I then explore the absence of a common framework of developmental stages in the field's familiar group development models. The models instead cluster into three categories, which I have called "performance," "emotional climate," and "revolt" models. These models claim to characterize shared patterns of development across groups but in fact do not converge into a generalized cross-model developmental scheme. I argue that we must look carefully at the divergence among the models rather than glossing over their differences.

To pursue this analysis, I return to several major studies to speculate about the influence of the context of the research on the shape of the final model. I also revisit Tuckman's (and others') methodological critiques of any cross-study generalizations about group development. This discussion leads to the conclusion that generalized group development models obscure more than they clarify and that we should look for a new type of model to describe the phenomenon better. I point out that the literature on groups contains ample arguments for why group development should be seen as a dynamic process contingent on a variety of forces internal and external to the group. I then outline a set of factors influencing group development that should be included in a new type of group development model.

The attempt here is severalfold: to explore and validate the theoretical foundations of the concept of group development, to acknowledge the theoretical and methodological questions that have been ignored in the generalized group development models, and to expand the idea of "theory" beyond the notion of a universal model, so that group development researchers can pursue a more dynamic and setting-specific exploration of how and why groups develop.

EXPLORING THE "DEVELOPMENT" IN GROUP DEVELOPMENT

Psychologists have explained many aspects of human life by proposing the existence of universal principles of individual development. Levinson et al. (1978) assert in presenting their work on adult development, "It is now generally accepted that all lives are governed by common developmental principles in childhood and adolescence and go through a common sequence of developmental periods. At the same time, each individual life has its own special character and follows its own special course" (p. 3).

Human "development," then, means that people move through a predictable series of changes over time; the patterns of change hold across individuals but contain variations determined by the unique circumstances of each life. Theories of individual development, despite the different arenas in which they are applied (from infant to adult development), work at the macro level, identifying gross changes over time rather than setting a detailed blueprint for every human life.

To test the viability of the concept of development at the group level, I started by exploring the work of five well-known theorists of individual development. My purpose was to derive a set of criteria or assumptions that could be said to define "development" or developmental theory. These researchers were chosen for the collective range of application of their work and for their prominence: Melanie Klein has illuminated how emotional development in infancy influences emotional health later in life; Piaget has created theories to explain the intellectual development of children; Kohlberg's work focuses on moral development in children and adults; Erikson and Levinson have analyzed the continuous changes into and through adult life.

Questions should be raised by the application of individual-level models to groups. Am I arguing that groups should develop in ways that mimic individual developmental stages? Although many writers on group theory have speculated about this analogy (Slater, 1966; Hartman and Gibbard, 1974; Kaplan, 1974), I do not intend to pursue it here. What I am interested in exploring initially is whether researchers on groups have followed the criteria set out by developmental psychologists in evaluating their data on group development, or have they (implicitly or explicitly) set out alternative definitions of development?

Six Criteria for Developmental Theory

Based on authors' discussions of the criteria shaping their own theories (Brown, 1965; Erikson, 1963, 1980; Klein, 1983, 1985, 1986; Kohlberg, 1984; Levinson et al., 1978; Piaget, 1973), I have identified six general assumptions behind individual developmental theory:

1. individuals pass through a common sequence of stages as they grow older;

2. the work of each stage builds on the work of the former;

3. the stages have distinct features or structures;

4. change from one stage to another or within stages is not continuous but episodic;

5. development represents a process of individuation, or of clarifying the individual's boundaries with the external environment;

6. development is driven by the interaction of biological, psychological, and social forces on the individual.

In the discussion that follows, I explore the relevance of these criteria to group development theory, reviewing the assumptions about "development" underlying group development models.

1. Sequence of stages. Developmental psychologists insist that their data show a set of stages of "invariant sequence" (Kohlberg, 1984). For Klein, this criterion is unarticulated; however, it is implicit in her writings that the normal infant moves through several "positions" to reach the Oedipal complex in the second year (Klein, 1986, 1985). For the four other writers, a fixed sequence of stages is named as essential to the theory.

The congruence of the group development literature with "developmental" theory can be challenged on this criterion (although it is important to recognize here that some developmental psychologists do not utilize stage theories: see, for example, Gould, 1978, on adult development). Gibbard, Hartman, and Mann (1974b), for example, have argued that some group researchers reject the stage theory of group development and instead portray groups as oscillating continuously among issues. They contrast these "recurring cycle" models with "linear progressive" and "life cycle" models of group development (p. 83). However, I believe the case is not as clear as they would like to make it. With the exception of Bion (1961), all of the authors they cite as offering recurring-cycle models (Schutz, 1958; Slater, 1966; Bales, 1955; Mills, 1964) have in fact described stages of group development.

To explain this seeming incongruity, it is important to note the distinction between models of group development and models of group process. The fact that Bion (1961) and Whitaker and Lieberman (1964) do not offer stage theories of group development does not mean that these writers rejected the idea that groups develop in predictable patterns. They simply concentrated on describing a different phenomenon—group process: Bion the oscillations among basic assumption and work modes and Whitaker and Lieberman the resolution of conflicting wishes and fears. Smith and Berg (1987) address the two topics separately. While the authors focus primarily on process (how movement or "stuckness" happens in groups), they also suggest a progression in the sequence in which major paradoxes arise for groups as they move through time.

Thus, it is fair to say that most researchers who have approached the question of group development have concluded that groups pass through a progression of stages over time.

2. Stages build on each other. In general, writers on individual development argue that developmental stages build directly on each other; the quality of work in each stage depends on how well or poorly the work of the previous stages was done. However, these authors disagree on whether or not to ascribe a normative value to the relationship of each stage to its predecessor. Levinson et al. (1978) declare their theory "nonhierarchical," meaning that the tasks of one period in the human life cycle are no better or more advanced than the tasks of any other period (p. 319). Kohlberg (1984), in contrast, assumes as a criterion of his theory the "displacement of lower stages by higher stages" (p. xxx); for him, moral development means moving toward better guidelines for judging right and wrong.

Writers on group development use a similar framework, suggesting explicitly or implicitly that the stages build progressively on each other or that the activities of one stage allow the group to address the tasks of the next stage. Hartman and Gibbard (1974), for example, write:

> The reaction to the uncertainty of the initial phase, with its regressive components, leads to an extreme reaction of exclusionary mechanisms. This process leads in turn to the inclusive preoccupation and the utopianism of the next phase. This phase denies and in a sense stimulates the competitive sexuality of the third phase, which brings with it more exclusive and differentiating mechanisms. This competition in turn threatens the solidarity needed to face termination and to deal with the sadness and regrets accompanying the end of a group (p.174).

The question of a hierarchy of stages is, as in the literature on individual development, in dispute. In some group development models, the assumption is that a group "progresses" over time—toward better performance (Tuckman, 1965), toward maturity in relationships (Gibb, 1964), toward overcoming obstacles to valid communication (Bennis and Shepard, 1974), or toward boundary awareness (Slater, 1966). Other models are descriptive: Kaplan (1974) and Dunphy (1968), for example, outline a stage-to-stage pattern but do not argue that later stages are "better."

3. Stages represent distinct structures. For the five developmental writers, each stage has distinct features that compose an interdependent whole or "structure" identified with each stage. Levinson et al. (1978) describe a "life structure" that is built in each period of adult life.

Despite their insistence on the distinctness of the stages, however, developmental psychologists have recognized their inability to discern in their data clean boundaries between one stage and the next. Although they see the stages as age-linked, the authors allow for significant variation in the age at which a stage is entered or departed. Most writers speak of an integration process, in which the work of previous stages is folded into the work of the current stage. Each stage is distinct, but contains elements of other stages. Levinson et al. (1978) explain this apparent paradox: "In the actual process of development . . . each period is 'interpenetrated' with the others. The current period is predominant, but the others are present in it. . . . The life cycle is an organic whole and each period contains all the others" (p.321).

In most group development models, the stages are seen as having features distinct enough to allow their differentiation from each other. However, as in the individual developmental model, most writers see evidence that stages overlap and contain elements of each other. Bennis and Shepard (1974) write that "lower levels of development cocxist with more advanced levels" (p. 141) and describe the presence of several themes in each stage: "We are here talking about the dominant theme in group life. Many minor themes are present, and even in connection with the major theme there are differences among members" (p. 133). Boundaries between stages are recognized as indistinct, and at least two models (Srivastva and Barrett, 1988; Dunphy, 1968) include transition phases between stages.

4. Change is not continuous. None of the developmental psychologists proposes a smooth, continuous change process. Change is depicted as occurring in spurts, with periods of stability or even stuckness alternating with periods of dramatic transformation. According to Piaget (1973), a variety of factors can "hasten or delay the appearance of a stage, or even prevent the manifestation" (pp. 50–51).

Gersick (1988) describes the pattern of movement she saw in her groups similarly as a "punctuated equilibrium" rather than a continuous process. This description fits the models of virtually all the group development researchers reviewed here except Tuckman, who does not explain how changes from one stage to another take place. Gibb (1964) describes a process of sudden spurts of change amid plateaus; Bennis and Shepard (1974) suggest that a group can get stuck at any stage and not progress farther. Thus, theorists in group and individual development share the view that movement from one stage to another or even within a stage happens episodically rather than continually.

5. Development is a process of individuation. Levinson et al. (1978) see increasing individuation, or "changes in a person's relationship to himself and to the external world" (p. 195), as the process underlying individual development from infancy through adulthood. In their words, the individual forms progressively clearer boundaries between himself and the world and has a firmer grasp on reality: "He forms a stronger sense of who he is and what he wants, and a more realistic, sophisticated view of the world: what it is like, what it offers him and demands from him" (p. 195). Erikson (1980) and Klein (1983) also define development as an intensifying view of reality, or a clearer relationship between self and outer world.

Although some writers see group development as movement toward a more effective and efficient means of performing a task (Tuckman, 1965), most agree with the "developmental" formulation. They describe group development as the process by which boundaries are clarified and group members experience a heightened sense of group identity. This idea is expressed in terms of a progressive process of learning about self and others (Smith and Berg, 1987), an increasing sense of autonomy and ability to overcome anxiety (Srivastva and Barrett, 1988), increased interdependence among members (Gibb, 1964), and a "gradual encroachment of light on shadow," in which conscious bonds between members are substituted for unconscious ones (Slater, 1966, p. 176).

6. Development is driven by interacting forces. The psychologists surveyed here agreed that development is driven by the interaction of biological, psychological, and social forces on the individual. The "engine" of development, the driving force, is characterized differently by the five authors, however. Erikson (1980) hypothesizes a kind of biological blueprint for development; Kohlberg (1984), however, argues that environmental forces are paramount.

For Levinson, Erikson, and Piaget, the aging process, or the passage of time, drives development. Erikson (1963) and Piaget (1973) propose that the psychological and intellectual development of children is tied to physiological advances (teething, talking, and increasing muscular coordination, for example). Levinson et al. (1978) and Erikson (1963) extend this argument to the adult years, noting that the experience of age and mortality drives key developmental stages such as the midlife transition.

Group researchers see the intersection of analogous forces as being at the root of group development. Some writers stress the intrapsychic experience of individuals (basically, how group members manage anxiety) as crucial (Hartman and Gibbard, 1974; Whitaker and Lieberman, 1964; Dunphy, 1968). Others focus on the relationships between group members and group leaders (Bennis and Shepard, 1974; Slater, 1966). Still others stress environmental forces as key to development (Gersick, 1988; Tuckman, 1965).

Almost all models, however, contain an implicit acknowledgment of the interaction that is recognized directly by several writers (Smith and Berg, 1987; Dunphy, 1968; Srivastva and Barrett, 1988): that all three forces—members' internal experience, roles and relationships in the group, and the group's external environment— interact to influence group development.

Summary

An examination of five prominent theorists' work yields a set of criteria that define "development" at the individual level. While the authors I surveyed differ on some points—particularly on the hierarchical nature of stages and on the forces that drive development—overall, their work provides a consistent model of developmental processes.

The application of these criteria to the group development literature demonstrates that researchers in group theory have observed the analogous process in groups. Their understanding of "development" matches the assumptions of the major developmental psychologists; thus, the utilization of the general concept of "development" to describe changes in groups over time seems defensible. The next question becomes: are the generalized group development models of Tuckman (1965) and others, which present a set of stages characterizing development in all groups, useful and valid representations of group development processes?

SEARCHING FOR A GENERALIZED MODEL

Once we have recognized the claim of generalized group development models to describe a sequence of stages through which all groups move over time, even a preliminary look at the best accepted of the models raises an interesting and difficult question: if the models are generalizable across groups, why are they so different? As I will demonstrate, there is significant disagreement among them about the characteristics and sequence of stages. In fact, examining the divergence of the models, it seems strange that so many group development models have coexisted in the literature for so long. For the purposes of this argument, I will illustrate the extent and nature of these disagreements; I will further suggest that important insight into the group development process can be generated by probing into, rather than glossing over, the differences among the models.

Categories of "Unified" Models

Table 1 summarizes the stages proposed in a variety of relatively well known group development models. To sharpen the analysis of cross-model differences, I have collected the models into three categories, according to the language researchers used to name the stages they observed. I assume here that language reflects the central interest of the researchers in approaching group development: the performance of the group, the group's emotional climate, and the dynamics of revolution in the group.

The *performance* models contain an implicit assumption that groups resolve process issues as preparation to competent task performance. The best known of these models is Tuckman's (1965) synthetic framework, which culminates in a stage of optimum task performance ("performing"). In this model, one can see a clear hierarchy of stages. Recognizing the influence of emotional issues raised by the dissolution of a group, Mills (1964) included a termination phase, as did Tuckman in his revision of the model with Jensen (1977). Lacoursiere's (1980) survey model also contains a termination phase. However, all these models can be seen as depicting group development primarily as "progress" towards more efficient or effective group work.

The *emotional climate* models contain no stage of optimal performance, but rather describe a progression of emotional concerns in the group. The general pattern observed by these authors moves

Table 1. Stages In Group Development

Study	Stages				

Performance Models

Study					
Mills (1964)	The encounter	Testing boundaries and modeling roles	Negotiating norms	Production	Separation
Tuckman (1965)	Forming	Storming	Norming	Performing	
Tuckman and Jensen (1977)	Forming	Storming	Norming	Performing	Adjourning
Lacoursiere (1980)	Orientation	Dissatisfaction	Resolution	Production	Termination

Emotional Climate Models

Study				
Schutz (1958)	Inclusion	Control	Affection	Affection-control-inclusion
Dunphy (1968)	Early Period (1) Maintain external norms (2, 3) Warfare		Later Period (4) Transition (5, 6) Concern for affection	
Kaplan (1974)	Dependency	Power	Intimacy	
Bennis and Shepard (1974)	Phase I: Dependence (1) Dependence-flight (2) Counterdependence) flight (3) Resolution-catharsis		Phase II: Interdependence (1) Enchantment-flight (2) Disenchantment-flight (3) Consensual validation	

Revolt Models

Study				
Slater (1966)	Leaders seen as gods	Leaders seen as fallible	Revolt	Post-revolt guilt
Hartman and Gibbard (1974)	Uncertainty-revolt	Group fusion-utopia	Competition-intimacy	Termination

from dependency (as group members deal with formation) to antagonism (as group members deal with differences in authority and influence in the group) to intimacy (as group members realize their affection for each other). The stages build hierarchically toward closer member-member relations and increased self-revelation. There is no explicit recognition of termination dynamics in the language of these models, although Schutz sees his fourth phase as driven by termination processes.

What I have called the *revolt* models are based on Slater's (1966) proposal that groups proceed predictably toward a rebellion against the leader(s). Here the focus is on member-leader dynamics. Hartman and Gibbard (1974) see the revolt as occurring much earlier than Slater does; their model adds a utopian stage after the revolt, whereas Slater sees the revolt as followed by guilt. The Hartman and Gibbard scheme then follows the pattern of the emotional climate models in moving to competition and intimacy and ending with a termination phase.

Although there are some similarities across the three clusters of models and among individual models, Table 1 shows that there is as yet no universally accepted developmental framework for groups. In fact, there *is* no generalized model. However, the well-known models have not been recognized as challenges to each other. There has been no attempt to reconcile their claims as generalized models with their divergence from each other. Given the initial analysis of this chapter, we must also recognize that the concept of group development itself is probably not the cause of the cross-model variation—group researchers have used the term *development* consistently and appropriately.

It is instructive to ask why the field has not resolved this dilemma by discovering one model that captures the phenomenon better than the others. This would require a close look at the underlying research to establish if there are theoretical or methodological reasons to accept some models and reject others. However, there is no obvious evidence that any of the studies underlying the models are fatally flawed; the stages seem to be reasonable interpretations of the data. Therefore, we need to look beyond the validity of the individual studies and instead explore the models themselves.

Explanations of Divergence among the Models

We could hypothesize, on the basis of what we know about the research represented in Table 1, that the different patterns of development offered as "universal" stemmed as much from factors outside the groups in the different studies as from incorrect or divergent interpretations of comparable patterns in the data. As Tuckman (1965) himself pointed out, researchers worked in a variety of settings with different kinds of groups. For at least these ten studies, the type of group, the training of the researcher, and the circumstances of the research can arguably explain some of the variation among the models.

For example, some researchers (Slater at Harvard, Hartman and Gibbard at the University of Michigan) studied undergraduates, an adolescent population in perpetual rebellion against adult authority. It is not surprising that these instructors recognized phases of active revolt in their groups' development, especially given that their research was conducted in the 1960s and early 1970s.

Three of the authors in the emotional-climate-model category (all except Dunphy) dealt exclusively with therapy groups, encounter groups, and T-groups. Given the purpose of these groups and the training of the researchers, it seems reasonable that the models derived from these studies would focus primarily on the development of interpersonal relationships in the group. It is difficult to explain the absence of a termination phase in these models, especially given that researchers noted termination dynamics in three of the four studies (all except Bennis and Shepard) (Lacoursiere, 1980). Perhaps the researchers' concern with intimacy as the "goal" of these groups led them to discount the disruption of termination processes. Because some therapy groups continually change membership rather than disband, it is also possible that leaders experienced in therapy groups were not attuned to termination as a separate phase.

As a final example, we need to look at why Tuckman, in surveying research dominated by studies of therapy groups and T-groups, consciously maintained a task-achievement (or "performing") perspective in his model. In part, this may reflect his desire to make room in the model for those studies in his survey that focused on task as well as process. It is also tempting to speculate that his final synthesized model reflects the task-performance concerns of the Office of Naval Research, the funding agency for the research.

My intent here is not to discredit the work of these researchers by asserting that their results were nothing more than artifacts of the circumstances under which the research was conducted. First, most of this work has stood up over time. Second, there are too many anomalies in the patterns I describe above to build a decisive case: for example, Dunphy, who created an emotional climate model, and Mills, whose model has a "production" stage, both worked with groups of undergraduate students. My purpose is, instead, to illustrate how the context of the research—the type of group and the training of the researcher, at minimum—could have influenced the ultimate shape of the models. What is called into question here is the *generalizability* of the models—their claim to be universal group development models—rather than the validity of each model in describing the developmental pattern of the groups in the study.

On the basis of this discussion, it seems unwise to generalize about group development based on models derived from research conducted with one type of group in one setting. Nor, will I argue, is it defensible to survey a wide variety of studies and aggregate them into a generalized model. The argument against such a practice, interestingly, is developed most fully by Tuckman (1965). In the next section, I will summarize the arguments Tuckman and others have raised against generalized models that spring from surveys of group research. The conclusion of this analysis is that the validity of the generalized group development model cannot be defended.

Questions of Validity

Both Tuckman (1965) and Lacoursiere (1980) articulate convincing arguments that call the validity of generalized group development models seriously into question. Tuckman's article raises two key points, both of which are essentially criticisms of the comparability of the studies aggregated into the model. The first is expressed directly, as he probes the methodological weaknesses in and differences among the studies he has included in this survey. The second point is made implicitly, in the way he structures his argument. He notes two distinct research streams, exploring the development of group structure (or relationships among members) and the development of group problem-solving abilities, and discusses them separately.

Tuckman (1965) criticizes the methodology of the studies in his own survey on numerous counts: his sample contains research on different-sized groups in different settings; he has collapsed data from laboratory groups into data from natural groups because of uneven sample size; some researchers in the survey generated conclusions based on single-group observations while others looked at several groups; and the researchers played a variety of roles in the groups from which data were reported. In general, he reports, independent variables were not adequately controlled in the studies and therefore cross-study generalizations are unwarranted.

Lacoursiere's (1980) list of caveats is similar: the data in his exhaustive survey of group development studies may include only a partial history of the group or it may report a group's entire life cycle of activities; assumptions behind data collection vary greatly (for example, what variables are measured and how they are measured); and techniques of data analysis reflect a variety of theoretical and methodological approaches. On the basis of his and Tuckman's discussion, it is difficult to defend on methodological grounds the comparability of the studies in their surveys.

To give just one example in support of their criticism: Hartman and Gibbard (1974) derived a scheme of group development stages based on changes in affect recorded over time via a structured scoring system administered by former members of the group. Dunphy (1968), on the other hand, divided the group's life arbitrarily into three-week stages and then described the characteristics of each such "phase," on the basis of group members' weekly reports of their experiences in the group. Even if data collection techniques for these two studies were assumed to be congruent (a difficult assumption), the concept of "phase" built into data analysis in these two studies renders the two uncomparable. Yet the two have been aggregated into Tuckman's (1965) and Lacoursiere's (1980) models.

This discussion illustrates that, even if researchers had been looking at the same type of group in the same type of setting for the last forty years, comparability problems would arise in the methodological differences among the studies. The validity of generalized group development models, given all these differences, must be severely questioned. Researchers have been approaching groups in radically different roles, using different theoretical frames, asking different questions, gathering different types of data, and subjecting it to different types of analysis. In the face of this variety of research design, which has been explicitly acknowledged by the major authors, cross-study generalizations should be resisted.

The second point that casts doubt on the validity of generalized group development models has frequently been raised in the group development literature and then ignored or explained away. Tuckman (1965) acknowledges that "group development" may mean something different depending on whether the researcher looks at how a group approaches a task or at how interpersonal relationships change over time. However, rather than pursuing the implications of this distinction, he erases the differences between these two streams of research in his unified model.

Dunphy (1968) argues that such separation is not necessary. He recognizes the differences between the two research traditions, but states that methodological sophistication allows generalizations across all kinds of groups pursuing any number of tasks (from laboratory exercises to therapy). Others have not acknowledged clearly the distinctions between group development in socioemotional versus task accomplishment terms. Gersick (1988), for example, places her work in a theoretical framework that includes "emotional climate" models. However, as she reports her data, it appears that she attended exclusively to how her groups developed toward the accomplishment of a concrete task.

It is difficult to accept the argument for generalizing across the literature on group problem-solving and task accomplishment to studies of group process in therapy groups and T-groups. The theoretical traditions behind the two research streams are quite different; problem-solving studies largely spring from social psychology (see Ross, 1989, for citations in this tradition), while process research comes from clinical psychology and social systems thinking. In addition, there are difficult, if not unresolvable, methodological issues raised by the aggregation of findings from these two traditions. A researcher attending to development of task behaviors in a group (Gersick, 1988, is a good example) will gather data different from that collected by someone researching developing affective patterns or group metaphor as a window into group development (for example, Srivastva and Barrett, 1988).

Reflecting on this discussion, one can enumerate the valuable insights that have been lost in the collapse of research results into a generalized group development model. The objective seems to have been to create a framework that erased all the variation in development patterns among groups. Differences between development in task and process terms have been washed out rather than clarified, and methodological choices in research on groups have been ignored instead of explored and criticized.

Most importantly, in the drive to generalize, researchers have not sought to explain in detail the complexity of forces shaping the development of specific groups. Researchers directly observing groups have not used their data to ask several crucial questions: what forces will shape a group's development and how will they be expressed in the group? Given that so much of the literature relevant to group development points to groups as complex phenomena influenced by the dynamic interaction of individual, group, and systemic-level factors, it is remarkable that the generalized group development model, which washes out this complexity, has persisted.

If the generalized group development model is inadequate, what kind of model could better capture the phenomenon? In the section that follows, I will outline the framework of a different kind of group development model, one that builds on the concept of development as a dynamic process. I will also suggest the factors that should be included in such a model.

MOVING BEYOND THE UNIFIED MODEL

Open systems theory (Miller and Rice, 1975) provides a framework for rethinking group development. The evolution of the group as a system should be affected by internal characteristics (of the group as a whole and of individual members), as well as by the relations of the group with its environment. The group as a system will evolve over time in interaction with internal changes as well as ongoing environmental processes. The model required to capture this phenomenon could be called a dynamic contingency model: "dynamic" because development occurs over time, and "contingency" because the path of development is contingent upon the complex interaction of a large number of variables.

Support for a Dynamic Contingency Model of Development

Theoretical support for a dynamic contingency model of development (based on open systems theory) can be found in the concept of development expressed in the individual development literature surveyed earlier. Those theorists, like writers on group development, initially sought to create models that would be generalizable across individuals. However, in testing the reliability of their research, they encountered and addressed problems with the universality of their models. The acknowledged limitations of their models provide support for a dynamic contingency model of development.

Development is a process by which a system (in this case, the individual) adapts to internal and environmental forces. Individual development is driven by the interaction of biological, psychological, and social factors (although theorists disagree about the relative power of these factors in shaping development). Researchers found that these factors interacted to produce relatively predictable patterns of change in individuals over time.

When variation in those factors increased, however, researchers on individual development found that their models broke on down. Piaget, for example, struggled with the invalidation of his model in cross-cultural settings. Levinson acknowledged that his model was of limited applicability for women, as his study population was male (Levinson et al., 1978). The applicability to women of Kohlberg's stages of moral development has been challenged (Gilligan, 1982).

These findings indicate that the complex forces driving development at the individual level interact in predictable ways only when the study populations and their environments are relatively homogeneous. Differences in national cultures (which may be reflected in the biological, psychological, *and* social forces acting on individuals) apparently create more variation than the models can capture. In addition, other cross-group differences (for example, between genders—see Stewart's [1976] work on women's adult development) also appear to create distinct differences in the interaction of developmental forces. Recent research on racial differences in adult and career development (Herbert, 1985; Thomas, 1986) suggests that race is also an important factor influencing individual development.

Applying these findings to groups, it seems logical that similar types of groups in similar environments could share patterns of development. However, the group as a system is even more complex than the individual; in addition to environmental influences, it is also affected by the dynamics among numerous interacting subsystems (individuals, pairs, and subgroups). Thus, the group is likely to be subject to a large number of interrelated forces. Variations among groups' internal characteristics or external circumstances, therefore, are likely to alter greatly the character, magnitude, and expression of developmental forces. As a result, patterns of group development are likely to vary widely.

If we cannot say exactly how groups will develop, however, we should at least be able to identify general categories of factors that will shape development (analogous to the biological, psychological, and social factors at the individual level). As we saw, group development writers have discussed intrapsychic forces, relationships among group members, and environmental forces as influencing development. However, group development has not been formally modeled as a process contingent on the dynamic interplay of this or some other set of forces. In this section, I will suggest the factors that might be included in a dynamic contingency model of group development.

Factors Influencing Group Development

On the basis of individual development, open systems, and other theories about groups, we can predict that the group development process should be affected by three general factors: the group's relations with its environment, internal relations among subsystems (reflecting individual, interpersonal, and group-as-a-whole issues), and the group's temporal boundaries.

Environment. The argument for including environment as a factor driving group development has been made powerfully and pervasively in the literature on groups. Research on intergroup relations has illustrated the impact on group process of the group's "embeddedness" in a larger institutional setting (Alderfer and Smith, 1982). The work of sociotechnical and group effectiveness researchers suggests the means by which a group's context impacts on the group's process and output: in the *authority relations* between the group and the organization (Turquet, 1974) and in the definition of the group's *task* (Katz and Kahn, 1978; Hackman and Oldham, 1980).

Internal relations. The literature also tells us to look inside the group to see forces that will determine patterns of development. The *composition* of the group is mentioned throughout the literature as a key variable, in terms of homogeneity of group members (Hackman and Oldham, 1980), skills (Hackman and Oldham, 1980), and personality (Bennis and Shepard, 1974). Tuckman (1965) and Lacoursiere (1980) suggest that group *size* is a factor. Finally, *subgroup relations* and *leadership dynamics* are commonly recognized as forces that shape development (Bennis and Shepard, 1974).

Temporal boundaries. Time must be included as a factor in a dynamic model. Tuckman (1965), among others, has suggested that the lifespan of a group is an important variable to consider in group development. The life of a group may last a few hours or generations (for example, a family); however, like other living systems, group lifespans are finite. Given the power of termination dynamics (as recognized in the existing group development models, in individual psychology [Lifton, 1983] and in organizational research [Van Steenberg, 1988]), we could predict that developmental patterns would be influenced by members' experience of the end of the group. In addition, the *temporal context* in which the group operates should be considered, as group and environmental dynamics are likely to be affected by seasonal cycles, for example, or historical events.

This quick outline of the factors influencing group development gives a sense of how a new kind of group development model could open up, rather than close down, discussion of the variations among developmental patterns in different groups. By focusing on one of the proposed factors, researchers can, first, test its influence by varying that one dimension in a study (for example, running several groups similar in most respects except size). Second, researchers can begin to draw more specific conclusions about how the influence of each factor is expressed in the group: for example, how are termination dynamics expressed in three-day- as opposed to three-week-long groups? A model that spells out the complexity of the developmental process permits more systematic exploration of the phenomenon.

This type of model also holds greater utility for managers and others who work with groups than does a generalized model. The generalized model describes a predetermined process; the dynamic contingency model shows the active relationship between group development and variables at the individual, group, and organizational level. The "fit" between task and group can therefore be improved as managers recognize the constellation of factors that will influence the life of a group. A thorough understanding of the ways that the group's environment influences development allows the manager of a task force, for example, to make more informed choices about how and how often she or he intervenes in the work of the group.

CONCLUSIONS

A review of the generalized group development model, as exemplified by Tuckman's (1965) model leads to two main conclusions: that groups do "develop" in the sense of the concept established in the individual developmental literature, and that group researchers have not yet accounted for the variations in developmental patterns that arise in different types of groups. Group development researchers have been searching for uniformity in the content and sequence of stages across *all* small groups. With all the energy invested in the creation of these group development models, there has been virtually no explicit recognition of or search for common theoretical criteria underlying the process of group development.

The benefit of a dynamic contingency model is that it will

allow us to explain and predict specific developmental patterns in a variety of types of groups. The type of model I have described here creates a starting point from which future research and practice can evolve.

It is important to point out that this argument does not question the usefulness or validity of much of the tradition of research on group development. The work of Slater (1966), Bennis and Shepard (1974), and others is compelling; however, we need to see their work as representing the development of *specific* groups in *specific* contexts and to think critically about the applicability of their findings to different groups in different settings. The central problem in the group development field has not been weak or unimaginative research: it has been the drive to generalize when theory tells us that generalization is unsupportable.

The implications of this analysis warrant reflection and interpretation: why has the field preferred simplified models to models that reflect the complexity of the phenomenon? Until we have a detailed intellectual history of the tradition, we can only speculate: because social science researchers and practitioners are, like other people, attracted to clarity? because our clients and students expect us to have "correct" answers? because a simple model is more likely to be widely remembered and cited than a complex contingency theory?

The answer could also lie in the fact that the field itself has been in dormancy, having peaked in the late 1960s. For twenty years, the assumptions underlying the literature have not been seriously questioned, although the theory has continued to serve as a foundation for teaching and training. This may have been because research on experiential groups has been out of style, or because academic politics have created an environment in which group researchers feel forced to defend their tradition at all costs. In this atmosphere, it is difficult to pursue critical theoretical questions.

Active criticism, however, is essential to the reemergence of theoretical work in the field. The hope expressed in this chapter, as in the rest of this volume, is that new research will move the field out of dormancy, building critically and appreciatively on the theoretical groundwork that has already been laid.

Chapter 7

Application Work in Group Dynamics Instruction

DAVID A. THOMAS

INTRODUCTION

Application work is the means by which participants in experiential group dynamics courses are provided the oportunity to learn how knowledge of group dynamics is relevant to understanding their own and others' behavior in organizational settings, and to the development of actions for the management of human behavior. The explicit aim of application work is to facilitate the transfer of learning to the back-home environment. Theories of experiential learning often emphasize application as an important element (Kolb, Rubin, and McIntyre, 1974; Johnson and Johnson, 1975; Rice, 1969; Schein and Bennis, 1965). Descriptions of courses and conferences, however, have depicted application as a difficult and often overlooked element of experiential learning events (Barber, 1987; Rice, 1969). Research has also shown that participants in group dynamics courses and conferences often show little change in behavior once they return to their organizational settings (Bolman, 1970), and that they have difficulty applying to the organization what they have learned.

My own concern with application work, in the context of experiential group dynamics courses, began several years ago with a conversation between myself and a second-year M.B.A. student, Cedric, who was in the midst of completing a group dynamics course taught in another department. Cedric's comments to me were as follows:

"Professor Thomas, I know that you have done a lot of work in group dynamics. Tell me, how do you exist in this organization when you are able to see all these dynamics and you can't use any of [what you know]?" (A long, thoughtful pause.) "Well, I guess you really can't see [the dynamics] in the real world, because people are busy doing a real task. . . .

"I've learned a lot about myself in the class and for that it was worth it, but I don't have a clue as to how I would use any of this in a real organization."

This conversation proceeded with my asking Cedric what he found most useful about the course and then having him ponder the parallels that existed between the group dynamics environment and other settings of which we had common knowledge. Before leaving, he agreed that he saw some similarities and definitely could imagine ways that people might behave differently based upon understandings gained in experiential group dynamics courses, but he did not seem very convinced.

His final comment to me was, "Maybe it will come together at the end of the course, because the last class is on application." I remember feeling that if it had not "come together" by that point, it probably wouldn't "come together" as the result of the coming week's lecture.

This brief conversation moved me to think about how instructors of experiential group dynamics courses assist students in applying to organizational settings what they learn and why application work is given so little attention in the context of experiential learning. Why was application work most often left till the end of the course and sometimes neglected altogether? Could instructors make it easier for students to see the parallels and to take action, or was the benefit of this learning confined to the realm of personal growth?

This chapter presents these deliberations and draws upon what we already know about experiential learning and organizational behavior to create a framework for increasing our ability to integrate application work with the primary task of here-and-now learning in experiential groups. In this chapter, the tendency to neglect application work is described as the product of historical factors, the tensions inherent in the work of facilitating experiential learning, and the practice of placing application at the end of the course. Following this, several elements of instructor knowledge and course design critical to effective application work are discussed.

THE NEGLECT OF APPLICATION WORK

Historical Roots of Application

The two traditions of group dynamics work that have influenced the model developed at the Yale School of Organization and Management both had their roots in the attempts of researchers to understand and improve the quality of life in organizational settings, and not in advancing technologies of personal growth. The T-group tradition originated in the efforts of Kurt Lewin and his associates to improve race relations in a community (Lippitt, 1949; Alderfer provides a detailed discussion of this in Chapter 9). The British Tavistock Institute tradition of group relations conferences is rooted in the efforts of behavioral scientists at the Tavistock Institute to grapple with structural and psychodynamic issues of organizational life (Bridger, 1987). The first Tavistock Group Relations Conference included a field project as part of its application work (Trist and Stofer, 1959).

From the early 1960s through the mid 1970s, tensions existed within the National Training Laboratory (NTL) between those who wished to extend the organizational and action research focus of Lewin's early work and those who felt the emphasis of the organization's work should be on the development of human potential. The former group included such luminaries of applied behavioral science as Richard Beckhard and Warner Burke. The latter group included several of the prominent thinkers on group development and interpersonal dynamics, Herbert Shepard, Robert Tannenbaum, and John Weir among them.

As the central technology of the institute, the T-group, gave birth to more sophisticated techniques of fostering personal growth that were grounded in the examination of individual and interpersonal level dynamics, organizational development (OD) developed as the application branch of the work. In 1964 the OD Network was formed. Consistent with the ethos of the late 1960s, NTL focused primarily on the personal-growth aspects of experiential learning, while the OD Network pursued the development of methods for intervening in, and changing, organizations.

The result of this split could be seen in the basic design of the primary NTL course offering, the Human Interaction Laboratory. Very little of the content in this lab addressed group and system level dynamics. The focus was primarily toward individual and interpersonal level phenomena. The implication of this history for current efforts at application work is that those who were trained in the NTL tradition of group dynamics may not have been taught the importance of group- and system-level concerns and how to make these part of the learning experience. It will be argued later that such a deficiency inhibits the instructor's ability to help students do application work.

The Tavistock group relations conference was imported to the United States by the A. K. Rice Institute, which was based at the Washington School of Psychiatry. As a result, the conference tradition was embraced by the psychiatric community, and much of the emphasis on sociotechnical systems and organizational consultation was lost, as less emphasis was placed on the application of learnings to broader organizational concerns. The American version of Tavistock group relations conferences has instead emphasized unconscious group processes, especially as they relate to authority relations. Interestingly, the version of sociotechnical research that gained prominence in this country (represented in the work of Louis Davis, 1975, and the traditions that emerged at UCLA and Purdue) did not revolve around concepts of psychodynamic processes, as was true of the early sociotechnical-system design work of Tavistock associates such as Trist and Bramforth (1951) and Rice (1963).

This split between unconscious group level processes and the structural aspects of organizations and systems is in many ways similar to the split between the OD and personal-growth elements of NTL. Both the NTL personal-growth and A. K. Rice Institute traditions have an inward focus that deemphasizes the connection to and understanding of organizational behavior.

This discussion suggests that the lack of explicit attention to organizational application is not merely the isolated choice of instructors. It is likely that those whose training in group dynamics is based on the U.S. traditions of the NTL personal-growth movement and the psychiatrically based Tavistock tradition may find they have not been trained to think systematically about application to organizational settings. Thus, group dynamics instructors may need to examine the nature of their training to assess the extent to which they have been taught to consider application and to do application work that is aimed at increasing individuals' capacities to work within organizational settings.

The Nature of Experiential Work

History is not the only factor that drives the lack of attention that organizational application work receives in the context of group dynamics training. Inherent in the task of experiential learning is the focus on learning in the "here and now"—that which is occurring in the present and being generated from the interactions of study group members. This here-and-now focus is sharpened by the role of the group consultant, who aids the group in studying its own dynamics. The nature of application work moves the individual from the here-and-now focus to the transfer of learning to other settings, and is thus a complex undertaking for both instructor and students.

Bion (1961) points out that individuals have contempt for learning about themselves. Not infrequently, group members will voice their reluctance to engage in the here and now by challenging the consultant to show its relevance for operating in the "real world." The instructor, by responding to this challenge, runs the risk of colluding with the flight from the work.

This danger of collusion is real, yet it is also possible that the here-and-now focus can become a defense against the instructor's engaging his or her own anxieties about the applicability of this knowledge to work in organizations. When instructors delve into issues of application, they lay themselves open to legitimate questioning about the relevance of course content and the accuracy of their interpretation of an event. The instructor who takes seriously the application of course learning must be willing to accept such a challenge and face the possibility of being unable to help a student make an application to an important element of his or her organizational role or experience.

A second aspect of the self-analytic study group that complicates application work is its ostensible lack of resemblance to other kinds of work groups. Groups formed for the purpose of self-study lack the normal overlay and exigencies of a production-oriented group in a formal organization. Furthermore, individuals often experience the self-study group as stripped of a concrete task and feel deprived of a "tangible" role. Awareness of these differences can become so magnified that the similarities escape both members and consultants. Thus, individuals may lose sight of the fact that the fundamental social processes of the study group are inherent in all other work groups.

The likelihood that the consultant can assist the group in doing application work under these conditions is determined, at least in part, by his or her understanding of the self-study group as an organization embedded in a larger social system with the same properties as other organizations. If instructors cannot convey this perspective to group members, the fantasy that the group experience mirrors no other will limit the benefits of participation to personal growth; students will not see the connection to organizational settings nor be able to understand situations in which they are not primary actors.

The Location of Application Work in Course Designs

A review of the literature on designing experiential courses in group dynamics shows that application work has traditionally been placed at the end (Rice, 1965; Bunker et al., 1987). Miles (1975) argues that participants should first become immersed in the here-and-now work of the T-group before beginning application work, because they are best able to apply what they learn once they are thoroughly grounded in the group experience. In his model, application work consists of a set of activities designed to help students draw back-home parallels to what occurred in the group. However, Lippitt and Schindler-Rainman (1975) maintain that application work is most effective if integrated throughout the group dynamics course.

The best-articulated theoretical explanation for placing application work at the end of a session is put forth by theorists from the Tavistock tradition (Rice, 1969). The learning event is viewed as an open system with an import-conversion-export process that, for the task of self-analytic study, requires shifts in psychological orientation and task focus at the boundary between each pair of the three processes. When individuals are about to be exported back out of the temporary learning organization into the environment, the focus should move toward explicit application work.

While this theoretical reasoning flows logically from an open-systems approach to sociotechnical system design, problems emerge when the conveners and designers of events must consider the allocation of time to various activities. What does it mean when application receives two hours in a three-day event, or one class period in twenty-four, and all at the very end? It is likely that, unless prior work has occurred to help group members see the connections between their course learning and behavior in organizations, the application work at the end of the session will be quite ineffective.

Before moving forward, it should be understood that this criticism is not meant to imply that application work should be given equal time in relation to the here-and-now work of the experiential group-dynamics course. It should, however, be given equal seriousness and deliberation in the design of the learning event. The remainder of this chapter is concerned with providing the reader a framework for considering the integration of application work into the experiential group-dynamics course.

INTEGRATING APPLICATION WORK: THREE ESSENTIAL ELEMENTS

It is not enough simply to wish to make application a part of group-dynamics instruction. Application must be integrated into the curriculum in light of three considerations. First, the instructor must have a coherent theory of the structural properties of organization that encompasses an understanding of behavior at multiple levels. Second, the connection between application and the experiential learning process must be clear. Third, if application is to be integrated into the curriculum and not merely added onto it, the topic must be addressed in a manner that accommodates the developmental stage of the experiential group. Each of these considerations and its relationship to designing application efforts will be discussed below.

A Theory of Organization and Human Behavior

Earlier, I argued that the historical development of group-dynamics training in this country has meant that application work is not likely to be a major part of group instructors' training, and thus not part of what they subsequently teach. Also, the disciplinary training of group dynamics instructors is frequently not concentrated in the study of organizational dynamics as it occurs at multiple levels, but in individually oriented models of psychological work. The instructor of a group-dynamics course, though believing the learnings to be relevant to organizations, may therefore operate without an explicit theory of individual, group, intergroup, and system-level dynamics.

It is obvious from the chapters presented in this volume that such a perspective has been an integral part of the Yale tradition of group-dynamics education. The most critical of these shared elements of organizational theory can be delineated. Briefly, organizations are open systems (Katz and Kahn, 1978; Lawrence and Lorsch, 1967), composed of interdependent groups of two varieties

(Alderfer, 1987): organizational groups, defined by the institution's needs with regard to accomplishing its primary task, and identity groups, those defined by the historical, cultural, and biological characteristics of its members. Individuals join and maintain membership in the organization through the assumption of roles, both formal and informal. These roles are connected to and shaped by the group and intergroup relations of the organization.

The primary management task at any level of the system is boundary management. Boundaries are the physical, spatial, temporal, and psychological states that differentiate elements of one human system or set of interdependent activities from those of another. Miller and Rice (1967) define four types of organizational boundary management that are of central concern: regulation of (1) the organizational boundaries within the environment, (2) the task or technical system, (3) the emotional and sentient group boundaries, and (4) the boundaries between task, sentient, and organizational boundaries.

The importance of managing the relationship between the organization and its environment is often viewed only with regard to the management of the temporal and spatial aspects of the import and export boundaries. However, the instructor of the group dynamics course is continually managing the psychological elements of the organization-environment relationship, because members import their external experiences and paradigms for interaction into the learning group. This, then, requires the instructor to attend to relations at the boundary between the technical, or task, system and the external environment of the laboratory experience in the here-and-now.

A coherent theory of organization is important to application for three reasons. First, in order for students to transfer learnings from the course to other organizational contexts, it is necessary for them to understand the organizational properties of the experiential learning environment. I have already mentioned that without explicit attention to this topic, individuals are likely to focus on the ways in which the group-dynamics setting is bizarre as a work context. Instructors can create awareness of its commonality with other organizational settings by introducing theoretical concepts that speak to the key dimensions of organizations outlined above (such as open systems, boundary management, and role theory), while drawing examples from formal work organizations and the group dynamics course. This helps to form a foundation for subsequent application work of the bridging nature that Miles (1975) describes.

Second, the greater the extent to which the group consultant is able to see dynamics of the group as parallel to other organizational phenomena, deriving from structural properties common to the learning environment and other organizations, the greater his or her capacity to integrate application into the consultation process. For example, consider the manner in which the consultant attends to racial dynamics in the experiential group. Frequently, discussions about race are focused on the biases that lead individuals to treat others in a particular manner. Interpretations generally stay at the individual level, and, if scapegoating is part of the dynamic, the group level. Seldom do instructors explicitly explore the connection between the task roles of group members or consultants and the management of racial identity in the organization. However, the organizational model underlying this tradition suggests that, to the extent to which racial groups are salient and sentient in the organization, the boundaries between them must be managed in order for effective taking of the task role to happen. Exploration of this kind offers a much more sophisticated and organizationally applicable set of learnings than the exclusive focus on bias or racial scapegoating. It even opens opportunities to examine racial dynamics in racially homogeneous groups.

Third, an explicit theory of organization calls the instructor's attention to the nature of the managerial role that he or she occupies, especially the boundary management functions that must be fulfilled. This is important to the participants' learning at two levels: first, in the creation and maintenance of an appropriate learning environment and second, in the strength of role modeling as an influence on what individuals learn. Thus, instructors, through their attention to various aspects of course management, signal to group members the model of organization from which they work, and therefore how group dynamics can be applied to "real" work situations.

Experiential Learning Theory

There are two essential aspects of learning in a group dynamics course that are important for the instructor to understand when attempting to integrate application work into the design of the event. The first is, how do individuals learn experientially, and what elements of this process are essential for application work to be effective? The second is, where does learning take place, and what options are available to the instructor for shaping learning, both within and outside the self-analytic study group?

Kolb (1984) has described the process of experiential learning as a cycle consisting of four elements. First, *concrete experience*

(CE) is the actual encounter that the individual has in the here-and-now. This experience then becomes the focal point around which he or she develops a subjective understanding of the event and makes abstractions from it to a particular class of phenomenon. The second element is *reflective observation* (RO), in which the individual examines what has comprised the experience and develops a personal understanding of its meaning. An individual's feelings are an important part of this process; rather than focus on the generalizability of the meaning ascribed to the experience, its personal validity is emphasized. The third element is *abstract conceptualization* (AC), which is the process of making logical deductions and generalizations from the data. Abstract conceptualization can be thought of as a period of theory building or acquisition. The final element of the cycle is *active experimentation* (AE)—the process of applying theory (abstract conceptualizations) to actual events in order to foster a greater understanding of them, to solve problems, or to implement change.

According to this perspective, in order for learning to take place, individuals must be open to it (CE). They must be able to reflect on their experience and derive personal meaning from it (RO). Also, they must be able to integrate their experiences and reflections into a theory (AC). Finally, they must be capable of drawing on these conceptualizations to develop the basis for subsequent action (AE) (Kolb, 1984, p. 30). The difficulty in completing this learning cycle in one educational enterprise is that individuals are required to engage in learning activities that are diametrically opposed on two dimensions: abstract versus concrete and active versus reflective. This is coupled with the fact that individuals tend to have learning style preferences and are likely to emphasize some of these activities over others.

Kolb has pointed out that some subjects and modes of teaching emphasize particular elements of the learning cycle over others. If learning is to be a holistic and adaptive process, all four elements of the learning process must be incorporated into the structure of its design.

Porter (1987) points out that experiential learning often leads to an overemphasis on concrete experience and reflective observation, while there is inadequate attention to the issues of abstract conceptualization and active experimentation. This has dire consequences for application work, because abstract conceptualization and experimentation are most crucial to it.

On first examination, following the prescriptions of Kolb's learning theory might seem simple: there must be sufficient abstract conceptual material presented in the course and demanded from students in their writing assignments. The issue, however, is more complicated when students must make application to dynamics occuring in organizations and to events in which they are not actors, as well as to those in which they are.

One of the major difficulties in designing courses to include application work that has an organizational focus is that much of the here-and-now learning is associated with a very strong set of feelings that students find hard to generalize to other people or settings. To facilitate the abstract conceptualization process, the instructor can help the student to hold the emotions and the personal meaning ascribed to an event long enough to conceptualize at two levels. The first is individual—what was learned about the self in this context? The complete learning cycle can take place at this level without a connection to a context beyond that of the instruction. The second level is: what was learned that is generalizable to other contexts and contingencies? Achieving abstract conceptualization at this level requires an awareness of the structural properties of the group dynamics environment so that appropriate comparisons can be made to other organizational settings.

Too often, even when applying the Kolb model of learning, instructors focus narrowly on helping students make sense of the here-and-now group experience, while active experimentation is encouraged only within the group dynamics course context. Group-dynamics instructors often feel they have followed the learning model because they observe that course participants experiment with new behavior and derive logical abstractions about their experience. This may explain why, despite reporting the group experience to be personally valuable, individuals are frequently at a loss to define its relevance to work situations.

An important, but seldom addressed, issue in developing an understanding of how people learn, is: where does learning take place? Gillette (Chapter 1) offers the distinction between on- and off-line learning. On-line learning occurs in the context of the experiential learning group, while off-line learning occurs during activities that are part of the instruction, but not in the experiential group, and also when the individual is outside the boundaries of the course.

The primary opportunities for explicit application work are in the shaping of off-line learning experiences. The instructor must, however, be careful to connect the issues of application to on-line experience and dynamics emerging within the group. This task may be difficult, because students may resist efforts to generalize and abstract from the experience.

An understanding of on- and off-line learning can also be helpful in guiding the instructor to anticipate and influence what types of individual learning agendas will be imported and exported across the on-line–off-line boundary. For example, students can be asked to do reflective work outside the course to identify similarities with and differences from their experience and behavior in the on-line group experience. This assignment is likely to shape what comes back into other on-line experience, as well as what might be attended to in lecture and discussion periods. Written assignments are another form of off-line activity that can facilitate application work and that shape the nature of what is brought to the on-line experience.

During the on-line experience, application work is influenced by the nature of interpretation and metaphors used by instructors. Interpretations can be made that call attention to behavior patterns in the external world that are reflected in the here-and-now of the group. Prompting group members to think about what they have imported into the group from elsewhere often generates off-line reflections as individuals search for these patterns in other parts of their lives.

For example, a group member in the on-line experience led a rebellion against the consultant. The consultant intepreted this behavior in terms of a connection between the group's here-and-now experience and covert assaults on authority figures in organizations. As a result, the student was motivated to examine his behavior and, off-line, he reflected on his past practices. Doing so moved him, through reading and a paper assignment, to do some conceptual work on the implications of this situation. Later, the student recognized these dynamics within his work organization and attempted a constructive confrontation with the leadership rather than a covert and ultimately destructive assault. Thus the learning cycle began during the on-line experience and, shaped by the consultant's metaphor, was completed through off-line activity.

What has been discussed here points to a way of thinking about the experiential learning process that facilitates application work. However, efforts to attend to application must be integrated with the overall learning activity and must be consistent with the dynamics of the course.

Group Development

Several theories describe the development of self-analytic study groups (Tuckman, 1965; Bennis and Shepard, 1956; Mann, 1967; Lundgren, 1971—McCollom critiques these models in Chapter 6). While each of these theories has its particular emphasis, all have

three common elements. First, the initial phase of group development is characterized by participants' preoccupation with issues of
inclusion in and orientation to the group. Second, this initial phase
is followed by a period in which the group struggles with issues of
power, status, and control. Third, at some point in the group's life,
assuming healthy resolution of earlier issues, the group comes together in a manner that allows for the expression of more varied
and intimate feelings. Group cohesion and identification are also
high during this period, which facilitates the here-and-now work of
the learning task. Relatively few theorists have focused on the termination phase of groups, but this is also an important period of
group life (see Chapter 8 for a more detailed discussion of this phase).

Each phase of group development presents special issues and
oportunities for application work. Successful integration of application work throughout the group dynamics course is dependent
upon an understanding of these issues.

The initial phase of orientation, or inclusion, poses difficult
issues for the integration of application. It is especially important
in this phase that instructors not abandon engagement in the here-
and-now work by focusing on the relevance of the course to outside
settings. However, organization work *can* be done in the early phase
of the group's life. This should be a time for sowing the seeds for
the explicit application work to be done later. The instructor should
make a clear statement in written material and in introductory sessions that application will be explicitly addressed.

Choices about lectures are also important here. Application
can be facilitated by early intellectual input, including presentation
of an organizational model, application of the model to the instructional environment, and introduction of the experiential learning
model. The central focus of this period is still on bringing members
into the course, but the organizational issues represented by the
class as a human system are clarified.

The phase in which the group works most diligently with its
power and control issues is perhaps the most amenable to application
work in the here-and-now. During this phase, members often make
assumptions about the external groups that individuals represent,
confer status on them accordingly, and engage in behavior that mirrors power tactics used in other organizations. Through interpretation, attention can be called to these maneuvers while working
in the here-and-now group experience, and in lectures, by using
examples drawn from organizational settings.

It is perhaps the most difficult task for both staff and participants to work with issues of application during the stage of intimacy.
It is during this period of group life that members are most connected

to one another and convinced of the instructor's competence. In this respect, members may be resistant to moving away from the experience in the here-and-now. Difficulties for the instructor can arise from his or her enjoyment of the "love fest" atmosphere that members create and the positive and potent projections that he or she receives from the group.

Application work attempted during this phase can be beneficial, however, because it is often here that members are most open to feedback and committed to self-reflection and scrutiny. This can be a good time to have members work on back-home issues of their choosing with the support of other group members. The practice of leaving application work until the very end of the course is frequently ineffective because members have started to disengage with one another or may withhold feedback for fear that there is little time to repair any unanticipated damage to the relationship. However, if the work of application is started sooner, it is more likely that participants will feel comfortable with it as they move to termination and life after the course.

Termination is most frequently marked by feelings of loss and anticipation of life after the group. Often members regress, exhibiting behaviors associated with their early ambivalence about joining. Instructors also find themselves experiencing these same emotions, as well as doubt about the impact of their work. One reaction to these feelings may be a collusive attempt by group members and instructors to deny the impending termination. Instructors encourage this flight from reality by pushing members to explore "thoroughly" and express their feelings about leaving, often extending this venting into the periods set aside for lecture and discussion. As a result, other work, especially application, may be pushed out.

It is rare that the final lectures of a course include an explicit examination of how group dynamics learnings fit into a broader consideration of organizational dynamics. This may happen because the professor chooses to stay with issues that keep members connected to the group instead of helping them transition out of the class. One tool that has been developed to help students in making this transition is the role analysis exercise (Barber, 1987; Reed, 1976). In this exercise, members are asked to make application of their learnings to a particular organizational role that they either presently occupy or have held in the past. Role theory is then offered as a conceptual framework for application issues.

CONCLUSION

Application is an important, but difficult and often neglected, aspect of group dynamics training. Instructors' tendencies to omit or neglect the topic stem from the lack of emphasis on application that may have been in their own training and from the inherent demands of the here-and-now focus of the experiential group.

The perspective on application offered here focuses on increasing students' abilities to apply group dynamics learning to formal organizational settings and to situations in which they are and are not actors. This view suggests that application work can be attended to throughout the group dynamics course and not be included merely as an exercise at the end. However, this integration needs to be done in a manner that does not subvert the here-and-now aspect of experiential learning. Successful integration requires an explicit model of organizations that connects human behavior and issues of task and boundary management, an understanding of experiential learning, and knowledge of group development.

Increasing students' abilities to apply their learning about groups is as much a matter of framing and focusing attention as it is the inclusion of specific exercises, lectures, or assignments. The choices about what to include in readings, how to manage the boundaries of the course, and what kinds of interpretations and metaphors to offer in the on-line experience all shape the ultimate readiness and willingness of students to work at the development of their own grounded theory of group dynamics, a theory that can be available over the long term to guide their efforts to diagnose and influence group behavior in formal organizations.

Chapter 8

Termination in Groups

VICKI VAN STEENBERG LaFARGE

It's four o'clock. The last lecture of the spring semester has just ended in its typically awkward way. Some students rush out the door as if fleeing from the Devil himself. Others, fewer in number, stop by to say an uncomfortable "thank you" to which I respond with equal discomfort. As I gather my papers to leave the classroom for the last time, I am once again struck by the ambivalent feelings that seem to characterize my response to endings in general, and to last classes in particular. On the one hand, I am relieved that the class is over. I will not miss the regular pressure to perform and the seemingly endless need to grade and evaluate. On the other hand, I will miss the surprises that the class has brought, the creativity it has forced from me, and the occasional "Eureka" events when a student suddenly sees the world from a new perspective.

Musing on my ambivalence, I also must squarely face my sense of frustration, and perhaps of incompetence, at once again failing to provide a truly satisfying closure to the classroom experience. Along with congratulating myself on the learning the course provided, I become entangled in a web of missed opportunities and emotional and intellectual loose ends with which I fear I have left myself and my students to struggle.

Upon reflection, I find that my response to the ending of this particular class is fairly similar to the responses of my colleagues ending other classes. It is also similar to the response of the class members. There is a certain inevitability to our reactions, born out of the character of the phenomenon in which we are involved: the termination of a group experience. These reactions are also characteristic of individuals involved in all kinds of terminating groups—

in a task force that has finished its work, in a work group eliminated in a corporate restructuring, or in a social group that is breaking up.

This chapter is an attempt to explore further the complex processes that are inherent in the termination of groups. In particular, it focuses on the responses of members of terminating groups to their ambivalent feelings of grief and relief and to their conflicting desires for resolution and dissonance. Last, it explores the way in which the complexity of these termination issues is influenced by, among other factors, the context in which the group resides. In this chapter, I use examples from the final phase of several representative groups to illustrate the more general termination dynamics that do, upon close inspection, characterize most groups in the process of ending.

AMBIVALENCE IN GROUP LIFE

One window into the complexity inherent in the termination of a group is the concept of ambivalence; that is, the "existence of mutually conflicting feelings or thoughts . . . about some person, object, or idea," (*American Heritage Dictionary*, 1982). This ambivalence characterizes life in the group not only at the group's termination, but also from the moment of its inception and throughout its existence. Referring to groups as inherently paradoxical in nature, Smith and Berg (1987) describe individual group members as experiencing "the group as being filled with contradictory and opposing emotions, thoughts, and actions that coexist inside the group. As group members struggle to manage the tensions generated by these contradictory and opposing forces, the essential process dynamics of group life are created" (p. 15). (See Chapter 5.)

In their work on group development, Bennis and Shepard (1974) describe these process dynamics in terms of the ambivalent orientations of group members toward the issues of dependence and interdependence, power and love, and authority and intimacy. These ambivalences are "the central problems of group life" (p. 152). Group interaction revolves around the struggle of group members to come to a meaningful resolution of the tensions around one ambivalent orientation in order to move to another phase of development with a new set of tensions.

Stock and Lieberman (1974) frame the issue of ambivalence in group life in terms of a "group focal conflict" or "preconscious conflict between two opposing motives" (p. 58), whose opposition the group must struggle to resolve. Group members may, for example, struggle with the simultaneous wish to be included in the group and fear of being overwhelmed by the group. When faced with this simultaneous wish and fear in its members, the group directs its energy toward creating a solution that both satisfies the wish and alleviates the fear to the maximum extent possible. Stock and Lieberman depict group life as a "flow from one focal conflict to another" (p. 59). As adequate solutions develop for one focal conflict, either the solutions themselves give rise to a new focal conflict or a previously unrecognized conflict emerges.

Given the inherent ambivalence in group life, an important step in understanding termination processes in experiential groups involves an exploration of the source and nature of the group members' conflicting feelings about the ending of the group. One way to do this is to frame the discussion in terms of the contradictory tensions experienced by group members at the approaching termination of the group.

The Tension between Grief and Relief

The most obvious tension in a terminating group is probably that produced by its members' ambivalent feelings of grief and relief. Both individually and collectively, group members face the termination of the group with an uncomfortable mixture of sadness and happiness. The happy relief comes in response to the anticipated end of the often difficult experiences and relationships that are part of group life. The sadness comes from the approaching loss of these same relationships and experiences. For its members, an ongoing group is not merely another number in the course catalog or block of time in a busy personal or professional schedule. It is a living entity.

The extent to which a group becomes a significant, living entity for its members is revealed in the way in which they refer and react to the group throughout its existence. For example, the experiential learning group in a group dynamics class becomes more than just a classroom exercise for most of its members. It becomes the focal point for their lives for at least one semester. In the words of one student, "I organize my week around this class. It seems like I never stop thinking about it." At times, the group becomes a "Venus flytrap, sucking out all of my juices." At other times, it is a "comfortable friend." Whether they view it as flytrap or friend, however, the members undoubtedly imbue the group with a life and personality all its own.

The creation of a life and personality for the group is not limited to students in classes in group dynamics. One member of a support group for new mothers described the group as "my surrogate mother. I come here to be nurtured. It [the group] replenishes all that I'm giving out to [her child]." Perhaps reflecting the inherent ambivalence in group life (or perhaps my own perversity), I saw the same group not as a nurturing mother, but more as a loved, but competitive, older sister with whom I was wary of sharing my inadequacies as a new parent.

Grief. For its members, the fact that the group takes on a life of its own makes its approaching termination an occasion for sadness and grief. Termination means that the living, breathing, personality-filled entity that the group has become for its members must "die." Members respond to the approaching death of a group much as they would respond to the approaching death of an individual. They recapitulate the group's life by remembering its beginnings and progress with a "terminal review" much like that noted by Mann (1966) in self-analytic groups. They express their feelings about the group and its members and fantasize about the ways in which the group will continue to be a part of their lives. They may also speak with anger and frustration about the premature death of the group, which precludes further accomplishments. In essence, members mourn the group.

The mourning for the group may take many forms. In a structured experiential group dynamics class, the mourning is likely to take place both in regular group meetings and in the interactions of members outside the group. In my new mothers' support group, we reviewed the life of the group in our often tearful final meetings and in a farewell dinner for our group leader. The members of a committee on which I served marked its passing with a laughter-filled wake, highlighted by a slide show of hilarious and poignant moments in the group's history.

As part of the mourning process, individual group members express both positive and negative feelings about the group for the membership as a whole. Those group members elected to carry positive feelings focus on the constructive aspects of the group and its evolution. They are likely to mourn the impending loss of roles, relationships, and learnings that have been important to them. During termination, their discussions of the group take on the quality of a eulogy for a dead friend. They often express the group's desire to have the group continue in order to perpetuate a meaningful, important aspect of its members' lives.

Members carrying negative feelings also grieve at its approaching termination. However, instead of mourning what will be lost, they mourn for what might have been. They express the grief of the group over missed opportunities, broken promises, and unresolved issues. They may wish for the group to continue in order to meet its members' unfulfilled expectations.

During the termination of the group, members expressing opposite views of the group (that is, the group as worthwhile and positive, or the group as negative and unsuccessful) often seem to be at loggerheads. Their arguments center on the need to persuade the opposing member, or subgroup, of the correctness of their view of the group's existence. Unable to recognize the ambivalence in their own mixed positive and negative responses to the group, these opposing individual members and subgroups have difficulty recognizing and discussing the common feelings of grief and sadness that bind them together at the group's termination. Equally inaccessible to them is their shared wish for the group to continue, either in its present form or in some new manifestation. Instead, this shared wish to have the group continue may manifest itself in unconscious fantasies of pairing.

As described by Bion (1961), a pairing group comes together around the hope for a messiah who will save the group from disintegration. Hartman and Gibbard (1974) view the defensive aim of the messianic fantasy to be "to . . . avoid group death and a sense of failure" (p. 330). Pairing is, therefore, a basic assumption that lends itself to the terminating group. Faced with the ending of the group's existence and the impending dissolution of the group's boundaries, members search for a way to ward off the inevitable. Unable to accomplish this objective consciously, they attempt to do so at an unconscious level.

To illustrate pairing at termination, I will briefly describe an environmental task force of which I was a member. The purpose of this small task force was to produce a report on a complex environmental issue. Our meetings, which were often intense and full of disagreement, became particularly stormy as the report deadline approached. Two members of the group, a man and a woman, became spokespersons for opposing points of view about practically every question before the group as well as about the worth of the group's overall effort. At the group's final meeting, at which we were to present our report to the board for approval, an interesting series of coincidences occurred. Neither of the two group members originally charged with presenting the report was able to do so. One was called out of town and the other had laryngitis. At the last minute, the group appointed the opposing subgroup leaders to present the report. (In retrospect, this was not a particularly good strategic move in light of the previous difficulties the man and woman had had in working together.) In spite of their differences, they did a brilliant job, and as a group we basked in a sense of accomplishment. We also elected our presenters to take the report the next step in the process, thus creating a pair that would save the group from our unconscious fears of extinction.

Relief. At the same time that (and, in part, because) group members are struggling to resolve unconsciously, or perhaps consciously understand, the apparently conflicting positive and negative expressions of grief and loss over the group's termination, they also experience the opposite side of the grief-relief tension. They look forward to the group's passing.

The group that has been a "comfortable friend" has also been a "Venus flytrap." Learning has been at various times stressful, confusing, and painful. The responsibilities of membership and the degree to which the group has dominated the lives of its members have not always been welcome. The end of the group means an end to the pain and drudgery that are as characteristic of most groups as excitement and opportunities for learning. In the words of one group dynamics class member, "I won't exactly be sorry not to have my entire week focused on figuring out what happened in last week's group and anticipating next week's."

Expressing relief at the ending of the group is often quite difficult for members. Wishing the group "dead" is viewed as an act of disloyalty and a potential negation of the value of the life of the group and of its membership. Because it denies the desire to continue working to create a perfect group, relief is more frightening for members than the reservations expressed in the context of grief over missed opportunities. And although relief at the group's demise may often manifest itself in expressions quite similar to those promoted by grief and sadness over missed opportunities—in that both tend to highlight negative aspects of the group's existence—it is quite different. It welcomes and wishes for the termination of the group's existence rather than mourning the group's passing.

The ambivalent feelings of grief and relief are uncomfortable for members. As so often happens with ambivalent feelings, group members tend to project one side or the other of the ambivalence elsewhere. While the mixed positive and negative feelings and expressions of grief tend to stay within the group (expressed by seemingly opposing mourning subgroups), relief at the group's termination is often projected outside the group. Group members talk about how happy their spouses or significant others will be about the ending of the group and its incessant demands. In the mothers' support group, one woman said, "I think my husband is secretly delighted that we're ending. I always stood up for myself a lot more after our meetings." Sometimes, the sense of relief is projected upon the outside system in which the group is embedded. According to a group dynamics class member, "What happens in here has a big effect on the rest of the school, I think . . . [everyone] breathes a collective sigh of relief when this course ends." Recognizing the collective relief that exists within the group around termination is more difficult than projecting it elsewhere.

Attempts by members or interventions by group facilitators aimed at exploring the group's ambivalent feelings of grief and relief are often rejected and misunderstood. Uncomfortable with their ambivalent feelings of grief and relief and frightened that the approaching end of the group will not allow for a resolution of these feelings, members avoid and resist interventions that address these mixed feelings and fears. One member of a terminating volunteer committee said that he was of mixed minds about what the group had accomplished and whether he was delighted or depressed about our last meeting. Other group members, in a style typical to the group, blew raspberries to drown his ambivalence out. A particularly respected and thoughtful group member supported these group members by adding, "No postmortems. Once you've done it, don't think about it." In effect, the group members had refused to explore their mixed feelings and had effectively silenced the one member who had expressed them openly.

Efforts to understand the dynamics of grief and relief also often get lost in the complexity of the issues with which group members are grappling. During termination, members must begin to recognize the similarities in the apparently dissimilar positive and negative manifestations of loss and grief at the termination of the group. They also must understand their common yearning for the continuation of the group, which is expressed as mourning over both missed opportunities and the ending of a positive experience. At the same time, the group members must begin to untangle and differentiate between apparently similar negative expressions about the group, some of which express mourning for the group and some of which express relief. In a group dynamics class devoted to exploring group processes, one member described the terminating group and her feelings about it as "snarled ball of yarn with no beginning and no end."

The Tension between Resolution and Dissonance

Another tension inherent in termination is that caused by the group members' contradictory desires for resolution and for dissonance. On the one hand, the terminating group yearns for a resolution to all its differences and unsettled issues. On the other hand, members fear that this resolution will mean a negation of their individuality. They seek to maintain themselves in the group's dissonant elements.

Resolution. At first glance, the desire for resolution during the impending termination of a group is perhaps the more comprehensible of the group's competing needs. Resolution implies consonance, agreement, a solution to problems, and an end to irritating differences and divisions. For a terminating group, the push for resolution is somewhat akin to a dying patient's desires to right old wrongs, see friends for the last time, and put the financial and emotional house in order. It provides a comforting sense of completion.

The desire for resolution and completion is reinforced by the commonly held notion that a "good group" or a "successful group" is one which has little disagreement and whose members always like and respect one another. No one wants to end the group experience believing that they have been a member of a "bad group." Therefore, the terminating group struggles to create itself in the image of a mythical, resolved, or "good" group.

The yearning for resolution is not only a manifestation of the group's desire to end well, but also a response to its fears about termination and an attempt to strengthen its dissolving boundaries. Faced with the aloneness inherent in the termination of the group, its members struggle to tighten boundaries by reducing differences, reincluding peripheral or ostracized members, and achieving oneness. Perhaps these newly strengthened boundaries will allow the group magically to fend off its impending disintegration upon termination. If this is not successful, the group at least will have achieved a cohesiveness that protects its members from the fear of isolation raised by the specter of termination. They are part of a tightly bounded entity that they can bring with them upon termination, albeit psychologically rather than physically. The group becomes a neat emotional package that the member can easily carry into the groupless future, thus easing the pain of separation. Obviously, carrying an unresolved group package with loose ends streaming behind it is much less satisfactory and more difficult.

The terminating group's push for resolution is similar to the fantasies of mystical fusion described by Hartman and Gibbard (1974) as occurring at the beginning and termination of a group when its boundaries are most fragile. With fusion, the group hopes to establish "the peace, tranquility, and magical fullness of the early mother-child symbiosis," and flee from conflict and differentiation, which are "inevitably accompanied by ambivalence and separateness" (p. 319). With resolution, the group hopes to achieve a comfort and oneness that will help its members, and perhaps the group itself, survive the separation and isolation inherent in termination.

Dissonance. In the terminating group, however, the goal of resolution is a double-edged sword for its members. Although resolution may promise an attractive end to conflict and feelings of isolation, it may also require an uncomfortable loss of individuality and freedom of expression. Members in a resolved group may find themselves unable to express thoughts and feelings that run counter to the mood of the group, for fear of endangering the much-yearned-for sense of resolution and oneness. A group bent on resolution attempts to swallow up its members and their differences just as Chronos swallowed up his children. Fears of being swallowed up by the terminating group complicate its members' yearnings for resolution and push them to struggle for dissonance as a way to maintain their individuality.

The desire for dissonance manifests itself in many ways in a terminating group. The most obvious is in angry disagreement among members. Subgroups form around a range of issues both real and imagined, and are unable to find any ground for agreement, or even for understanding. This dissonance-induced anger makes it particularly difficult for the group to explore such issues as the apparently opposite expressions (positive and negative) of mourning and loss discussed earlier. The need to maintain individuality through anger and disagreement overwhelms the need to understand.

The anger that helps to maintain dissonant elements in the group may also reflect the attempts of group members to ease the pain of separation. The impending dissolution of the group and the distance (either physical or psychological) between members that termination inevitably brings is a complicated issue for members. While they may welcome an existence separate from the group, they may also fear isolation. One way to manage this fear is to attempt to bring the psychological group with them in the neat, resolved package discussed earlier. Another way to address the fear, which coincidentally meets members' needs for dissonance, is to make the group less attractive. An angry group that is rife with unresolved conflicts is rarely attractive to its members. Separating from such a group (at least on a conscious level) is hardly painful.

Although anger is perhaps the most obvious way for terminating groups to meet their desires for dissonance, it is also common for the group to respond to this need by maintaining silence. By not responding with either agreement or disagreement to the opinions and overtures of fellow members, silent members act to keep the group from truly coming to the resolution of unfinished issues. Although the group may act as if "silence means consent," members instinctively realize that this is not true. The atmosphere of the group becomes clogged with unspoken differences and a pervading sense of numbness.

In many ways, the tension between the need for resolution and the need for dissonance forces the group to recapitulate many of the issues it struggled with during formation. On the one hand, members long to be included in a cohesive and comfortable group that will protect them from their fears—either fears of a powerful and capricious leader, or fears of the disappearance of the group itself. On the other hand, members resist inclusion for fear that the boundaries of a tightly drawn, cohesive group will strangle them and leave them unable to function as individuals.

In an experiential learning group, the similarity in the group's reactions to formation and termination makes it difficult for a group leader or member to intervene effectively to help the group explore the tension between desires for dissonance and resolution. To group members, the recapitulation of these issues around inclusion and individuality often makes the group seem as though it has learned nothing and made little progress. The group becomes mired in a paralyzing sense of inadequacy and frustration and its members distrust their ability to learn. It is important for the group members to realize, however, that the impetus for revisiting inclusion and individuality comes from the impending termination of the group's boundaries rather than from their formation.

The ambivalent tension that group members feel over their conflicting desires for resolution and dissonance is characteristic of a terminating group. As they struggle to understand their reactions to termination, group members find themselves pulled in directions and acting in ways that are difficult to comprehend. Inevitably, the terminating group is neither resolved nor dissonant enough to satisfy completely the conflicting desires of its membership.

TERMINATION IN CONTEXT

Although the tensions around grief and relief and desires for resolution and dissonance exist in any terminating group, the goals and environment of the group certainly influence the nature and character of the group dynamics around these issues. A group with no strict authority structure, such as a mothers' support group, may end without ever directly exploring ambivalences about the group and its termination. Over time, members in my group, "pulled" by other responsibilities, just began to leave. Remaining members grieved at their departure and expressed fear about the group's dissolution. Any relief felt at the group's inevitable termination was expressed unconsciously by the failure of remaining members to recruit new mothers. Issues of resolution and dissonance became moot as members carrying the group's desires for dissonance were first to leave the group. For an experiential learning group, however, exploration of the group dynamics and the feelings of individual group members are required of its members by the authority structure of the course.

The terminating group's struggle to explore and understand its ambivalent feelings of grief and relief and desires for resolution and dissonance is made particularly complicated if the group's end is both predicted and mandated. Unlike many self-analytic groups that experience a series of unscheduled mini-terminations as members leave and new members join, experiential groups in academic environments (like some special task forces and ad hoc committees) are driven by a calendar. Group members know the limits to the group's mortality on the day it is born.

This scheduled and mandated end to the group has a number of influences on the dynamics of termination. Perhaps most obviously, it is likely to become the source of a significant amount of generally unconscious anger in the group toward those in authority. For example, an experiential learning group that has become increasingly independent of its instructor during the course of the semester must suddenly face the reality of its complete dependence around a tremendously significant issue: its own dissolution. Frustrated by this forced regression to a more dependent state as well as by their inability to reverse the inevitable termination of the group, members experience a great deal of anger toward the instructor. In general, however, they are unable to identify the source of their angry feelings. If they express anger to the instructor at all, it is around what the instructor did not do (for example, create a nurturing learning environment or intervene in a helpful way) rather than around what the instructor is doing (that is, destroying the group).

However, at the same time that group members are mourning the loss of the group and are angry at the instructor's (or in other instances, the boss's) role in creating this loss, they also are grateful to the instructor for scheduling the end to the group's existence. The part of each member that welcomes the termination of the group is thankful for its clear-cut ending. Without this scheduled termination, the group members themselves would be forced to confront more completely their mixed feelings of grief and relief and come to an individual, or group, decision about the life and death of the group. Fantasy, one-dimensional images of the group as cohesive and loved by all members, or fragmented and despised, would need to give way to a reality where some members wished to maintain the group while others wished to end it. When termination is scheduled by those in authority, the group can avoid this confrontation with reality.

In the predictably perverse nature of the groups, this grateful reliance on the instructor or boss to terminate the group is in itself a cause for resentment. While members of a task force may welcome the boss's ability to terminate the group, they also find that this ability is an uncomfortable reminder of both the boss's power and the group's desires to be dependent. The group becomes angry at itself for its manifestation of dependency needs and angry at the boss for providing an occasion for exposing those needs.

Whether the group members welcome the termination of the group or mourn its loss, scheduled termination becomes a symbol of the boss's or instructor's ability to control events in the life of the group and an unpleasant reminder of the evaluating role of those in authority. On the other hand, an unscheduled termination may prompt the group to blame the boss or instructor for his or her inability to control events influencing the life of the group. In either case, termination is likely to prompt a return to group concerns about dependence, counterdependence, and independence that were focal early in the group's life. In many ways, this is similar to the recapitulation of inclusion and individuality issues discussed earlier. While the impetus for the reawakening of dependency issues may be quite different in the terminating group than it is in the forming group, the group's reactions to the issues may be quite similar. It is therefore sometimes difficult for the terminating group and its instructor or boss to understand that the group has not merely regressed to some previous stage in its existence.

The terminating group's location in a particular environment may heighten not only authority issues, but also the effects of termination itself. For example, group dynamics courses are generally part of an advanced graduate curriculum. This means that students in the course are often near the end of their academic careers and facing issues of termination not only in the experiential group but also in other aspects of their lives (see Chapter 11). Ambivalent feelings of grief and relief and desires for resolution and dissonance, which are characteristic of a terminating group, are also characteristic of student responses to leaving school. Sadness and excitement or looking forward and looking back may be themes that exist for its members outside the group as well as within it.

Simultaneous endings both inside and outside are likely to amplify termination dynamics for individual members and for the group as a whole. Because the boundaries around the group are permeable, members constantly bring outside issues with them into the group, just as they bring group issues to the outside. When the substance of these issues coincides, group members are likely to experience them with particular intensity. The group no longer is an escape from the rest of the environment, nor is the outside environment an escape from the group. In the words of one group member, "I can't get away from endings. . . ."

The intensity of amplified dynamics can make the termination of the group particularly stressful for members. Obviously, the amplification means that members carry a heavy weight of emotions. They grieve for more than one loss. They struggle to maintain their identity in more than one group. In addition to bearing an exceptional emotional load, group members are also likely to experience the weight of confusion. Understanding their responses to termination is difficult when group members must struggle to identify the sources of these responses and then correctly locate them inside or outside of the group.

The location of the group in a particular setting and the possibility of a resonance between system dynamics and dynamics within the group may require quite active intervention from those in authority in order to help the group members understand their reactions to the tensions inherent in termination. In particular, group members may need help in exploring and clarifying issues of authority and dependency prompted by termination. Without this intervention, group members may respond by reaffirming their independence from authority in the most effective way available to them: refusing to learn in the group and failing to complete final projects or assignments. In addition, the group may need help in exploring issues of termination that are present in the larger context.

Rather than focusing exclusively on termination processes as they present themselves in the group, a consultant, instructor in a small-groups class, or even a boss must frame interventions that tie the dynamics of the group into those in the larger system. This prevents group members from becoming overwhelmed by the multiple terminations in which they are involved and allows them to function productively.

TERMINATING ON TERMINATION

As I finish this chapter, it strikes me that terminating a paper is no easier than, and quite similar to, the termination of a group. Rereading the paper, I become embroiled in my ambivalent reactions. Relief at having completed a sometimes onerous project is coupled with a certain nostalgia at finishing it and a definite frustration at what it does not accomplish. On the one hand, I hope that it will blend well with other chapters in this book. On the other hand, I want it to be completely original. Unable to design a suitable ending that ties together the themes in the chapter, I return to the introduction in hopes of inspiration. I feel alternately frustrated by the deadline imposed by the editors and grateful that the impending deadline has forced me to finish.

The terminating group has a similar experience in ending its process of creation. Faced with the dissolution of the group, its members react with ambivalent feelings of grief and relief and apparently opposing desires for resolution and dissonance. In addition, the issues raised by termination push the group to revisit and rework a number of themes experienced previously. All these reactions are complicated by the dynamics of the particular environment in which the group is embedded.

Given the complexity of termination processes, it is little wonder that endings in general, and of groups in particular, are often confusing, difficult, and fraught with ambivalence.

CREATING A CONTEXT FOR GROUP LEARNING

Chapter 9

Conditions for Teaching Experiential Group Dynamics

CLAYTON P. ALDERFER

INTRODUCTION

Teaching experiential group dynamics effectively means providing learners with a psychologically secure setting in which to observe their own and others' behavior as it occurs and to examine concepts and theories that provide understanding for the events that take place. Establishing a psychologically secure setting involves minimizing the chances of casualties developing from the learning activities and maximizing the opportunities for participants to have a rich and worthwhile experience. Effective teaching, therefore, involves a favorable mix of experience and conceptualization and of safety and challenge about one's self and others.

This chapter defines and explains what I believe to be the five key conditions for teaching experiential group dynamics effectively. They are (1) selecting participants for the course, (2) focusing on here-and-now behavior in experiential sessions, (3) organizing conceptual material based on a developmental conception of groups, (4) evaluating the intellectual work of students, and (5) managing the intergroup relationships embedded in the educational environment. Each of these conditions consists of a combination of technique and theory. I developed my convictions about the importance of the five conditions over a twenty-year period.

Although the five conditions can be derived from embedded intergroup relations theory (Alderfer and Smith, 1982), a close connection between theory and technique has not always existed. Often the technical problem and its solution existed prior to framing the practice in terms of theoretical concepts. For the sake of historical accuracy, the chapter treats the conditions more concretely and pragmatically than if theory had preceded practice.

The teaching of experiential group dynamics occurs both in university and cultural-island settings. My experience includes working in both kinds of situation. In recent years, however, the largest proportion of my work has occurred at the Yale School of Organization and Management, where my colleagues and I have been importantly influenced by what we have learned about the special characteristics of that environment.

Even though, on some variables, a university is very different from a cultural island, both kinds of settings are embedded in more comprehensive suprasystems. The technical problems associated with the five conditions occur in both kinds of situation. The reasoning applied to each of the problems derives from the same body of theory. But for some conditions, solutions to the problem differ by setting. Emphasis in this chapter will be on the practices that we have evolved at the Yale School of Organization and Management.

Before turning to a discussion of the five conditions, however, the chapter frames the historical and philosophical bases from which the more concrete discussion proceeds. Experiential group dynamics developed at a particular point in history and reflected the social and intellectual state of those times. The developments are embedded in a flow of events and ideas as well as in particular institutional settings. I begin with an account of that background.

HISTORICAL AND PHILOSOPHICAL BACKGROUND

In both the physical and the social sciences, technological advances—sometimes known as inventions—bring new opportunities for increasing knowledge (Conant, 1964). Inventions evolving from physical science, for example, include the clock, the telescope, the microscope, the nuclear accelerator, and the digital computer. The historical period over which we are conscious of these developments includes several millennia (Boorstin, 1983). Social science, on the other hand, is a newer cultural form, whose time span of existence is a matter of centuries. Psychology and sociology have life histories on the order of a single century—with the beginning of the twentieth century marking a turning point in terms of notable increases in the number of individuals whose lifework is participating in these disciplines. The last one hundred years have witnessed the invention of psychoanalysis, the psychological test, the social survey, and the social psychology laboratory.

Generally, investigators view the work of social science mainly as a dialogue between theory and data (Merton, 1967). Social technology, however, plays a key role in how the dialogue unfolds. Researchers begin their work with some degree of conceptual formulation, and they then proceed to seek data in order to support a theoretical position or to choose among competing explanations (Kaplan, 1964). The accumulation of anomalous data—findings that do not fit extant frameworks—may eventually stimulate a crisis and ultimately a shift in the dominant paradigm guiding research and teaching a body of knowledge (Kuhn, 1962). As individuals, social scientists vary in their preferences and skills for data gathering (the empiricists) and theory building (the conceptualizers).

Advances in social technology enter the theory-data dialogue in two places. In the first, a novel social form makes it possible to obtain new types of data or to improve significantly the quality of data one has previously been gathering. Thus, the invention of psychoanalysis provided access to unconscious material about personality that prior to the invention was less available. A new technology may also become possible because of theoretical advances and, in this manner, serve as a kind of demonstration experiment for showing how the phenomena of interest behave (Webb, Campbell, Schwartz, and Sechrest, 1966). Thus, as psychoanalytic theory developed, the treatment method became the means to illustrate key concepts and a path to uncovering anomalous findings, which in turn led to proposed changes in theory (Kohut, 1977). Figure 1 shows in diagrammatic form the interdependency of technology, data, and theory.

The experiential learning group is a social invention of the mid-twentieth century. Horrifying events in World War II provided an important stimulus for what seem to have been independent and yet related developments in the United Kingdom and the United States. Both settings were concerned about bringing social science knowledge to the problem of learning about leadership and discovering better ways to combine social research and effective action.

During World War II, the British psychoanalyst Wilfred Bion established a theoretical system about groups as a result of his efforts to treat people who had become psychological casualties from the fighting (Bion, 1961). Bion's theoretical formulation about group behavior became the basis for inventing the Tavistock study group and conference design and conducting the first group relations conference in 1957 (Rice, 1965). Behind Bion's theory of groups rested Melanie Klein's object relations theory of personality development

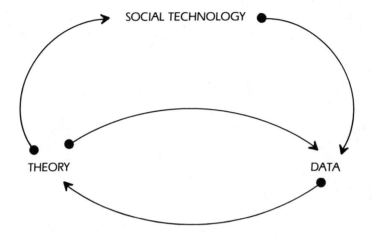

Figure 1. Interdependency of Social Technology, Data, and
    Theory

(Klein, 1960). Thus, in Britain, the tendency was for theory to precede
technique in the development of the experiential learning group as
a social technology. Klein (1960), however, in giving a summary
statement of her concepts, noted that her theoretical advances were
made possible in part through the development of a play technique
that enabled her to treat very young children by psychoanalytic
methods.

In contrast, events in the United States tended to place advances in social technology ahead of theory. Leland Bradford described how the origins of laboratory education evolved from his
own efforts to improve the methods of adult education during the
depression, from the experiential social psychological research on
leadership styles conducted by Ronald Lippitt, Kurt Lewin, and
Ralph White, and from explicitly stated desires by leaders in business
and government to improve the skills people brought to dealing with
others (Bradford, 1967). In fact the name taken for the small group,
which became the central learning unit, was the "T-group," a short-
ened form for Human Relations Training Group. The first experiment with laboratory education in the United States, sponsored by
the American Jewish Congress and the Connecticut Interracial Com-
mission, was held in New Britain, Connecticut, during the summer

of 1946. The crucial breakthrough came when people began to exchange feedback about the effects of interaction in groups (Bradford, 1967). The discovery about the "electric effects" of feedback, as Bradford put it, became a central feature of laboratory education methodology.

One can observe a variety of similarities and differences between the British and the American inventions of experiential learning groups. Although the British name their event a conference and the Americans call theirs a laboratory, both institutions are similar in that they locate the setting for learning away from normal day-to-day activities. The NTL people call the setting a *cultural island,* and the Tavistock professionals use the term *residential conference.* Both methods evolved from a combination of psychotherapy and education, and both were designed to serve educational rather than psychotherapeutic purposes. How education and therapy combined, however, differed between the two traditions. NTL initially began with explicitly and exclusively educational objectives and over time developed a style of laboratory that bordered on psychotherapy and was called personal growth or "therapy for normals" (Argyris, 1967). The British version emerged from a psychotherapeutic tradition and, perhaps as a result, never mixed the explicit objective of learning about groups with the conscious aim of helping individuals to change. The theoretical bases for the American therapeutic elements were diverse and included Rogerian, gestalt, and existential frameworks. The British were, to a large extent, unified in their acceptance of the Kleinian perspective. On the relationship between psychotherapy for individuals and experiential education about groups, the National Training Laboratories as an institution had their intellectual and behavioral boundaries less clear than did the Tavistock Institute—an aspect of the two traditions connected to their separate yet related invention of the experiential learning group.

The potential for learning about groups from experiential methods was not just an educational innovation. The social technology also spawned a new path for studying groups—in both field organizations and social research laboratories. Offering possible benefits to both teaching and research, experiential methods found their way into university settings by the 1950s.

By the middle 1960s, the experiential learning group was in use for educational and research purposes in three parts of Yale University. In the then Department of Administrative Sciences, Chris Argyris, who at the time had a close connection with Leland Bradford and the NTL Institute, introduced T-groups for both undergraduate and master's level graduate education. In the Department of Psychiatry, Fritz Redlich and Boris Astrachan, who had developed relationships with A. K. Rice, made group relations training an element of psychiatric education. The third location was in the Department of Sociology, where Theodore Mills (1967) established a group dynamics laboratory that was quite similar to the model developed by Freed Bales at Harvard.

In the administrative sciences and psychiatry departments, experiential group dynamics education was tied closely to preparing students for careers that combined thinking and action. Graduates of administrative sciences went toward careers in management and consultation, and the psychiatric residents, upon completion of their formal education, entered careers in community and administrative psychiatry. Both the NTL tradition, as exemplified by Argyris, and the Tavistock tradition, as portrayed by Rice, included action research in the field with organizations (Argyris, 1962, 1970; Miller and Rice, 1967). The Bales and Mills tradition was more closely tied to academic sociology and social psychology, with the major emphasis being on knowledge for its own sake. It was largely devoid of action research with organizations.

As the sociologist Kurt Back (1972) noted in his cultural analysis of the encounter group movement, the 1960s were characterized by the predominance of values associated with some forms of laboratory education. With the end of the decade came a decided reduction in the religious fervor that had briefly captured experiential education activity. In the ensuing years, two of the three Yale departments dropped their commitments to teaching group dynamics by experiential methods. First, Mills left Yale to join the State University of New York at Buffalo, and the sociology department did not replace him with a person of similar interests. Next, the psychiatry department, which increasingly fell under the domination of the biological researchers, eliminated their group relations training for psychiatric residents. The organizational behavior group within administrative sciences, however, maintained and enriched their array of courses that employed experiential group methods. In 1974, when the department was folded into the newly established School of Organization and Management, the capacity to offer courses using experiential group methods became part of the fabric of Yale's newest professional school.

My own history with the Yale Organizational Behavior Program covers both the time when the Department of Administrative Sciences was offering experiential group dynamics and the more recent period since the founding of the School of Organization and Management. As a doctoral student, I began my work in the field closely associated with Chris Argyris and Fritz Steele from the Yale program. After completing the Yale program and leaving to teach at

Cornell, I entered the NTL Applied Behavioral Science Intern Program, which included work with Warren Bennis and Henry Reicken. Later, on returning to Yale as a faculty member, I participated in a faculty seminar on groups that included learning Tavistock theory and method and examining the similarities and differences between the NTL and Tavistock (Alderfer and Klein, 1978). Thus, by the time the Yale School of Organization and Management began in 1974, I had had extensive exposure to both schools of thought under favorable conditions, although my connections were closer to NTL than to Tavistock.

SELECTING STUDENTS FOR THE COURSE

Regardless of whether the events occur at a university or on a cultural island, the temporary system that makes laboratory education possible must provide a means for selecting participants. The two types of settings, however, differ in the implications for what people are chosen and how they are picked. People who journey to a remote location in order to participate in a learning experience of from several days to two weeks often do not know each other in advance and rarely see each other afterward. Students who enroll in a course participate in the same community before, during, and after the educational experience. Selection processes must respond to these differences.

The concerns about who can benefit from the learning, however, are the same in both settings. We want to detect casualty-prone individuals and prevent their participation. As much as possible, by means of written and oral communication, we want to inform all potential participants about the nature of the experience they will face, so they can make informed choices about whether they want to join.

In both the university and cultural-island settings, participants should be volunteers who receive an accurate account of the experience they are about to join and then actively choose to join because they want the kind of education offered. Cultural-island settings are more likely to receive members who have been sent to repair what bosses perceive as behavioral deficiencies, and university courses are more likely to sign up people for reasons other than educational. People who do not want to attend or whose objectives are to change themselves dramatically are likely to become casualties (Lieberman, Yalom, and Miles, 1973; Kaplan, Obert, Van Buskirk, 1980).

Students who wish to take the interpersonal and group dynamics course receive an account of the course activities and requirements. They are encouraged to ask questions about what they have heard, and then they are asked to respond in writing to a contract, which specifies a number of issues about which faculty members ask for comments. The students' written contract gives their reasons for wanting to take the course, indicates that they agree to attend all group sessions unless confronted by a personal emergency, asserts that they accept the goal of the course to combine experiential and intellectual learning, and confirms that they understand the course is not intended as a substitute for psychotherapy.

The last issue alone, or in combination with the individual's statement of purpose, identifies individuals who are potential group casualties. If a student's response to this line of inquiry is evasive, as would be shown by giving an abstract account of the difference between education and therapy rather than by making a personal statement that he or she wants to take the course for educational, not therapeutic, purposes, then we exclude the applicant from the course. If a person is ambiguous in his or her response, saying that he or she is not sure of the line between education and therapy, and might be inclined to use the group experience for therapy, then staff members invite the person for an individual interview. During the discussion, the student's reasons for wanting to take the course are reviewed and the faculty member makes an assessment about whether the person is likely to get into psychological difficulty as a group member. Over the years, we have come to have a high order of confidence in the validity of these questions for identifying individuals who are potential group casualties, because individuals whose reponses are questionable at the time of admission and who are admitted almost always turn out to be those who come closest to becoming casualties in the group.

From the people whose contracts are acceptable, we eliminate individuals at random, if more people are available than there are places in the course. Depending on the age, race, gender, ethnicity, and educational program of applicants, we sometimes stratify before the random elimination occurs. In order to protect individuals against the structural aspects of scapegoating, we try to make sure that no well-defined category of person is isolated within a group.

Students who request an explanation about why they did not get into the course are given up to an hour with a faculty member to explain matters. For some the answer is relatively simple, "Your contract was fine, but you lost out in the random number draw."

For others, the discussion is more complicated. In these cases, the faculty member reviews the student's contract, shows her or him which statements were a source of concern, and explains why the presence of such statements in combination with the faculty member's understanding of how people get into difficulty in experiential groups led to the decision to exclude the person from the course.

Understandably, these discussions are sometimes uncomfortable. In them, I attempt to convey three kinds of messages. First, to the extent that the student shows evidence of feeling hurt and angry, I try to acknowledge those feelings in as accepting a manner as I can. Second, I indicate that although we have a high order of confidence in the capacity of the learning contract data to predict who is likely to get into difficulty in the group, I also indicate that any prediction is fallible—especially for a specific individual. Depending on what happens in the conversation, I may say the words, "In your particular case, it is possible that the decision was a mistake." The acknowledgment of potential fallibility, however, is not a basis for reopening the decision about any particular individual. On the average, we exclude two or three applicants per semester because their contracts lead to concerns about their becoming casualties. Recently, however, we excluded twelve people in a single semester for this reason.

In the university setting, providing for conversations with the people not admitted respects the individuals and helps to manage the relationship between the course and the wider environment. Generally, only a fraction of the people eliminated ask for such conversations, so the burden is not great. When people choose to discuss why they did not get into the course, staff members assist the individuals in coming to terms with their frustration. That process serves the people involved, and it reduces the likelihood that they will feel the need to take their complaints to other authorities, who may not decide to talk to the course staff, if they have doubts about whether the students were properly advised.

FOCUSING ON HERE-AND-NOW BEHAVIOR IN EXPERIENTIAL SESSIONS

Regardless of whether experiential group therapy education occurs on a cultural island or in a university, staff members need a clear sense of what they are doing when they speak in the experiential sessions. Within the professional group that does this kind of work, there is no single widely agreed-upon orientation. Differences to some degree vary with learning objectives for experiential groups and with the theories practitioners employ. The focus on here-and-now behavior of group members does *not* vary directly with the setting in which the experiential group occurs. However, the concrete nature of what members say and do—according to the theory of embedded intergroup relations—is likely to vary depending on the setting in which the group is located. Thus the content of staff members' interpretations of here-and-now events may differ by setting, but the focus on the behavior of people in the room does not.

At the start of the first group session, I say something like "The purpose of the group sessions is to provide members with an opportunity to learn from the experience of behavior as it occurs in the here-and-now. I will comment on what is happening in the room when I think it will help people to learn." In subsequent group sessions, the signal to start working is turning on the tape recorder.

As it turns out, both NTL and Tavistock traditions pay attention to "here-and-now" behavior in the group (Argyris, 1962; Bion, 1961). But the concrete material to which representatives of the two traditions attend is different. The major focus in the NTL tradition is on *interpersonal* behavior and relatively *conscious* emotions. For example, "John, you put your head between your hands and turned away after Melanie finished talking to you. Do you want to tell the group what you were experiencing?" In the Tavistock tradition, the major focus is on *unconscious* assumptions, fantasies, and communications as they appear in the *group* as a whole. For example, referring to the same episode as the previous comment, the staff member might say, "The group might wish to examine the tensions that seem to be present between male and female members of this group."

My own learning about the significance of here-and-now behavior proceeded in a series of steps. Early in my doctoral training, I had worked with Chris Argyris's (1962; 1965 a,b) behavioral scales designed to measure interpersonal competence. Argyris developed the scales both to assess the quality of interpersonal relations among executives in day-to-day organizational events and to analyze the learning processes in experiential groups. Since working with this system had been an important part of my doctoral education, I was aware of both the strengths and limitations of the system. As a result of my growing experience as a group relations trainer and as an organizational consultant, I became increasingly convinced of the value of being able to discuss events as they occurred as a way of helping people to learn about their own and others' behavior. After completing my doctorate and moving to Cornell, I collaborated with Thomas Lodahl, who also worked within the NTL tradition, in conducting a systematic study designed to compare the predictive power of a behavioral scale measuring "openness" with a behavioral scale measuring "here-and-now" (Alderfer and Lodahl, 1971). The openness scale was derived from the Argyris measures, while the here-and-now scale was aimed to operationalize the concept of here-and-now that appeared in both NTL and Tavistock literatures. At this time, I had only a reading knowledge of the Tavistock work and was not at all sure that the concrete use of the term for their purposes would be identical to mine. I was encouraged, however, by the idea that the same term appearing in two closely related literatures might have similar behavioral referents. Table 1 shows this scale.

Results of the empirical study showed the here-and-now scale to be superior to the openness scale by every comparison. The here-and-now scale distinguished between the behavior in laboratory ed-

Table 1, Scale for Measuring Here-and-Now Behavior

Scale Value	Behavioral Form and Example
5:	Conversation about present group members today. Example: "I noticed that John has been silent today."
4:	Conversation about present group members at previous meeting. Example: "This group seemed depressed last meeting."
3:	Conversation about others in the course or school. Example: "Is everyone aware how many second-year students are missing classes to attend job interviews?"
2:	Conversation about people outside the course or school. Example: "There has been another drug-related killing in the streets of New Haven."
1:	None of the above. Example: "I would like to have a discussion on the subject of abortion. Who in this group believes in it?"

ucation and a conventional human relations class and detected changes over time within both kinds of classes as a result of planned interventions, and the openness scale did not (Alderfer and Lodahl, 1971, p. 56). At the level of group sessions, we found relatively high correlations between here-and-now behavior and involvement ($r = .64$, $p < .003$), perceived transfer of learning ($r = .66$, $p < .002$), and comfort with feelings ($r = .74$, $p < .001$) (Alderfer and Lodahl, 1971, p. 66) and no significant correlations between openness behavior and these same attitude measures.

These empirical findings raised severe questions about whether the focus on openness behavior and interpersonal competence, the more general concept of which it is a part, contributes to the kinds of learning for which experiential learning groups are especially well suited. An emphasis on learning how to be "interpersonally competent" tends to set into motion dynamics between staff and participants that do not serve the aim of encouraging participants to be responsible for their own learning. Instead, it encourages people to copy trainer behavior. It pushes staff members toward a role and relationship that do not encourage participants to find their unique ways through the dilemmas and paradoxes of group life. Chapter 12 presents a discussion of the conception staff as model, including the problems associated with that framework.

DEVELOPMENTAL PHASES IN GROUP LIFE

In the professional literature of experiential group dynamics, there is a widely held hypothesis that groups with well-defined beginnings and endings pass through predictable phases during their development and demise. Not all agree with this hypothesis. Those particularly committed to the Tavistock tradition are perhaps less likely to agree. As part of Chapter 12 in this book, I offer a formulation suggesting that how staff members respond to naturally occuring group events influences the extent to which and clarity with which groups pass through developmental phases.

Whether an experiential group is set in an academic environment or on a cultural island, however, does not by itself affect the validity of the phase movement hypothesis. In either kind of setting, the suprasystem in which the program is embedded can exert a deleterious influence on group development by intruding through the group boundaries or provide a benign environment in which the group boundaries are supported. I recall, for example, a time in the late 1960s at an NTL laboratory in Bethel, Maine, when local officials spoke to staff members to prohibit personal growth labs from conducting exercises on the town green after these activities had occurred. That had an impact on staff-participant relations in the laboratory and thereby affected group development. When a public announcement stated that nontenured faculty members in Organizational Behavior at the Yale School of Organization and Management would be terminated without review when their contracts expired, that event had a powerful impact on the experiential classes being taught by those faculty members and subsequently affected the development of their groups.

From an intellectual point of view, organizing the course around the framework of phases in group development provides a coherence that otherwise might be lacking. The framework provides an order to topics addressed in readings, paper assignments, and lectures. It also offers a theoretically based focus for understanding what occurs in the experiential group sessions. Staff members need only to accept group development as a working hypothesis to employ the framework. It is quite possible to formulate lecture material and paper assignments in the style of a dialogue about the validity of the working hypothesis.

In a university, where the first value is intellectual understanding, the benefit of having such a framework is significant. On a cultural island, where generally there are fewer expectations for teaching general (in comparison to personal) knowledge, neither participants nor the suprasystem are as likely to be concerned about whether they can find an overall framework with which they can organize their experience. Yet I believe staff members in both kinds of settings operate more effectively if they work from a tentatively held comprehensive theory than if they observe only from a short-term time perspective (Smith and Berg, 1987).

A framework that I use based on the orderly series of phases in group development is summarized in Table 2. This formulation draws on the Bennis and Shepard (1956) theory of group development, the Whitaker and Lieberman (1964) focal conflict theory of groups, and the Alderfer (1976) theory of changing boundaries and relationships. As with any reasonable notion of developmental phases, this one does not assume sharp or unequivocal movement from one period to the next.

Periods of transition contain elements of both preceding and subsequent phases. Regressions occur, particularly during transitional times. Thorough and complete movement through all phases may not occur. Experiential groups, running over the course of a university semester, have a clearly defined beginning and ending. There is usually some kind of midsemester break, such as Thanksgiving or spring vacation, to signal the impending termination of the group. This does increase the probability of the phases unfolding in a manner that is consistent with the theory. The intellectual structure of the course plays a role as well, but it is unlikely to be as straightforward as one might imagine.

One effect of making the intellectual structure of the course explicit is to invite students to behave in a manner that "proves the theory is correct": that is, to obey what they consciously or unconsciously might believe the instructors want. But there are also counterforces to these inclinations. At the conscious level, there are repeated invitations to criticize the theory and to propose revisions. Less conscious are the well-known tendencies in all of us to show that our behavior cannot be predicted—especially by social scientists! In addition, not all instructors who teach this course are equally convinced of the validity of the developmental theory. Providing support for a conception of developmental phases are the moments when events conspire to illustrate the theory so dramatically that even the most committed doubters announce their conversions publicly.

In Table 2, the phases of group development are defined in terms of the boundary or relationship that is being formed, the primary emotion that tends to be evoked, the wish and fear combination associated with that emotion, and the modes of coping with the wish-fear tensions that tend to emerge. At the outset, the question is whether the group will form—that is, whether members will give up enough of their individuality to be responsive and responsible to collective needs and, in turn, whether the group will fashion solutions to its problems that permit members to retain a sense of individuality while becoming members in good standing. During this period, questions about the mandatory-attendance rule for group sessions are rooted in this struggle as are debates about whether members "can" discuss events from the group with their significant others.

Closely tied to the issues of group formation are authority and influence dynamics; the staff members, after all, are the authors of the mandatory attendance rule. Attempts to renegotiate that rule, to find its limits, or to enforce it blindly all contain messages about authority in the group. When the staff does not take on the customary teaching role during group sessions, a vacuum is created, and members or subgroups of members step in to fill it. Often during this period, one can see members who seem to represent the staff perspective on issues ("There must be a good reason for mandatory

Table 2. *Phases of Group Development*

An experiential group is a temporary system with a definite beginning and end. In this way it differs from many other groups. A precise beginning and ending help to clarify the visibility of developmental phases.

PHASE	BOUNDARY OR RELATIONSHIP ISSUE	PRIMARY EMOTION	WISHES	FEARS	MODES OF RESOLUTION
Group Formation	forming the psychological group; being in or out	anxiety; discomfort	to be in; to be autonomous	to be out; to be overwhelmed	staying out selectively; partial inclusion; total immersion
Influence	giving and receiving negative emotions	anger frustration	to express aggression; to be influential; to be dependent	to hurt; to be hurt; to accept influence	remaining quiet; competing; carving role (turf)
Intimacy	giving and receiving positive feelings	tenderness; love; affection	to be close; to receive affection	to be vulnerable; to be unworthy of affection	staying away; stepping close; slowly disclosing fully
Termination	eliminating the group boundaries	grief; sadness	to be harmonious; to be complete; to be free of group pressures	to be incomplete; to be splintered and fragmented	fantasizing; slowing down; working through

attendance"), and also members who clearly resist ("Johnny really had his heart set on a job with McKinsey, and they gave him only class time for an interview").

If members have not discussed their thoughts and feelings about the staff, there is nothing like the due date of the first paper to remind people that they are members of a course with a real authority structure. The issue is further rekindled when the first papers are returned with comments and grades. For this reason, staff members commit themselves to getting the papers read and returned in a timely fashion.

The move from a focus on authority and influence in the group to an emphasis on intimacy is often marked by some member saying out loud something like "Can people believe that we only have six more sessions of this group?" The fact that the group will end in the near future tends to allow members to realize that they have developed committed relationships with one another, that some people have spoken about matters that involve significant personal risk, and that some people feel gratified by what has happened in the group, while others remain frustrated by unmet expectations. There are questions of intimate feelings among members, real or fantasized sexual relationships, and hopes to reproduce the warmth some have experienced in the group in other areas of their lives. Also present are the statements of those who feel uncomfortable with more intimate conversations and who act to be sure the group does not become too close during this phase.

Termination is a phase that evokes sadness both about the impending end of the group and about opportunities for learning and growth missed by the group. The dominant experience may be one of gratification for all that the group has been, coupled with sadness that it will end. Or it may be one of anger and frustration—usually aimed directly or indirectly at the staff—for the myriad ways in which the group did not meet members' expectations. Usually both kinds of feelings are present, and their expression, in part, serves as a kind of life review of the group by its members. The process as well as the content of the final meetings have some tendency to reproduce in microcosm the major facets of what the group experience was for its members. Various forms of both frustration and admiration for the staff are usually part of that picture. Groups die in a variety of ways: some stop working in advance of the termination time; some work strenuously to the very end; and others experience a kind of slowing down of vital functions that precedes the actual end.

EVALUATING THE INTELLECTUAL WORK OF STUDENTS

A course in a university that prides itself on high academic standards takes place in an environment different from those of a human relations laboratory on a cultural island or a group relations conference in a residential setting. Although laboratory or conference environments include lectures and offer people an opportunity to read between sessions, they present no demands that learners demonstrate intellectual understanding of interpersonal and group dynamics. Universities, on the other hand, have expectations that courses will teach and students will learn a defined body of knowledge and that students will be graded on the basis of their mastery of course content. To abide by the laboratory or conference norms about evaluation is to violate normal university expectations about grading.

The issue is further complicated by the "personalness" of the learning and the intricate relationship between learning and the student-faculty relationship. The subject matter of the course includes emotional issues, such as leadership, authority, and intimacy. Moreover, whether acknowledged or not, most professionals know that their relationship with students affects the learning process. Thus, if one is really honest with oneself, one accepts the hypothesis that when there are difficulties with students learning, this has an effect on and is affected by the relationship between students and teachers. (I happen to believe that this proposition holds for any learning environment, but it is a little easier to deny it when the subject matter is mathematics, economics, or accounting than when it is interpersonal relations and group dynamics.) If one is committed to competent and fair evaluation of students' mastery of the intellectual material, how does one do so within the environment of a university without undermining the learning conditions that are necessary for experiential learning to occur?

Some universities—and Yale is among them—provide an option that we did not take, which is to grade the course on a pass/fail basis. To adopt a pass/fail grading system is to give two undesirable messages, tacitly and explicitly. The first of these messages is that what we teach in group dynamics cannot be organized and evaluated as a systematic body of knowledge. This simply is not true. The second message is that we are unwilling to step up to the difficult task of doing evaluations. In a course with authority relations as one of several central topics, what are we teaching if the authority figures in the course avoid one of the major responsibilities of being a university faculty member?

Thus, the decision was to evaluate academic performance on the same marking scale as any other course in the curriculum. With that decision made, the question became what instruments to use for evaluation. Ruled out quite explicitly was student behavior in class. In the course syllabus and during the introduction to the course, we stated clearly that, to the best of our ability, what students did during class sessions would not be a basis for their grades. This meant that they could neither help nor hurt their grades by how much or how little they talked or by what they said or did not say. We ruled out student behavior as a basis for grades in order to reduce the likelihood that the authority relations in the class would be influenced by students' sense that saying the "right" or "wrong" thing in class would affect people's grades. We also wished to reduce the faculty's unconscious temptation to use transference and countertransference reactions as the basis for grades. As a further guard against these kinds of difficulties, on the course syllabus we explicitly invited students to discuss their reactions to grades if they believed errors had been made. If these discussions did not prove satisfactory, provision was made for students to obtain a second opinion from another faculty member who was qualified to teach the course.

During the entry process, students were required to agree to attend *all* of the group sessions, barring personal emergency (defined as serious illness, family crisis, or unavoidable accident). No such requirement was stipulated for the lecture sessions. We reached the decision to require attendance at the group sessions from our own experience with university norms. When that requirement was not in force, a pattern of roughly one student missing each session developed. As a result, groups lacked adequate cohesion, and those who did attend regularly became obsessed with wondering why others did not. The theoretical point is that without the mandatory attendance rule, the group boundary did not become strong enough to provide the security needed for learning to occur. The attendance requirement for group sessions distinguished this course from virtually all others, while not having such an expectation for the lecture sessions made it similar to more traditional classes.

Having ruled out class behavior as a basis for grades, we established that three written papers of eight to twelve pages, turned in on a regular basis throughout the semester, were to be the sole basis for grades. The papers were to relate events from the group sessions to concepts presented in the lectures and readings. Each paper called upon students to *describe* thoroughly and accurately what occurred and then to *analyze* these events using the various theoretical positions to which they were exposed. In the paper assignments, students were invited to propose revisions in the theory based on events that occurred in the class or to use events that occurred in the class as a basis for comparing one theory with another. To assist students with maintaining a source of descriptive data about the course, each group session was recorded on audio tapes and deposited on closed reserve in the library for use only by members of groups who generated the behavior. We also encouraged students to keep diaries of their experiences with the course and to view their own feelings and fantasies as well as their behavior as data for analysis.

The class structure gives time on a weekly basis to both intellectual and experiential learning. The papers, in turn, call upon students on a regular basis to integrate the two modes of learning by writing. Student paper writing is a solution to a major technical problem within the professional experiential learning community. Invention of experiential methods in part represents a reaction to traditional lectures or case methods for teaching about human behavior and groups. Research literature from the late 1960s and early 1970s includes a series of articles that contrast lectures or cases with laboratory methods (for example, Argyris, 1965a, b; Bolman, 1970; Alderfer and Lodahl, 1971). One theme of this research was that experiential methods were superior to traditional methods for teaching about emotions and effecting behavioral change. A second theme—less pronounced but nonetheless present—was that experiential methods alone without adequate provision for intellectual learning drive out theory (Alderfer and Lodahl, 1971). In fact to this day, many experiential group leaders resist the notion that experiential and intellectual learning can be integrated and demonstrate a kind of perverse pride in being anti-intellectual. Given this history of tension between experiential and intellectual learning, it is possible that students who apply to take the course will have a similar confusion. Therefore, we ask all who wish to be considered for the course to commit themselves to the integration of the two types of knowing and use the papers as a means to measure how well they do that work.

MANAGING INTERGROUP RELATIONSHIPS EMBEDDED IN THE EDUCATIONAL ENVIRONMENT

Whether on a cultural island or in a university, the experiential group dynamics educational program is located within a larger suprasystem. On the cultural island, the higher authorities are likely to be the sponsoring organization, such as the NTL or Tavistock Institutes. Under these circumstances, the immediate authorities are likely to understand the work and to appreciate the conditions necessary to do it well (although I must add that my experience includes more than one case when this decidedly was not true). As one moves away from the immediately adjacent suprasystem to the local community, however, the degree of understanding and support is likely to decrease. In a university, the circumstances are likely to be somewhat different. The immediate suprasystem consists of the department and school, which I have known to vary in support from highly benevolent to quite malevolent. When the immediately surrounding system is benevolent, then one generally need not be concerned about deleterious effects from wider suprasystems. But when there are problems with department or school authorities, the difficulties can be quite severe in terms of establishing the conditions necessary to do the work well. Understanding the suprasystem dynamics is framed as a problem in embedded intergroup relations; managing those relationships is part of the staff responsibilities for doing the work (Alderfer, 1986).

Within the Yale School of Organization and Management and the Yale Graduate School of Arts and Sciences, the course was open both to management and doctoral students. For management students, it was an advanced offering within the organizational behavior track. For organizational behavior doctoral students, it was a core course that could be omitted if a student expressed a preference to do so. Doctoral students usually took the course in their first year, and management students usually took it in their second year. Doctoral students who wished to develop special research and teaching competence with clinical methods had, in their third or fourth years, served as teaching assistants in the course. Thus, whenever the course was given, it was likely to be populated by students from at least two different and clearly identified programs. In addition, it was possible that there might be first-year management students as well as people from other graduate programs (for example, Forestry,

Public Health, Nursing, Drama, Psychology) at Yale who became members of the course. Thus, the *individuals* who joined the course quickly became known (or were already known) to each other by their *group* memberships in particular classes of academic programs. Students learned to recognize that they thought of themselves and were thought of by others as representatives of particular programs and classes within programs. In addition, some students who entered from the same year and program had established relationships with one another among subgroups. Each of these group memberships and the relationships among them shaped the intergroup relationships that the wider educational environment imposed onto the course.

In addition to the organization group memberships that the Yale environment conferred upon students, the individuals also belonged to a variety of identity groups as a consequence of their gender, ethnicity, race, and age (Alderfer, 1986). Compared to the national management school average of approximately 25 percent, for example, the proportion of Yale students who were female ranged between 38 and 50 percent. The proportion of organizational behavior doctoral students who were female, in recent years, had been 50 percent or higher. The organizational behavior faculty, on the other hand, were 75 percent male, and the senior faculty were 100 percent male. Among American ethnic and cultural groups, Jews accounted for approximately 30 percent of the class. Black Americans, black Africans, Asian Americans, and Asians each accounted for between 5 and 10 percent of the class. To the extent that the information was available when the groups were formed and there were sufficient numbers, we attempted to form groups in such a way as to be sure that individuals who represented particular identity groups were not isolated. We also attempted to form the staff in such a way as to provide as much diversity and support for underrepresented groups as possible.

As the School of Organization and Management grew and the popularity of the course increased, we faced a variety of challenges and problems. In 1980, we introduced the group-on-group design as a means of doubling the number of students who could take the course in a given section. The design consisted of each section (1) having two groups of twelve members each; (2) dividing the time so that each group in turn was the participating group for 50 minutes while the other group observed, followed by a ten-minute break between periods, after which the groups reversed roles; and (3) concluding with 30-minute total class discussion. Staff for this design was usually one faculty member with an organizational behavior doctoral student teaching assistant. The design makes it possible to learn about the intergroup dynamics of the two experiential groups as well as about the group and interpersonal levels of analysis.

Van Steenberg and Gillette (1984) have given a detailed account of this design in action, complete with examples of the kinds of learning that are possible at each level of analysis. I originally learned about the design in 1966 from Barry Oshry, who introduced it at the National Training Laboratories as a technological innovation without a theoretical framework to accompany it. In those days, I recall thinking of the design as a means to observe new and different features of group life—much as a biologist might employ a new kind of microscope that made it possible to see previously invisible elements of an organism. When we introduced the design at Yale, in 1980, it was in conjunction with an intergroup perspective on group dynamics that had been developing from a variety of research and consultation projects (Alderfer, 1977, 1986; Alderfer and Smith, 1982).

Further pressures to increase the number of students who could take the course led to teaching two sections during a semester for the first time in the spring of 1987. From 1980 through 1986, we had offered the course as a single section with its group-on-group design in both fall and spring. Embedded intergroup relations theory predicted that there would be a significant difference between whether the two sections were treated as if they were independent or had a relationship with one another. Conventional thinking about teaching multiple sections of the same course generally assumes (whether or not people actually believe) independence among sections. Embedded intergroup relations theory predicts otherwise (Alderfer, 1986). Faculty members teaching the parallel sections have a choice about whether they jointly manage the interdependency or cope independently with the consequences of not working together on the intergroup relationship between the sections. In this case, Jack Gillette and I, together with our teaching assistants, acted to treat the entire course as the interdependent system that it was.

Joint work included holding a single course preview, meeting to select students for the course, deciding together which students would be assigned to sections and to groups within sections, holding a total class opening session for the course, meeting together during the breaks of each experiential session, and, approximately halfway through the semester, designing and conducting an experiential event that involved both sections and all four staff members. One of the dramatic results of the total-course exercise was that we discovered that the students identified a good-to-bad rank ordering that crossed the section boundaries and covered all four of the experiential groups in the course. If one had questions about the interdependence between the two sections or about the interpenetration of the wider educational environment upon the course, this finding reduced those doubts. Staff members saw it as no accident that in an environment such as Yale, whose values are preoccupied with prestige and status, a set of peer groups of students would need to form a rank ordering among themselves and that this ranking would be correlated with the rank of the professors teaching the respective sections of the course. If there were not already a concept of identification with the aggressor, one would be led toward inventing one (Freud, 1936). What is somewhat different about this situation, however, is that the unconscious identification occurred at the group level, not just for individuals. Ranking the experiential groups was achieved by a collusive agreement involving the four groups themselves, the two sections, and the course as a whole. The learning value of this event was not lost by the students who, for the most part, were able to tolerate the discomfort involved in seeing what they had done.

As the popularity of the course grew, we faced pressures to increase the number of faculty members who were available to teach it. Normally, one would think of this mainly as a benefit, but in this situation, the consequences were far more mixed. The fact that organizational behavior courses in general, and the experiential courses in particular, were popular with management students was a source of disturbance to many faculty members at the school. Administrative people in the school faced requests from students for more faculty resources to be devoted to teaching the course, and at the same time they heard senior faculty members from other disciplines regularly complaining about the amount of resources already devoted to organizational behavior at the school.

I also believe that it is important to acknowledge that both the intellectual and the professional standards for doing experiential work nationally are not high. As a result, it is simply not easy to find faculty members who are capable of operating at the level of theory and practice called for by this and other courses in the curriculum. One solution to this problem that has been posed periodically—without, of course, being identified as such—is to assign the course to faculty members who are less than adequately qualified. In the long run, this solves both the problems of student demand and of faculty complaints. If the course is not adequately taught, students will have less desire to take it, and there will be a valid basis for administrators to agree with faculty members who wish to reduce resources for organizational behavior. From time to time, it has been necessary to intervene both with colleagues and with deans in order to insist that we do not compromise on the quality of preparation and experience called for from faculty members who teach this course. This intervention into the wider educational environment is necessary in order to maintain adequte control over the staff group boundaries for the course. The action derives from the same theory that we use within the course and involves acting in the faculty-administrative part of the environment in a complementary fashion to what we do when we select students for membership in the course (Alderfer, 1980; 1986).

Being attentive to selecting faculty for the course does not end the process of assuring that staff members are adequately prepared to meet the demands of teaching. The staff also functions as a group and therefore finds its own group dynamics importantly influenced by all the forces that also shape the participants' experiences. As a result, the staff needs to be capable *as a group* of observing and managing its own interpersonal and group processes. When this condition is not satisfied, the probability of individual participants becoming scapegoats (and then casualties) for unresolved staff tensions increases substantially (Kaplan, Obert, and Van Buskirk, 1980). In addition, those issues that the staff members cannot address among themselves are less likely to become topics from which participants can learn. Thus, when the staff members cannot examine their own behavior, the chances of establishing a psychologically secure setting for experiential learning are substantially lower. (A more extensive discussion of this subject can be found in Chapter 12.)

CONCLUSION

This chapter describes and analyzes what I believe to be the essential conditions for teaching an experientially based interpersonal relations and group dynamics class embedded within larger suprasystems. The particular context was the Department of Administrative Sciences and the School of Organization and Management at Yale University during the period from 1968 to 1988. The general framework applies equally to cultural-island and other university settings.

The historical background provides a formulation of the epistemological context within which I believe this learning has occurred. It is based on a series of learning cycles characterized by the diagram in Figure 1. In the middle 1960s, I began mainly with a focus on the experiential learning technology as it had been developed through the NTL Institute for Applied Behavioral Science and interpreted by interpersonal competence theory as formulated by Argyris (1962) and group development theory as stated by Bennis and Shepard (1956). From that point, I drew upon the clinical data that emerged from my own practice and the systematic research findings that were produced by a variety of studies, including my own. In the 1970s, as a result of sustained encounters with the Tavistock theory and method and my own fieldwork with organizational diagnosis and change, I broadened my working conception of leadership, authority, and groups. This was also a period in which I began a sustained interest in intergroup theory, which continues to this day. As my conception of intergroup theory developed, I found that it began to influence how I thought and acted in relation to the conduct of the Interpersonal Relations and Group Dynamics course. By the 1980s, I was making design changes and other interventions, not just stimulated by pragmatic needs or opportunities, but also derived from theoretical propositions.

The period from 1971 to the present has been one of constant turbulence within the wider educational environment within which the Interpersonal Relations and Group Dynamics course has been located. During the period from 1971 through 1988, Yale has had four presidents (Brewster, Gray, Giamatti, Schmidt), seven provosts (Gray, May [twice], Goldstein, Brainard, Nordhaus, Turner), and the School of Organization and Management has had five deans (Donaldson, Hazard, Malkiel, Peck, Levine). Coping with these disturbances, which can be conceptualized as data about intergroup relations and leadership, provided yet another opportunity to revise and use the theory in the living laboratory of one's own organization and further to test its utility. The net effect employs comparable theory and method in field and laboratory and relates to phenomena that range from the individual through group and intergroup relations to complex organizations. The cumulative effects of this learning have been very significant for me personally and for many others who have been involved in the course as students and staff.

Chapter 10

Group Relations Training
in Context

JAMES KRANTZ

INTRODUCTION

Learning about group dynamics can be both exhilarating and horrifying, especially when learning through the vehicle of one's own experience. Doing so requires people to peel back the surface veneers of self-presentation and mutually protective etiquettes to examine the hidden agendas, covert processes, simplifying myths, primitive fantasies, and intense anxieties that underlie group life. Unconscious processes are exposed as the source of creativity and destructiveness. Participants are confronted with their own beliefs and identifications, aggression, passions, longings, and the sources of vitality and withdrawal that are elicited in the process of joining a group, taking up a role, working with authority, and authorizing others.

Ordinarily these phenomena are held at bay, out of awareness, as groups and organizations get on with their tasks. Allowing them to surface and providing means of illuminating them requires a set of conditions and a "technology" for understanding that has certain features. Taken together, these conditions must create a learning context that provides the necessary conditions of protection and vulnerability such that one can learn and be challenged without being overwhelmed or unduly threatened. Without a "good enough" balance of protection and vulnerability, these efforts will be unable to avoid the various, and deadening, forms of inauthenticity and superficiality that result when people find themselves unsafe or unchallenged in self-study endeavors. These conditions create a "transitional space" (Winnicott, 1953), which exists between the real world of work with its risks and the inner world of pure fantasy—conditions that enable people to experiment, grow, and creatively learn in relation to important features of the world.

The purpose of this chapter is to examine some of the contextual factors that influence this balance by exploring the similarities and differences that characterize two established and effective approaches to educating people about group dynamics—the so-called Tavistock conference, on one hand, and the tradition of group dynamics education that has evolved at the Yale School of Organization and Management (SOM), on the other.

I am writing this chapter, in part, because I bridge both traditions. Because my perspective stems from my experience, some autobiographical information may be useful to the reader here. As an action researcher I work in the Tavistock tradition of open-systems approaches to organizational inquiry. The systems approach focuses attention on the relationship between a system or sub-system and its environment rather than trying to understand things atomistically. It follows from this perspective that any enterprise aimed at studying group processes will be shaped by the environment in which it exists.

Prior to joining Yale's SOM, my experience in group relations training had been entirely in the context of freestanding conferences organized along the "Tavistock model."[1] When I began teaching group dynamics at SOM, I was faced with adapting to the forces, constraints, and dynamics that arose from teaching group dynamics both in an academic setting and, more particularly, in a management school. Teaching group dynamics within a management school, to enrolled students, situates the self-study enterprise in a fundamentally different environment from the "freestanding" group relations conference. Much of the thinking in this paper represents my own sense-making process of translation and adaptation to a new setting.

TWO MODELS COMPARED

Two models of group self-study are compared in this chapter in an effort to elucidate more general issues that stem from the context in which group study is embedded. The self-standing con-

---

[1] I use this term advisedly. "Tavistock" represents several models and approaches to sociopsychological, sociotechnical, and socioecological work. In connection with education in group dynamics in this country, the term, however, has largely come to signify the approach to understanding group life explicated by A. K. Rice (1965). The term is used in this sense here.

ference provides opportunities for learning about group processes by establishing temporary institutions for periods of from three days to two weeks. These conferences take applicants who come for this purpose, and draw upon an open-systems framework that uses psychoanalytic thinking to understand the covert dimensions of the temporary institution. At the end of the conference, the enterprise is dissolved. (See A. K. Rice, 1965, for a detailed description of this model. Many other models and approaches to studying group processes exist. The ideas developed in this paper will be most useful in application to others using some form of group-as-a-whole model from a psychodynamic perspective [Wells, 1985].)

The SOM course combines experiential and more traditional didactic modes by alternating the twice-weekly classes. On one day the students meet in a regular class format, on the other the twenty-four students meet for an extended session in which twelve meet with the two consultants for an hour while the others watch, and then the groups reverse. (For more detail on this course, see Chapter 9 of this volume or Van Steenberg and Gillette, 1984). The course is usually comprised of students from the same year, and when the course is over they blend back into other school activities.

Theoretically, the two models are quite similar. Both draw on foundation beliefs in the usefulness of open-systems theories and depth psychology approaches. Both work primarily from a group-as-a-whole perspective. Though the conceptual frameworks underlying both traditions are quite similar and compatible, providing learning opportunities about group dynamics in the two contexts is quite different. (Although practitioners of neither tradition work in conceptual unity, for the purposes of this paper I believe the differences are less relevant than the commonalities.) This comparative discussion centers around four areas. "Task and Context" looks at differences between the freestanding conference design and locating group relations training in ongoing educational institutions. "Staff Roles in Context" examines how the embedded context generates multiple and complex roles for staff. "The Students and Their Aims" acknowledges the impact of different membership aims that are brought to the self-study process. The final section, "The Role of the Enterprise in the Institution," is devoted to considering the role and meaning of the group dynamics training enterprise within the management school institution.

Task and Context

A perspective on the evolution of group relations training. An early foundation of laboratory education was an emphasis on creating "social spaces" within which people were freed from many of the social constraints on thinking, feeling, and acting that govern ordinary contexts. Given this opportunity, participants could experiment with their behavior and create ongoing cycles of learning, insight, and novel experience. A variety of technical considerations went into creating the conditions necessary to establish this safe environment.

One design principle for laboratory education that gained currency was that of holding these events in neutral, "off-site" locations with people who were not in participants' natural work groups. Trainers believed these conditions, termed "social islands" by Kurt Lewin (Bradford, 1967), would provide enough safety to allow for the emergence of distressing experiences or behaviors that are feared to be unacceptable. Because it is the unacceptable that is kept locked away in the unconscious, laboratory education models focusing on the study of the unconscious and irrational bits of experience adopted this design principle. If participants were protected from the real and imagined censure that would result from exposing unconscious processes in their natural settings, designers of these events believed they would be more likely to make themselves vulnerable to the exposure, anxiety, and doubt that arise from such inquiry. The original Tavistock conferences in England reflected this concept, as did the conferences developed in the United States by the founders of the A. K. Rice Institute.

As interest in different approaches to experiential group study diffused through professional and academic networks, efforts were made to experiment with these models and their application. As for the Tavistock model, "freestanding" conferences of varying lengths were developed, focusing on particular dimensions of group life, such as male-female relations or diversity, or oriented to certain professional and occupational groups, such as government officials or educators.

In addition, efforts were made to use the experiential technology in different settings and under different conditions. These developments grew along two lines. One was attempts to mount conferences—or conference-like events—within regular work organizations, with memberships comprised of employees. With few exceptions, these experiments were unsuccessful, and now "in-house" conferences in this tradition per se are rarely, if ever, attempted. The use of this particular conference technology, with its emphasis on regression, has been found to be dysfunctionally disruptive to the sponsoring organizations.

Studying group dynamics in the here-and-now evokes primitive dimensions of unconscious life and along with it powerful emotions that are often suppressed in natural work organizations. Once elicited, these emotional processes could not be "contained" within the in-house conference, and were exported into the ongoing operational life of the organization. A motivating hope for hosting these conferences was that the greater sensitivity and awareness, the immediacy, and the directness that develop in the conference would be exported into the ongoing operations of the organization and thereby provide the cultural mechanisms for productively managing the increased emotional intensity and vitality. This hope was ill founded—other, less regressive approaches, designs, and technologies aimed at using the same insights in helping organizations have been far more successful.

Another development involved experiential group relations training within teaching institutions. Many efforts have been made to introduce what is often thought of as the Tavistock open-systems model or other group-as-a-whole approaches to exploring group dynamics experientially into the classroom. While many of these experiments are either so cursory or sufficiently truncated in one way or another that they provide only a superficial taste of the aims of this experiential learning method, other efforts, such as those discussed in this chapter, have succeeded in providing students with deep and intensive theoretical and experiential learning.

I believe that one reason teaching group dynamics has been more successful in school settings than in other sorts of work organizations is that there is a basic congruence between the primary task of the group relations conference and that of the school: both are concerned primarily with learning.

The impact of context on the task of learning. The general task congruence tells only part of the story, however, because the most dramatic and important difference between the two models stems from the differences in the primary task or tasks that each enterprise pursues. The defining characteristic of the freestanding group relations conference is that it can be designed and implemented with an extraordinarily sharp focus on a single primary task of providing learning opportunities. The consistent adherence to that focus provides a "work boundary" or referent against which interpretation of unconscious processes can be made. This is not to suggest that the staffs of these conferences are always able to adhere to this highly focused task. Social island conditions, however, permit conferences to work toward such a focus, in which it is useful to understand *any* deviations from this sharply focused task interpretatively, as representing the expression of underlying anxiety.

The training program within the school, in contrast, does not pursue the learning task so single-mindedly, or ruthlessly, as it often seems to conference members. The purposes of the course must conform to the mission of its immediate school environment, which includes not only teaching and learning but credentialing and, in the case of a professional school, professional socialization as well. By its very nature, the embedded group relations training program is more varied and diffuse in its purposes, a fact that creates a different array of opportunities and constraints than those of the free-standing conference.

In systems theory it is axiomatic that the attempt to pursue more than one task diminishes the effectiveness with which any single task can be achieved. As resources—emotional, intellectual, financial, and material—are deployed against multiple tasks, fewer are available for each. Additional resources are required to manage the inevitable conflicts and strains that emerge in the effort to contain multiple aims. Understanding differences between the traditional conference modeled along social island design principles and the program embedded in the school environment requires an appreciation of this fact. Differences in design choices—in the extent to which the more primitive aspects of group and mental functioning can be accessed and in the conscious and unconscious constraints imposed on the enterprise—all flow from this essential difference, which can be understood in terms of the different environments within which these enterprises exist. As a result, the struggle to accomplish the task through balancing protection and vulnerability takes on a different character in each context.

The role of grading might be an instructive example. In free-standing conferences the conference management says explicitly that it will not report to anyone the behavior or participation of conference members. To do so would be to work on a task other than providing learning opportunities. Not only would this diminish the sense of protection afforded by social island designs, but it would violate the group-as-a-whole conceptual framework. Since the staff is committed to working through the open-systems, group-as-a-whole framework, individuals can be understood only in terms of what they represent or "carry" for the group.

Of course "social island" conditions are never pure or total. In the case of group relations conferences, for example, staff and members often share overlapping networks outside the conferences. Thus the evaluations staff and members have of each other, while not

formalized, are exported, at times, with varying degrees of awareness. On the other hand, to the extent to which this occurs it can
be seen as a deviation from the mutually agreed-upon task of the
conference, and thus becomes interpretable as a form of defense.
This is not to say that it always is handled as such, but the focused
task definition of the freestanding conference allows for it.

With the embedded group relations course, however, the situation is different. An important part of the school's mission is to
export students recognized as having certain skills, and credentialing
is an important part of students' reasons for matriculating. Organizations in the school's immediate environment that hire students
often make decisions based on their performance. Grades are often
used, at least on the surface, as a means of differentiating students
according to performance.

In keeping with the school's multiple missions, professors in
group dynamics must assign a grade to the students. This poses
something of a dilemma: how can students be expected to challenge
authority, explore persecutory anxieties, and explore their irrational
processes if they are to be graded on their participation?

A structural solution is used to provide the protection necessary to enable experiential learning. Students are not graded on the
basis of the study group or even on classroom behavior, but on the
basis of assigned papers alone. From the group-as-a-whole perspective, doing this ultimately begs the question because it implies the
papers are less of a "group product" than other instances of members'
behavior. In fact, from this conceptual vantage point, a paper represents the group's influence as much as the roles that individuals
find themselves in. For the purposes of grading, however, the whole-
group focus must be relinquished, and for this part of the course the
professor must work at the individual level of analysis.

Thus the management school context creates a set of conditions that requires working at multiple levels of analysis. New avenues for learning are opened. To be sure, the tension between the
individual and group levels mirrors an element of organizational
reality that can offer important learning to students about the ambiguities and uncertainties of organizational life. Managers and administrators must relate to both individual and group performance.
They are faced with discerning when an individual's behavior represents his or her group, and they must develop ways of handling
the ensuing tensions.

The added complexity of the credentialing process has costs in
terms of depth of inquiry into the group as an entity. Important data
and experience from the group as a whole gets channeled into a
dyadic, and largely private, connection between student and profes-

sor. Sometimes students use the movement between levels of analysis defensively by lodging their capacity for inquiry and self-reflection largely in the papers and avoiding the exposure of bringing it into the experiential sessions.

At the same time, establishing an individual-level relationship creates learning opportunities that are precluded when working solely on the group-as-a-whole level. Students are able to refine their capacity to work conceptually, to work on linking experience and theory, and to deepen their capacities to formulate hypotheses through their dyadic relationship to the professor (which typically develops through the papers).

Managing the movement between different levels of analysis and working to prevent defensively motivated oscillations between levels are challenges to students and teachers alike. The context creates a need for teachers of these courses to develop and refine this skill.

Transactional and contextual environments. Looking conceptually at differences between the environments of the two group training formats brings to mind a distinction first put forward by Emery and Trist (1973b) between the task, or transactional environment, and the contextual environment of an enterprise. The task environment refers to the immediate operational environment and consists of all organizations, groups, and people with whom the enterprise has specific relations on both the input and output sides. In contrast, the contextual environment consists of the relations that do not directly enter the world of the enterprise's own transactions. Events in the contextual environment may at any time intrude into this world, constructively or destructively, predictably or unpredictably. The two types of training events essentially share the same contextual environment. It is in the transactional environments—their immediate contexts—that the critical differences emerge.

The transactional environment of the freestanding conference consists of a relatively few "stakeholders." These include, principally, the sanctioning organization (such as the A. K. Rice Institute), the potential membership, and the administration of the host site. This relative sparseness of constraints and interdependencies gives the conference management maximal control over conference boundaries. Members serve as vehicles for importing the contextual environment into the conference, which is how microcosms of the wider society are re-created and studied within the conference.

To be sure, the contextual environment intrudes into the school-based group training program as well. These self-study groups serve equally as social holograms, bringing in all of the salient group, institutional, and intergroup relationships that are represented by the group memberships of students. But in this model, the self-study group's experience is mediated by a powerfully complex, interdependent, and unmanageable transactional environment—the school itself.

The denser the environmental web, the greater the transactional complexity, and the larger the number of stakeholders, the greater will be the social constraints on an enterprise. Complexity in the transactional environment creates a measure of social constraint on the endeavor. The impact of this transactional environment requires the group study enterprise to conform to the more diffuse and varied set of tasks, creating a set of adaptive requirements that constrain, on one hand, but also create further opportunities for learning, on the other.

Any organization or enterprise must establish a sphere of activities recognized by its immediate environment. This constitutes its "distinctive competence" (Selznick, 1957), or niche. Recognition of this competence, or contribution, can be granted only by the interest groups or interested publics that are affected by its activities. Their support is a requirement for the continued existence of the enterprise.

While for the freestanding conference this recognition is based on the authorization of some sort to mount a conference, sanction to hold it somewhere suitable, and a voluntary membership, in the embedded groups course the mandate is far more complex, multifaceted, and constrained by institutional missions and, inevitably, intergroup politics. Thus, this enterprise has, in its transactional environment, the fluctuating norms and intergroup dynamics of the faculty.

Staff Roles in Context

The multiple tasks that comprise the core purposes of the educational institution are inevitably encoded into the relationships between members who take up work roles in the institution. This section looks at how embedding group relations training in an educational institution generates multiple roles for staff that must be understood and managed in order to protect the primary learning task of the course.

Because the school environment is so multidimensional and each professor has multiple group memberships within the school, conflicting demands and competing interests inevitably affect one's ability to teach. Moreover, different dimensions become salient in often unpredictable ways at different times. Three of the many complexities introduced by these interdependent roles are highlighted in this section.

1. Group relations training creates multiple and at times conflictual role constellations. Given the multiple, and at times conflicting, missions of an academic environment, faculty members wear more than one hat. Within the school environment we are, at various times, teachers, researchers, evaluators, and administrators. Students, too, are attempting to manage complex ambiguities in their roles. The processes involved in credentialing, achieving, and going ahead in their chosen professional fields can be at odds with the goals of learning and development: one favors the appearance of knowing and completeness while the other requires exploring one's ignorance and lack of knowledge. "Pleasing the teacher" can have both self-defeating as well as adaptive features.

Providing an effective group dynamics course requires "unbundling" some of the multiple role relations that are contained within the teacher-student relationship so that more focused role relationships can be imported into the course. As discussed above, this is accomplished partly through the course design, which locates the evaluation function in the didactic portion of the class (which includes paper writing), a different subsystem from the experiential portion, in which the here-and-now consultative/interpretative function is contained.

Moving back and forth between these different functions can be daunting for students and teachers alike. The tendency to confuse the differing role requirements of student/group member and consultant/teacher is strong, and the quite different emotional textures underlying the different role relations pose important ambiguities in student-teacher relations. Learning to manage and use these ambiguities and using them in the service of learning has been the major challenge to me in moving from working only in freestanding conferences to teaching group relations within a school context. I will illustrate these points by briefly discussing three such role dilemmas.

Consultant-Evaluator. Students take the course for credit as well as for learning, and the consultant is in the position, at the end of the course, of evaluating students. Often group members experience interpretation as judgment and attack, leading them to create in fantasy an image of authority as punitive and critical. Interpreting this can lead to fruitful exploration of persecutory anxieties that underlie authority relations in group life. However, interpreting the image of consultants as evaluators is complicated by the close proximity of the formal evaluator role, which is filled by the same person.

Questions of the consultant/teacher's capacity to keep the two roles distinguished comes sharply into view in this type of design. Will the professor be able to contain his feelings within the experiential subsystem and use them in the service of learning? Or is he likely to act out his feelings toward students in experiential groups by unconsciously downgrading the students' thinking in the papers? If so, then it is hardly safe to explore this possibility, and an essential element of the necessary protection is covertly removed.

Teacher-Consultant. Experiential self-study groups contend with enormous deprivation and frustration due to the withdrawal by authority figures from the ordinary structures and procedures that satisfy a range of dependency needs, such as being given leadership and guidance from above. The resulting regression surfaces irrational unconscious forces for study and inquiry. In classroom teaching, however, dependency needs are met to a far greater degree. Students "take" classes that teachers "give"; readings are "handed out," explanations "provided," lectures "given," and discussions "guided."

Desires to confuse the two arise as defensive responses by both faculty and the students. For faculty members, the opportunity to escape from the painful aspects of such depriving work provides a strong pull to rework issues from the experiential sessions in the classroom, where the authority relations are less overtly primitive. For students, it is an opportunity to "really get what he can't tell us on Mondays," as one student put it.

Complicating the management task is the need to build links between the two elements of the course. The SOM course places a strong emphasis on the ability to bridge theory and data. Experiential work is regarded as an opportunity for students to ground their theoretical/conceptual learning in experience and, alternatively, for students to illuminate their experience by internalizing a set of useful concepts and orientations.

To do so without encouraging defensive intellectualization or primitive, dependent reliance on texts to substitute for experience in the experiential sessions can be tricky. Similarly, building the links without encouraging a fantasy-driven effort to rework experiential group issues in the safer, more nurturant, and less regressive atmosphere of the classroom is one of the most formidable challenges faced in trying to offer a course like this.

Another tension in the dual teacher-consultant role stems from anxieties inherent in the teaching role. In teaching, one's self-esteem and sense of mastery can easily be tied up with a sense that students are learning, a connection that is far more dangerous when consulting to self-study groups than when in the classroom. I have often found myself wanting to teach rather than interpret, to help rather than work with the students, and to "make sure" they understand something in the experiential sessions. While this is often a powerful dependent pull on consultants in any self-study settings, the nearby presence of the teacher-student relationship predisposes me to be pulled into these wishes more readily than in freestanding conferences.

Teaching Assistants–Students. Unlike the usual teaching assistant role, TA's in SOM's group dynamics course take on a highly collegial role. They consult along with the professor in the experiential sessions, and are expected to work with the same range of intense projections. The authority boundary between consultants and students in the group attracts transferential fantasies and projections and puts the TA in the position of having to adhere to the same sort of emotional abstinence and detachment that any group consultant must.

This creates substantial confusion and anxiety because the TA, for the greatest part of his or her work life, is a member of the students' task and sentient groupings. On the concrete level, TA's have to withdraw from other students emotionally, are discouraged from socializing with them, and are expected to govern their relations with other students by the sort of confidentiality that is necessary to provide sufficient conditions of safety for students to engage in this work. This can put a strain on existing relationships, as well as remove a TA from sources of support. Because this experience is a stressful and anxiety-laden one, it is particularly costly to dilute a student's support system while she or he is working as an apprentice in this role. I have found it advantageous to work with students who have support systems outside the school and whose lives are not entirely centered in the school.

On the dynamic level, the pressure of an authority figure in the groups who is also a student in other roles evokes powerful fantasies and anxieties. With a male professor and female TA—the usual configuration—it is quite daunting for the group to explore in much depth its maternal transference to the TA because she was chosen from, and is still in most contexts a member of, their same sentient group. To be paired with one of the daughters, in fantasy, raises the specter of incestuous strivings. Thus these groups are often characterized by an unusually anxious avoidance of the maternal transference.

2. *Group relations courses potentiate a set of intergroup relations with other classes, faculty, and students.* The transactional environment of the course is a complex and densely interdependent

one, comprising a wide variety of individuals and groups; some groups, like departments, are permanent, and others, like classes, are temporary. The conditions required to establish a successful group dynamics course differ from those required to conduct a traditional course. To the extent to which these conditions can be negotiated, the course will adopt procedures and policies that are divergent from the set of usual governing procedures. These negotiations, in themselves, are complex intergroup events.

In the SOM course, the entry process is shaped not only by the school's administrative procedures, but by additional requirements we feel are necessary to protect and foster this sort of work within the school. We ask students to submit written statements concerning their interests and intentions, and we make judgments about which "contracts" are acceptable—both in terms of protecting the course and in terms of protecting students for whom this type of setting may not be right. Only after filtering these statements and establishing categories stratified by certain demographic variables do we randomly select students.

Making these choices and judgments goes against the grain of typical class enrollment procedures. And, as one might expect, it evokes powerful emotional dynamics. Sometimes students feel unjustly excluded and will mobilize a network of support for their cause, which can involve other faculty, students, or administrators. The pressures brought to bear can be strong, especially for junior faculty members, and all of these exchanges involve not only the effort to exert interpersonal influence, but whatever intergroup relations are manifested in the dyad as well. Especially where cross-unit or interdepartmental rivalries exist, these issues can serve as an irritant, or vehicle for historic tensions between groups. Pressures to make alterations or special arrangements for certain students during the entry process can be great for junior faculty members when approached by senior ones. The disturbing feelings that can be evoked around this process can excite tensions between groups, especially where there are preexisting tensions grounded in ideological, methodological, and political issues.

In addition, other classes exist in the transactional environment of the group dynamics course that are affected by what is happening in the group dynamics course. Subgroups of students from other courses bring their shared experiences from earlier terms into the class, and subgroups of students are also simultaneously taking other courses together. I have often wondered what it means for another class to contain a small group, say four or five, students who are in the midst of such an interpersonally intense experience. While there has been almost no inquiry into this, partly because of the norm of confidentiality, I am quite sure the reciprocal influences are great.

3. *Role relationships that have been deeply touched by the primitive, regressive, transferential dynamics elicited in group relations training are exported back into the transactional environment.* Self-study groups often go through remarkable journeys, facing the loving, creative, joyful dimensions of the unconscious as well as the destructive, envious, and bitter. Along the way powerful feelings, intimate relations, and archrivalries are experienced and, hopefully, examined. The regression-inducing leaderlessness of the groups elicits equally powerful transferential dynamics that, when acknowledged and examined, establish a sense of intimate connectedness between teachers and students.

Whatever learning is exported by and in the students, these relationships between peers, between teacher and TA, and between the teacher and students are exported as well back into what is, conceptually at least, the transactional environment of the course. The other contexts in which these relations occur are receptive, to varying degrees, to the sort of consciousness elicited by group dynamics training. As this kind of awareness is brought into other relations among students and between students and teachers, these relationships must then be harnessed to other work tasks in courses, advising, mentoring, and administrative processes.

The Students and Their Aims

The potential participants of either the embedded course or the freestanding conference are a crucial stakeholder group in the course's transactional environment. Important differences between the two models of group relations training stem from characteristics of the participant groups. Freestanding conferences attract a diverse group of people, mostly strangers to one another ahead of time, who come from a variety of fields, with a variety of interests, and in different stages of their adult development. In the management school there is far less diversity, and the students are part of a cohort before and after the course.

In contrast to the anonymity of social island conditions, group dynamics courses work with people who have already established collegial relations before the course and will have them—although altered by the experience—afterward. This diminishes the level of protection that students can be offered, and creates a felt constraint on what can be revealed. At times, this is used defensively, such as in fantasies of how much damage will be done in the future if a bit of information is revealed about a person in the course. Or, alternatively, there is a defensive belief that if only students didn't have these outside ties, then they could work freely without inhibition in exploring their unconscious processes. At the same time, the impact on ongoing relationships within the school, and potentially beyond, is a real possibility.

Another powerful cohort affect is the fact that all of these students are simultaneously going through an important, and stressful, life transition (Van Steenberg and Gillette, 1984). One of the most important factors inducing this homogeneity is a shared purpose among all students: namely, to learn about the impact of group relations on taking up managerial roles. The course is designed on the assumption that learning to work with unconscious processes is an essential element of being an effective manager.

Consequently, many of the students bring their aspirations for success and ambitions for achievement into the course, believing that what they may learn will serve them well. Often students bring with them archetypal images of leaders that are based on heroic assumptions about learning to control or master groups. Many of these images stem from, or are reinforced by, dominant myths and images in the business community. Many management students unconsciously identify with maverick business innovators and visionaries who are lionized by the popular press, and come to see leadership as the result of having won a competition (Mant, 1983; Gilmore and Krantz, 1989).

Confronting the profound interdependence of leadership and followership, the conflict in each individual between work motivations and basic assumption motivations, and their own conflicting attitudes toward both work and basic assumption leaders can be disturbing to the student with heroic self-images of leadership.

THE ROLE OF THE ENTERPRISE IN THE INSTITUTION

Group Dynamics and the Management Curriculum. Looking beyond design issues, important questions arise concerning the meaning of such an enterprise within a school environment. Many writers on group process (for example, Alderfer and Klein, 1985) have described the way in which affect, leadership, and different group functions are distributed throughout a system. Following on this insight, questions arise as to what it is that group dynamics contain on behalf of the system. What does the course represent for students and/or faculty?

The answers to these questions form an important basis for the work of teachers and students attempting to understand the unfolding group process. While the precise meanings change over time and fluctuate with shifts in the transactional environment, I wish to suggest some hypotheses as a way of exploring some of what the students, teachers, and the course "carry" for the system.

Group dynamics, and other organizational behavior courses, are the "place" in management schools where irrationality is explored. Feelings, belief systems, subjectivity, interpersonal relations, attitudes toward authority, and unconscious group identifications are at the core of understanding group relations. Ambivalent feelings toward these features of social and organizational life are inevitably enacted in the relations between the courses and their wider environment. The ever-changing political terrain can lead one side of this ambivalence to be dominant at different times.

One feature that stands out for students is that they are undergoing a process of professional socialization. Socialization—the inculcation of patterns of behavior and habits of mind—is at core a dedifferentiating process. Many students are disturbed by the effect that the stress and the particular focus of management education have on their selves as whole persons. Many fear the loss of vitality or the effects of conformity pressures characteristic of so many business environments. This is symbolized by the job-search process, during which so much of the diversity in dress and personal presentation gives way to remarkably consistent dress and manner.

Many students experience considerable anxiety concerning the evolution of their "selves" through this process, and particularly concerning the potential loss of important and vital parts of themselves to the socialization process. One hypothesis I have is that group dynamics is often used by students to reclaim and develop parts of their selves in relation to management education. Group dynamics is implicitly used by some to counteract the deadening aspects of professional socialization and, in fantasy, to counter these same forces in the future by reclaiming and developing important parts of the otherwise ignored self in relation to management education.

Group dynamics also represents, in part, the feminine bits of the managerial role. Group dynamics is concerned with the role of connectedness and feelings in collective life, and sensitizes students to those bits of the managerial role calling on an appreciation of the very real human drama represented by groups of people trying to accomplish something together. People tend to leave with a more empathic understanding of their own and others' struggles to work and live together. Because group dynamics represents the feminine bits required to take up managerial roles fully, the ambivalence felt about these bits is also enacted in relation to the enterprise within the institution.

Furthermore, studying group dynamics requires people to consider how "reality" is inherently social and anchored in belief systems rather than being an attribute of the "objective world." In this sense the very existence of group dynamics serves as a critique of the philosophical positivism dominant in management schools. According to this theory of knowledge, authority can be conferred only on "objectively" verified knowledge. This knowledge must be established externally to personal experience, which is considered idiosyncratic, subjective, unreliable, and downright unscientific. Thus, whatever data occurs in the context of personal experience is not regarded as an appropriate part of professional practice. Along with this notion of professional practice as the application of scientific methods (developed in the rigorous, controlled atmosphere) to practical problems in search of solutions is the notion that the problems are *given* or *emergent* from the situation itself. They are discrete, definable, operationalizable, and inherent in the world.

This approach to knowing banishes irrationality to the realm of the unprofessional. As a norm it leads to the splitting off of the irrational, and its consequent projection into "less professional" groups. The cost of this strategy, as we learn so painfully in group relations conferences, is massive depletion of the self.

By centering on the irrational, subjective, and experiential dimensions of organizational life, group dynamics serves as an implicit critique of the positivist epistemology around which so much management education is centered. Group dynamics then comes to represent this debate within the faculty and shapes the faculty intergroup relations that surround (and are necessary to sanction) the course.

Group Dynamics and Social Defenses in a Management School Culture. Management schools aim to teach students to take up managerial roles in contemporary organizations. Successful management requires a variety of sensitivities and skills, including analytic ability, leadership capacity, interpersonal awareness, an understanding of authority, and a sense of person-in-role. As with developing any professional practice, one must learn core technical skills as well as develop ways of getting one's knowledge used in organizational settings.

Managers have always faced uncertainty and ambiguity in their efforts to deploy resources—uncertainty concerning both the transactional and contextual environments as well as unpredictable internal conditions. In recent years, however, the destabilization of environments and the emergence of enormously turbulent conditions has led to situations of great uncertainty for managers, with attendant anxieties.

In consulting to organizations, I often find myself noting defensive maneuvers employed by work groups to simplify a complex and often terrifying reality confronting them. This can often take the form of what Bion (1961) called "basic assumption dependency," in which groups turn to a person, idea, text, or technique as if it were a magical solution that conferred certainty and understanding on inherently uncontrollable and ambiguous situations.

Another hypothesis I want to put forward about the business school environment is that the emphasis on analytic methods, based in positivist epistemology, gets *used* as a social defense (Menzies, 1961) to fend off some of the anxiety and doubt that are elicited in the course of confronting the uncertainty and ambiguity at the heart of management practice. By social defense, I am referring to an aspect of organizational life—an ideology and methodology in this instance—that is used to reinforce psychological defenses against anxiety in addition to task-relevant purposes. While social defenses shield members from painful feelings, they can also lead to dysfunctional or maladaptive organizations.

An increasing number of voices in the academic literature (for example, Mulligan, 1987; Behrman and Levin, 1984), the popular press (for example, Peters and Waterman, 1982), and daily newspapers question the asymmetrical emphasis on analytic techniques in business schools. Many are speaking to the need for people with greater "people skills" and more effective leadership ability, specifically those attributes that are not technical nor rooted in rationality, nor amenable to positivist approaches.

Considering the role business schools play in their wider environments leads me to another hypothesis: namely, that the rampant positivism in business schools reflects a psycho-dynamic role the schools play for the business community. In spite of the evidence, which calls for a more well-rounded approach to management education, business schools are moving surely in the direction of reliance on analytic and technical training as an expression of the (defensive) wish in the business community that uncertainty can be controlled.

The study of group dynamics cuts to the heart of this defensive process: experiential group learning reflects the ambiguity and un-

certainty that accompany all social processes and endorses the validity of (inter)subjective experience as data concerning social
context. As is the case when any defense, social or individual, is
undermined, group dynamics instruction is accompanied by increased anxiety, splitting, projection, and denial.

To whatever degree analytic techniques and Positivist ideol-
ogies are being mobilized as social defenses then, by implication,
group relations training and what it represents will find itself in an
increasingly unfriendly, hostile atmosphere. For teaching group dynamics in a management school environment, teachers will need to
understand these issues to appreciate the anxiety inevitably imported into their classes and, equally, to appreciate the political
forces that surround the presence of courses that call important
social defenses into question.

CONCLUSION

In this chapter I have explored some central issues I faced in
bridging two traditions of group relations training—the Tavistock
model freestanding conference and the SOM course on group dynamics—and have raised some resulting appreciations about the role
of group dynamics education in management schools. In going from
the freestanding approach to an approach embedded in an academic
environment, I was faced with adapting the technologies and frameworks to the demands, constraints, and opportunities inherent in a
new environment. While the need remains to provide the right balance of protection and vulnerability so students/members are safe
enough to learn about disturbing phenomena and yet are challenged
sufficiently to be meaningfully stretched, the conditions within
which this balance must be struck are substantially different. Finding the necessary balance is a function of the unique constellation
of factors, or codeterminants in systems terms, that comprise a given
system.

Chapter 11

Teaching Group Dynamics as a Visitor: Boundary Management from the Outside In

EDWARD B. KLEIN

INTRODUCTION

This chapter explores how larger organizational dynamics are reflected in a group process course (Rioch, 1977) and how obstacles initially encountered in teaching the course led to opportunities to enhance effective learning. What is unique about this contribution is that it is written from the perspective of a teacher who was an outsider. This chapter also illustrates how the group process changes as the outsider becomes more of an insider. It compares two experiences teaching group dynamics: first, when the author was outside, an unknown, somewhat controversial, dynamically oriented psychologist, and second, when he was a more inside, known, accepted, and popular professor.

Both courses were taught in 1985 when I was a visiting professor at the Yale School of Organization and Management (SOM). In each course I had a Christian female doctoral candidate in her thirties as a teaching assistant (TA). Having never taught an experiential course before, I found it an illuminating experience, which provided insights into how systems (Miller and Rice, 1969) issues—such as a dramatic strike at the university, staff and student "outsiderness," and class makeup by gender, age, and stage of adult development—affect the management of course boundaries and the subsequent group process.

THEORY

Systems

Systems theorists agree on the centrality of the boundary concept and that every group has boundaries that distinguish it from the environment. Moreover, the group leader's role involves boundary identification, maintenance, and, most important, regulation (Astrachan, 1970). There is a constant interaction between the group and the environment, which can be understood as a throughput process with *input, conversion,* and *output* phases. The group is affected by the environment (that is, society) in terms of values, norms, roles, and other social characteristics, including gender, age, and race.

Systems writers tend to agree that each group member plays a role influenced by the larger society, but can move toward individual authority, autonomy, and growth. There is also some agreement that groups go through various stages of development, often involving forming, dependency, authority relations, intimacy, mutuality, and independence (see Chapter 6). Current systems theory suggests that four levels of analysis are needed to account for group life: intrapersonal, interpersonal, group-as-a-whole (Singer et al., 1975) and intergroup (Rice, 1963; Alderfer, 1970). The fourth level is particularly important in understanding an interdependent process group embedded in a larger university culture.

Adult Development

Over the past decade, developmental research has shown that adults go through alternating transitional, change-oriented stages and stable, structure-building stages (Levinson et al., 1978). Recently there has been criticism of gender and racial bias in adult development research and dismissal of age-specific stage theory (Gilligan, 1982; Rosenfeld and Stark, 1987; Wade and Tavris, 1987). Nevertheless, adult development theory has been useful in understanding thirty-year-old women (Roberts and Newton, 1987), white women attorneys (Duff, 1980), black female administrators (Malone, 1981), black men (Murray, 1982; Herbert, 1985), career systems for men and women (Lebowitz, Farren, and Kaye, 1986), and phases of the mentoring relationship (Kram, 1983). Adult development theory has also illuminated clinical work in the first (Klein, 1980) and second

(Nemiroff and Colarusso, 1985) half of life. Stage theory should be helpful in further understanding the learning of women and men students at SOM, particularly since so many are in The Age Thirty Transition and I was in the Age Fifty Transition. Indeed, it is difficult to conceive of teaching about group processes without a developmental perspective, since the participants' stages of adult development should influence the dynamics in the course.

These theoretical frameworks underlie the analysis in this chapter. Specifically, it is divided into input, conversion, and output phases and elaborates central themes organized at four levels of analysis.

1. At an intrapersonal level, the age and stage of adult development of students and staff influence the group dynamics (Levinson et al., 1978). For instance, the broader the developmental range of students, the more varied should be the issues brought into the course; a class with a more restricted developmental range should be limited in its concerns.

2. At an interpersonal level, peer relations will be the focus of the group if the class is exclusively drawn from one unit of the university. That is, if all members are SOM students, they should have an intragroup or peer view, while a class drawn from throughout the university should have an intergroup perspective.

3. At a group level, the proportion of students by gender and race determines the group tone. This chapter investigates whether a relatively homogeneous class by gender is marked by paternalism and/or tokenism (Kanter, 1977), while a more heterogeneous class exhibits less stereotyping in group processes.

4. At an intergroup level, systems issues such as time of year, "outsiderness" of students and staff, and larger political concerns influence the saliency of issues. In educational institutions, termination processes predominate in the spring, when students are in a transitional stage about to start new jobs and/or careers. A very disruptive strike of female employees and the "outsiderness" of the staff contributed to unclear boundaries and fewer women in one course, which enhanced a macho tone, splitting, and scapegoating. In the second course, an insider staff, the absence of a strike, an equal number of men and women students, and a well-bounded and -managed enterprise led to a more moderate, worklike tone and male-female collaboration.

COURSE PREPARATION

Initial entry as a visiting professor began during my first fall semester at Yale, where I taught one of four sections of a "required" process course for first-year SOM students, entitled "Individual and Group Behavior" (IGB). Each section was large (forty-eight students); the course was held during an extremely trying clerical and technical workers' strike. My section, in part as a reflection of the disruptive strike and my psychological background and style, was viewed by students in a somewhat unfavorable light. In the second (spring) semester I was scheduled to teach group dynamics, but was unable to obtain what I was told was a requirement for effective teaching: a female Ph.D. candidate in organization behavior (OB) to function as a teaching assistant. After a full month of frustration, I was finally able, through A. K. Rice Institute contacts outside Yale, to locate a woman Ph.D. candidate in social psychology at another Ivy League university. She had been a member at the A. K. Rice Institute national conference two years before, where I had been the conference director.

The TA and I met at my office a week before class. We reintroduced ourselves, and I eagerly told her my impressions of SOM as a social system and some of the history of the group dynamics course. We then tentatively planned a course outline, based primarily on the existing SOM model.

GROUP DYNAMICS I

On the first day, I introduced the TA as a competent, accessible professional. It was noted that the course contained an equal number of lectures and experiential sessions, and that the experiential sessions involved a group-on-group design with both participation and observation periods. All process sessions were taped for students to use for observational reports and monthly papers. The goals were to generate an in-depth understanding of group process, including formation, authority relations, covert dynamics, intimacy, gender and race relations, termination, and the application of group behavior to large-scale organizations.

Students would have to use their experiences to learn in the course. Everyone had to attend all experiential groups *and* lectures, confidentiality was to be maintained, and the course was not a substitute for therapy. Applicants were told that it is very difficult to both experience and learn, and also that there would be one extended experiential Tavistock session with an outside consultant in the middle of the semester (a traditional part of the course). Finally, applicants were informed that grades are based on three papers that attempt to integrate experience and theory, *not* on classroom behavior, observation reports, or group performance.

Class Composition/Input

Only twenty-one students showed up at the first class session, in contrast to higher numbers in previous years in which the course had been taught. Twenty students signed up for the course by writing up a learning contract and explicitly accepting the class conditions, noted above. Three of the six women applicants came up to talk to staff at the end of the first class. The one dropout was a non-SOM woman, an important indication of things to come.

The resulting class had fifteen men and five women. Fifteen were SOM students. Unexpectedly, a quarter of the class were non-SOM students. These students were from five different Yale departments or schools. Four of the five non-SOM students were men; three of them were Jewish. The one non-SOM woman was a Jewish fifth-year Fellow in child psychiatry. There were four SOM women, three whites and one Asian American. The eleven SOM men included four Jews, two first-year students from my IGB section, one Asian American, and four white Christians, one of whom was an English citizen. The class members ranged in age from twenty-two to fifty, with most being in the Age Thirty Transition (Levinson et al., 1978).

My hypothesis is that the outsiderness and psychological background of the staff, along with the disruptive strike of female employees the previous semester, led to there being fewer women students in the class than expected (SOM was 50 percent female by design). The question for women applicants may have been one of safety in the course (staffed by outsiders), which was widely seen as encouraging psychological exposure. On the other hand, twelve of the fifteen male students shared some similarities with the Jewish visiting professor in terms of being non-SOM (four), Jewish (four), IGB-section members (two), or otherwise outsiders by nationality or race (two). Indeed, what marked this particular class was its great heterogeneity.

Class Process/Conversion

In the first few weeks the SOM administration asked us to change classrooms for the lectures, the bookstore couldn't locate the textbooks, and staff misrecorded one of the group tapes. There were two ten-person process groups, Group A with eight men and two women (one SOM and one non-SOM), and Group B with seven men and three SOM women. Both groups had the two staff members as co-consultants. In the process sessions, students either couldn't remember the teaching assistant's name, ignored her, or put her on a pedestal.

Women tended to be treated as tokens (Kanter, 1977), particularly in Group A with only two female students. The humor in this group reeked of a locker room; the men "called each other out." Group A had a number of particularly tall men who acted in a macho fashion. The SOM woman in Group A actively stimulated male competition and was competitive with a woman in Group B. Group A split their two women, with the SOM woman being viewed as hard and attractive, while the non-SOM woman psychiatrist was seen as soft and weak. Group B, with three women, had a less competitive tone, which was facilitated because the oldest male was a member.

Responding to the developing gender relations in the process groups in which women were being treated as tokens, we decided to make a change in the course design. Instead of using an outside black Tavistock consultant for an extended evening session (which would highlight race), we designed a modified four-hour session staffed internally in order to bound the course more firmly and make it a safer environment. (See Miller, 1959, for a discussion of system boundaries.) Each staff member worked alone with one group for an hour, then with the other group for another hour; this was followed by a review in the small groups and finally a longer plenary session with all students and staff members in a large circle. The purpose of the new design was to focus on reactions to, and comparisons between, male and female staff authority; we also wanted to explore gender relations among students and endorse the TA's role. In other words, we decided that, at this point, gender was more important than race. In the modified event, female authority would be endorsed and work would be kept within the group; we felt that an outsider would be disruptive to the ongoing educational/developmental process in a loosely bound group process course.

After the extended evening, the course boundaries became firmer, staff lectures were more personal (including one on the "Metaphors of Intimacy"), and student papers were less dependent on readings and more integrative. Formal student observations of group process were deeper and more creative (including a humorous script where members of Group A were given the identities of members of Group B). Class attendance was better and there was less lateness. This was possible because the course became a somewhat safer, bounded environment and there was greater awareness of interpersonal and group issues.

There was also a greater appreciation among class members of how the group reflected larger intergroup or systems dynamics. Examples included the concerns of non-SOM students being taken seriously, the repercussions of the strike, and, very powerfully, the influence of job interviews on group process. That is, some students came to class in their "interview outfits," usually dark blue suits. This raised issues such as who was being interviewed, who had multiple interviews, who already had offers with what companies, and who were the lonely outsiders who had not yet been interviewed.

The stresses of being adult students in a two-year, innovative management program were also addressed, particularly for those who had gone back to school after working for many years and in some cases having been very successful. As the course progressed, age became an important issue, especially near graduation. Most students, both SOM and non-SOM, would be graduating at the end of the term. Since most students were in transition from school to work and many in a developmental transition (the Age Thirty Transition), change was central. Therefore termination imagery was well developed. That is, students were ending one phase of life to go on to another. With job interviews going on, the large age range, and a fifty-year old student, termination was an especially rich issue. A critical review of the program and discussion of "Life after Yale" was facilitated by two application sessions focused on applying group process knowledge to large-scale organizations like the ones that would be employing most graduates. As the graduation boundary drew closer, transitions and change became more powerful issues.

Conclusions about Group Dynamics I

There are five major conclusions to be drawn from this experience. First, not having an outside consultant for an extended evening was a good decision in terms of firming up the class boundary, endorsing the TA's role, and focusing on gender issues both within and between staff members and students.

Second, having two nonwhites made racial discussions richer and raised group consciousness about race within SOM, Yale, and the larger society. The fact that neither was black may have made racial issues more acceptable; alternatively, as a male and female pair, they may have been skilled in presenting racial issues so that whites could listen, hear, and respond in a somewhat less defensive fashion.

Third, age and adult development issues were particularly salient in this course. Most students were in transition both occupationally and developmentally. The early locker-room humor of younger men, which was in part an immature expression of male bonding, moved to more mature expressions of caring toward the end of the semester. An especially moving discussion of aging was initiated by three students, one of the oldest women and the two oldest men. The discussion focused on both the dilemmas of being an older student and what the future held in store. In the last process group, the oldest male gave a candle to each person and lit them in a darkened circle. The males got blue candles, the females got pink, and the staff candles were larger. Giving out the different-sized and -colored candles can be seen as calling our attention to larger societal realities as the process part of the course ended.

Fourth, application work was excellent, since most students were actually graduating and life after school was a particularly pressing issue. Students were very active during the two application sessions and made lots of suggestions for topics. There was little denial of termination. We worked well together under the reality of decreasing time.

Fifth, there was scapegoating of the most "outside" student, even though the use of splitting and scapegoating as defensive maneuvers was explicitly discussed in lectures and interpreted in the process groups. As staff members became better known and accepted and course boundaries were experienced as firmer, students felt they could depend on us. Since everyone has mixed feelings toward authorities they depend on, the negative affect toward staff was projected onto a safer target—a student. In retrospect, the choice of the final target was not accidental. The target was the most "outside" person, the *only* Jewish woman and a Psychiatric Fellow, and therefore a "logical" role occupant. That is, she was most like me by religion, profession, and "outsiderness." In any case, we all painfully learned how and why splitting of affect and scapegoating occurs.

Postscript/Output

At the end of the semester, students fill out course evaluations. The student ratings and comments for Group Dynamics were overwhelmingly positive. On a scale of 1 to 7, the overall rating was 6.9. All of the students who handed in evaluations viewed the course in a positive fashion, with comments varying from "excellent", to the "best at SOM," to "one of the most profound learning experiences of my life." The major criticisms had to do with a lack of integration between the lectures and the process groups. Some students found the course so intense that they recommended it be held in the evening, since it would be difficult to attend another class after Group Dynamics. Overall, it was an extremely well received course.

TRANSITION

The dean asked me to teach the course again in the fall during my sabbatical year. I agreed only after assurances that a large stipend would be provided so that a competent teaching assistant could be employed. In addition, the same office, phone number, and stable secretarial support would be provided through the end of the academic year, five months *after* the course ended, so I could continue my ongoing research activities. I felt these were reasonable proposals, and all were eventually agreed to by the administration. These concessions suggest that I was now more of an insider.

This time an experienced woman Ph.D. candidate in organizational behavior who had previously been a TA in group dynamics volunteered to work in the course two months *before* it was to start. She and I revised the course overview, updated the readings, and included lectures addressing her interests in nonverbal behavior, the observational process, and organizational cultures. Indeed, the two of us functioned in a much more equal fashion than the TA and I had in the previous semester. The first group dynamics course had gotten very good press, and had been a major topic of informal discussion, so we announced a limit of twenty-four students.

GROUP DYNAMICS II

On the first day of class we were overwhelmed by fifty eager and often angry students. Students knew that there were limited openings, so they went to the dean to pressure him to get staff members to enlarge the class size. When the dean called asking me to take thirty-two students, I refused. A half-hour later he called again and asked me to reconsider. I finally agreed to take twenty-eight students, after some consultation. Taking four more students than originally announced led to subsequent questions about student legitimacy and faculty collusion with the administration.

Class Composition/Input

The fifty applicants seemed very homogeneous; all were from SOM. We picked out twenty-eight students, fourteen men and fourteen women. To create some diversity, we selected the one nonwhite woman, a New Zealand male, a Canadian male, a white American who had lived in Africa for many years, the one first-year student, a female lawyer, and a man who was in the military. The class included eleven Jews (six men and five women). The age range was twenty-five to forty-one years, with many students being in the Age Thirty Transition. Two process groups (A and B), each with fourteen students (seven men and seven women), were formed.

The presence of an inside woman TA who was a known Yale OB Ph.D. candidate, the success of the course the previous semester, and the fading memory of the strike enhanced the "insiderness" of the staff and contributed to the seminar being viewed as a well-bounded, safe enterprise. There was a much higher percentage of women applicants, more in keeping with the larger student population. Most of the students felt they were lucky, since twice as many applied as were accepted, although some may have wondered if they were one of the four "extras" admitted at the last minute.

This time we announced an extra, long evening later in the term, but not an outsider-staffed Tavistock event. The other major change was that I was out of town for the first lecture given by the TA, on "The Creation of a Group Culture." In the previous term, with so few students, an outside TA, unclear course boundaries, and my first-time exposure to the course, I wouldn't have considered being away. With an experienced TA and tighter class boundaries, it was possible to miss a lecture she was scheduled to give anyway.

As anticipated, it went well. As a reflection of the greater safety in the course environment for women, it should be noted that the TA, in preparation for her solo lecture, went jogging alone right before class in one of the least safe areas in New Haven! This was her "macho" way of showing she was strong and could survive as a woman in authority.

Class Process/Conversion

From the first of the five scheduled student observation reports on the group process, gender dynamics were highlighted in terms of female hostility toward males, male guilt, the roles men and women played in the A and B groups, and men's and women's relations to the staff. Early on, the TA's centrality, beauty, and competence were highlighted, a process that stirred strong reactions within the membership, resulting in a man's making a particularly offensive sexual remark. After this one outburst, somewhat reminiscent of the previous semester, the discussion of gender relations became more rational. The second night of observations included women indirectly attacking women by withholding or lack of support. By the third set of observations, the issue of race finally was raised by the one nonwhite student. But other observations by women about religion, social class background, marital status, dating, Ivy versus non-Ivy undergraduate college attendance, and physical size captured the class's attention.

The fourth observation night included an analysis of Group A women as never challenging the TA, the men as a bunch of macho "cowboys," and fighting across gender. Group B was characterized as having nonsupportive women and sensitive, bonded men, and as fighting within gender. Myths were explored, including the "perfect man," women's unity, unisexuality, and men as either macho or sensitive wimps. The fifth and last observation focused on termination, the death of one student's father, the passing of wine and candles, the TA's authority, rebirth, course evaluation, and fantasy versus reality. It was a rich evening.

The last two sessions were on application. Men asked for specific skills, such as how to point out strange behavior in groups without rocking the boat, how to play different roles in different groups, how group dynamics affect career choices, how to use groups for personal growth, how to work with gender relations in the workplace, and how to generate rules for effectively functioning groups.

Women were more concerned with how to *tactfully* point out group phenomena, how to bring gender dynamics to the attention of men in a work situation, how to bring out differences in a constructive manner, how to work with attraction, what to do with men who discount you (or exhibit power), for example, by looking at your breasts throughout a meeting, and how to find resources to continue the learning process begun in the course. Even at the end, the gender "issue" was carried more by women than men, as demonstrated by women's greater focus on gender in the application requests and sessions.

Postscript/Output

After the semester ended, three women handed in creative poems or songs about the course that they had written and/or performed in public. These postcourse events suggest that women were more engaged by the class than were the men students. This outcome makes sense, since the course was a firmly bound, safe environment in which gender issues were discussed; these women wanted to thank us and let the larger community know about it. These events again emphasized the staff's status as safe insiders.

Conclusions about Group Dynamics II

The second group dynamics course reflected a major concern of many students at SOM: gender. The course had an experienced TA, who spoke with her own voice. She helped revise the syllabus, gave excellent lectures, knew the culture, was on important institutional committees, identified with the school, and was a strong role model for women graduate students. Women students were clearly not tokens in the process groups in this course. Women spoke up, displayed work leadership on the ambiguous task of understanding group process, and often seemed more comfortable working on the task than men students did. Men appeared to be struggling to learn, feeling guilty, or fighting by being macho. With few demographic differences by race, age, discipline, or "outsiderness" among students, only interpersonal dynamics and gender discussions captured the group's attention. In part, because of group size (fourteen students—seven men and seven women—in each group), it was easier to hide behind gender as "the issue." Women students did not get picked on by men students; rather, some men were attacked for being macho, "military," or insensitive.

COMPARISON OF THE TWO COURSES

In the first, smaller group dynamics class, everyone was more exposed and it was harder to "pass" (in a university culture that promoted assimilation on the dimensions of ethnicity, religion, social class, gender, and race). The second class was larger, and so students could hide out. Competition among women was denied or minimized. Homosexuality was a secret in the school's culture, particularly since major corporations interviewed in the building and one could guess their attitudes toward homosexuality. However, with safe boundaries, homosexuality could be privately acknowledged but *not* publicly discussed in the groups in the second course. On the other hand, in the first course, with permeable boundaries and so many men, it was not safe to discuss different life-styles publicly *or* privately.

The TA in the first group dynamics course was married and lived forty-five minutes away; we tended to have dinner after classes, particularly the evenings of the group sessions, which called for a lot of review work. Students discovered where we ate and, toward the end of the course, pairs would show up in the restaurant. This gave the evening a family feeling, with the younger generation watching the elders dining. On the other hand, the TA in the second course was single, and we tended to confine our work to the office. I also had more of a mentoring relationship to the first than the second TA. The more personal staff relationships no doubt contributed to the intimite, incestuous, loosely bound quality of the first course, as the formal relationship probably contributed to the greater sense of equal participation by women students in the more tightly bound second course.

In sum, the heterogeneous makeup of the first course by age, stage of adult development, and "outsiderness" influenced the group dynamics of the class. With a broader developmental and social range, the class displayed an exciting variety of topic selection, greater emotion, and depth of discussion. There was in general less ageism, racial tokenism, or dismissal of non-SOM students. The concerns in the larger Yale community were taken seriously, no doubt because of the recently ended strike. The discussions of termination were much richer in the spring seminar, when students were actually in a transitional stage, about to graduate and start new jobs, occupations, and/or careers. The time of the year also enhanced adult developmental issues, since all the students were in a transition period, which stimulates appraisal or reappraisal of one's life and direction.

Dropping the outsider-consulted Tavistock evening helped to form a tighter boundary around the course and highlighted the woman TA's authority. Dividing the responsibility for class presentations, office hours, and grading, and encouraging staff openness about developmental issues, aging, narcissism, careers, money, and values underscored the role of the TA. But, realistically, the TA was seen as less of an equal. Also, the initially permeable course boundary, the small class size, few women, tokenism of women, the locker-room mentality (with its male intimacy and insensitivity toward women) all contributed to the scapegoating of the most "outside" student, who received deflected aggression meant for me.

The homogeneous nature of the second class, the popularity of the course, the acceptance of the professor, and the "insiderness" of the TA all led to an exclusive focus on peer relations and within-school dynamics. There was less paternalism and/or tokenism on the staff or between men and women students. There was a greater balance of the masculine and feminine and more female leadership in the fall course. There was no scapegoating of women students, but there was a minimizing of social and racial issues. One could argue that the second class would have been richer with an outside, black Tavistock consultant for one night, as it might have heightened racial awareness and gotten the class out of its singular focus on gender, the SOM issue. But, with no black students it seemed inappropriate.

The second class clearly explored gender relations at a greater depth than the first course. The first class was more exciting, exposed, and challenging. The second course was popular, larger, marked by psychosexual politics and greater rationality, soft in tone, and monotonous; there were unexplored hidden agendas. The rational tone and secrets in the class may have also reflected staff collusion with the system to increase class size. Hiding out may have been a response to unstated questions about staff integrity. Each course was good in its own way, the first for individual, developmental, racial, and social-systems issues, and the second for gender group identification and male-female work relations.

ACKNOWLEDGMENTS

I would like to thank Suzanne Fenwick and Marion McCollom, the teaching assistants, who contributed so much to the course, Claudia Fleming for her editorial suggestions, and Lorna Volk for her typing.

David Berg very generously shared the course materials, history, and his insights about teaching group dynamics at SOM.

EXPLORING THE EXPERIENCE OF CONSULTING TO GROUPS

Chapter 12

Staff Authority and Leadership in Experiential Groups

CLAYTON P. ALDERFER

INTRODUCTION

What does it mean to have authority and to exercise leadership in the conduct of experiential group dynamics learning events? For the purpose of this chapter, authority means the legitimate right to do work. Leadership, in turn, is doing the work called for by the staff in order to teach experiential group dynamics effectively. The purpose of this chapter is to provide my perspective on the question of authority and leadership as it has evolved from more than twenty years of experience in doing the work and is influenced by the perspective of embedded intergroup relations theory (Alderfer, 1986).

The chapter begins with an analysis of the capacities and preparation required of individuals who wish to lead experiential groups. Included are both emotional and intellectual capabilities. The second section examines what it means to accept a position of leadership in an experiential learning activity. Here the central issues are what individuals must be prepared to experience internally as they do the work, and what they must be prepared to do externally in order to act in accord with the demands of the leadership tasks. The third section analyzes staff leadership as a constellation of people acting interdependently. The central question is how to deal with the close connection between intragroup and intergroup dynamics of the staff as a group. Finally, the fourth section explicates the processes by which characteristic roles and styles emerge for staff members. Explanatory mechanisms encompass several levels of analysis including individual staff people, the staff and participants as groups, and the suprasystem in which the learning events are embedded.

CAPACITIES AND PREPARATION OF INDIVIDUAL STAFF MEMBERS

The first question about the selection of individuals for leadership roles concerns their capacities and preparation. What kinds of people with which kinds of preparation should take on the roles of leading experiential groups? The work of learning from experiential groups involves finding a favorable balance between emotional experience and intellectual understanding. Individuals who lead experiential groups should be selected because they show this kind of symmetry and have the potential for additional development.

Emotional Capabilities

The role of staff members in experiential events, when well executed, inevitably takes learners to emotional locations to which many have previously avoided going. In most instances, it helps if the staff member has been there before: that is, if staff members have had something like the personal experience that participants are about to have. To the degree to which staff members have had similar experiences, they are better equipped to anticipate what participants will encounter. To the extent to which staff members have effectively worked through and integrated the experience into their own senses of themselves, they will be able to maintain a satisfactory relationship to the phenomena and the participants, as members attempt to learn and to resist learning.

Staff members, like participants, search for a balance of approach and avoidance motives. They want neither to push participants faster and farther than they are prepared to go, nor to prevent people from taking steps they want to take and are prepared to handle. To be ready to work with the emotional dynamics of experiential groups, staff need to have *the capacity to accept and to engage a wide range of emotions in themselves and in others.* This capacity grows out of naturally occurring life events and becomes available for professional work through education and supervision (Erikson, 1975).

People who have been shielded by others from difficult life

events are not prepared for leadership roles in experiential group activities. Individuals who are unable to separate themselves and to maintain a sense of their own identities are also not prepared. Excessive use of defenses rooted in denial impedes learning. Lack of adequate ego boundaries prevents reflection. Staff members need to have a sense of both their emotional strength and their emotional vulnerability. Without a sense of his or her own vulnerability, a staff member will lack adequate empathy for participants—individually and collectively—when they are about to be overtaxed by staff interventions, when they are receiving undue pressure from group members, or when they are about to overextend themselves. Without a sense of his or her own emotional strength, a staff member will be predisposed to overlook or to flee from learning opportunities from which participants may benefit with minimal risk of harm.

The capacity to appreciate one's own strength and emotional vulnerability can be enlarged by serving as a participant in experiential learning events, by completing a course of psychotherapy or psychoanalysis, and by receiving competent supervision as a junior staff member while conducting experiential learning events. Perhaps it should go without saying that one does not serve as a staff member without first having been a participant, but it does occur. A staff member's ability to anticipate and to empathize with what participants experience is severely limited if he or she has not had a comparable learning experience.

A staff member's capacity to respond appropriately to unanticipated events depends importantly on her or his self-awareness. It is a demanding requirement, indeed, to ask of all fully qualified practitioners that they have had extensive psychotherapy or a personal analysis. I had a brief period of Freudian psychotherapy in my mid twenties and completed a four-year Jungian analysis between ages forty and forty-four. I believe that both of these experiences (and particularly the analysis) contributed importantly to my capacities as a staff member. The practitioners whose work I most respect often turn out to have had comparable experiences.

The effect of competent supervision for the junior person is to assist the new professional with integrating herself or himself into the role of staff member. (See Chapters 14 and 15.) Being a junior staff member locates one on the boundary between participants and the senior staff. From this vantage point, the junior person endures the hazards of both roles and some of the benefits. It is a most difficult role, and its value turns very much on the relationship that evolves between junior and senior staff members.

To the extent that the relationship serves the needs of both, involves the proper balance between acceptance and struggle, and adds to the range of receptivity and interpretation for the experience, the pair will serve participants more fully than either member alone. However, the effect on the group could be more regressive than progressive if the relationship between them is not adequate for the work to be done.

Intellectual Abilities

Experiential learning involves intellectual as well as emotional understanding. As events unfold, staff members need a basis in theory to understand and to monitor what is occurring. They need to be prepared to intervene during the unfolding activities, so that participants can examine the patterns of behavior and feelings that emerge from the learning situation. Staff members also need a way of thinking about and intervening to prevent damage to participants. They need to be able to see what is happening that is important to learning, to frame what is occurring within a body of explanatory propositions or theory, and to determine whether commenting is likely to aid learning or prevent damage more than remaining silent. If the decision is to speak, the comment needs to be formulated in a way that is likely to assist participants in their learning. To meet the requirements of the lecture portion of the course, staff members also need to be able to present the relevant theoretical material in a sound and coherent fashion. In sum, to be prepared intellectually to lead experiential groups, staff members need to have *the capacity to conceptualize what is occurring during experiential activities and to make comments that prevent damage and assist member learning.* This capacity grows out of staff members' exposure to and mastery of the relevant theory and empirical literature on experiential group dynamics.

There is a close connection between the emotional and the intellectual capabilities required of experiential group dynamics staffs. Well-prepared staff members bring extensive intellectual preparation with them to the work of leading. They keep the intellectual dimensions of their professional activity alive and growing by reading, by participating in classes and workshops, by conducting their own research, and by making their own attempts at theoretical advances. These activities contribute to a sense of their being vital intellectually as well as emotionally.

The processes of using theory and teaching concepts in the context of experiential group work involve balancing a number of important tensions. Whenever one takes theory seriously, one must at the same time acknowledge that any theory is limited in its capacities to explain and predict. If one is seriously engaged in scientific work or accepts the notion of "scientist-practitioner" as part of one's professional identity, then one is regularly looking for or trying to develop better theories (Kaplan, 1964; Kuhn, 1963). This quest is pursued in at least two ways: by remaining attentive to the empirical limitations of whatever theories one uses and by searching for improved conceptual formulations. These intellectual activities—here identified as residing with the staff—are, in fact, directly comparable to what participants who wish to learn do by attending the experiential activities. One key difference on these matters between staff members and participants is that for participants, the quest for improved intellectual understanding may be associated only with their connection to a particular workshop, while for staff members, the pursuit of theoretical advances is synonymous with ongoing professional development. A second difference is that for participants, less understanding is expected in advance of events than for staff members.

An additional distinction in connection with the use of theory pertains to the relative balance between eclecticism and reference to a single strong theory. Individual staff members vary in their preferences on this matter. My own leans more in the strong theory direction than toward eclecticism. Regardless of one's own relative position, however, a central problem remains. The twin hazards are between achieving some sense of coherence in understanding the phenomena one is observing and keeping an open mind in order to discover anomalous findings. If one's mind is totally open (which it never is), no intellectual coherence is possible. If one's theory determines the meaning of all observations (which empiricists fear), then the process one is going through is more properly called indoctrination than education.

In my opinion, the most desirable condition is *both* a strong theory, which one holds with a spirit of tentativeness, *and* an attitude of receptivity toward receiving information from particular individuals and groups on their own (not the theory's) terms. The aim is to find oneself regularly having a conversation between data and theory and, particularly, to be attentive to events that disconfirm whatever one's preferred explanatory hypothesis may be. Sullivan (1954) argued for the practice of always having at least two hypotheses at any moment—an orientation quite in the spirit of this discussion. This attitude, which one might term "being receptive with theory," can be further strengthened by how one makes comments.

The staff member begins by listening receptively. Initially, he or she attempts to be as theory-free as possible. Events occur, and the staff member begins to see a meaningful emotional and behavioral pattern. Upon "seeing" the pattern, the staff member should recognize that her or his theory or favorite empirical generalizations have been evoked by what is occurring. This does not necessarily mean one has decided to speak—only that one is making coherent meaning out of what is happening. Eventually, however, one will be inclined to speak. Formulation of the words can then be aimed both to show the connection between concrete events and theoretical position and to encourage participants to conduct additional inquiry, rather than to assume they have received the ultimate interpretation. In this way, staff members show outwardly to participants the conversation between data and theory that has been previously going on inwardly as part of their emotional and intellectual experience. Steps by which junior staff members develop increasing capacity to act in this manner have been delineated by Bradford (1980), and Berg and Smith (Chapter 5).

This formulation defining the joint emotional and intellectual capabilities required to be an effective experiential group leader state what is necessary for individual staff members to prevent harm and to promote sophisticated levels of learning from experiential group events. It seems that some individuals have these capacities to a remarkable degree, and others—including many thought to be highly intelligent by other standards—do not. One might say either that high conventional intelligence is a necessary but not a sufficient condition for doing this work well, or that leading experiential groups, in a manner similar to other kinds of clinical work with people, calls for a different order of intelligence.

In the spirit of the second alternative, one cannot omit noticing the similarity between what has been described here and what Howard Gardner (1983) has called the "personal intelligences." These he termed "intrapersonal intelligence" and "interpersonal intelligence." The first he defined as access to one's own feeling life and the second he called the ability to notice and make distinctions among other individuals and, in particular, their moods, temperaments, motivations, and intentions. In Gardner's way of thinking, the personal intelligences are of a different order from the sorts of verbal and mathematical abilities we most often think of as being measured by mental ability tests. High personal intelligences are essential for individuals who are to function effectively as experiential group leaders.

ACCEPTING THE LEADERSHIP POSITION

Having the capacities to serve as an effective experiential group leader is not identical with serving in the role effectively. In order to do the work competently, a person must also enter into the role and accept its demands. The colloquial language for this process is that one takes "what comes with the territory" realistically and with an attitude of receptivity. There are both internal and external components to accepting the leadership position. The internal portion refers to the leader's relationship to self-in-role, and the external portion pertains to the leader's relationship to the system in which the experiential educational subsystem is embedded.

THE PERSONAL EXPERIENCE OF HAVING AUTHORITY

Roles that involve someone being in charge of others share common properties. They establish a hierarchy in which some people are above others. The people in the lower position are to some degree dependent on those in charge. Those in charge are to some degree responsible for the welfare of those who depend upon them. The dependency relationship, however, does not end by recognizing how those in the down position rely on those in the up position. In fact, those in the dominant role also depend on those in the subordinate role. Leaders cannot be said to lead if followers do not follow; teachers cannot be said to teach if students do not learn. The result is that there is a mutual *dependency* between leaders and led—a dependency that implies that the two roles need each other in a most fundamental sense. Neither could exist without the other. For the purposes of this analysis, it would be misleading to substitute the word *interdependency* to characterize the qualities of relationship that are relevant here. Interdependency implies that the ways in which each party relies on the other are roughly equivalent. That is decidedly not the case when the roles in question are hierarchical. People in the up position depend on those in the down position differently from the way that those in the down position depend on those in the up position.

Participants in experiential group learning events generally are adults who themselves have significant leadership roles. As a consequence, they have had practice with both sides of hierarchical roles: they know the experience of being in the up position and of being in the down position. These same statements, of course, apply equally to the staff. But during the experiential group learning event, structurally staff members are in the up position, and participants are in the down position.

Senior staff members, therefore, need to accept the part of being in the up position, as do staff members in apprenticeship roles. They need to be prepared for participants to treat them as the people in charge. When their behavior does not meet normal expectations of participants—as often it will not—they need to be prepared to receive various expressions of frustration. When participants react to them as if they were previous authority figures in their lives, staff members need to be prepared to interpret these responses in a manner that encourages learning. When participants attempt to subvert their authority, they need to be prepared to cope with the turbulence that they and the entire group will experience. In general, they need to retain and employ their authority in the service of learning while remaining cognizant of the potential hazards to themselves and participants in how they use their power.

While understanding that participant responses to staff are evoked primarily by the role differences between the two groups, staff members need also to be prepared to examine how their own needs, preferred styles, and relationships with other staff members influence their responses. They need to be aware of how their identity-group memberships, based on age, family, race, ethnicity, and gender, affect participant reactions to them and, in turn, their reactions to participants. They need to recognize how their own perceptual apparatus influences what they observe about participants and how they interpret the data they obtain. As human beings occupying significant roles in the learning process, staff members regularly need to be attentive to how the same processes they are observing and analyzing in others are influencing themselves.

The Requirement to Manage Boundaries

The practice of leadership in the staff role during experiential group learning involves a number of essential activities. The first establishes a secure setting separate from day-to-day activities, so that participants and staff can attend to learning tasks (Bradford, 1967; Rice, 1965). The second is that the group leader takes a relatively nondirective stance during experiential sessions as a means to facilitate learning. In addition, most laboratories or conferences combine experiential sessions with lectures, and thereby result in staff members' behaving somewhat like conventional teachers as well. Establishing a separate setting, taking a nondirective role, and conducting lectures all involve the management of boundaries.

Establishing a setting in which work can be done is a key part of the leadership role in any organization. In theoretical terms, the ideas and actions that establish the setting are creating a boundary that distinguishes the learning system from its environment (Alderfer, 1976; Miller and Rice, 1967). Without authorization, the setting cannot be established. Once the setting is established, negotiations between the learning system as an entity and the suprasystem as environment reflect the strength and permeability of the boundary and the degree of benevolence or malevolence of the environment. The individuals who take initiatives to establish the setting—and, once it is established, to maintain it—are the leaders. They have the vision; they set the direction; they maintain the relationships that permit work to continue. Faced with challenges from the environment or threats from within, they respond; and, when the time comes, they terminate the undertaking. In these ways, the authority and leadership of the staff in experiential settings are similar to other organizations. The nature of the suprasystem, and therefore the content and processes of the negotiations, vary depending on whether the suprasystem is academic or a cultural island.

Formation of the separate setting is necessary for the nondirective stance of the staff to facilitate learning. The separate setting provides protection from many of the factors in our day-to-day existence that can impede learning. Staff members who act properly within their roles, for example, will neither reward nor punish participants for their behavior during learning events. This ingredient contrasts markedly with the norms of most other organizational environments, including schools, where people correctly anticipate that their actions are subject to more or less constant evaluation. The nondirective stance of the staff removes certain social defenses that in most conventional settings protect people from observing the consequences of their own and others' behavior and from dealing with those consequences. As a result, in the experiential learning setting, behavior, feelings, fantasies, and ideas that are otherwise invisible become observable.

During the experiential events, staff members offer comments aimed toward assisting learners to understand more fully what they are learning to see. These statements might be said to punctuate the free flow of events within experiential sessions in order to assist learning. Decisions by staff members about what to say and when to say it in experiential sessions, therefore, are decisions about how to form boundaries around events as they occur in the sessions.

Directly analogous to the decisions about comments within experiential sessions are choices about the location and content of lectures among sessions. Lectures provide the staff with the means to talk at greater length and to develop extended lines of reasoning about what occurs in experiential sessions. They also place participants in a more passive relationship to the staff, in which the tasks of the students are to take in, to examine, and to test the concepts presented in the lectures. The style of the lectures may vary in terms of how much speakers invite participants to question, to provide examples, or to disagree. Regardless of style, however, lectures are settings in which the speaker traditionally is in charge, and therefore they alter the behavioral pattern between staff and participants in comparison to experiential sessions. Choices about where to place lectures in the flow of events (how to punctuate the larger units of experience) and how to conduct the lectures (what to let in and what to keep out) are boundary-management activities by the staff.

Furthermore, when the experiential learning event is a course within a university and when the course involves paper writing (see Chapter 9), then the assignment of paper topics and the timing of the assignments is yet another occasion for boundary management by staff. The framing of topics establishes the cognitive boundaries within which the work is to be done, and the setting of due dates for when the work must be completed locates temporal boundaries by which students must abide or face sanctions. Paper writing thus is an extension of the same boundary-management function as staff comments and lectures. In addition, paper writing calls upon students to take a stand about what they believe intellectually. It therefore both requires and authorizes a kind of speaking not usually found in cultural-island settings. Framed in this manner, paper writing attempts to regulate the exchange among concrete experience, reflective observation, and abstract conceptualization (Kolb, 1964).

LEADERSHIP AS A CONSTELLATION

Staff members of experiential learning events rarely serve only as individuals. The need for at least two staff members in an experiential group event has several origins. An experiential group learning event is a highly complex undertaking. The social and psychological forces that come to play on people who serve in leadership roles are substantial and, on average, probably exceed what a single person can adequately manage, regardless of her or his ability and preparation. Additional staff members provide alternative perceptions of what occurs and the always valuable opportunity to discuss one's own experience and understanding with another person who is professionally prepared for the work.

Furthermore, from the perspective of embedded intergroup relations theory, the lone staff member will not be experienced only as an individual by participants (Alderfer, 1986). He or she will represent a group whose level in the hierarchy during the learning events is above participants and, quite likely, also a group whose educational technology is differentiated from other groups known to participants. Staff members thus represent more than one organization group to participants even if they work alone. In addition, staff members inevitably bring their identity group memberships (gender, race, ethnicity, age, and family) to the experiential events. Which groups and intergroup relationships will be salient will depend on the identity group composition of the participants (Alderfer, 1986). To take just one example, a white male forty-eight-year-old staff member will be experienced quite differently by a group of participants of similar race, gender, and age composition from the same staff member by a group of participants evenly composed of black and white men and women of varying ages.

The group and intergroup relationships between staff members and participants, therefore, cannot be reduced to the personal characteristics and interpersonal styles of the individuals. In composing a staff, one need not be passive with respect to these factors. To the extent possible, a staff group can be actively composed to reflect diverse identity groups. It is especially desirable for the composition of the staff group to reflect the same dimensions of diversity as those of the participant group.

The quest for diversity among staff members, from my point of view, necessarily combines with two other conditions in forming a leadership constellation. The first is that each individual possesses the emotional and intellectual capacities defined in the preceding section. The second is that the staff group as a whole agrees in a straightforward and mutually respectful fashion to deal with their own interpersonal and intergroup dynamics—which inevitably involve both organization group and identity group differences. When all three of these conditions—individual capacity, diverse composition, and an enacted commitment to relationship development among staff members—are present, then the probabilities of preventing harm and of achieving a very sophisticated level of learning among participants are very high indeed.

The underlying theoretical rationale for staff members' observing and reflecting on their own behavior, feelings, and thoughts is the construct of parallel processes (Alderfer, 1976, 1986). Accordingly, staff members may either bring to a group session a state of mind or pattern of behavior that they project onto the group without awareness and thereby inappropriately influence the group process, or they may unwittingly absorb the affective condition of the group and thereafter act in a manner that collusively maintains a pattern of blindness to underlying group forces. When staff members belong to the same larger system as students, it is inevitable that periodically they will bring effects (and affects) from that system into the group. Similarly, as long as staff members relate to the group as receptive human beings, they will pick up the emotional condition of the group, which in turn will affect their behavior. The objective of understanding and utilizing parallel processes is not to prevent these effects. Rather, it is to accept them as part of the work, first by observing them as they occur and then by interpreting their meaning. In this way, the operation of parallel processes can be employed to serve rather than to impede learning.

The chief tool of the staff in working with parallel processes is to provide adequate time to discuss with one another their own experiences that pertain or might pertain to the course. In advance of the group sessions, the staff meets to discuss what events in the larger system might show up in the group. This sort of discussion allows staff members to show one another the sorts of system issues that might be influencing them, and it also sharpens their capacity to listen to what the students might be carrying. Breaks between group sessions provide an opportunity for staff members to confer again with one another about what they are experiencing in the group sessions. Then, at the close of the group session, there can be a discussion period to reflect upon the entire course of events for the session and to identify the topics that might be most fruitfully explored in the upcoming lecture session.

An example of parallel processes in the staff group from a section involves the relationship between faculty person and teaching assistant during the early portion of the course. The empirical signs of the phenomena might be the doctoral student's experiencing the faculty member as distant and cold and as being unwilling to share her or his more extensive experience about how to work effectively with the group. The faculty member, on the other hand, might experience the assistant as immobilized and as acting more like a class member than as a staff member. The faculty member may feel an urge to remind the student that he or she is being paid to be a staff member and to inquire about what sorts of conversations the assistant is having with class members outside the course. This set of complementary experiences means that both faculty member and teaching assistant will experience tension in their relationship, rooted in their organizational group memberships as faculty member and doctoral student. If both are able to discuss this experience with each other, the odds are quite high that they will be able to understand its origins and discuss the group forces with the students that are affecting all of them. If, however, the staff members withdraw from the tensions or resort to blaming one another, then it is likely that a similar pattern will be observed in the class.

In order for these sorts of discussions to occur, staff members as individuals must be able to accept themselves as people subject to the forces, and the relationship among staff members must include the commitment and competence necessary to discuss such anxiety-provoking topics in a direct and forthright manner. These are not easy conditions to satisfy. A relatively small proportion of individuals and groups who do experiential group work meet them.

The dynamics of parallel processes touch people at both the individual and group levels of analysis. Particular people who become receptacles for certain kinds of disturbing emotions within a group usually bring individually based predispositions or valences toward occupying a certain role within groups (Bion, 1961; Ringwald, 1974; Gibbard, 1974). Then, as naturally occurring group forces come into play, the more predisposed people are more likely than the less predisposed individuals to pick them up (Lieberman, Yalom, and Miles, 1973).

But individual predispositions alone account for only a portion of the reasons why in groups certain roles emerge for particular people. Also important are a variety of group-level forces that affect the emergent role structure. The more a person's identity groups are represented among the staff group, for example, the less likely the person is to be experienced as deviant and therefore vulnerable to scapegoating. That proposition holds, providing that the staff group dynamics are whole, and the staff as a group is not pushing out particular members. However, to the degree that staff members are unable to address their interpersonal and group dynamics and the group develops a propensity to locate negative affect in particular members, this same process is likely to appear among members (Kaplan, Obert, and Van Buskirk, 1980; Kaplan, 1982, 1983).

In a similar manner, group-level processes leading to the development of particular roles for specific members may emerge from within the participant group. This is especially likely when members have preexisting relationships with one another as a result of having participated together in common or related educational programs for some time prior to entering the course. We have observed organization group effects based on which program students belong to, which year in the program they are serving, and what their informal standing among peers turns out to be. We have also observed identity group effects based on family, gender, age, ethnicity, and race. To the degree that the staff group has the requisite diversity within its boundaries, the parallel individuals will pick up these effects from the members. To the degree that the staff group is able to observe and to discuss these effects among themselves, they will be able to prevent them from cumulating to create casualty dynamics and to convert them into significant learning opportunities.

The term *leadership constellation,* as used here, was derived from the concept of executive role constallation as developed by Hodgson, Levinson, and Zaleznik (1965). Their use of the term was employed in the study of a senior executive group and referred primarily to the integration of complementary personalities and roles among three men who were the top executive group in a highly regarded mental hospital. In terms of level of analysis, their use of the term *constellation* focused primarily on individuals and their interpersonal relationships. Because two of the three men had particular functional responsibilities and the third was head of the entire hospital, one might say their concept of constellation also tacitly dealt with organization groups as well. But little was said about the identity group dynamics of their constellation. In terms of explicit theory, their orientation toward the complementarity of roles did not include group and intergroup levels of analysis. The term *leadership constellation,* as used here, therefore, builds upon their formulation and adds attention to organization and identity group dynamics to their focus on personality and interpersonal relationships.

THE DYNAMICS OF STAFF AUTHORITY

People who serve as staff members in an experiential group dynamics course are subject to forces from a variety of directions that affect their feelings, thoughts, and behavior—as is any person who serves in a leadership capacity in a complex social system. Staff members contend with the dynamics of their own personalities, with the consequences of their place in the hierarchy among faculty members, with the effects of their membership in diverse gender, racial, ethnic, and age groups, and with the quality of relationships they establish with other staff members in the course.

As individuals, staff members need to be receptive to psychological information and to hold in mind more than one interpretation about possible meanings of that data. They need to accept the authority inherent in their roles and to exercise that authority competently and compassionately. Staff members need to be sensitive to and respectful of their own and others' needs to establish and maintain mutually rewarding relationships with others, but their relationship needs cannot be so strong that they systematically omit data that are relevant to the theories-in-use or prematurely close off alternative interpretations of the data that they retain. They need to be able to maintain a sense of their own psychological wholeness amid intense and complicated group pressures, and, amid such group dynamics, they need to be able to speak about their own unique perceptions without demeaning others. They need a high order of self-awareness, especially on matters that pertain to their own inclinations toward splitting and projection. They need to understand and accept the meaning that their own gender, racial, ethnic, age, and family memberships have for themselves and the likely impact that these group memberships have for others with whom they have significant relationships, including both the staff and participants. Aspiring to these qualities calls for continuing effort. It is enhanced or diminished by the behavior of others, and may be expanded or contracted as individuals move through life stages.

Leadership Style and Role

Leadership style thus is not simply derived from an individual's personality, but rather is the result of people meeting and contending with the variety of group forces in a given situation. One result of these forces is that staff members may behave in restricted ways. Each simplified role has underlying group dynamic reasons for being evoked, and each is more tempting—consciously or unconsciously—to some kinds of personalities than to others. Because the prototypical roles that emerge for experiential group leaders reflect the operation of both group and individual processes, they each represent a *part*, but only a part, of the leadership role potential.

Each represents one kind of solution to the variety of conflicting forces that become located in a leader. They are important to understand because they serve as partial equilibrium points among the dynamic forces characteristic of groups. They are important to work with because of their diagnostic value to staff members in their attempts to promote learning and prevent casualties. As the various roles are presented to staff members, the challenge is neither to reject nor to embrace any one on a permanent basis, but rather to accept what is given to be examined and to be worked with on a temporary basis in the service of the aims for which the group and course were created. The professional literature, however, suggests that there are tendencies among some in the field to attach themselves to a single orientation and to behave as if it were the optimal solution. This finding should be surprising only if one believes that professional work in this field somehow makes one immune to the phenomena one studies and attempts to change.

One style that may emerge for an experiential group leader is that of a *distant high priest or priestess*. Taking this orientation, the leader places herself or himself above and outside the group and behaves as if he or she has access to an arcane mystical knowledge. To assist the group in its task of learning, the leader makes pronouncements and sounds like an oracle. We see evidence of this style in the writings of Wilfred Bion (1961), Margaret Rioch (1971), and Pierre Turquet (1974). This manner of role-taking recognizes that the leader is not a member, does (or should) have special knowledge and training, and needs to maintain a different perspective on group happenings from that of members, in order to do the work. A major hazard of this form of role-taking is that it suggests to members (and, more dangerously, to the leader) that he or she is above being human—that the leader is capable of escaping from the group's dynamics. Consciously or unconsciously, such leaders may treat the role as a defense against their own feelings of confusion, inadequacy, or loneliness. In the name of giving interpretations, they may project their own feelings onto the group. They thereby contribute to members' difficulties in learning, which they may in turn interpret back to members in a somewhat punitive fashion, thus further impeding the solution of members' problems.

The high priest or priestess role tends to occur from group forces when the authority of the group leader is reasonably well established and when the person is relatively silent at the start of the group. When the leader is functioning well enough, he or she understands these group forces and in fact uses her or his knowledge and skill to assist members' learning. He or she is reasonably in touch with her or his tendencies to feel superior as a person and is not inclined to phrase interpretations in language or tone that is condescending. As a result, members are more able to discover their tendencies to project godlike images (and this god can be good and bad) onto the leader.

A second emergent role for the group leader is that of *emotionally engaging magician*. The group leader who demonstrates this role becomes a highly attractive figure to a significant proportion of participants and may stimulate a kind of surrender by members of ego functions to the staff. Participants report how "impressed" they are with the leader's special insights and vision. This leader seems to take a special interest in certain members of the group, to stimulate fantasies (and sometimes the actual behavior) of sexual encounters, and either consciously or unconsciously to relate quite personally to group members. One sees evidence of this style of role-taking in the writings of William Schutz (1967), Philip Slater (1966), and Richard Mann (1975). The term *charismatic* is frequently used to characterize such a style, and the manner of role-taking to a considerable degree accepts the unconscious quest for a messiah by group members. The leader participates by a willingness (or, worse, by a desire) to tell people what they are thinking or feeling and receives at least a temporary gratification by the adulation associated with members' turning their psychological lives over to her or him.

The emotionally engaged magician style does form relationships of significance with group members and with the group as a whole. As a result, change through these relationships is possible. Individuals may have personally important insights about themselves and their relationships with others. The group as a whole may develop unusually cohesive bonds through their relationship to the leader. It is also possible, however, that the leader may become identified with the group and its members, not just in relationship to them. Under these conditions, the leader is no longer working with the group and its individual members but rather is using the group for her or his own gratification. These are the conditions where the leader is most likely to participate in the creation of casualties. She or he projects parts of the self onto group members, rejects, and thereby encourages the group to reject, members who take on the unacceptable parts of her or his personality. The rejected members then become group casualties (Kaplan, 1982).

A third emergent role for the experiential group leader is that of *member*. A leader who takes on this role accedes to desires on the part of members to make her or him one of them. He or she may do this psychologically by elevating the members to a place of equal status to the leader or by pretending that he or she is no more than a member. In the first case, the leader is bringing the members into the staff group; in the second, he or she is moving the staff into the member group. Either case tends to erase the boundary between staff and members. Writers who have reflected this orientation are Gibb (1972) and Egan (1970). The leader as member emphasizes the humanity of all people—including the individuals who are experiential group leaders—and speaks forcefully for such human values as spontaneity, self-expression, democracy, and closeness.

The leader as member acts as a peer with members. This view is a counterforce to the distortions that arise when the experiential group leader is elevated to a psychological position that implies that he or she is either above or beyond group forces or the struggles of members. The experiential group leader is a human being and, however well trained and self-aware, does not escape her or his version of the forces that affect group members. But by taking on the role of staff member—whether acknowledged or not—the experiential group leader accepts a significant degree of responsibility for the conduct of the course as a whole and for the welfare of individual members. Staff members, one way or another, are paid for giving the course, and members pay to take it. As a result, the leader gives up certain freedoms that accrue to people who are members.

The leader who acts as a peer colludes with forces within the group that make members into scapegoats, because often those dynamics involve deflecting angry feelings from a powerful leader to a more vulnerable member (Kaplan, 1982). Because the leader who acts like a member is in part fleeing from the responsibilities of being a leader, it is unlikely that he or she will step into the leader's role to interpret scapegoating dynamics. Doing so would bring on the very forces that adopting the peer role is designed to avoid.

The fourth emergent role for the experiential group leader is that of *model* or exemplary member. Most teaching roles, in some way or other—both consciously and unconsciously—operate by asking learners to imitate or emulate what the instructor does. If the staff person does not invite members to do this, they do so nonetheless as a natural phenomenon. Sometimes they do so without conscious awareness; sometimes they do so competitively to challenge other members or the leader; and sometimes they do so mockingly to make light of the struggles involved with learning. Identification is one of the basic means by which human beings acquire competence (White, 1963). Among writers about experiential group leadership, Argyris (1962) and Golden (1972) have discussed the leader as model for members.

A leader who is able to create conditions that foster learning and who can make interpretations that enable members to understand might be behaving in ways that members would benefit by copying. But there are a variety of hazards associated with encouraging members to do so. When a leader, either implicitly or explicitly, encourages members to act as he or she does, one is led to questions about whether this process does not result mainly in narcissistic gratification for the leader.

Several elements in the situation argue against leaders *actively* encouraging members to emulate their behavior. First, the member is a different person from the leader, and the leader's professional commitment is to work with members as unique human beings, not to attempt to remake them after the leader's own image. Second, the leader has a different role from the member's, and, to the extent that the leader is carrying out her or his role in a sound manner, the behavior of the leader is appropriate for that role. It is possible but not highly likely that the same behavior is also appropriate for the member's role. To encourage a member to copy a leader's behavior, therefore, is to treat the member as a leader and thereby to confuse the boundary between staff and students. Third, it is also possible that by seeming to reward a member for acting like a member of the staff, a leader may contribute to scapegoating of that person, as group members frequently find it easier to express angry feelings toward one another than toward staff members. In fact, members are attentive to each other's tendencies to identify with the leader and to copy leader behavior. Often the leader need do nothing to call this phenomenon to members' attention, because they do the work themselves.

On the other hand, there are circumstances when the appropriate staff behavior is to comment on the tendency of some group members to criticize other group members whose behavior resembles actions of the staff. This sort of interpretation serves at least two kinds of functions: first, it provides members with an opportunity to increase their awareness of the copying behavior, and second, it disrupts the unconscious inclinations of members to scapegoat one another. When students seem reluctant to comment on the most obvious kind of emulation, then a staff member might call it to their attention. For example, "The group seems to be ignoring the facts that tonight Simon's dress is nearly identical to Clay's, that Simon arrived early and sat where Clay usually does, and that Simon has been speaking in a manner that closely resembles the staff. I wonder if this has anything to do with the anger the group has been expressing toward Simon."

The four staff-to-student roles presented here represent simultaneous solutions—that may be temporary or permanent—to two major classes of forces that confront the staff member. The first of these is *interpersonal* and pertains to how close versus how distant psychologically the staff member becomes to the students, and the second is based on *group* membership and pertains to whether the staff member psychologically joins staff or student groups. The emotionally engaged magician role and the staff as member role reflect the staff member's becoming relatively close to the students, while the staff member as priest or priestess and the staff member as model represent the staff member's staying relatively distant from the students. Staff members as priest or priestess and as magician place themselves into the staff group, while the staff as members and staff as models place themselves into the student group. Figure 1 summarizes how the interpersonal and group dimensions converge to form the four roles.

Figure 1. Emergent Roles for Staff Members in Experiential Groups

| | | Psychological Group Membership | |
		Staff	Student
	Far	Priest and Priestess	Model
Interpersonal Distance	Close	Magician	Member

Roles and Factors Shaping Them

As an experiential group moves through developmental phases, forces within the group change, and, as a consequence, the balance of pressures on the staff change as well. How the staff responds to these forces, in turn, influences how, and with what depth and degree of understanding, the group and the individual members experience the developmental phases. Learning about authority, influence, and power, for example, is limited if the staff psychologically acts as if they are members of the student group. Learning about intimacy is limited if the staff remains distant and cold in their relationship to members. My own orientation is to attempt to be responsive to the changing emotional climate of the group.

In my own experience, there is little doubt that I belong to the staff group. As time passes, I tend to become somewhat closer to the members. Usually this process is not linear but is characterized more accurately as a series of steps. The movement from an emphasis on authority and influence to intimacy may be associated with a member demonstrating what seems like real empathy toward the staff. After a group has spent considerable time discussing their perceptions and feelings about the staff, a group member may say something like "I've really become aware of how difficult it must be to listen open-mindedly to all the different and disturbing things that members have to say about the staff." If this sort of thing happens, I respond in a manner consistent with the feelings evoked in me by the empathic statement. The form might be something like "I am certainly aware of the kind and strength of feelings people have expressed about the staff, including me. I have feeling reactions myself. You might have noticed a change in the color of my face. Mainly, however, I view these sorts of experiences as an important part of what learning is about, and am appreciative of people's willingness to report their perceptions and emotions."

If I have correctly perceived the students' understanding, then the group as a whole becomes a warmer environment, and intimacy becomes a more central element in the group's work. However, responding more warmly to a changing group climate involves psychological risk on the part of the staff. Staff who are unable to take appropriate risks limit the risks that class members can take and therefore the learning that is potentially available for the group as a whole. Because of the hierarchical nature of the staff-to-member relationship, it is unlikely that students will be able to learn about topics that staff members themselves cannot tolerate experiencing. Consciously or unconsciously, staff members send signals that prohibit the necessary talk. Class members may then project their own concerns onto others, as in the dynamics of creating casualties discussed above, or they may simply inhibit the exploration and discussion necessary for learning to occur.

The challenge for staff members during periods of intense emotionality is to accept and contain the feelings, while working to allow the group as a whole and individual members to choose how much and in what ways they wish to explore what can be learned. Qualitatively different kinds of feelings become more prominent as a function of the developmental phase. Inevitably, individual staff members vary in their capacities to deal with particular classes of emotions as a function of their life experiences and self-understanding. Individuals who have experienced the death of a loved one and who have worked on the feelings of grief associated with the loss, for example, will be better prepared to respond appropriately to the feelings associated with the termination phase of an experiential group. Analogous statements apply to the emotions central to the other phases of group development.

Various members of a leadership constellation are likely to be affected differentially by the emotions associated with each developmental phase, depending on the composition of the constellation, the composition of the membership, and the predisposition of the individual staff members. Imagine a situation in which the senior staff member is a white male, the junior staff member is a black female, the participant group has one black female member, and the remaining members are evenly split between white men and white women. Under these circumstances, the pressure on both black women will be substantial. It will be most important for the two staff members to be able to discuss the racial dynamics between them and to have a coordinated strategy for how to comment on racial dynamics within the group as a whole. If it falls to the junior black staff member, for example, to carry the burden of commenting on the racial behavior of the white members, the effects on the black female member and on the black female staff member are likely to be most unfavorable. Such a pattern would set the stage for the white members of the group to locate concerns about race relations solely within the two black people. Were this to happen, it would tend to undermine the authority of the black staff member and to increase the vulnerability of the black member to casualty dynamics.

Gender dynamics within the staff group and within the member group are likely to vary with the developmental stage of the group. In a situation in which there is approximately an equal number of men and women among participants and the staff includes both men and women, the effects of struggles about influence within and between genders are likely to be complex. Within the staff group, there will be concerns about how gender is affecting the relative influence of the individuals. Often this takes the form of staff members' wondering whether the group is hearing their interventions or acting as if words from the staff members were not spoken. If the senior staff member is male and the surrounding institution is male-dominated, it is quite likely that the male voice will be received more easily as an authority than the female voice.

A junior female staff member should not be surprised to find male members inquiring (perhaps outside class) about her availability for social activities, and the senior male is likely to observe female members being especially solicitous of his attention. Again, it is most important that the staff members be able to talk frankly with one another about their observations and to determine together what is the best strategy for interpreting gender-related efforts by members to deal with the authority of the staff group. The aim of these conversations is to establish conditions so that these kinds of dynamics can be observed and discussed by the group as a whole, and the influence of women and men in both staff and participant groups becomes relatively balanced.

In sum, the roles of individual staff members, the relationships among staff members, and the dynamics between the staff and participants vary by the developmental stage of the group, the personal readiness of individual staff members and the staff group as a whole to address the issues brought on by each stage of the group, the organization and the identity-group diversity of the staff and participants, and the comparable dynamics of the institution surrounding the group dynamics course. Being prepared to observe, understand, and intervene with this order of complexity is most challenging.

CONCLUSION

The requirements for people who accept staff roles for experiential group dynamics learning events are substantial. They call for extensively developed emotional and intellectual capabilities, for the willingness to accept and to carry out leadership tasks, for the readiness to work as part of a leadership constellation, and for the flexibility to adapt to changing circumstances while attempting to remain whole as human beings and realistically responsive to the events that occur. In trying to meet these demands, staff members can find many opportunities to continue learning. The order of understanding about human systems available from this work, in my opinion, is unmatched by any other known method and theory.

If there is a central axiom to approaching the work as it has been conceptualized here, it would be that no one escapes the interpersonal and group dynamic forces that experiential methods were invented to understand. Certainly staff members during experiential events influence and are influenced by the events they interpret. I believe that our ability to serve effectively in these roles is directly related to our willingness to accept and address our relationship to these forces.

Chapter 13

On Using the Self as Instrument: Lessons from a Facilitator's Experience

KENWYN K. SMITH

A central theme in the tradition of group dynamics explored in this book is the facilitator's capacity to use the *self* as an instrument. In this chapter I am moving this topic from the background role it has in the writings of many colleagues and making it center stage, placing it in the spotlight so we can examine what is added to members' learning about group dynamics *when the facilitator learns how to use the self as an instrument.* While all group members can benefit from developing this skill, here I am focusing on the facilitator's learning.

Using the self as an instrument requires a special commitment to introspection and personal scrutiny. It demands that the facilitator be intensely *connected* to the experiences of the group and simultaneously *separated* from them, a skill that provides the foundation of a very difficult, but necessary, task: *comprehending the whole of interaction patterns that one is a part of.* It requires sitting on the boundary between being "a part of" the group and being "apart from" the group.

The idea of using the self as an instrument has a long history in psychology, as it is the centerpiece of the psychotherapeutic concept of transference and countertransference. These are terms used to describe the unconscious tendencies of both client and therapist to relate to each other on the basis of a prior relationship, each transferring to the other the attributes of a previous significant individual with whom he or she is being identified (Lidz, 1968). For a patient, this usually involves treating the therapist as a substitute for someone with whom there are deep, long-standing, unresolved conflicts, typically a parent. For the therapist, the countertransference would involve, then, adopting a parental perspective toward that patient and acting in ways similar to parental relationships in the therapist's own life.

Three processes are required to know about transference and countertransference. The therapist must (1) reflect on his or her own emotions as they are evoked by the actions of the patient in the psychotherapeutic encounter (Erikson, 1964), (2) scrutinize his or her thoughts, constantly analyzing the possible meanings associated with the patient's behaviors, formulating hypotheses about the patient's experiences (Edelson, 1988), and (3) make his or her self available to be used as a transferential object in the patient's process of self-discovery (Lidz, 1968).

Freud (1959), broadening the application of these concepts, argued that all interactions among people in groups can be viewed as an interplay of both transferential and countertransferential processes. Taking this as a starting point, I am suggesting that everything that happens to, and within, the facilitator during group encounters can be fruitfully understood in these terms. I begin with the premise that the fabric of all experiential events is socially constructed, the texture being created out of what participants bring to their interactions with each other and with the facilitator, together with the interpretations attached to those interactions by the facilitor and the members, whose relationship is deeply symbiotic. The facilitator depends on the members of the group, on their behaviors and affects, both those expressed and those kept latent, for his or her interpretive material. At the same time, members, in depending on the facilitator for guidance and direction, even when it is not being offered, are mutually making the facilitator into a shared repository for their projections, projections that contribute a great deal to the group's character.

I wish to explore how we can enhance the quality of our facilitation through the use of our selves as transferential objects. I will discuss the three facets identified above—(1) our emotions, (2) our thoughts, and (3) the use of our personhood—illustrating and elaborating the key issues through the discussion of four case fragments. I have chosen these particular cases because of the common thread that connects them: what transpires within the facilitator mirrors, either directly or inversely, critical dynamics in the group being facilitated. By skillful examination of the self, one can tune into processes occurring in the group not yet accessible through direct observation.[1]

[1]The names of individuals and situations in all cases have been disguised to protect the anonymity of group members, but they are all based on my own and colleagues' experiences. I thank those colleagues who willingly let me refer to their experiences.

These cases illustrate four different ways the facilitator can use the self: (1) as an enactor of the opposite of what is being sought, (2) as an ally of the shadowy sides of group members, (3) as an unwitting agent in the group's unfolding dynamics, and (4) as the expresser of the destructive side of the group's unconscious.

The reflections of this chapter are based on the experience of facilitating self-analytic groups. My primary purpose working in such groups is to enable members to learn about group dynamics. While the group is the main focus, members are encouraged to reflect on how they think, feel, and act in group contexts, so there is invariably a personal growth dimension to the learning as well. And the encounters members have with each other are constantly placed under scrutiny so members can explore how their interpersonal interactions influence the group's development. Hence the facilitation I am discussing here is concerned with three levels: the group-as-a-whole, the interpersonal, and the personal. In addition, some of my interventions are undertaken to prevent the evolution of group processes that might be so counterproductive that potential learning will be overwhelmed by the attendant chaos.

Case 1: Please Reject the Me Who Wants Your Acceptance!

Many people crave acceptance but reject it when offered. As a group facilitator, I often become the person upon whom this desire for acceptance is projected. The issue is not really my acceptance, but rather that person's struggle with self-acceptance. It is, of course, something that is being imported into the group from elsewhere, but it also contains a key aspect of group life: the tendency to seek what is not available as a defense against accepting what is.

The wish for my acceptance usually results from the member's self-rejection. Hence, it is important for me as facilitator to keep my rejecting side active when *my* acceptance is being sought as a denial of self-acceptance. For no matter how accepting I may feel, I must be willing to reject the seeking of my acceptance as a substitute for self-acceptance. Very often the rejecting side of the person craving acceptance is being projected onto me, making my response inappropriately important. My task is to make possible the exploration of this projection, so that the member concerned does the critical work, starting the process of liberating self, and vicariously the group as a whole, from dependency upon the facilitator.

I will illustrate with an encounter I had with Margaret, focusing on how I used my self in the three ways I am discussing in this chapter—my emotions, my thinking, and my person. Margaret was a very competent professional woman who had earned my respect because of her many valuable contributions during the group's life. But she was having difficulty accepting parts of herself, a problem that became expressed as her fear that I might reject her.

In the group's last session Margaret turned to me and, clear out of the blue, told me she wanted my acceptance but was afraid I would not give it to her. My immediate response was to draw attention to what she might be projecting into this encounter, which I did by asking her what my acceptance would do for her and what my rejection would do for her.

Margaret responded, "If you accepted me it would validate me. If you didn't, it would be pretty devastating. But I think I would survive."

That last phrase about surviving grabbed my attention and led me to reflect on those times I have been tempted to try things beyond my capacities so that I can reaffirm that I am OK despite my obvious limitations. On those occasions, even though I fear rejection, I often act as though it is rejection I actually want. I began to wonder whether Margaret could be seeking my rejection so she could confirm her capacity to survive such a rejection.

I needed more information but, thinking it best to get Margaret focused on the issue of her acceptability rather than my acceptingness, I asked what she had done to earn my acceptance. She replied by talking at length about something she had done that she knew would displease me. There was a "confessional" quality to this revelation, leading me to wonder whether she was making these violations public so she would be rejected.

I began to think of the human negativism that seems to result from our doing the opposite of what we mean in order to mean the opposite of what we do, a problem resulting from our propensity to misplace "not" (Bateson, 1972). I thought of that wonderful illustration from *Alice in Wonderland*. Alice exclaims, "I see nobody on the road," triggering the retort, "You must have incredibly powerful eyes to be able to see nobody." In this case, the negation was applied, in grammatical terms, to the object (the person) rather than the verb (the actions taken by the subject). Of course, the message was meant to be "I do *not see* anybody on the road" (Smith and Berg, 1987). I thought about the tangled webs we create by negating the person rather than the person's actions.

Margaret seemed focused on the things she had not been doing rather than attending to those things she had done, and then using the things she was avoiding as a basis for understanding her experience while overlooking the things she had been actively engaged in. I suspected that her wish for me to affirm her was to compensate for her own acts of self-negation. I could recognize the special bind she was placing us both into and began to think about how to set up an encounter with Margaret so that she commenced the emotional work necessary to liberate herself from this Catch-22. One thing was very clear. There was nothing to be gained by my pointing this out to her directly. It had to be uncovered by her.

Searching for a way to use myself and my relationship with Margaret as a vehicle for her self-liberation, I asked her what she wanted from me. She replied that she had been learning a lot by watching others interact with me and that she craved some direct contact with me. Here was a clue: make it obvious that by settling for vicarious involvement via others' encounters she was cheating herself and guaranteeing that she only ever had secondhand experiences. I said as much, which really upset her, although she acknowledged that my assessment of her was accurate. I was eager to keep the pressure on her, so, after pointing out that, in order to accept her fully, I needed the freedom to reject, I responded, "I really do accept parts of you, but I reject other parts of you."

There was a long silence. I could now see my opportunity to use my self as a way to prompt the work Margaret needed to do. I liked Margaret, but in this facilitator role, direct expressions of personal feelings toward members must be done with great caution. It was very clear to me that what Margaret wanted from me was assurance that I thought she was OK. Yet I also knew that if I did express to Margaret the acceptance she sought, she would simply reject it as part of the process of discovering that it was her own self-acceptance that she was really looking for. I was now ready to take my initiative, knowing she would reject my acceptance. That, of course, was the point.

"Margaret, I want to tell you that I really like you."

After a very long silence, she replied, with a very embarrassed expression, "I have difficulty accepting that."

With a rather harsh tone I responded, "Then I will take it back!"

Not surprisingly, Margaret looked stunned. So I continued, "I don't like giving gifts that are not received."

This left Margaret having to acknowledge her own rejecting side. And that process of self-acceptance broke the cycle of her desiring my acceptance, which of course made it easy for me to reoffer my acceptance.

The next set of exchanges Margaret engaged in provided encouragement for others in the group to express their similar concerns over self-acceptance, which, as this group ended, created a warm climate of quiet acceptance.

This example illustrates how group members often pull the facilitator into a position that is the exact opposite of where they need the facilitator to be. This is detectable only when the facilitator keeps active inside him- or herself the opposite sides of what is being pulled. It may well be that the member is unknowingly inviting the facilitator into the position that if what is being asked for is given, it will reinforce the impossibility of that person's accepting what is being sought. As such a trap is being set, the facilitator needs to foster the interaction so that the pattern develops adequately and then to act in such a way that the pattern gets broken. This involves setting the stage for the member's participation in her or his self-liberation, willingly doing the opposite of what is ostensibly being asked her.

Case 2. Sadist, Meet the Group's Masochists!

It was the group's second session. Already Brent had become a complex character for the group. He was provoking strong feelings in others but in ways that left them confused. He was charming, and a lot of members were attracted to him. He willingly took on battles others wished they had the courage to engage, so members were proud to be associated with him. He was cruel, so members felt frightened by him, but strangely they often felt his cruelty was justified. When someone did tell Brent that his actions were hurtful, he was quick with an apology: "That is not what I intended—you must be misinterpreting my actions." One could almost hear the unspoken corollary: "My motives are pure, so if you are getting hurt, it must be something you are doing to yourself." And then his fellow group members would let the issue drop, as if an assurance that he did not intend to hurt anyone meant he was not being hurtful.

I found Brent's behavior to be outrageous. He dealt with me, the facilitator, as he did others, except that our interactions were so laden with authority issues that others viewed his mistreatment of me as justified. I felt Brent was being sadistic, and I found my own sadistic side engaged by him. I kept that easily in check, this being a familiar experience in the group facilitator role, but I had three concerns. The first was to protect those group members who were getting hurt by him, often in unknown ways. Second, I felt the group was getting stuck as members became increasingly paralyzed by Brent's insidiousness. And third, his dark side was casting such an enormous shadow over the group, I suspected others would be unlikely ever to explore their own shadowy sides. After I had compiled enough direct evidence of Brent's sadism to feel very sure of my ground, I interrupted proceedings.

I first asked him if he was aware of what he was up to in this group, only thinly veiling my own anger at his actions. He responded with a list of the good things he wanted for the group, things he saw himself dedicated to achieving. He showed no awareness of his shadowy side. I asked him if he could see any negative consequences of how he was going about what he wanted to achieve. He responded, "No!"

I got myself hooked. I fell immediately into the pattern of trying to point out to Brent some of the ways he had hurt others in the group. This went nowhere. He just did not see what I was getting at. To make matters worse, he treated everything I said to him as an accusation, responding very convincingly in the style of a skilled defense lawyer. Other group members seemed pulled into the jury role. And although some of them were also his victims, "acquittal" seemed increasingly likely. The fighting side of me was tempted to escalate my conflict with him, but I knew that would go nowhere. As I was getting ready to back down, Brent said something that triggered a critical strand of thinking for me: "You know, Kenwyn, what you are saying just does not fit my experience."

This word *fit* jumped out at me and led me to think about what it might mean in this setting. First, I thought Brent might be treating my statements in an isomorphic form, saying something like "I have these experiences and here you are trying to map your interpretations onto them and they *just do not fit*." So I wondered, "What happens when something does not fit?" If we are trying on clothes in a store and they don't fit, we discard them. Could Brent be saying, "I discard these interpretations you offer me because they do not fit?" That is always difficult to hear, and it prods me to try harder to create images that will fit so perfectly that they could not possibly be discarded.

Second, the idea of "fitting" is closely linked to the issue of adaptation. We all experience the demands to fit in, and when we do not, we become subjected to enormous pressures either to adapt or to leave. Pressures to adapt focus on the "nonfittingness" of the person concerned, not on "nonfittability" of the location in which the person is existing, even though the concept of fit is in fact a relational one. Could Brent's comment to me be a request to "let him be what he is" and to encourage me to "get the group simply to adapt to him"?

Third, I was drawn to think about Von Glassersfeld's (1984) discussion of fitting in terms of the metaphor of a key "fitting" in a lock. Von Glassersfeld noted that any key that opens a particular lock may be viewed as "fitting." And some keys will never open the lock, no matter how much we pull and twist.

Once this image of the key and the lock had occurred to me, I found a whole new way of hearing what Brent was saying to me. I began to assume that Brent was on my side in my attempts to help him out of the cycle he was in. And I heard his statement to me about what I was offering him as "not fitting" as a message to search for a different key, one that might help unlock what was imprisoning him. The moment I saw this, many options occurred to me, and I quietly waited for the right moment.

After one of his sadistic outbursts that group members seemed to take quite passively, I asked, "Brent, what is it like for you, being in a room full of masochists?" Of course I was now speaking not only to Brent but to the relationship between him and the others, to the partnership of sadism and masochism as it was evolving in this group.

The other group members seemed stunned by my question. Not Brent. A slight smile appeared on his face as he replied, "I kind of like it."

"Does it feel familiar?" I asked.

"Hardly! I am usually with other sadists."

"How does it go for you when you are in a room full of sadists?"

"I often get really hurt."

"Why? Is your own sadism not up to the task?"

"Usually not!"

"So you must be feeling pretty good that you can get all this practice at your sadism here when there are no sadists to match your skill!"

He gave a slight nod.

"Where did you learn the art of sadism?"

"In my family."

Now my interventions were moving him and the group along at a fast clip. No longer was there a struggle about whether my interpretations fit. They were fitting, not in the isomorphic sense, but in the key-in-the-lock sense. Every few sentences gave opportunity to open yet something else that had been closed. Also, I was no longer finding my own sadism engaged. I felt very much on Brent's side.

After Brent had done some significant exploration, I turned the attention to those I was labeling as masochists, and invited them to explore the ways they acted like voluntary victims looking for fights in which they could come out second best and then blame the world for its cruelty. The exploration with these group members is another story, into which I will not digress here. However, by the end of this discussion, all group members had learned (1) how those who passively absorbed Brent's abusive behavior were actively responsible for the pain they were experiencing and (2) that the emergence of the sadistic side of a group is fostered by the side that adopts the masochistic position. In addition, the need for me to protect the group faded, for now the group-as-a-whole experienced itself as much more capable of self-monitoring and self-regulation.

Through this case I want to emphasize how important it is for a facilitator to be willing to let self be so influenced that one's own shadowy side (such as one's sadism) becomes activated. This level of internal functioning stirs new ways to think about intervention. When members are drawn into very primal functioning as a result of their group experiences, the facilitator, as co-partner in the experiential exploration, must be willing to descend to similar depths of self to match what the members are having stirred within them. Then it may be possible to discover how to be an ally of the shadowy sides of group members and to make visible those patterns that are paralyzing to the group.

Case 3. Taunting and Triangulation

In both the previous cases I knew how I was using my self. By being open to my emotions and through intense thinking, I came to understand how I could take actions to be a critical instrument in the group's life. In this third case, while I was attending just as much to my own feelings and was intellectually very engaged, I came to discover how I had been actively used by the group as an agent in the unfolding of its dynamics, admittedly with my willing collusion, but without my awareness of what was happening. It was only after it had occurred that I understood.

The context was more complex than that of the previous cases, the class being a group-on-group design (one group works while the other observes, then the two groups switch roles). The first session of Group A began with members introducing themselves. Each person chose to identify him- or herself in terms of some of the groups he or she belonged to, saying status-enhancing things like "I am a Stanford graduate pursuing a career in investment banking." I was soon bored, and sensed the energy was draining from the group. This led me to suspect members might be introducing themselves in terms of their status in the external world as a way to manage their anxiety about whether they were going to become persons of importance in this group.

After several people had introduced themselves in this manner, I chose to speak for the first time, pointing out that members faced a choice about whether to introduce themselves by reference to their lives external to the group, or in terms of how they were experiencing the awkwardness and pain of the new beginnings they were embarking upon in this first group session. After a long silence, some members began to express resentment over what I had said, acting as though my comment, intended to be helpful, had been an indictment of everything they had done so far. Some members began verbally attacking me for "stopping our introductions"! Others countered in support of what I had said. Within the hour, two factions had galvanized, one taking the position "Kenwyn is trying to be helpful, even though he is isn't," while the other was adamant in arguing, "He is simply trying to create conflict for us to learn from."

I felt both factions were taunting me, one side trying to get me to say what I meant, despite the fact that I had meant exactly what I said, while the other side tried to make it clear that I had not meant what I had said. My inner response during this time was a briny mixture of both anger and amusement. Part of me wanted to join the fight I felt I was being invited into but, knowing this would be pointless, I refrained. My relationship with the group was turning into a triangular situation with me and the two emerging subgroups, and I felt anything I said ran the risk of simply galvanizing these two factions by making me into an enemy.

My sense of being taunted reminded me of Bateson's (1936) discussion of tribal initiation rituals, where rival factions of men, rather than fighting directly with each other, instead bullied the novices. As one faction intensified the initiation abuse, the other countered with even more extreme behavior until the initiation of the novices became primarily an arena for the ventilation of the tensions among the adult men.

Bateson (1936) explains this pattern in terms of social splitting, where one part of a system takes on certain attributes on behalf of the whole, leaving others free to adopt different attributes, again on behalf of the whole. This seemed to be happening with Group A. As the two subgroups became increasingly entrenched, the position of each part heightened the differentiation from the other. The splitting within Group A was essentially *horizontal* (Smith's [1989] relabeling of what Bateson called symmetrical splitting) in that each faction viewed the other as a rival and wanted to have its position accepted as *the* reality for the whole of the group: an impossibility, given that neither subgroup was about to capitulate. Horizontal splitting typically leads to cycles of escalation, and I began to wonder how this would play out with Group A.

While the membership of Group A was arranging itself into two subgroups, I felt my relationship with the class as a whole was also being driven by a process of splitting. However, in contrast to the subgroups' horizontal pattern, this splitting was *vertical* in nature (Bateson's term was complementary), in that different roles developed that together made up a whole (such as master-apprentice or exhibitionism-spectatorship). In vertical splitting, if one side is not engaged, the other also fades. But, on engagement, the pattern escalates. For example, as the submissive becomes more passive, the dominant becomes more assertive, and vice versa. In this case, the paired relationship was I as authority figure and the groups as dependent students.

Bateson (1936) observed that when horizontal interactions become extreme, they are often swapped for vertical ones, and vice versa. It suddenly dawned on me that *I might be able to use the intensity of the vertical feelings I was experiencing with this group as a barometer of the strength of the horizontal tensions brewing within its midst that were being displaced and relocated in their relationship with me.* It seemed perfectly reasonable that tensions between me and the group would take on a vertical form, given that the authority relations between facilitator and members sets in place from the outset the dependency dynamics associated with master-apprentice-type relations.

While I held this as an emerging thought, Group B (whose members had been observing Group A during its initial experience) commenced its first session. One person, in the most gentlemanly of tones, began as follows: "I suggest we start by determining whether the facilitator will be allowed to stay in our group." My immediate inner reaction was to cream him. My thoughts (which I kept to myself) were "You think you can get rid of me! Who do you think you are! If you want a fight, go ahead. We'll pretty quickly sort out the men from the boys here." I kept silent. I could see that I was being drawn into a vertical fight with Group B. But this was happening from the outset, whereas with Group A the vertical splitting between me and the group seemed to grow out of the members' internal horizontal splitting. So I began to ask myself what horizontal split this might be indicating. The most puzzling thing was that I had not even had an encounter in this group before this had happened. So it had to be a result of what was being imported into the group.

The most obvious issue was the potential for intergroup conflict between Groups A and B inherent in the group-on-group design. Group B usually begins with members expressing the hope that they will do better than Group A, whose first session they have just observed and whose actions seemed regressive. Hence the beginning of Group B's life is essentially *intergroup* in nature with their wanting to be not Group A, in contrast to Group A's fundamentally *intragroup* beginning.

Both groups moved into a vertical posture with me, but for very different reasons. Group A's resulted from its *internal* horizontal split, whereas Group B's came from an *external* horizontal pattern with Group A. They had seen Group A as having immense difficulty with me, and vicariously concluded that Group A's troubles were caused by me. Hence, having judged that Group A had done poorly, the only obvious way for Group B to do well was to dispose of me. Since there were no opportunities for direct contact between these two groups, I suspected Group B was engaging in a vertical struggle with me as an expression of the horizontal struggle they were creating with the other group.

The suggestion that I should be removed from Group B, presumably physically, did not seem inappropriate to any of their members, though some had other things they wished to pursue. Quickly the group split into two parts: those who felt disposing of me should be top priority, and those who felt it was futile because I probably could not be disposed of anyway. These two factions moved rapidly into a horizontal posture toward each other, and in no time this group internally was in much the same condition as Group A. Group B's determination to be different from Group A insured that Group B became very much like them.

In this second situation, I came to recognize that horizontal tensions among Groups A and B became translated into a vertical struggle between the membership of Group B and me, the facilitator, which then became enacted as internal horizontal splits within their group. In contrast, in the first situation, the vertical relationship between me and the group seemed to be a consequence of the internal horizontal splitting of that particular group.

In this setting I retrospectively worked out for myself how my relationships with both groups were mirroring both their intragroup and intergroup dynamics. But my discoveries were too late to make meaningful interventions in these particular groups so that the members could uncover these dynamics for themselves while they were occurring. So in this case the critical learning ended up being predominantly for myself, though I was able to catalyze retrospective insight for some members on this issue. However, in the groups I have run since then, I have observed this same pattern numerous times and have been able to detect its character while it is coming into being and hence make appropriate interpretations so members can learn from it as well.

The key learning from this experience is that as a facilitator I often find myself unwittingly pulled into a vertical struggle. I can now recognize this as signaling the emergence of a horizontal split *within* the membership that is being displaced into my relationship *with* the members. The pattern about to materialize may be in one of two forms: (1) it may be the emergence of *intragroup* conflict indigenous to that group at that time, or (2) it may be *intergroup* conflict that is being set up by the second group as it attempts to avoid the traps it observed the first group falling into. Of course, it is just as likely that the unexpressed and unexplored vertical struggles *between* the facilitator and the membership will be displaced and relocated *within* the membership, emerging as a horizontal split.

Case 4. Keeping the Rapist Contained

One dominant aspect of the theory presented in this book is that group members frequently take on and enact certain processes on behalf of the group as a whole, leaving others free to express different aspects of the whole. This becomes especially pertinent when we consider what goes on in the unconscious life of the group. If unconscious group dynamics are emerging into awareness and the whole group is defended against them, then they will become manifest in unexpected ways and often in distorted forms.

One domain of a group's unconscious life that is difficult to manage and where this regularly occurs is when members feel sexual attraction. When sexual feelings surface, the unconscious relationship between the female and male sides of the group as a whole often becomes loaded into, and expressed through, the interpersonal exchanges between the members experiencing the attraction. Hence, what the particular members do or don't do with their sexual feelings for each other becomes a major concern for the whole group. For if the attraction gets expressed, it may be releasing something for the whole group, and if it is repressed, it may be incubating these unconscious processes further, setting the stage for their erupting some other time, some other way.

This is especially complex when the attractions are between a member and the facilitator, for other members are usually vicariously involved to the point that what "happens" to another is experienced as having actually happened to them. These attractions contain powerful authority and transferential elements. So it is critical the facilitator knows how to use them as a window into the unconscious, projective dimensions of the group that are being embodied in the attractions of these particular members. And, of course, it is devastatingly dangerous for the facilitator to give sexual expression to these attractions, for such actions are sure to assault deeply the unconscious life of the group as a whole, and members not involved in any direct way are likely to be psychologically damaged, probably in unrecognizable ways.

In concert with the above reasoning, if the facilitator can access the unconscious dynamics of the group and internally work with them in a constructive way, this may dissipate their destructive force. This helps free the group members from becoming embroiled in the chaos of enacting them and thereby turn down the volume of these emotions, as it were, so they can be actually learned from. What usually happens is that these sexual feelings become overwhelming, and members get into exchanges they do not know how to handle and thus defend themselves against the critical lessons latent in these attractions. If it is possible for the facilitator to do critical internal work on these unconscious group dynamics, it will be work done on behalf of the group as a whole. I will illustrate with an occasion when I was a subordinate member of a two-person team, with my senior colleague being a woman. In this case the work involved both deep introspection and interpersonal exchanges with this senior female colleague.

In the early meetings of the group the women members were very dynamic and active. We understood this as being stirred by the sentient ties they automatically had with the senior woman facilitator. But the men seemed emasculated and depressed. And this was getting to me. It was hard being a male in this group because the women were so powerful and the intensity of their contributions was difficult to match, and, like the male participants who had so often been in a predominantly male world, I found myself with the uncomfortable feelings of being overshadowed by the women. Their energy and competence seemed to be experienced by us men as an assault on our masculinity. It was a struggle, but I eventually got around to acknowledging this in the group, and I made several interpretations based on this feeling, but none of the male group members seemed willing to concede such feelings.

At one point I found myself unexpectedly thinking about myself as a rapist and fearing the consequences of not keeping that rapist contained. These thoughts about being a potential rapist were deeply disturbing to me, for they provoked me to examine feelings about my own psychosexual development, and no matter how hard I tried, it was impossible to push them out of my mind. I felt scared, anxious, and guilty. This was not a part of me that I accepted, and I was feeling overwhelmed by the sense of urgency and importance of the "containing" I felt compelled to do. Eventually, I gave up fighting these feelings and started to explore what they meant, both for me in particular and for men in general. I began reading a very provocative book about rape.

As I became more and more absorbed in this exploration, I chose to discuss these feelings about sexuality and violence with my senior woman colleague during our planning and review meetings. This conversation brought us close, for she conceded often experiencing such difficult-to-discuss feelings when in the subordinate role, and then feeling particularly vulnerable on raising them in the staff meetings. This acknowledgment helped me a lot. I began to see that some of my feelings might be a product of the group roles that I had been falling into and the power of the female energy in the group. However, at this time I had no awareness that I might be actually picking up unconscious aspects of the group's life.

This was a difficult time for me in the group in another sense, for I began to doubt my competence as a facilitator. I was often raising issues no one seemed willing to discuss, leading me to wonder whether I was simply importing my personal struggles into the group. It was increasingly difficult for me to keep my own boundaries and the group's clearly distinguished in my mind. I felt badly about this and wondered whether I might be really off target in my understanding of both the group and myself.

Then I learned that one of the group members, Harvey, an older married man, had weeks earlier sexually propositioned Donna, a younger, single woman. At the time Donna experienced this as an assault, though she chose to keep it to herself. When I eventually heard of this I began to realize that the theme of sexuality and assault had been something that was actively going on in the group, even though it had been out of my field of conscious awareness. This led me to recognize that what I had been going through might well have been unconsciously connected to the larger dynamics of the group that I could not recognize.

As the group proceeded, Donna elected not to discuss with the group that she had been propositioned or that this had made her feel assaulted, although she did write about it in one of her required course papers. In most ways she worked it out by herself, and this enabled her to remain more contained and less vulnerable than she might have been had she taken on the "victim" role in the group.

In the final group session Harvey publicly apologized to this woman
for his sexual proposition. This occurred in an integrous way, for
everyone experienced it as his issue, not Donna's. And the emotional
work Harvey ended up doing in the group around his propositioning
of Donna, and her experience of assault, seemed to be relatively free
of group baggage.

Afterward, I wrestled with the speculation, which at this time
can be no more than a speculation, given that this was just one case,
that the emotional struggles I had been going through concerning
"keeping the rapist contained" were actually done on behalf of the
group as a whole. And given that we facilitators brought that element
of the group's unconscious into the light of day and dealt with these
forces directly in our interactions with each other, our emotional
work freed the group from having this unconscious element of its
life loaded into Harvey and Donna's exchange. Certainly how this
event played out in this group was very different from what we
commonly see. Usually the woman who is the object of the assault,
rather than the male assailant, ends up bringing the experience into
the group. And then she can be seen by the other group members
as the one creating the problem, because she raises the difficult
feelings that others have tried hard to suppress. Her affect is con-
strued as disproportionately exaggerating what occurred, and she is
rejected.

That did not happen in this case. Donna worked out a way to
keep her feelings contained and was confident that the proposition/
assault was Harvey's issue and not hers. She felt no imperative to
attack Harvey publicly, to expose herself unnecessarily, or to force
him to do emotional work he was not ready for. This created an
emotional spaciousness, so that when Harvey was ready, he, and
not Donna, did his work.

This experience has led me to understand that when I make
myself available to tap into and be acutely influenced by the unconscious forces active in the group, that it is possible for me, as
the facilitator, actually to do work on behalf of the group, freeing
the other group members from having to deal with that aspect of
the group's work. In this sense, when the facilitator deeply exposes
self to the unconscious forces of the group, and then actually does
critical emotional work on behalf of the group, the facilitator's self
is being used as an expresser and releaser of the destructive sides of
the group's unconscious.

Of course, it is a judgment call as to whether it is wise or
appropriate for the facilitator always to be available in this way, for
by doing such group-based work, he or she may "save" the members

from having to deal with these issues for themselves. On the other hand, doing the unconscious emotional work for the group can be an extraordinary contribution if it minimizes the likelihood of psychological damage and lessens the emotional burden on members, freeing them to explore and learn from these complex feelings.

CONCLUSION

The groups discussed in this book are those created for the purpose of education, promoting members' learning both about the group dynamics they are embroiled in and also about the causes and effects of their behavior in the experiential group. In this chapter I have been arguing that the central aspect of the group facilitator's role is knowing how to use self as an instrument, and describing some of the lessons my experiences have taught me.

The starting point to *using self as instrument* is to be fully open to whatever emotions well up within the facilitator, even if they are threatening and would normally be censored. Then intense intellectual work is required, actively seeking new patterns for understanding what is transpiring in the group. The third requirement is then to work out, on the basis of the feelings and thoughts that are surfacing, how to make active use of one's personhood as a catalyst for group development and member growth.

In the light of the above, it is clear that the facilitator role cannot be treated in a formulaic way. The prescriptions of "dos" and "don'ts" that facilitators internalize during their own training provide merely a foundation upon which the actual discovery of what to do in the setting can be based.

There are three dominant principles I offer as a conclusion to this chapter. The first is that the facilitator will be made into the repository of a wide array of projections by group members. By making self available to absorb and mull over these projections, the facilitator is being given the equivalent of the clay the potter needs to create his or her artifacts. These projections can be taken in, mirrored back, rejected, or ignored, depending on the understandings that the facilitator develops. However, facilitation starts with tuning into these projections.

The second is that what comes at the facilitator from the members and the group as a whole may be the exact opposite of what is going on or is required from the facilitator. Many aspects of groups and their members operate on what has been labeled the schizo-phrenic pattern: conveying the opposite of what is meant in order to mean the opposite of what is conveyed. The facilitator must calibrate self to explore whether what is being received is the mirror image or opposite of what is intended or required.

The third is that what one is experiencing internally may be a mirroring, in microcosm, of what is happening in the group as a whole. This microcosmic reflection of the group's dynamics, when it can be acheived, gives the facilitator a powerful window into the unconscious dynamics of the group, and provides an array of options for the facilitator that are not otherwise available.

Chapter 14

The Process of Authorization for Consultants-in-Training: A View from the Threshold

MARK LEACH

During the second semester of my doctoral training in organizational behavior, I co-consulted to and assisted in teaching a masters-level course in group dynamics. At first I felt only minimally entitled to fill the position. I had, just the year before, been a student in such a group and remembered vividly the mysterious and often opaque world of the unconscious in which the lead consultant and his TA seemed to function. As I entered my first session as a co-consultant, I was not at all sure I would have anything to say, or if my experience and knowledge would translate into a useful competence.

However, I increasingly came to feel I had a legitimate claim to the role of group consultant—that I was justified in holding myself out as one who could help others learn about group dynamics. And to my periodic surprise, the legitimacy of my claim to that role was increasingly recognized by others: students in the class, the lead consultant, other faculty members, graduate students, and colleagues at work. The observations in this chapter are based on my experience of feeling increasingly entitled to fill the role of study group consultant.

At some point, every study group consultant makes a transition from group member to staff member.[1] While I still stand near the threshold between the two roles, I want to explore the dynamics of this transition. What establishes the legitimacy of the new consultant's claim to the role?

[1]. Following the distinction between study groups and T-groups described by Klein and Astrachan (1971), I use the term *study group* to denote groups with a psychoanalytic emphasis. Such groups are based largely on the work of Melanie Klein, Wilfred Bion, A. K. Rice, and the theory and method of the Tavistock Institute in London. By contrast, the *T-group* approach is based on the work of Kurt Lewin, and has been widely popularized by the National Training Laboratories Institute for Applied Behavioral Science.

I suggest that becoming authorized in the role is the result of four processes: (1) establishing position power, (2) behaving competently, (3) authorizing oneself, and (4) authorizing group members. Paradoxically, since these processes are also essential to the consultant's task of "providing group members with learning opportunities" (Klein and Astrachan, 1971, p. 668), the group consultant becomes authorized to do the work by doing the work. I also suggest that, contrary to the individualistic assumptions of our culture, authorization of the consultant-in-training is not solely the product of the consultant's individual efforts; it requires a complex set of behaviors and attitudes on the part of other individuals, groups, and institutions.

I offer these observations from my experience in the spirit of theory generation, and am not proposing a formal theory of authorization. I hope that these reflections will be useful to other new consultants and to others in the systems in which consultants are trained.

PRELIMINARY DISCUSSION

The Context of My Training

The study group consultant's work exists in a context that includes an institutional setting and a multiplicity of roles, group memberships and relationships. I want to outline several aspects of this context that, in my experience, influenced the authorizing process.

The course. I was a first-year doctoral student in organizational behavior when the professor of an M.B.A. and doctoral course in group dynamics invited me to be her teaching assistant. The professor (whom I will refer to as my supervising consultant) was a thirty-seven-year-old white woman. I am white and was thirty-one years old at the time. The class of eight women and seven men students ranged in age from twenty-two to forty-nine, and represented a variety of religious and ethnic identities. All were white except one North African student. Some were full-time students, but most studied part-time and had several years of work experience. All had some prior academic training in organizational behavior.

The first two hours of the three-hour-weekly class were devoted to experiential learning, using a group-on-group design. One group worked with the two consultants in an inner circle, while the second group sat in an outer circle observing; these roles were reversed in the second hour. The third hour was given to lectures, discussion of course readings, and application of theory to students' work settings.

My supervising consultant was responsible for the majority of the course design, most lectures, all administrative details, and determination of final grades. I had input on course design and readings, and was responsible for co-consulting to the groups, preparing several lecture/discussions, grading half of the students' papers, and consulting on my own to several study-group sessions at a day-long institutional event. My supervising consultant and I had a one-hour planning session prior to each class, and spent about one and a half hours debriefing afterward.

The multiplicity of roles. Because I was simultaneously a first-year doctoral student and a TA, I occupied multiple roles during the semester. In relation to the university, I was a *student, employee* (the university paid my salary as a TA), and *agent* (the university delegated to me as a TA its responsibility to provide educational services).

In relation to the course instructor, I was simultaneously in the roles of *student* (she was my independent study advisor and a faculty member in the Department of Organization Behavior), *colleague* (she and I constituted the staff group in relation to the class and were co-consultants during the experiential group sessions), and *subordinate* (she was my immediate supervisor, and it was through her that my institutional authority as agent of the university came).

In relation to students in the class I had two primary roles. During the experiential group sessions I was in the role of *consultant.* When I lectured, led class discussions, graded papers, or held office hours, I was in the role of *instructor.* The processes of authorization in my two primary subroles, consultant and instructor, were interdependent in that failure to establish my formal or informal authority in one of the roles would have undermined my authority in the other. Authorization in each role entailed different personal challenges, skills, and kinds of relationships. In this chapter I will focus mainly on my authorization in the consultant role.

Conceptual Issues

Authorization and power are conceptually inseparable. Indeed, authorization can be understood as a process of empowerment.[2] By power I mean "an actor's ability to induce or influence another actor to carry out his directives, or any other norms he supports" (Etzioni, 1971, p. 5). One becomes authorized when one's power is legitimized or sanctioned by others and by oneself. As such, authority is not an entity or a possession of an individual; it is a social construction that is "built or created" (Smith and Berg, 1987, p. 134). Authorization is a constant process of social negotiation in which actors sanction other actors' power.

Authority can be either *formal* or *informal*, depending on the nature of the power being legitimized. Formal authority is based on what French and Raven (1959) call position power: "the capacity to influence because of the prerogative of the office or role within the organizational structure" (in Eddy, 1985, p. 88). In the academic setting, an instructor's position power is derived from his or her position in the university hierarchy and is manifest in his or her prerogative to establish time, space, and membership boundaries around the class, give assignments, determine grades, and so on. An important aspect of this position power is what Etzioni (1971) calls "remunerative power." Because of their position, instructors have control over resources about which students care, such as desirable grades and good recommendations. Students legitimize an instructor's position power in contracting to take a class.

Establishing *informal authority* requires the legitimizing of "expert power" and "referent power." Expert power is the capacity to influence others because of one's knowledge, and referent power is the capacity to influence others because of one's personal characteristics (French and Raven, 1959). For example, in choosing to pursue the task as defined by a study group consultant and to make use of the learning opportunities that he or she provides, group members legitimize a consultant's expert and, in some instances, referent power. Group members are also free to reject the task and learning opportunities, and so fail to grant informal authority to the consultant.

Consultants may also be granted informal authority based on normative power: "power [that] rests on the allocation and manipulation of symbolic rewards and deprivations" (Etzioni, 1971, p. 5).

---

[2]. I have chosen to retain the more archaic and (to a generation steeped in the jargon of liberation and human potential movements) less palatable word *authorization*. To many, *authority* is oppressive and bad, but *being empowered* is noble and good. While the contexts may differ, the processes are similar.

Positive response from a superior is such a symbolic reward for some people. The group member or consultant-in-training who works to gain the approval of the supervising consultant legitimizes his or her normative power.

So, authorizing means establishing the legitimacy of one's power, can involve both formal and informal means, and involves the sanctioning of power at many levels of a system. In my case these levels included class members, department faculty members, peers in my program, and representatives of the university. I will now examine the four processes of authorization that I identified as central to my own authorization: establishment of my position power, demonstrating competence, authorizing myself, and authorizing group members.

1. AUTHORIZATION THROUGH POSITION POWER

Within the university setting—and in all other study group settings—the consultant's task requires establishing position power. I identified two processes involved in establishing the position power of the consultant-in-training. The first, formal assignment to the role is the earliest process to occur and is the most obvious element of authorization. The second, setting boundaries around that role, is more subtle but equally important. Each of these dynamics requires the participation of the consultant-in-training, his or her supervisor, and agents of the institution in which the consultant is being trained.

Position Power via Formal Designation in the Role

My position power originated with the university and was channeled to me through my supervising consultant (who hired me for the position) and through the department dean, who approved my appointment. In return for being granted this position power, I agreed to sanction certain institutional powers of the university (such as the power to define semester boundaries, appoint faculty members, and require the grading of student performance).

This formal appointment gave me a second position in the institutional hierarchy and a double identity as both student and staff member. This second identity allowed me to do tasks that as a student I would not have been authorized to do and gave me access to certain resources of the university (salary, office, phone, copy machine, et cetera). It also permitted me to allocate institutional rewards and punishments in the form of term-paper grades. At the time, this formal authorization seemed to me like a suit of new and unfamiliar clothes: an alien and uncomfortable identity that I put on with the role and that neither felt nor looked like my familiar self.

My position power established me as part of a "staff group" with my supervising consultant, while previously we had had only separate group affiliations as student and faculty member. This staff-group boundary allowed her and me to share personal issues that would usually not be discussed between people at different hierarchical levels and that were required by our mutual task. Formal designation in the role was the first step in establishing the psychological boundaries around this staff group.

In relation to students, my legitimized position power served three functions. First, creating a staff group allowed exploration of intergroup authority dynamics in the experiential sessions. Second, it signaled to students the supervising consultant's belief that I had adequate skills for the role. Given members' fears of being emotionally damaged in a study group, this stamp of approval probably helped confer on me a higher initial level of trust than would have otherwise existed. Finally, my position power legitimized my participation in certain staff tasks—such as grading papers and leading class discussions—that as a student I normally had no authority to do. To be clear, these tasks only became "formal prerogatives of the office" (French and Raven in Eddy, 1985, p. 88) through negotiation and contracting between the supervising consultant and me. This process of boundary setting around the role constitutes the second step in establishing one's position power.

Position Power via Boundary Setting

The extent of one's influence based on office or role is set partly by nonnegotiable requirements of the role, and in part by negotiated boundaries. The authority to set limits around what is negotiable lies with the unversity and with the supervising consultant as prerogatives of their power.

For example, definition of the overall task was not a negotiable item in determining the limits of my role. The task was to contribute to students' learning about group dynamics through experiential and didactic means. If I rejected this essential boundary around the role (for instance, by trying to turn the class into a therapy group), the supervising consultant could revoke my position power. Within this metaboundary, I negotiated with the supervising consultant to establish my participation in course design, consulting, lecturing, grading, and other tasks that would define my role. It was not until later in the semester that I fully appreciated the contribution that conscious boundary setting around my role made to my authorization. Had I negotiated for less responsibility I would have certainly diminished my authority in the perception of students, my supervising consultant, and myself. The reverse is probably true as well. The irony is that the consultant-in-training knows the least about what is necessary for authorization at exactly the time when he or she makes some of the most important decisions affecting that authorization.

The setting of boundaries around my role simultaneously determined my degree of formal authorization and contributed to the work. Establishing formal authority, however, is only the beginning of the authorizing process. Informal authority is at least as important, and is certainly more complex.

2. AUTHORIZATION THROUGH COMPETENT BEHAVIOR

Behaving competently is an essential requirement for informal authorization. The consultant-in-training must legitimize his or her expert power by exhibiting existing competence and developing new competence. I am using "competence" in the sense described by White (1959) to mean "effective interaction with the environment." For the consultant-in-training, effective interaction means the ability to provide learning opportunities within the interpretive framework established by the lead consultant of the study group. (For example, it would not be competent to consult from a Tavistock framework in a group that was constituted as a T-group.) Despite many people's belief that competence is a personal attribute, the following discussion illustrates that exhibiting and acquiring competence require the collaboration of many actors.

Exhibiting Existing Competence

The consultant-in-training legitimizes his or her expert power by having and developing skills required for the task, and by making these skills visible. The urge to hide one's skills as a new consultant can be strong. The time when one is behaving most competently may also be the time of greatest resistance and challenge by the group, and so of greatest personal anxiety for the consultant. For me the most challenging aspects of exhibiting my competence were (1) "staying in role" (Klein and Astrachan, 1971), (2) scrutinizing *all* levels of the system, and (3) being visible to students.

Staying in role. Staying in the consultant role is like staying on a bicycle. While learning, you must give it constant attention, and when attention wanes, you fall off and get a little banged up. Fortunately, spills are rarely life-threatening, and staying in role gradually becomes, if not automatic, at least habitual. Staying in role requires a *constant focus on the task.* For me it eventually took the form of always asking myself, "What, in this particular situation, will contribute most to learning?" For example, once a study group was struggling with the issue of supposed domination of the group by its female members. On the suspicion that there was a group fantasy about the emasculation of powerful males by the female lead consultant, I commented that perhaps the group believed she had made me into a eunuch. I believe this was a faithful answer to the question "What would contribute most to learning?" but it was certainly not an answer to the more comfortable question "What would reduce my anxiety right now?"

Another aspect of staying in role is *managing boundaries around the role.* For me, this meant resisting the temptation to be coaxed out of role by study group members. Opportunities for this were plentiful. For example, in my first solo consulting during an institutional event, two group members greeted me with different versions of "Hi, Mark, how 'ya doing?" In addition to being a casual greeting, it was also a test of my willingness to abandon my staff role and join in the group wish for flight from the task. While I occasionally shared this wish, I could not give in to it without undermining my informal authority. On other occasions, students would directly question me about an interpretation, asking for clarification or repetition. Not to respond—in those instances where I thought not responding was best for the group's learning—was extremely difficult. The consultant-in-training who is also a student may feel the tug to rejoin the student group especially strongly.

Staying in role also requires *constant application of the in-*

terpretive framework. While using one's feelings as data is an essential aspect of doing good interpretive work, it is not a substitute for a well-grounded theoretical perspective. The framework we used in our work gave primary attention to group-level phenomena and interpreting fantasy, defense, and basic assumption themes. Since my supervising consultant and I were rooted in the same theoretical tradition and received our initial training from some of the same people, there was little disagreement about the framework to be used. Consistent application of an interpretive framework could be problematic without such similarities among the staff. Exhibiting competence involves applying the interpretive framework not just to the group, but to all levels of the system in which one is being trained.

Scrutinizing all levels of the system.

Application of the interpretive framework obviously requires scrutiny of oneself and of the group. But before my experience as a consultant-in-training, it was less apparent to me how much the work also involves scrutiny of the larger institutional context and of the co-consulting relationship. Failure to be attuned to these dynamics reduces the legitimacy of the consultant's expert power by restricting the group's learning. For instance, at one point in a study group I experienced it as dangerous to offer an interpretation that differed from one my supervising consultant was pursuing. This was four weeks into the semester, and I had not had such a feeling before. During our debriefing, we realized that we were acting out—as representatives of the student and faculty subgroups within the organizational behavior department—a range of conflicts that had nothing directly to do with the study group. (I will return to this example later.)

Because the consultant's task requires honest intellectual and emotional communication across an authority boundary, examining the relationship with the co-consultant can feel risky to the consultant-in-training. Despite our temporary membership in the same staff group, my co-consultant was concurrently my supervisor and a potential authority figure in future settings. I came to appreciate how carefully my co-consultant managed her own boundaries in sharing only those personal thoughts and feelings that pertained directly to the work. Had she also used our relationship as a place to discuss strictly personal issues, it would have created a deeper personal connection. Such a connection, she felt, would complicate some of my future decisions as a graduate student—such as choosing dissertation and exam committee members.

At the debriefing following our first co-consultation, I felt coerced, not by my supervising consultant but by the task. It clearly demanded that I share feelings about myself, the supervising consultant, and the class much sooner than I normally would, even in a relationship with a peer. In addition to the sense of risk, I admit to exhilaration in crossing the previous authority boundary to engage in emotionally and intellectually stimulating work with a female professor. (One benefit study group consultants may get from their work is some satisfaction of intimacy needs in a highly controlled setting. Some consultants' insistence that co-consultant teams be of mixed gender may be based as much on heterosexual pairing fantasies as on the rational reasons usually offered.)

Without exploring our own dynamics of conflict, competition, attraction, anger, dependence, and so on, we could not help group members explore these dynamics. Risky, exhilarating, or otherwise, competent behavior in the role requires such scrutiny. Learning and informal authorization depend upon it. Scrutiny of the co-consultant relationship cannot be done alone, and demonstrates again the paradox that one is authorized to do the work by doing the work.

Being visible. Exhibiting competence requires that someone be there to see it. The degree of informal authorization obtained by the consultant-in-training depends on his or her ability to negotiate for responsibilities that will test and demonstrate competence to the lead consultant and to study group members. In my situation, this involved co-consulting to the weekly study groups, doing a solo consultation with each group, preparing a lecture/discussion, holding office hours, and grading papers. While some of these activities had more to do with authorizing me in my role as an instructor than as a consultant, the general point remains. The consultant-in-training must be visible in order to be authorized.

Consultants-in-training enter their first consultancy with widely varying skills and experience, and even seasoned consultants face new situations from which to learn. In this sense, all consultants are "consultants-in-training." But consultants being authorized for the first time have a larger increment of competence to acquire. Thus, developing new competence is the second aspect of behaving competently that contributes to the authorizing process.

Developing New Competencies

There are two things I wish I had known earlier in my first consultancy about how to develop new competence: first, that such development requires authorizing one's supervising consultant and communicating that to him or her, and second, that making mistakes can contribute to authorization.

Authorizing one's supervising consultant. Conceptually, this means legitimizing the supervising consultant's expert power, allowing the supervising consultant to influence one's training because of his or her presumed competence. Authorizing one's supervising consultant is initially a matter of blind—or at least nearsighted—trust. This trust is paradoxical in the sense described by Smith and Berg (1987): "One needs to trust others, but development of that trust depends on trust already existing" (p. 115). More concretely, authorizing one's supervising consultant requires being open to a new role model and occasionally giving up control in the interest of growth.

In the first weeks after agreeing to work with my supervising consultant, I had a hard time trusting that she could teach me what I needed to know. My concerns surfaced indirectly in misgivings about my choice to leave the university where I had done my masters work. While I was only dimly aware of my hesitancy to authorize my supervising consultant, she was very sensitive to it. At one point prior to the start of the semester, she said defiantly, "I can teach you anything the people at Yale could!"

At least three factors contributed to my initial unwillingness to authorize my supervising consultant. First, I had great respect and admiration for the man who had been the lead consultant in my own study group when I was a student and had a hard time accepting his "replacement." Creating a working relationship with my supervising consultant seemed at the time to require rejecting my previous mentor. Second, this previous instructor was my only role model for how to do the consulting work. I was reluctant to place myself in the consultant role without taking with me what I had internalized of his approach. To face the anxiety of entering a study group for the first time as a consultant, I felt I needed the protection of a familiar and trusted internalized authority. Opening myself to the authority of a new person threatened to deprive me of this protection. Third, because she was female, I may have discounted the lead consultant's ability to instruct me. (Said differently, because I was male, I discounted the lead consultant's ability to instruct me.) This may have been common sexism, but it points to a broader question of the limits of anyone's ability to be a role model for a person of the opposite sex. I will return to this theme in more detail.

One route to—and a tangible result of—authorizing one's supervising consultant is giving up control in order to grow. Some of my greatest learning experiences occurred when I let go of my own approach to a task and followed my supervising consultant's advice. In one instance, I prepared a lecture on Bion, Klein, and basic assumption theory. It was clear and thorough and I was proud of it. (Its thoroughness was also my main defense against the anxiety of presenting my first lecture.) Twenty minutes before the class, I met with my supervising consultant to review my presentation. She commented that the thoroughness of the lecture left little room for the class to share what they had learned from the readings, and that it might simply feed their dependency. She suggested I present a bare outline of the main themes, and then facilitate a discussion to flesh out the ideas. It was a relief to anticipate turning over to the students more responsibility for the learning, but I felt uneasy abandoning the control offered by my carefully drawn plan. The discussion went well, and I discovered the thrill of building on students' interests and energy as a vehicle for facilitating learning. Had I not authorized my supervising consultant, I would have missed this experience.

Making mistakes. One also acquires new competence by blowing it—at least in moderation. During the first session of the semester, the group's anxiety was high and its confidence in the consultants and in the process still low and untested. I made an interpretation of a fantasy theme that was meekly assented to by one group member, and then resoundingly rejected by many of the rest as confusing and insensitive. Whether or not the interpretation was sound, my timing was poor. I had not established enough credibility with the group for them to be able to accept and work with the observation. Instead, I provided an excuse for the group to flee from the task and to temporarily devalue my fledgling authority. My supervising consultant later helped me explore why and how I made the interpretation, and effectively reframed errors as opportunities to learn instead of reasons to be gun-shy about potentially volatile or incorrect interpretations. In her words, "It isn't incompetent to make mistakes; it's incompetent not to learn from them." In this light, becoming authorized requires behaving competently, not perfectly, and involves learning as well as performing.

Establishing position power and behaving competently each has to do primarily with authorization of the consultant-in-training in the eyes of others—an institution, colleagues, and students. But a crucial part of authorization is legitimizing one's place in the role in one's *own* eyes. It requires a change in self-perception.

3. AUTHORIZATION THROUGH AUTHORIZING ONESELF

Authorizing oneself is a developmental process. For me, the process consisted of four stages: (1) "unfreezing" (Lewin, 1951, pp. 228–229) my existing view of myself; (2) identifying with role models and external authorities; (3) differentiating from these role models and external authorities; and (4) acting independently and interdependently. The process was not as linear as this framework implies, since certain stages recurred and entire cycles of the process occurred in microcosm.

Since the process involves an evolution from dependence through counterdependence to interdependence, the process mirrors the movement of some study group members' learning and is analogous to the process of a child growing up. (Maybe it *is* a process of growing up.) We all learn to live by living, and develop our power by using it. Group members become authorized to learn by learning (which is the members' primary task), and consultants become authorized by doing that which provides group members with learning opportunities (which is the consultants' primary task). Authorizing oneself is an inherently relational activity. Successful movement in this process is as much dependent on one's personal history and mentors as it is on one's individual efforts.

Unfreezing One's Existing Self-Concept

Becoming authorized as a consultant-in-training requires a substantial change in self-concept. The role of the full-time graduate student is characterized, in part, by dependence, low power, low status, and passivity. One receives course assignments, produces work for judgment by superiors, and receives grades and financial assistance. One's most creative and assertive acts are still made from a receptive and exploratory stance. (Robert Frost said education is hanging around until you've caught on.)

In entering the TA and co-consultant role, these aspects of my life were temporarily suspended or modified. I became an instructor as well as a learner, giver of grades as well as a receiver of them, target of authority projections as well as a source. Developing a new identity as well as changing the old one involved several stages.

Dependent Identification with Role Models

Forming a new identity after unfreezing the old first meant identifying with others who were established in the field. I did this by expressing views and behaviors I had internalized from my own previous study group consultant, and by minimizing differences with my supervising consultant.

My previous study group leader was my only role model for consulting to study groups. From him I learned a personal style while in role, an intellectual framework, and a vocabulary for interpretation. For example, during my first two or three sessions, I adopted his nonreactive facial expression and sought opportunities to use interpretations he had used. I consulted mainly by asking myself, "What would he do or say in this situation?" There was little of me in the work during my first session or two, and I felt most capable and secure when I sounded most like him. During this brief "mimicking" period I avoided meeting or talking to my previous group consultant. It wasn't until I had settled into a more personal style that I felt free to call or visit him. Perhaps I didn't want to be presented with evidence that I was behaving fraudulently.

During this early phase I also sought to fulfill my new role by minimizing differences with my supervising consultant. I made sure the class knew we were both trained at the same university and made a point with her of emphasizing those times when I agreed with her. This was less to impress her than to reassure myself that I had a right to be involved in this enterprise. During the first weeks I also *created* similarities to her—some related to the task and some not. I negotiated for responsibilities that would make my role as much like hers as possible. I also changed some of my personal style and approach in the study groups to be more nearly like hers and waited to build on her interpretations.

This shift in identification from my previous instructor to my supervising consultant was simultaneously a step toward authorizing myself and a first step in authorizing her. At the end of the second class session, I was impressed as I watched her manage the lecture/discussion hour. Remembering her comment about being able to teach me anything the instructors at Yale could, I thought, with a great sense of relief, "She's right, she *can* teach me everything I need to know about this work." Although I perceived myself as a capable beginner and learner, I was clearly still feeling very dependent.

The degree of my need to identify with her was also evident in behaviors *not* related directly to the consulting role. For example, when we met over supper to debrief the first study group session, we shared a pizza and a salad. I commented at the time that it felt like communion, that we were feeding off the same source in our theory and training. Also, we initially avoided discussing the terms of the independent study course that I was doing under her supervision. This would have highlighted the discrepancy between us in authority and expertise. Creating these similarities functioned to form my self-image as a study group consultant and to strengthen the boundary around the newly formed staff group that the two of us composed.

Counterdependent Differentiation from Role Models

Imitated behaviors based on identification quickly felt unauthentic to me, and were inadequate to meet new situations arising in the study groups. I became increasingly aware of differences between me and my supervising consultant. I see this as a counterdependent phase, since I was mostly aware of how I was unlike my supervising consultant and not yet very focused on what I brought to the work as an individual. For instance, in the third week of the semester my supervising consultant was prodding me for clarification of the terms of my independent study project. Justified as she was, I initially found this reassertion of her superior position power irritating. Two other examples of this emerging differentiation are worth noting.

In the fourth week of the semester, I recognized feeling competitive with my supervising consultant about the accuracy of our interpretations. I didn't know why, but I also felt that if my interpretations were different from hers, I would be in danger. In debriefing the session, I realized that I, as a student, was angry with her, not as an individual but as a member of my department's faculty. I had heard the day before that a fellow student had decided he hadn't the time or energy to complete the degree, and had withdrawn from the doctoral program. I liked this student and felt angry with the faculty for "killing off" a member of my group by setting requirements he couldn't meet. By implication, my supervising consultant could kill me off in the group if I disagreed with her. During my earlier, more dependent, phase, I would not have allowed myself to recognize this difference with my supervising consultant or the feelings connected to it.

In the fifth week of the semester, one study group was wrestling with my supervising consultant's authority in the group, and began using images and metaphors that hinted of racial and sexual domination. In working to understand the group's dynamics, she and I had to confront the seeming impossibility of understanding each other's experience because of our gender difference. I felt sad and angry at this realization—in part because this chasm between men and women *is* sad and infuriating, and in part because it weakened the identification I was relying on to establish my self-image as a consultant.

Differentiating from my supervising consultant eventually led to an event that felt like rebellion. Six weeks into the semester, just before our usual preclass staff meeting, I called my previous group dynamics instructor to ask him for information about an upcoming A. K. Rice seminar. At the beginning of the staff meeting I told my supervising consultant about my conversation with my former instructor. In response, she asked why I felt a need to "go to the source" to get my questions answered. She said she felt that she was as good a source for the information as he was, and that the way I announced my conversation with him brought him into our staff group in a way that felt intrusive. At the end of our meeting, and throughout the class session that followed, I felt distant and isolated from my supervising consultant.

Debriefing after the class, we struggled to understand what was happening. Initially I was unsure of why I wanted to bring my previous instructor into our staff group, and my supervising consultant understood my behavior as a refusal to accept her authority because she was a woman. We eventually realized that we each had wanted my supervising consultant to be capable of providing all I needed in a mentor and were resisting recognizing the inherent limitation in our relationship: as a woman, she could not be a role model for how to do this work as a man. It wasn't true that she "could teach me anything the people at Yale could": for one reason, they were male and she was not. In coming to this recognition I initially felt I was betraying my supervising consultant. I had to reject my unrealistic view of her unlimited ability to help in my authorization as a consultant. As a doctoral student subject to her authority, recognizing and acknowledging this limitation had the emotional charge of a rebellion, not of simple, rational discovery.

The authorizing process will usually require working *across* identity group boundaries, and always requires working across an authority boundary. My "rebellion" episode made it clear that there are some aspects of the work that are especially difficult to learn in cross-identity-group mentoring relationships. Beyond the limitations imposed by gender differences, there are other differences of age, personal history, temperament, and so on that make one consultant's authorization process different from any other's. While mentors are essential in facilitating the authorizing process, the individual consultant must find ways to incorporate his or her unique characteristics into the work.

Unfreezing, identification, and differentiation were necessary but insufficient aspects of my self-authorization. Ultimately, I defined myself as a consultant not only in positive or negative relation to role models, but by drawing on my own experience and characteristics.

Acting Independently and Interdependently

This aspect of self-authorization does not mean that one rejects all similarities with one's role models and supervising consultant. It means recognizing similarities and differences and exploiting the differences in the service of the group's learning. Acting independently and interdependently means integrating one's uniqueness with what one can learn from others.

Concretely, for me, this meant (1) trusting my feelings as valid data; (2) using my age, gender, and position in the hierarchy as bases for group learning; and (3) pursuing my own interpretations. This was when I felt most empowered (read "authorized") and when my interpretations seemed to have the most impact on the group.

This lonely step of finding one's own voice and integrating it with that of others requires courage: the kind of courage Paul Tillich calls "the courage to be" (Tillich, 1952). This courage is paradoxical in the sense described by Smith and Berg (1987). They say, "Only when one is floundering with all the uncertainties of not knowing what to do, feeling totally without courage, can one's actions be courageous. It is much like faith. One cannot believe unless one has doubts" (p. 149). Self-authorization requires being in touch with all the subjectivity of one's particular experience, doubting its relevance, and then using it to create learning that would otherwise vanish with the doubt.

A Final Note on Authorizing Oneself

The process of establishing a new self-concept involves anxiety as well as empowerment. The anxiety comes from fears of retribution and isolation rooted in the task's demand for boundary setting and differentiation. Some of these changes in identity are temporary and are in place only as long as one is in the role. Others require more fundamental and personal shifts that may be permanent.

I felt the fear of retribution most strongly in relation to study group members. In interpreting group dynamics, one discusses the undiscussable and excavates the buried. Since study group members often perceive these comments as judgmental or punishing, there is an element of betrayal involved for the consultant-in-training who is part student and part staff—like being a scab crossing the picket line, a whistle-blower going public, or a double agent revealing his or her duplicity. The level of my anxiety was usually in direct proportion to the accuracy of my interpretation. I also had fantasy fears of retribution about upsetting the "natural" hierarchy of authority. I was doubly guilty: first, for being subordinate to a woman, and second, for assuming an authority position over class members much older than I. One study group was never able to confront directly why I was the TA instead of the forty-nine-year-old group member who was also senior to me in the doctoral program. The group constantly tried to replace me with this man until *I* came to believe I had a legitimate claim to my position as consultant.

The anxiety of isolation was in relation to students, mentors, and my family of origin. In creating an authority boundary between me and other students, I temporarily deprived myself of my primary group membership. In aspiring to authorization as a consultant, I set myself up for evaluation and possible rejection by the gatekeepers of the field. In differentiating from my supervising consultant, I risked conflict with and isolation from her. And I faced destruction of my privileged relationship with my supervising consultant as the temporary staff boundary dissolved at the end of the semester. Finally, the working-class orientation to authority that I had learned from my father seemed increasingly incompatible with becoming authorized as a consultant, or seeing myself as a professional and an academic. The reshaping of that orientation was functional in my new role, but it meant distancing myself from the man who raised me.

Becoming authorized by establishing position power, behaving competently, and authorizing oneself are all crucial aspects of the authorizing process. But, paradoxically, one cannot be fully authorized without authorizing others.

4. AUTHORIZATION THROUGH AUTHORIZING GROUP MEMBERS

It is impossible to be authorized as study group consultant without authorizing the other actors in the system in which one is being trained. I have already discussed how the consultant agrees to legitimize certain institutional powers in return for position power. And I have emphasized the importance of legitimizing one's supervising consultant early in the relationship. However, one's authorization as a consultant also requires that the consultant authorize the student members of the study group. Again, it is apparent how the dynamics of authorization are fundamentally socially created. One cannot authorize others without their conscious or unconscious cooperation.

Authorizing a group's members means legitimizing their power to take advantage of learning opportunities and to provide such opportunities for themselves and each other. To not authorize them in this way is to keep group members dependent on the consultants. This is not competent consultant behavior, and so undermines the informal authorization of the consultant-in-training. How does the consultant-in-training authorize group members and thus contribute to his or her own authorization?

Trusting group members. The consultant must trust the group members' desire and ability to be involved in the task. This basic trust underlies all the other ways in which the consultant-in-training authorizes group members.

Resisting members' desire for dependency. The consultant-in-training must not succumb to the many manifestations of group members' desire for dependency—such as projections of omnipotence or exhibitions of confusion and helplessness. Since this desire is especially strong at the beginning of the group, it coincides perfectly with the time when the consultant-in-training may feel most in need of affirmation, and most uneasy about having separated him- or herself from other students.

Letting members be competent. Consultants authorize group members by providing members with opportunities to acquire and demonstrate competence in understanding group dynamics. In my setting, these opportunities were provided through participation in study group sessions, independent group work during institutional events, and through group presentations to the class. Consultant recognition of competent work by students helps students reclaim their split-off and projected competence from the consultants, assists the authorization of group members, and ultimately helps authorize the consultants.

For example, at one point a study group seated themselves so as to move me out of my usual position and into a seat next to the supervising consultant. She and I each made interpretations that recognized not only the difficulties the group was having relating to our authority, but also the exploration of their own authority that was implicit in the gesture. By not punishing them for their "insubordination" and by giving them room to explore the bases for their action, the group was authorized to learn. I emerged from the session feeling greater legitimacy in my role for having responded to the incident not as a personal attack, but as an opportunity for the group to explore its relationship to the consultants.

Accepting one's decreasing influence. Finally, the consultant-in-training authorizes group members by accepting his or her decreasing influence as the groups become less dependent and more competent. It may be analogous to the "empty nest syndrome" in which parents feel lost and irrelevant when their last child leaves home. I first felt it during a day-long institutional event during which the two study groups worked alone and then in an intergroup setting. Some good task leadership emerged in each group, and the groups were able to use the interpretive framework on their own to facilitate their learning. This empty-nest feeling increased toward the end of the semester as the groups were able to work productively on group issues with less interpretive help from the consultants. In addition occasionally to feeling irrelevant, I also felt gratified to see group members able to use their own skills to make learning opportunities out of their interactions.

CONCLUSION

I have shown how (in my experience) the process of authorization for the consultant-in-training depends on four main dynamics: (1) establishing position power, (2) behaving competently, (3) authorizing oneself, and (4) authorizing group members. Each of these dynamics contributes either to one's formal or informal authority, and none can be set in motion by the consultant alone. Each of the four dynamics of authorization is also a requirement for doing the work of the consultant. One cannot do the work without being authorized, and one cannot become authorized without doing the work.

Throughout the system in which one is being trained, temporary and permanent shifts in identity and self-concept evoke strong feelings, including guilt, resentment, exhilaration, rejection, inclusion, confusion, empowerment, isolation, omnipotence, and dependency. How different actors in the system deal with these temporary and permanent identity shifts has a major impact on the ability of the consultant-in-training to become authorized.

Supervising consultants and consultants-in-training differ in their expertise, position power, and sense of being entitled to the role. These differences are real and should not be erased. But all of us in this field are in a constant process of being authorized and authorizing others—in the service of our own learning and of those who contract for our services. Ironically, authorization of the study group consultant is at its most complete when group members create their own learning experiences and the need for the consultant is low.

Chapter 15

Reflections on the Development of a Supervisor

DAVID N. BERG

The portrait of an ideal supervisor, that has evolved from my trainees struggling to define such an entity and from my readings and observations, is a multifaceted and complex one. He/she should be ethical, well informed, knowledgeable in his/her theoretical orientation, clinically skilled, articulate, empathic, a good listener, gentle, confrontative, accepting, challenging, stimulating, provocative, reassuring, encouraging, possess a good sense of humor, a good sense of timing, be innovative, solid, exciting, laid back—but not all at the same time—the supervisory mode and mood should be appropriate to the trainee's stage of professional development and level of professional maturity.

—Florence Kaslow (1986)

The question, of course, is just exactly how does one get from here to there, presuming that the ideal is achievable. The answer is, in many ways, unique to each individual who seeks to develop his or her supervisory approach. In attempting to contribute to the development of a less experienced colleague, each of us is bound to confront the main channels as well as the backwater eddies of our own personalities. Our ability to work with ourselves often defines the quality and limits of our work with others. Yet theory and experience suggest that we can identify patterns in the development of a supervisor.

What little has been written on supervisor development focuses on descriptions of the various stages or levels of development (Hess, 1986; Stoltenberg and Delworth, 1987). And while a great deal has been written about the struggles of the trainee during supervision, less attention has been given to the dynamics of the supervisor's experience in learning to do the work.

This chapter is my attempt to add some reflections and some information to the search for patterns of supervisor development. I am primarily concerned with supervision that takes place in the context of an ongoing experiential learning group. I have also chosen to focus on the dynamics internal to the supervisor as he or she struggles to do supervisory work. It is clear to me that other dynamics (group, intergroup, systemic) exert a powerful influence on the development of a supervisor and his or her relationships with supervisees, but in this paper I examine these forces from the perspective of the internal experience of the supervisor. Since it is a personal account, there will be an intimate contamination of what is idiosyncratic to me and what may be more generally true about supervisor development. At various points throughout the chapter I will pause to reflect on the possible influence of my personality on my experience, observations, and interpretations, but it will often be left to the reader to determine the "general" validity of what follows.

SUPERVISION AND THE SUPERVISOR

Although the focus of supervision and the literature on supervision is the supervisee—his or her skill development, identity development (often called "self-work"), and relationship to the supervisor—it is clear that the supervisor, too, is involved in a process of developing both a set of supervisory skills and a professional identity as a supervisor. This requires supervisor "self-work" that is commensurate, in many cases, with the work of the supervisee. This self-work includes the supervisor's willingness to inquire into the nature of his or her involvement in the supervisory relationship and the ways in which he or she is affected by the supervisory process.

Especially early in a "career," the supervisor's own professional development can be a major, if not dominating, factor in the supervisory process and its outcomes. It is often the case, for example, that a young assistant professor teaches with an even younger teaching assistant a group dynamics course of the type described in this volume. The assistant professor now adds the struggles of "being a good supervisor" to the challenges of teaching a good course, developing a professional identity and managing his or her own work.

If the supervisory relationship were *just* an additional professional burden, it could be postponed for a few years. However, this assistant professor probably realizes that his or her own development can be fostered in the supervisory role. As a result, a relationship that often focuses on the development of the supervisee inevitably includes a full measure of supervisor development as well. The same can be said when the supervisor is more senior, though too often he or she is regarded as a constant in the supervision equation, a "professional" whose behavior is influenced primarily by the differences in who is being supervised and under what conditions. Throughout my experience, the work I did with supervisees proceeded in tandem with the work I struggled to do with myself as I encountered issues in the supervisory process that had been, at best, only concepts before.

A Definition of Supervision

Formally, supervision can be described as a process in which an experienced professional takes explicit responsibility for aiding the professional development or practice of a colleague. Usually, but not always, (1) the supervisor is older than the supervisee, (2) the supervisee is in a novice phase of his or her professional development or is experiencing particular difficulty in carrying out his or her professional work, (3) the work of supervision is carried out "alongside" ongoing professional work that serves as the topical focus of the supervision, and (4) there is some payment for the supervisory work, either in the form of tuition or fee. The goal of this process is (and should be) focused on the supervisee and can be expressed as follows:

> To aid in the development of the supervisee's professional "voice," one that is informed by theory as well as practice; is appropriately dependent upon accumulated knowledge yet independent enough to integrate the skills, identity, characteristics, and creativity of the individual with this knowledge; and includes a healthy albeit responsible willingness to be critical of existing knowledge in the face of new experience or personal research.

Supervision in Experiential Groups

The approach to the study of group dynamics discussed in this book carries with it an implicit description of supervision. There is universal agreement that supervision is carried out according to the model of instruction or therapy in use (Alderfer, 1988). In this sense supervision is a "meta-" process, the application to the training process of the theory and method used in the teaching or consulting work itself. Consulting to experiential groups, for example, involves helping a group understand, emotionally and intellectually, the processes that affect its internal life. These processes inevitably include conscious as well as unconscious dynamics that arise in response to authority relations, group composition, group development, and the group's embeddedness in a larger social system. The method used by the consultant to facilitate the learning of the group has, at its foundation, the development of a self-scrutinizing environment that includes both the consultants and the group members. To this environment are added intervention, interpretation, and conceptual work, first by the consultants and ultimately by the other group members as well.

Supervision in such an undertaking also involves the creation of a self-scrutinizing environment that includes both the supervisor and the supervisee. As in the consulting relationship, the supervisory relationship is concerned with both the conscious and unconscious dynamics that arise as the supervisory relationship struggles with parallel issues of authority, composition/identity, development, and embeddedness. And, like the consulting relationship, the work of interpretation and conceptualization is, hopefully, increasingly shared with the supervisee over the course of the supervision. The process of supervision in training consultants who will work with groups is therefore an application of the "group consultation" theory and method to the training relationship itself. It is likely to uncover covert and unconscious processes alive in the supervisory relationship and create "work" for the supervisee, the relationship, and the supervisor. It is with the development and evolution of the supervisor's self-work that the remainder of this chapter is concerned.

In presenting some of the developmental issues I see arising for supervisors, I will draw primarily on my own experience as a supervisor during the past ten years. My supervision work has been done in an academic environment. In most cases, I have worked with one or sometimes two supervisees in teaching a graduate course on group dynamics. In a few cases I supervised a graduate student who was teaching his or her own group dynamics course in which I had no direct involvement. There is a debate about the appropriate supervisory model that centers on the question of whether or not the supervisor should work with the trainee in the classroom or therapeutic session. I believe this is an important debate but one that should be wary of "either/or" pronouncements.

In my case, most of my supervisees were involved in their first group consultation experience, and our joint work allowed them to watch my actions and to examine my choices. It also provided us with a hierarchical working relationship so that both of us could experience the struggles, personal and collective, inherent in making such a relationship productive and satisfying. Since the group consultant is always engaged in this kind of face-to-face relationship with group members, the parallel supervisory relationship seemed especially appropriate. It was (and is) also the case that, as a member of a university faculty, I felt directly responsible for classroom instruction and did not feel that it was appropriate to turn over the direct teaching and consultation function to a novice consultant. I will return to this topic later. At this point let us turn to the reflections on self-work that I have accumulated during my work as a supervisor.

ISSUES IN LEARNING

Ekstein and Wallerstein (1958) used the phrase *issues in learning* to describe those issues in a supervisory relationship that affected the supervisee's ability to learn the theory and practice of psychotherapy. They also noted that it was important for the supervisory process to analyze and understand these issues, since the "issues in learning" that seemed to disrupt the supervisory process almost invariably paralleled disruptive issues in the therapeutic relationship. I would suggest that the topic can be more broadly applied to include those dynamics within and between the people involved in any supervisory process that threaten the training goals of the supervisory relationship. It is my experience in teaching group dynamics that the "issues in learning" in supervision often mirror dynamics occurring within or between group members and group consultants and therefore are especially important topics for analysis and discussion. In keeping with the focus of this chapter, I have chosen to discuss three such issues in learning that are, in my experience, particularly salient for the supervisor.

Authority for Learning

It is the espoused belief of most supervisors, I think, that the supervisory relationship should be an opportunity for learning for both the supervisor and the supervisee. This belief includes the realization that the learning objectives of the two people are different, but that each has something to gain from a mutual commitment to self-scrutiny and an ongoing reflective analysis of their involvement with the group. Putting this belief into practice is not always easy.

For the supervisor, the performance pressures as well as the formal responsibility for the course often overwhelm his or her ability (or willingness) to adopt a learning stance on the supervisory experience. The same, of course, can be said to characterize the supervisee's struggles to learn, but in most cases the supervisee actually *does* have more to learn about consulting to groups than the supervisor, and the relationship *is* a training experience for the supervisee. This is the rub. My struggle is to allow myself to learn not just about the supervisee and the group, but about myself and my own participation in the staff relationship as well. In order to do this, I must be able to see and accept the supervisee's authority to teach me something. This I subscribe to in principle, but it is something I often resist in practice.

Learning from the supervisee carries with it all the difficulties involved in professional learning (the experience of ignorance or vulnerability, feelings of incompetence) and, in addition, can disrupt the often tacit understanding between supervisor and supervisee that the former teaches and the latter learns. For me, the disruption of the supervisory "hierarchy of learning" was most acute when I was most concerned about my ability to be a supervisor. At these times, recognizing the authority of the supervisee, no matter how circumscribed, threatened the image I had of my own embryonic supervisory authority. Even now, the more successful the supervisory relationship, the more I must confront my resistance to the developing competence of the trainee. The more he or she develops the confidence and skill to carry out the work of a group consultant, the more likely it is that he or she will be able to inquire into the dynamics and meaning of our relationship and my participation in it.

Why is it important that I continue to struggle to learn from the supervisees I work with, even while we are in a relationship that is primarily devoted to their learning? There are a number of answers. First, the supervisee is in a unique "middle position" in our work, enabling him or her to see me and the group in ways that are different from my own. His or her view of me can aid us in the difficult task of examining *my* projections and transference reactions, and this in turn contributes to the work of the course and the work of supervision. To the extent that my projections have a defensive quality, it is likely that I will resist analyzing them in more or less sophisticated ways. Unless I can develop a relationship with the supervisee in which *I* feel safe and trusting enough to learn, there is a risk that I will use my authority in the relationship to defend myself against seeing my own unconscious involvements. In addition, the supervisee's hierarchical position between the group members and the supervisor can provide the staff with a more empathic connection to the experience of the "real" learners, thereby improving our understanding of the group. If I consistently resist learning from the supervisee, I risk losing crucial insight into my own and the group's unconscious life.

A second reason to strive for some degree of mutuality in the learning process is that what I learn about myself can be a valuable tool in carrying out my work as a supervisor. As a number of behavioral scientists (Alderfer, 1987; Bradford, 1980; Smith, Chapter 13, above; Berg, 1980) have noted, one's own reactions are often a window into the reactions of others. The development of the "self as instrument" is a continuous process of learning about one's conscious and unconscious reactions in different settings with different people. If I do not allow myself to learn about my reactions and behaviors in the supervisory relationship, I cannot examine the meaning of those reactions and behaviors for the supervision and for the group.

Finally, it may seem obvious to say that a supervisory relationship, like any relationship, loses its vitality when one or both of the people involved shut down the possibility of learning in the relationship. In supervision, the hierarchical relationship between supervisor and supervisee means that if (or when) the supervisor shuts down the possibility of learning, the supervisee is likely to "learn" to do the same thing. This not only jeopardizes the supervision and the particular group dynamics course in which the supervision is occurring, it also jeopardizes the supervisee's understanding of the role of consultant or facilitator. Consciously, none of us wants to give the message that a well-trained group consultant closes him- or herself off from learning that involves less experienced people. The possibility of sending this message is ever-present.

I do not mean to suggest that a supervisor is *either* open to learning or not. In fact, my experience is that I close down as the supervisory relationship passes through different issues and open up again if we have successfully expressed and explored them. But my struggle, over time, has been to recognize that the authority for teaching and learning resides in both of us, not equally but complementarily, and to allow myself genuinely to be a learner and a supervisor at the same time.

Control

Related to the issue of the authority for learning is the issue of control. In its simplest terms, the issue of control can be expressed by the question "When and under what conditions am I willing to let go?" Here again, the reasonable answer seems to be that it is appropriate and desirable to share control of the group sessions and the supervision process incrementally, as the supervisee develops his or her confidence and skill. Initially, the supervisee will look to the supervisor to structure the sessions (even if this "structure" is relatively unstructured). As the relationship develops, control of the content and process of the supervision sessions becomes shared. This answer, however, belies some of the complexity of the issue. Isn't it necessary for the supervisor to exert some control over the supervisory process? When does too much control undermine the development of the supervisee? When is too little control an abrogation of professional responsibility? What does the inequality in experience, formal authority, and responsibility mean for the distribution of control?

My internal conversations designed to answer these questions have changed over the years. At first it was even hard to allow the conversations to occur. I knew these were important issues, but my concern with being able to control the outcomes of my course and my supervision produced a consistent bias toward the control residing with me. I rationalized this choice, which at the time seemed to me like a response to my own anxiety about succeeding in new roles, by acknowledging that the supervisee, like the group dynamics class, should not be *given* authority and control; he or she must work for it. Control that is given without being earned carries with it the subtle undermining effects of paternalism. This rationalization has some validity, but my choice about retaining control was rooted as much in my own anxieties and inexperience as in my considered opinion about the dynamics of supervision.

As I learned more about myself as a teacher and a supervisor I felt the urge to control the outcomes lessen. At the same time, I began to discover that "letting go" had some deeply personal implications for me, and so my struggle with the questions stated above took on new meaning. The institutional gave way, somewhat, to the intrapsychic. This has been a difficult struggle and one that continues. "Control" may not evoke the same depth of response from others as it does from me, but I am sure that there is at least one "issue in learning" for all supervisors that will engage deeply personal material. Needless to say, it is in the service of the supervision for the supervisor to recognize and work on this issue, and he or she may need to do it alone or in a therapeutic relationship outside supervision.

Another side of this topic is the issue of self-control in supervision. Much could be written about the self-indulgence of supervisors who abuse the supervisory relationship, but it would be a mistake to "split" the world of supervisors into those with self-control and those without it. What do I do for example, with my needs for colleagueship and intimacy in my relationship with a supervisee? Is it in his or her best interests to hear about the stresses in my professional environment? What about meeting friendship needs through supervision? These questions are not easy ones to answer either, but here I find myself with a few "rules" to follow. First, these are *my* questions to answer. "Sharing" with the supervisee the responsibility for answering these questions is itself an answer, and not necessarily the best one. It is incumbent upon me to think through and/or discuss with others the risks and benefits to the supervisory relationship of these kinds of choices. Second, if I find that I am *not* thinking about the implications for the supervision of allowing more of my personal and professional life into the supervisory session, this is a clue to possible denial and delusion on my part. Third, when I am in doubt I exercise caution. This may be an example of my preference for supervisor control, but it has been my experience that while it is always possible to increase the level of disclosure in supervision in the service of the goals of supervision, decreasing the level of disclosure or working through a "mistake" of inappropriate supervisor disclosure is often difficult, ineffective, or detrimental to the supervisory relationship. Finally, too much self-control can be almost as debilitating to a supervisory relationship as too little.

As I describe it, there is a balance around the question of control that is often hard to find. It is my impression that I have approximated that balance in a series of near misses, sometimes exercising too much control, sometimes exercising too little. It is as if the perfect balance would, paradoxically, rob the relationship of some of the material with which it needs to work. Yet I believe it is important that I keep seeking this balance even as I become aware that it may be impossible to achieve.

Dependence and Independence

The dependency of the supervisee in supervision is a given. It is a clinical topic in the group dynamics class as well as in the supervisory relationship. It is an accepted topic and one that is acceptable to both the supervisor and the trainee. The dependency of the supervisor, however, is less openly acknowledged and discussed, but the supervisor is dependent too. At a very minimum, the supervisee's behavior can make the work in the group dynamics class more or less difficult, more or less interesting, and more or less successful. In more subtle ways, the supervisor who is a co-consultant and co-instructor depends on the supervisee's willingness and ability to struggle with unconscious forces in the group in ways that contribute to rather than detract from the learning of the group members.

In supervision, too, the supervisor is dependent upon the supervisee. There is no supervision without the supervisee (what if you offered a supervisory opportunity and nobody signed up?!), and the quality of the supervisory experience is determined to a large extent by the supervisee. Finally, the supervisor may depend on the supervisee for appreciation, understanding, and acceptance. The supervisee often has a more intimate look at the supervisor's thoughts, feelings, decisions, and struggles than do most other students and colleagues. This may make his or her understanding and acceptance all the more meaningful. If we are dependent on other people, in whatever ways, for the experience of accomplishment, contribution, and importance, then the supervisee plays a significant role in the supervisor's life.

This dependency is often difficult to accept in all but the most abstract ways. And even as I begin to accept my dependency on the supervisee, for example, I find myself seeking ways to minimize it. Sometimes I try to teach my way out of my dependency. In these situations, often my anxiety has been heightened by the fact that the person on whom I am dependent is *different* from me: younger, female, ideologically different, black, or Hispanic, of different ethnic background. So my coping strategy is to teach these trainees how to be more like me. My irrational hope is that by transforming them into someone *who would act the way I would*, I ease my anxiety about my dependency. I use my power in the supervisory relationship to attempt to control and minimize my feelings about my dependency.

Why is it so difficult to accept this dependency that I summon such defenses in spite of "knowing better"? I think it is because our implicit images of dependency involve parents and children, the strong and the weak, the helpful and the helpless, the less vulnerable and the more vulnerable. A supervisor's dependence on a supervisee violates the accepted "order" in these images, and since our images of mutual or "top-down" dependency are not as well developed, we may feel that something isn't right. How can the supervisor be weak, childlike, helpless, and vulnerable? It is very hard individually to change the images we carry in our minds, so instead we work against our interests in a productive supervisory relationship to change the feelings of dependency.

The struggle is to allow ourselves, as supervisors, to feel our dependencies and to explore and examine those feelings and their impact on our supervisory work. This is made especially difficult because supervision too often points only at the supervisee's dependency for analysis. I am likely to "miss" my own reactions in my attention to the dependency in the supervisee. For example, a supervisee makes a "technical" mistake during a group dynamics experiential session and in supervision I become "preachy" in my efforts to explain the nature of the error, not because I consider this the best way to handle the situation but because the event has heightened my feelings of dependency on the supervisee and I react. As I try to assert my helpfulness, I subvert and run the risk of submerging the issue altogether.

The acceptance of my dependency on the supervisee does not equate to a refusal to acknowledge my own source of independent action and thought. As a supervisor I am both dependent and independent. I must be able to draw on my experience so that I can speak not only in the moment of the current relationship, but with a perspective informed by theory and by my experience as a supervisor. The struggle here is to develop a trust in one's own independence that makes it possible to say the unpopular, the unspeakable, or the unsettling when such things need to be said. Consider the example of the supervisee who wants to be a colleague but not a student and who accuses me of not being open enough, disclosing enough, willing enough to learn. It is my opinion that what is best for the work of supervision always involves an awareness and examination of differences (including but not limited to hierarchy) rather than a dismissal, denial, or trivialization of these differences. In this situation, it is my work to affirm our difference rather than deny it and to work toward understanding its influence on our work, our relationship, and each of us individually. The supervisor's independence of voice enables him or her to explore the issue raised by the accusation instead of or in addition to exploring the experiential events that underscored it.

IDENTITY ISSUES

In this section I would like to focus on the involvement of one's identity in the supervisory process. By "identity" I mean those group memberships that contribute to the way I respond and react and the ways others respond and react to me. I have chosen to include a discussion of these identity issues because I have become increasingly aware of their influence on me and on my work as teacher and supervisor. Ten years ago, for example, in a course on individual and group behavior in organizations, I devoted one two-hour class to *both* race and gender dynamics in organizations. My teaching assistant at the time, a black graduate student, suggested that one could teach a whole course on these group identity issues and their impact on organizational life. I remember saying that we should do more in subsequent years but that there was "content" that had to be covered in such courses. Over the years, my opinions have changed. The content of organizational behavior and of group dynamics is infused with the dynamics of gender, race, ethnicity, hierarchy, sexual preference, age, and other group memberships. In fact, it may be impossible to study group dynamics without attending to these intergroup influences since, unless we can examine them, we will be forced implicitly to embed them in our theories.

The same can be said of supervision. Until recently, little mention has been made of racial and gender dynamics in supervision. Of course even less has been said about the role of the supervisor's identity in his or her development in the role. In the following paragraphs I will discuss what I have learned about identity issues that have been alive during my development as a supervisor. My group memberships are present and alive in the other sections of the paper, but in this section they are front and center. What follows are some observations and conclusions from a supervisor who is white, American, male, Jewish, thirty-nine years old, a husband and father.

Toward Transcendence?

For a long time now, I have experienced and observed the power of group memberships to influence individual thought, feeling, and action. In my teaching of group dynamics, for example, I am increasingly aware that my reactions, metaphors, associations, and evaluations are powerfully rooted in my various group identities and are called up when specific group memberships are made salient by behavior in the group. This is as true for me as it is for the group members. I am also aware that the groups I work with choose certain metaphors about me to express their unconscious fears and struggles because my identity (for example, Jewish, male) evokes these metaphors (for example, rabbi, concentration camp inmate or guard). The same phenomena appear in supervision. Two psychological processes seem to be occurring simultaneously: (1) I am expressing my identity in the way I make sense of the world, and with that expression comes the hope that this identity will be accepted, along with the fear that it will not; (2) I am finding ways of using the identities of others (and the history of intergroup relations between "their" groups and "mine") as a vehicle for expressing my own anxieties.

The dilemma is that I would prefer that *others* not use what they learn about my identity to express their own fears, and yet part of the legacy of my group memberships is a set of reactions to others that causes me to use them. In supervision I have tried to act on my commitment to examine these two processes as they co-occur, and this has led to the discovery of yet a third dynamic. In reflecting back on my relationships with supervisees, I realized that I had developed the belief that through hard *interpersonal* work in the context of supervision, the two of us could actually transcend our group memberships, their influences on us, and their historical relationships with each other. I did not actually say these words, but I behaved as if they were true when I began to expect that the boundary around the supervisory relationship would be stronger than any boundary around any of the *supervisee's* "other" group memberships. The wish was so powerful that I actually saw this transcendent boundary emerge. It was a rude shock when I discovered that this was not the case, that graduate students still talked to other graduate students about how to manage my reactions as a faculty member, black supervisees still consulted with black colleagues about how to manage my reactions as a white person, and women still talked to other women when deciding how to manage my membership in the male group.

It is one thing to believe that group memberships exert powerful influences on us; it is another to come to grips with the fact that the interpersonal relationship called supervision always takes place in the context of the group identities of the people involved. This is not to suggest that no interpersonal relationship can develop between supervisor and supervisee. Rather, I am beginning to understand that the interpersonal relationship can grow and develop only when each person is able to understand and discuss the role of group memberships in his or her life and in the life of the other.

These group memberships help keep supervision (and consultation to groups) from being a stagnating, clone-producing activity.

One final note. I have discovered that even when two people share a group membership that is important to both of them, there remains the possibility that their different ways of being *within* the group (different racial, gender, or ethnic identity, for example) can function in the same ways that differences *between* groups do. Two white men who view their "whiteness" differently may find themselves using this difference to explain or justify other issues that arise in their relationship. In some contexts, this within-group identity difference can be made extremely salient for the people involved, as in the case of the only black faculty member supervising the only black graduate student or the only female consultant supervising the only female trainee. The pressures in these situations to magnify the within-group differences in response either to the system's desire to "split" the minority group members or to the needs of the people involved to develop and establish a *personal* identity in the system can be immense. In these situations, like the situations in which the identity differences are across groups, it is extremely important to keep talking about the influence of individual identity on the supervisory relationship as well as the influence of the supervisory relationship's identity on the larger social system.

I Said That?

There have been numerous times when as a supervisor I said something that I wish I hadn't said, felt something I wish I hadn't felt, or done something I wish I hadn't done because of what is revealed about me. I may, for example, have made a sexist or racist comment or displayed an insensitivity to a supervisee's or group member's ethnic or religious background. Inevitably these "unwitting" disclosures became the focus of discussion in supervision, and in most cases we discovered something about me, about our relationship, or about the dynamics alive in the group with which we were working. There have also been times when I wished the other person were different: more sensitive, less attractive, more Jewish, less personal. It wasn't that I wished these supervisees would *do* something different; I wanted them to *be* something different, to change their identity. I wanted them to be different because the way they were raised difficult issues for *me* about *me*.

My ability to accept the supervisee's identity and to support him or her in integrating that identity into the role of group consultant is constrained by my own self-acceptance. What can make supervision difficult for the supervisor is that in the supervisory relationship I sometimes encounter who I am in unexpected ways. Thus, the first struggle is whether I can accept this information in the supervisory setting. I may be embarrassed or defensive or concerned about my ability to supervise in the aftermath of the disclosure. Only after I can accept the information can I struggle with what this information says about who I am.

There is a parallel here with the supervisee's experience, for I suspect that the fear of disclosing something embarrassing, "unacceptable," or "unprofessional" is a constant companion during the process of professional training. This produces a special dilemma for the supervisor. If I am successful in *never* saying the "wrong" thing, I probably contribute to the supervisee's reticence about saying anything original, controversial, prejudiced, ignorant, et cetera (for fear of its being "wrong" and therefore unprofessional). If I do say things I wish I hadn't, I might disclose information that would cause the supervisee to question my competence as a supervisor. Mercifully, it is nearly impossible to be "correct" all the time in all relationships, and so we are periodically presented with the opportunity to develop a way of learning from those moments when in conversation with someone else we discover something about our own identity.

Attraction to the Role

Supervising the development of a group consultant is related to but not identical to supervising the development of a psychotherapist. One area of overlap, however, is that in both cases it is extremely important to consider the transferential and countertransferential dynamics in the supervisory setting. Because the supervision of group consultants is *not* a therapeutic relationship, it is sometimes harder to include this examination in the supervisory process. There is much to be learned about these dynamics for the supervisors and supervisees alike. I will not try to review those dynamics here. Instead, I would like to highlight one manifestation of these dynamics that remains a constant challenge for me in my supervisory work.

One of the most difficult aspects of analyzing the supervisory relationship involves disentangling the supervisee's feelings about the supervisor from his or her feelings about the supervisory role. The value in separating these feelings lies in the importance of examining the supervisee's reactions to authority, since these reactions can provide insight into the supervisee's struggles with taking on the role of an authority figure (in the group) and into the authority dynamics between the group and the staff as a whole. One difficulty in disentangling these two sets of feelings is that it is sometimes hard to enlist the supervisor in the analysis.

Most of us are more able to see the influence of "the role" when the supervisee's reactions are negative. In this case, the self-esteem needs of the supervisor qua human being are sympathetic to a timely attempt to examine how much of the negative feelings coming from the supervisee are directed at the role rather than at the person. When the supervisee's reactions are positive (sexual attraction, idealization, humbling respect, and admiration), the self-esteem needs of the supervisor can join forces with the supervisee's desires not to examine these feelings, thereby spoiling them. After all, who wants to discover that a supervisee's respect and affection are for the power and status of the role rather than the analytic and empathic qualities of the person? In my experience, the early stages of a supervisory relationship make it easier for me to analyze the role aspect of a supervisee's positive regard simply because he or she knows precious little about my person. But as relationships develop the work gets harder. Respect and affection based on our personal relationship now enter into the supervisee's feelings, as does my desire to be liked by someone who knows me. Yet transferential attraction to the role may be alive and well, given the continuing differences in power, status, and experience. The more battered my self-esteem, the more susceptible I am to an uncritical acceptance of a positive transference. My own work is to stay alert to the connection between my self-esteem and the analysis of the supervisee's feelings toward me. The struggle is that my own emotional needs may get in the way.

On Being Part of a System

One of the themes in this book is that what happens inside groups is influenced by what happens around them, in the social systems in which they are embedded. In supervision, the relationship between two individuals and the groups they represent is embedded in the relationships between these groups in the larger social system in which the supervision takes place (Alderfer and Smith, 1982). In some instances, the dynamics in the larger system may determine the agenda of supervision.

Consider three illustrations. In one case, the faculty has recently decided to enforce a long-standing but rarely enforced policy that affects teaching assistants in their roles as students. The supervisory session begins with a heightened awareness of the power differences between the supervisor and the supervisee that originates in the dynamics of the larger system to which both belong. In this case, it becomes clear that belonging to a larger system also means that the people involved in supervision may have more than one role relationship with each other. Faculty-student relations can have a dramatic effect on supervisor-supervisee relations.

In another case, a threatened strike by clerical and technical workers at a university forced the supervisory relationship to consider how to handle the boundary around the group dynamics class (should students be forced to cross picket lines to come to class?) and how to handle the boundary around their supervision (will supervision be held on campus in the event of a strike?). Since the supervisor and the supervisee may be in very different relationships with the university, the decisions at the larger system level affect their supervisory relationship.

Finally, there is the situation in which a black supervisee comes to supervision after a faculty group that includes his white supervisor has just voted not to promote the only black faculty member in the program, a faculty member that he (the supervisor) and many others believed was exceptionally well qualified. How do the supervisor and the supervisee address the heightened saliency of race relations in their supervisory relationship? The necessity of examining the role of racial dynamics in their work together and in their work with the group has been underscored by events in the larger system.

In all three of these cases, the dynamics of embedded intergroup theory include an interesting and complex variation because the members of the supervisory "system" were also active participants in the larger social system (as a teaching assistant, faculty member, clerical supervisor). It is therefore much more difficult for the supervisory relationship to wall itself off from the larger-system events by pointing to what "those s.o.b.'s" are doing, even though both people may want to avoid examining their participation in these larger-system events. When "we" and "they" converge, the agenda of the larger system becomes the agenda for supervision.

Any supervision that is embedded in a larger system will inevitably face and struggle with these influences. In some cases these larger system events provide grist for the supervisory mill, real-life events that serve to evoke powerful, covert issues alive in the supervision. In other cases these events are merely distractions from the work of supervision. In still other situations, these events call upon the supervisor to attempt to take an active role in monitoring the larger system dynamics, intervening when possible and necessary. This active role might involve everything from engaging in a protracted discussion with the business office about the special demands made on teaching assistants in a group dynamics course to raising with the dean and faculty unpopular criticisms of the school's affirmative action efforts. This active stance is one that is often hard for me to accept, since it requires engaging a system outside the supervisory relationship. But I have come to understand the importance of my attempts to manage the larger system.

It may be necessary, for example, for me to engage in the management of the larger system because I may be the only member of the supervisory relationship who can (through my membership in certain faculty groups). I find that it is both important and difficult to participate in larger-system management when I am feeling that I will have no impact. At these times, it is tempting to join the supervisee in feeling helpless and angry. If I join the supervisee's feelings, I have done my part to deny our differences: in this case, our different levels of power and authority in the system. In addition, our collective sense of helplessness will inevitably impair our work in the group and our collective ability to consult to the group's internal relations and to its external relations with other parts of the system.

Another reason to consider acting in the larger system on behalf of the supervisory relationship is that such action is a realistic part of being a supervisor. It is, after all, the supervisor's responsibility to create conditions in which supervision can occur. This doesn't mean that the supervisor has *all* the responsibility for attending to the larger-system issues, but it also doesn't mean that he or she has no such responsibility. All too often, especially in academic training, the message transmitted is that it is acceptable and appropriate to divorce supervision, teaching, and research from the work of managing the institution *as if* what happens around the professional work is inconsequential or irrelevant. This has not been my experience.

The last reason for considering active involvement in the dynamics of the larger system is that one's behavior in the larger system can sometimes be a powerful force in the conduct of supervision. If I espouse certain approaches to supervision (training), group dynamics (managing groups), intergroup relations (race and gender relations, labor management relations), yet as a system member remain passive and uninvolved when these issues confront my organization, what message am I passing on to the supervisee who works with me?

COLLABORATION

As I review the reflections and insights in this paper, one of the themes that runs through the discussion of supervisor development is that much of the supervisor's self-work is tied up with the struggle to acknowledge, explore, and work with the differences between the supervisor and the supervisee, differences in hierarchical position, experience, identity, role, and personality. The goal of supervision is to create a relationship in which people who are different can learn from each other and from their differences in particular.

Collaboration can be thought of as a creative connection across difference. In this sense, a supervisory relationship is an example of one of the most difficult forms of collaboration, a connection across differences in experience, power, age (often), and status that aspires to be a creative learning experience for both parties. For the supervisor this collaboration presents challenges around authority, control, and identity that are not easily engaged nor easily navigated. I would argue, however, that these challenges are at the heart not only of the supervisory work, but of the supervisor's professional work as a whole.

ACKNOWLEDGMENTS

I would like to thank Clayton Alderfer, Bill Kahn, Jim Krantz, Marion McCollom, and Sharon Rogolsky for their thoughtful comments on an earlier draft of this chapter.

BIBLIOGRAPHY

Albanese, R. (1975). *Management: Toward Accountability for Performance.* Homewood, Ill.: Irwin.

Alderfer, C. A. (1988). "Gender Relevant Concerns in the Supervisory Process." Unpublished comprehensive examination, University of Massachusetts at Amherst.

Alderfer, Clayton P. (1970). "Understanding Laboratory Education: An Overview." *Monthly Labor Review*, vol. 93, pp. 18–27.

—— (1976a). "Boundary Relations and Organizational Diagnosis." In Meltzer and Wickert (eds.), *Humanizing Organizational Behavior.* Springfield, Ill.: Thomas.

—— (1976b). "Change Processes in Organizations." In Dunnette (ed.), *Handbook of Industrial and Organizational Psychology.* Chicago: Rand McNally.

—— (1977). "Group and Intergroup Relations." In Hackman and Suttle (eds.), *Improving Life at Work: Behavioral Sciences Approaches to Organizational Change.* Santa Monica, Cal.: Goodyear.

—— (1985). "Taking Our Selves Seriously as Researchers." In Berg and Smith (eds.), *The Self in Social Inquiry.* Beverly Hills, Cal.: Sage.

—— (1986). "An Intergroup Perspective on Group Dynamics." In Lorsch (ed.), *Handbook of Organizational Behavior.* Englewood Cliffs, N. J.: Prentice-Hall.

—— (1988). "Teaching Personality and Leadership: A Course on Followership." *Organizational Behavior Teaching Review.* vol. 12, no. 4, pp. 12–33.

Alderfer, Clayton P., and C. L. Cooper (1980). *Advances in Experiential Social Processes*, vol. 2. New York: John Wiley and Sons.

Alderfer, Clayton P., and Edward B. Klein (1978). "Affect, Leadership, and Organizational Boundaries." *Journal of Personality and Social Systems*, vol. 1, pp. 14–33.

Alderfer, Clayton P., and Thomas M. Lodahl (1971). "A Quasi Experiment on the Use of Experiential Methods in the Classroom." *Journal of Applied Behavioral Science*, vol. 7, pp. 43–70.

Alderfer, Clayton P., and Kenwyn K. Smith (1982). "Studying Intergroup Relations Embedded in Organizations." *Administrative Sciences Quarterly*, vol. 27, pp. 35–65.

The American Heritage Dictionary, 2nd College Edition. (1982). Boston: Houghton Mifflin.

Argyris, Chris (1962). *Interpersonal Competence and Organizational Effectiveness.* Homewood, Ill.: Irwin-Dorsey.

—— (1965). "Explorations in Interpersonal Competence," I and II. *Journal of Applied Behavioral Science*, vol. 1, pp. 58–83, 255–269.

——— (1967). "On the Future of Laboratory Education." *Journal of Applied Behavioral Science*, vol. 3, pp. 153–183.

——— (1970). *Intervention Theory and Method*. Reading, Mass.: Addison-Wesley.

Astrachan, Boris M. (1970). "Towards a Social Systems Model of Therapeutic Groups." *Social Psychiatry*, vol. 5, pp. 110–119.

Back, Kurt W. (1972). *Beyond Words: The Story of Sensitivity Training and the Encounter Movement*. New York: Russel Sage.

Baker, F. (ed.) (1973). *Organizational Systems: General System Approaches to Complex Organizations*. Homewood, Ill.: Irwin.

Bales, R. Freed (1950). *Interaction Process Analysis: A Method for the Study of Small Groups*. Reading, Mass.: Addison-Wesley.

——— (1955). "Adaptive and Integrative Changes as Sources of Strain in Social Systems." In Hare, Borgatta, and Bales (eds.), *Small Groups*. New York: Knopf.

——— (1958). "Task Roles and Social Roles in Problem-Solving Groups." In Maccoby et al. (eds.), *Readings in Social Psychology*, 3rd edition. New York: Holt, Rinehart, & Winston.

——— (1970). *Personality and Interpersonal Behavior*. New York: Holt, Rinehart, & Winston.

Barber, W. H. (1987). "Role Analysis Group: Integrating and Applying Workshop Learning." In Reddy and Henderson (eds.), *Training Theory and Practice*. Arlington, Va.: National Training Laboratories.

Bateson, G. (1936). *Naven: A Survey of the Problems Suggested by a Composite Picture of the Culture of a New Guinea Tribe Drawn from Three Points of View*. Cambridge: Cambridge University Press.

——— (1972). *Steps to an Ecology of Mind*. New York: Ballantine.

Behrman, J., and R. Levin (1984). "Are Business Schools Doing Their Job?" *Harvard Business Review*, vol. 62, no. 2.

Bellah, R. N., R. Madsen, W. M. Sullivan, A. Swidler, and S. M. Tipton (1985). *Habits of the Heart*. New York: Harper & Row.

Benne, K. (1964). "History of the T-Group in the Laboratory Setting." In Bradford, Gibb, and Benne (eds.), *T-Group Theory and Laboratory Method*. New York: John Wiley and Sons.

Benne, Kenneth D. (1968). "From Polarization to Paradox." In Bennis, Schein, Steele, and Berlew (eds.), *Interpersonal Dynamics*, 2nd edition. Homewood, Ill.: Dorsey.

Benner, P. (1984). *From Novice to Expert*. Menlo Park, Cal.: Addison-Wesley.

Bennis, Warren G., and Herbert A. Shepard (1956). "A Theory of Group Development." *Human Relations*, vol. 9, pp. 415–437.

Bennis, W. and H. Shepard (1974). "A Theory of Group Development." In Gibbard, Hartman, and Mann (eds.), *Analysis of Groups*. San Francisco: Jossey-Bass.

Bennis, Warren G. (1964). "Patterns and Vicissitudes in T-Group Development." In Bradford, Gibb, and Benne (eds.), *T-Group Theory and Laboratory Method*. New York: John Wiley and Sons.

Berg, David N. (1978). "Intergroup Relations in an Outpatient Psychiatric Facility." Unpublished doctoral dissertation, University of Michigan.

Berg, David N., and Kenwyn K. Smith (eds.) (1985). *The Self In Social Inquiry*. Beverly Hills, Cal.: Sage.

Berg, David N. (1980). "Developing Clinical Field Skills: An Apprenticeship Model." In Alderfer and Cooper (eds.), *Advances in Experiential Social Processes, vol 2*. New York: John Wiley and Sons.

Bion, Wilfred R. (1955). "Language and the Schizophrenic." In Klein, Heimann, and Money-Kyle (eds.), *New Directions in Psychoanalysis*. London: Tavistock.

Bion, Wilfred R. (1975). "Selections from Experiences in Groups." In Colman and Bexton (eds.), *Group Relations Reader. Sausalito*, Cal: GREX.

—— (1956). "Development of Schizophrenic Thought." *International Journal of Psycho-Analysis*, vol. 37.

—— (1961). *Experiences in Groups*. London: Tavistock.

Bolman, Lee G. (1970a). "Laboratory versus Lecture in Training Executives." *Journal of Applied Behavioral Science*, vol. 6, pp. 323–335.

—— (1970b). "Some Effects of Trainers on Their Groups." *Journal of Applied Behavioral Science*, vol. 7, pp. 309–325.

Boorstin, Daniel J. (1983). *The Discoverers*. New York: Random House.

Bradford, D. L. (1980). "A Model of Trainer Development." In Alderfer and Cooper (eds.), *Advances in Experiential Social Processes, vol 2*. New York: John Wiley and Sons.

Bradford, Leland P. (1967). "Biography of an Institution." *Journal of Applied Behavioral Science*, vol. 3, pp. 127–143.

Bradford, Leland P., Jack R. Gibb, and K. D. Benne (eds.) (1964). *T-Group Theory and Laboratory Method*. New York: John Wiley and Sons.

Bridger, H. (1987). "Courses and Working Conferences as Transitional Learning Institutions: A Tavistock Institute Approach to Training." In Reddy and Henderson (eds.), *Training Theory and Practice*. Arlington, Va.: National Training Laboratories.

Brown, E. (1979). "Intimacy and Power." *Voices*, vol. 15, no. 1, pp. 9–14.

Brown, Roger (1965). *Social Psychology*. New York: Free Press.

Bunker, B. B., T. Nochajski, N. McGillicuddy, and D. Bennett (1987). "Designing and Running Training Events: Rules of Thumb for Trainers." In Reddy and Henderson (eds.), *Training Theory and Practice*. Arlington, Va.: National Training Laboratories.

Caplan, R. D., and K. W. Jones (1975). "Effects of Workload, Role Ambiguity, and Type A Personality on Anxiety, Depression, and Heart Rate." *Journal of Applied Psychology*, vol. 60, no. 6, pp. 713–719.

Cartwright, Dorwin, and Alvin Zander (1968). *Group Dynamics: Research and Theory*, 2nd edition. New York: Harper & Row.

Colman, Arthur D., and W. Harold Bexton (eds.) (1975). *Group Relations Reader*. Sausalito, Cal.: GREX.

Colman, A. D., and M. H. Geller (eds.) (1985). *Group Relations Reader, 2*. Washington, D. C.: A. K. Rice Institute.

Conant, James B. (1964). *Two Modes of Thought: My Encounters with Science and Education*. New York: Trident.

Coser, L. (1956). *Functions of Social Conflict*. Glencoe, Ill.: Free Press.

Davis, M. D. (1973). *Intimate Relations*. New York: Free Press.

Diamond, Michael, and Seth Allcorn (1987). "The Psychodynamics of Regression in Work Groups." *Human Relations*, vol. 40, no. 8.

Dicks, H. V. (1963). "Object Relations Theory and Marital Studies." *British Journal of Medical Psychology*, vol. 36, pp. 125–129.

Duff, N. (1980). "Early Adult Development in Women: The Case of the Woman Attorney." Unpublished master's thesis, University of Cincinnati.

Dumas, R. (1975). "The Seed of the Coming Free: An Essay on Black Female Leadership." Unpublished dissertation, Union-Antioch Graduate School.

Dunphy, Dexter (1968). "Phases, Roles, and Myths in Self-Analytic Groups." *Journal of Applied Behavioral Science*, vol. 4, no. 2.

Eddy, William (1985). *The Manager and the Working Group*. New York: Praeger.

Edelson, M. (1985). "The Hermaneutic Turn in the Single Case-Study in Psychoanalysis." In Berg and Smith (eds.), *The Self in Social Inquiry*. Beverly Hills, Cal.: Sage.

Egan, Gerard (1970). *Encounter: Group Processes for Interpersonal Growth*. Belmont, Cal.: Brooks/Cole.

Ekstein, R., and R. S. Wallerstein (1958). *The Teaching and Learning of Psychotherapy*. New York: International Universities Press.

Emery, F. E. and E. L. Trist (1973a). "Causal Texture of Environment." In Baker (ed.), *Organizational Systems: General Systems Approaches to Complex Organizations*. Homewood, Ill.: Irwin.

Emery, F. E., and E. L. Trist (1973b). *Toward a Social Ecology*. New York: Plenum.

Erikson, Erik H. (1958). "The Nature of Clinical Evidence." In Lerner (ed.), *Evidence and Inference*. Glencoe, Ill.: Free Press.

—— (1963). *Childhood and Society*. New York: Norton.

—— (1964). *Insight and Responsibility*. New York: Norton.

—— (1975). *Life History and the Historical Moment*. New York: Norton.

—— (1980). *Identity and the Life Cycle*. New York: Norton.

Etzioni, Amitai (1971). *A Comparative Analysis of Complex Organizations.* New York: Macmillan.

Evan, W. M. (1966). "The Organization Set: Toward a Theory of Interorganizational Relationships." In Thompson (ed.), *Approaches to Organizational Design.* Pittsburgh, Pa.: University of Pittsburgh Press.

Feinberg, G., and R. Shapiro (1980). *Life Beyond Earth.* New York: Morrow.

Frank, J. (1974). "Training and Therapy" In Bradford, Gibb, and Beene (eds.), *T-Group Theory and Laboratory Method.* New York: John Wiley and Sons.

French, John, and Bertram Raven (1959). "The Bases of Social Power". In Cartwright (ed.), *Studies in Social Power.* Ann Arbor, Mich.: Institute for Social Research.

Freud, Anna (1936). *The Ego and the Mechanism of Defense.* New York: International Universities Press.

Freud, Sigmund (1959). *Group Psychology and the Analysis of the Ego.* New York: Norton.

Friedlander, Peter (1975). *The Emergence of a UAW Local, 1936–1939: A Study in Class and Culture.* Pittsburgh, Pa.: University of Pittsburgh Press.

Fromm-Reichmann, F. (1959). "Loneliness." *Psychiatry*, vol. 22, no. 1, pp. 1–5.

Gabarro, John (1983). "Acton-Burnett, Inc. (A) (B) and (C)." 9-484-005, -006, and -007. Boston: Harvard Business School.

Gardner, Howard (1983). *Frames of Mind: The Theory of Multiple Intelligences.* New York: Basic Books.

Gersick, Connie (1988). "Time and Transition in Work Teams: Toward a New Model of Group Development." *Academy of Management Journal*, vol. 31, no. 1.

Gibb, Jack R. (1972). "The Search for With-ness: A New Look at Interdependence." In Dyer (ed.), *Modern Theory and Method in Group Training.* New York: Van Nostrand Reinhold.

Gibbard, G. (1974). "Individuation, Fusion, and Role Specialization." In Gibbard, Hartman, and Mann (eds.), *Analysis of Groups.* San Francisco: Jossey-Bass.

Gibbard, Graham, John Hartman, and Richard Mann (1974a). "The Individual and the Group." In Gibbard, Hartman, and Mann (eds.), *Analysis of Groups.* San Francisco: Jossey-Bass.

Gibbard, Graham, John Hartman, and Richard Mann (1974b). "Group Process and Development." In Gibbard, Hartman, and Mann (eds.), *Analysis of Groups.* San Francisco: Jossey-Bass.

Gibbard, Graham, John Hartman, and Richard Mann (1974c). "The Dynamics of Leadership." In Gibbard, Hartman, and Mann (eds.), *Analysis of Groups.* San Francisco: Jossey-Bass.

Gibbard, Graham S., John J. Hartman, and Richard D. Mann (eds.) (1974d). *Analysis of Groups*. San Francisco: Jossey-Bass.

Gibbard, Graham S. (1975). "Bion's Group Psychology: A Reconsideration." Unpublished manuscript, West Haven Veterans Administration Hospital, West Haven, Conn.

Gillette, Jonathon H. (1985). "History in the Here-and-Now." In Berg and Smith (eds.), *Exploring Clinical Methods for Social Research*. Beverly Hills, Cal.: Sage.

Gilligan, Carol (1982). *In a Different Voice*. Cambridge, Mass.: Harvard University Press.

Gilmore, T., and J. Krantz. "The Splitting of Management and Leadership as a Social Defense." Forthcoming in *Human Relations*.

Golden, William P. (1972). "On Becoming a Trainer." In Dyer (ed.), *Modern Theory and Method in Group Training*. New York: Van Nostrand Reinhold.

Gould, Roger (1978). *Transformations: Growth and Change in Adult Life*. New York: Simon and Schuster.

Greenspan, I. S., and F. W. Mannis (1974). "A Model for Brief Intervention with Couples Based on Projective Identification." *American Journal of Psychiatry*, vol. 10, no. 131, pp.1103–1106.

Hackman, J. Richard, and Greg Oldham (1980). *Work Redesign*. Reading, Mass.: Addison-Wesley.

Hackman, R. (1985). "On Seeking One's Own Clinical Voice: A Personal Account." In Berg and Smith (eds.), *Exploring Clinical Methods for Social Research*. Beverly Hills, Cal.: Sage.

Hall, Edward T. (1973). *The Silent Language*. Garden City, New York: Anchor Press/Doubleday.

Hartman, J. J., and G. S. Gibbard (1974). "A Note on Fantasy Themes in the Evolution of Group Culture." In Gibbard, Hartman and Mann (eds.), *Analysis of Groups*. San Francisco: Jossey-Bass.

Hayles, R. V. (1978). "Psychological Health among Culturally Different Families." Presented at 4th Congress of the International Association of Cross Cultural Psychology, Munich.

Hayward, J. (ed.) (1949). *John Donne: Complete Poetry and Selected Prose*. London: Nonesuch.

Hearn, J., and W. Parkin (1987). *"Sex at Work": The Power and Paradox of Organizational Sexuality*. New York: St. Martin's.

Herbert, James I. (1985). "Adult Psychosocial Development: The Evolution of the Individual Life Structure of Black Male Entrepreneurs." Unpublished doctoral dissertation. Yale University.

Hess, A. K. (1986). "Growth in Supervision: Stages of Supervisee and Supervisor Development." In Kaslow (ed.), *Supervision and Training: Models, Dilemmas, and Challenges*. New York: Haworth.

Hodgson, Richard C., Daniel J. Levinson, and Abraham Zalenik (1965). *The Executive Role Constellation: An Analysis of Personality and Role Relations in Management*. Boston: Division of Research, Harvard Business School.

Hofstadter, D. R. (1980). *Gödel, Escher, Bach: An Eternal Golden Braid*. New York: Vintage.

Homans, G. (1950). *The Human Group*. New York: Harcourt, Brace.

Hughes, P., and G. Brecht (1975). *Vicious Circles and Infinity*. New York: Penguin.

Jaffe, D. S. (1968). "The Mechanism of Projection: Its Dual Role in Object Relations." *International Journal of Psychoanalysis*, vol. 49, pp. 662–677.

Janis, Irving. (1972). *Victims of Group Think*. Boston: Houghton Mifflin.

Jaques, E. (1974). "Social Systems as a Defense Against Persecutory and Depressive Anxiety." In Gibbard, Hartman, and Mann (eds.), *Analysis of Groups*. San Francisco: Jossey-Bass.

Jaques, E. (1955). "Social Systems as a Defense Against Persecutory and Depressive Anxiety." In Klein, Hermann, and Money-Kyle (eds.), *New Directions in Psychoanalysis: The Significance of Infant Conflict in the Pattern of Adult Behavior*. New York: Basic Books.

Jenkins, D. C. (1971). "Psychologic and Social Precursors of Coronary Disease." *New England Journal of Medicine*, vol. 284, pp. 224–266, 307–317.

Johnson, D. W., and F. P. Johnson (1975). *Joining Together: Group Theory and Group Skills*. Englewood Cliffs, N. J.: Prentice-Hall.

Kanter, Rosabeth M. (1977). "Some Effects of Proportions on Group Life: Skewed Sex Ratios and Responses to Token Women." *Journal of Sociology*, vol. 82, pp. 965–990.

Kaplan, Abraham (1964). *The Conduct of Inquiry: Methodology for Behavioral Science*. San Francisco: Chandler.

Kaplan, Robert E. (1982). "The Dynamics of Injury in Encounter Groups: Power, Splitting, and the Mismanagement of Resistance." *International Journal of Group Psychotherapy*, vol. 32, pp. 163–187.

——— (1983). "The Perils of Intensive Management Training and How to Avoid Them." *Professional Psychology*, vol. 14, pp. 756–770.

Kaplan, Robert E., Steven L. Obert, and William R. Van Buskirk (1980). "The Etiology of Encounter Group Casualties: 'Second Facts.'" *Human Relations*, vol. 33, pp. 131–148.

Kaplan, Sidney, and M. Roman (1963). "Phases of Development in an Adult Therapy Group." *International Journal of Group Psychotherapy*, vol. 13.

Kaplan, S. (1974). "Therapy Groups and Training Groups: Similarities and Differences." In Gibbard, Hartman, and Mann (eds.) *Analysis of Groups*. San Francisco: Jossey-Bass.

Karpman, D. (1968). "Script Drama Analysis." *Transactional Analysis Bulletin*, vol. 26.

Kaslow, F. W. (1986). "Supervision, Consultation, and Staff Training: Creative Teaching/Learning Processes in the Mental Health Profession." In Kaslow (ed.), *Supervision and Training: Models, Dilemmas, and Challenges*. New York: Haworth.

Katz, Daniel, and Robert L. Kahn (1978). *The Social Psychology of Organizations*, 2nd edition. New York: John Wiley and Sons.

Kernberg, O. (1980). *Internal World and External Reality*. New York: Jason Aronson.

Klein, Edward B. (1980). "Change Is Normal: Adult Development Theory and Research with Clinical Applications." In Karoly and Steffen (eds.), *Improving the Long-Term Effects of Psychotherapy: Models of Durable Outcome*. New York: Gardner.

Klein, Edward B., and Boris M. Astrachan (1971). "Learning Groups and Study Groups." *The Journal of Applied Behavioral Science*, vol. 7, no. 6.

—— (1972). "Learning in Groups: A Comparison of Study and T-Groups." *Journal of Applied Behavioral Science*, vol. 7, no. 6.

Klein, Melanie (1932). *The Psycho-Analysis of Children*. New York: Delta.

—— (1946). "Notes on Some Schizoid Mechanisms." *International Journal of Psycho-Analysis*, vol. 27, pp. 99–110.

—— (1955). "On Identification." In Klein, Heimann, and Money-Kyle (eds.), *New Directions in Psychoanalysis*. London: Tavistock.

—— (1959). "Our Adult World and Its Roots in Infancy." *Human Relations*, vol. 12, pp. 291–303.

—— (1960). *Our Adult World and Its Roots in Infancy*. London: Tavistock.

—— (1983). "Some Theoretical Conclusions Regarding the Emotional Life of the Infant." In Riviere (ed.), *Developments in Psycho Analysis*. New York: DaCapo.

—— (1985). "Our Adult World and Its Roots in Infancy." In Colman and Geller (eds.), *Group Relations Reader 2*. Sausalito, Cal: GREX.

—— (1986). *The Selected Melanie Klein* (ed. Mitchell). New York: Free Press.

Klein, Melanie, and Susan Isaacs (eds.) (1982). *Developments in Psychoanalysis*. New York: Da Capo.

Klein, Melanie, and Joan Riviere (1964). *Love, Hate, and Reparation*. New York: Norton.

Kohlberg, Lawrence (1984). *The Psychology of Moral Development*, vol. 2. New York: Harper & Row.

Kohut, Heinz (1977). *The Restoration of the Self*. New York: International Universities Press.

Kolb, D. A. (1984). *Experiential Learning: Experience as the Source of Learning and Development*. Englewood Cliffs, N. J.: Prentice-Hall.

Kolb, D. A., I. M. Rubin, and J. M. McIntyre (1974). *Learning and Problem-Solving in Organizational Psychology: An Experiential Approach*. Englewood Cliffs, N. J.: Prentice-Hall.

Kovel, J. (1970). *White Racism: A Psychohistory*. New York: Pantheon.

Kram, Kathy E. (1983). "Phases of the Mentor Relationship." *Academy of Management Journal*, vol. 26, pp. 608–625.

Kretch, D., R. S. Crutchfield, and E. L. Ballachey (1962). *Individual in Society: A Textbook of Social Psychology*. NewYork: McGraw-Hill.

Kuhn, Thomas S. (1962). *The Structure of Scientific Revolutions*. Chicago: University of Chicago Press.

Lacoursier, Roy (1980). *The Life Cycle of Groups*. New York: Human Sciences Press.

Lasch, C. (1979). *The Culture of Narcissism*. New York: Norton.

Laughlin, H. P. (1970). *The Ego and Its Defenses*. New York: Appleton-Century-Crofts.

Lawrence, P., and J. Lorsch (1967). *Organizations and Environment*. Boston: Harvard Business School Press.

Le Bon, G. (1895). *The Crowd*. New York: Macmillan.

Lebowitz, Z. B., C. Farren, and B. L. Kaye (1986). *Designing Career Development Systems*. San Francisco: Jossey-Bass.

Levine, R. A., and D. T. Campbell (1972). *Ethnocentrism*. New York: John Wiley and Sons.

Levinson, Daniel J., C. M. Darrow, Edward. B. Klein, M. H. Levinson, and J. B. McKee (1978). *The Seasons of a Man's Life*. New York: Ballantine.

Lewin, Kurt (1951). *Field Theory in Social Science*. New York: Harper & Row.

Lidz, T. (1968). *The Person*. New York: Basic Books.

Lieberman, Morton A., Irvin D. Yalom, and Matthew B. Miles (1973). *Encounter Groups: First Facts*. New York: Basic Books.

Lifton, Robert (1983). *The Life of the Self*. New York: Basic Books.

Likert, R. (1967). *The Human Organization*. New York: McGraw-Hill.

Lippitt, R. O. (1949). *Training in Community Relations*. New York: Harper and Bros.

Lippitt, R. O., and E. Schindler-Rainman (1975). "Designing for Participative Learning and Changing." In Benne, Bradford, Gibb, and Lippitt (eds.), *The Laboratory Method of Changing and Learning*. Palo Alto, Cal.: Science and Behavior Books.

Lott, A. J., and B. E. Lott (1965). "Group Cohesiveness as Interpersonal Attraction: A Review of Relationships with Antecedent and Consequent Variables." *Psychological Bulletin*, vol. 64, pp. 259–302.

Louis, Meryl (1980). "Surprise and Sensemaking: What Newcomers Experience in Entering Unfamiliar Organizational Settings." *Administrative Sciences Quarterly*, vol. 25.

Luft, Joseph (1970). *Group Process: An Introduction to Group Dynamics.* Palo Alto, Cal.: Mayfield.

Lundgren, D. C. (1971). "Trainer Style and Patterns of Group Development." *Journal of Applied Behavioral Science*, vol. 7, pp. 689–708.

Mahler, M. S. (1972). "On the First Three Subphases of the Separation-Individuation Process." *International Journal of Psychoanalysis*, vol. 53, pp. 333–338.

Malin, A., and J. S. Grotstein (1966). "Projective Identification in the Therapeutic Process." *International Journal of Psycho-Analysis*, vol. 47, pp. 26–31.

Malone, B. (1981). "The Relationship of a Black Female Administrator's Mentoring Experiences and Career Satisfaction." Unpublished doctoral dissertation, University of Cincinnati.

Mann, Richard D. (1966). "The Development of the Member-Trainer Relationships in Self-Analytic Study Groups." *Human Relations*, vol. 19, pp. 85–115.

—— (1975). "Winners, Losers, and the Search for Equality in Groups." In Cooper (ed.), *Theories of Group Processes*. London: Wiley.

Mann, Richard D., with Graham S. Gibbard and John J. Hartman (1967). *Interpersonal Styles and Group Development*. New York: John Wiley and Sons.

—— (1983). *Leaders We Deserve*. Oxford: Basil Blackwell.

McCollom, Marion (1987). "Subcultures and Stories: Reflections of a Multicultural Reality in Organizations." Unpublished doctoral dissertation, Yale University School of Organization and Management.

Menzies, I. (1961). "The Functioning of Social Systems as a Defense Against Anxiety." *Human Relations*, vol. 13.

Menzies, I. (1975). "A Case-Study in the Functioning of Social Systems as a Defense Against Anxiety." In Colman and Bexton (eds.), *Group Relations Reader*. Sausalito, Cal: GREX.

Merton, Robert K. (1967). "The Bearing of Sociological Theory on Empirical Research and the Bearing of Empirical Research on Sociological Theory." In *Social Theory and Social Structure*. New York: Free Press.

Miles, Matthew B. (1975). *Learning to Work in Groups*. New York: Teachers College Press.

Miller, Eric J. (1959). "Technology, Territory, and Time: The Internal Differentiation of Complex Production Systems." *Human Relations*, vol. 12, pp. 243–272.

Miller, Eric J., and A. Kenneth Rice (1967). *Systems of Organization: The Control of Task and Sentient Boundaries*. London: Tavistock.

Miller, Eric, and A. Kenneth Rice (1975). "Selections from 'Systems of Organization'." In Colman and Bexton (eds.), *Group Relations Reader*. Sausalito, Cal: GREX.

Miller, J. C. (1974). "Aspects of Tavistock Consultation." Unpublished doctoral dissertation, Yale University.

Miller, James G. (1978). *Living Systems*. New York: McGraw-Hill.

Mills, Theodore M. (1964). *Group Transformation: An Analysis of a Learning Group*. Englewood Cliffs, N. J.: Prentice-Hall.

―――― (1967). *The Sociology of Small Groups*. Englewood Cliffs, N.J.: Prentice-Hall.

Morgan, G. (1986). *Images of Organization*. Beverly Hills, Cal.: Sage.

Mulligan, T. (1987). "The Two Cultures in Business Education." *Academy of Management Review*, vol. 12, no. 4.

Murray, M. M. (1982). "The Middle Years of Life of Middle Class Black Men." Unpublished doctoral dissertation. University of Cincinnati.

Nemiroff, R. A., and C. A. Colarusso (1985). *The Race Against Time: Psychotherapy and Psychoanalysis in the Second Half of Life*. New York: Plenum.

Newcomb, T. M. (1961). *The Acquaintance Process*. New York: Holt, Rinehart, & Winston.

Nobles, W. W. (1974). "Africanity: Its Role in Black Families." *The Black Scholar*, vol. 5, no. 9, pp. 10–17.

―――― (1976). "Formulative and Empirical Study of Black Families." *Black Family Project*. San Francisco: Westside Community Health Center.

O'Day, R. (1974). "The T-Group Trainer: A Study in Conflict in the Exercise of Authority." In Gibbard, Hartman, and Mann (eds.), *Analysis in Groups*. San Francisco: Jossey-Bass.

Olmsted, M. S., and A. P. Hare (1978). *The Small Group*. New York: Random House.

Oshry, Barry (1978). *Power and Systems Laboratory in Organization Behavior*. Boston: Power and Systems, Inc.

Perls, F. (1970). *Gestalt Therapy*. New York: Basic Books.

Peters, T., and R. Waterman (1982). *In Search of Excellence: Lessons from America's Best Run Companies*. New York: Harper & Row.

Piaget, Jean (1963). *The Origins of Intelligence in Children*. New York: Norton.

―――― (1973). *The Child and Reality: Problems of Genetic Psychology*. New York: Grossman.

Porter, L. C. (1987). "Game Schmame! What Have I Learned?" In Reddy and Henderson (eds.), *Training Theory and Practice*. Arlington, Va.: National Training Laboratories.

Quinn, R. F. (1977). "Coping with Cupid: The Formation, Impact, and Management of Romantic Relationships in Organizations." *Administrative Science Quarterly*, vol. 22, pp. 122–145.

Redlich, F. C. and Boris Astrachan (1975). "Group Dynamics Training." In Colman and Bexton (eds.), Group Relations Reader. Sausalito, Cal: GREX.

Redl, F. (1942). "Group Emotion and Leadership." Psychiatry, vol.5, pp. 573–596.

Reed, B. D. (1976). "Organizational Role Analysis." In Cooper (ed.), Developing Social Skills in Managers. London: Macmillan.

Reed, B. D., J. Hutton, and J. Bazulgette (1978). Freedom to Study: Requirements of Overseas Students in the United Kingdom. London: Overseas Student Trust.

Rice, A. Kenneth (1963). The Enterprise and Its Environment. London: Tavistock.

——— (1965). Learning for Leadership: Interpersonal and Intergroup Relationships. London: Tavistock.

——— (1969). "Individual, Group, and Intergroup Processes." Human Relations, vol. 22, pp. 565–584.

Ringwald, John W. (1974). "An Investigation of Group Reaction to Central Figures." In Gibbard, Hartman and Mann (eds.) Analysis of Groups. San Francisco: Jossey-Bass.

Rioch, Margaret J. (1970). "The Work of Wilfred Bion on Groups." Psychiatry, vol. 33, no. 2, pp. 55–56.

——— (1971). "All We Like Sheep—(Isaiah 53:6): Followers and Leaders." Psychiatry, vol. 34, pp. 258–273.

——— (1975). "Group Relations: Rationale and Technique." In Colman and Bexton (eds.), Group Relations Reader. Sausalito, Cal: GREX.

——— (1977). "The A. K. Rice Group Relations Conference as a Reflection of Society." The Journal of Personality and Social Systems, vol. 1, pp. 1–16.

Roberts, P., and P. M. Newton (1987). "Levinsonian Studies of Women's Adult Development." Psychology and Aging, vol. 2, pp. 154–163.

Rosenfeld, A., and E. Stark (1987). "The Prime of Our Lives." Psychology Today, vol. 21, pp. 62–72.

Rosenfeld, H. W. (1952). "Notes on the Psychoanalysis of the Super-Ego Conflict of an Acute Schizophrenic Patient." International Journal of Psycho-Analysis, vol. 33.

——— (1954). "Considerations Regarding the Psycho-Analytic Approach to Acute and Chronic Schizophrenia." International Journal of Psycho-Analysis, vol. 35.

Ross, Raymond (1989). Small Groups in Organizational Settings. Englewood Cliffs, N. J.: Prentice-Hall.

Scheidlinger, S. (1964). "Identification, the Sense of Belonging and of Identity in Small Groups." International Journal of Group Psychotherapy, vol. 14, pp. 291–306.

————— (1968). "The Concept of Regression in Group Psychotherapy." *International Journal of Group Psychotherapy*, vol. 18, pp.13–20.

Schein, Edgar (1969). *Process Consultation*. Reading, Mass.: Addison-Wesley.

————— (1980). *Organizational Psychology*. Englewood Cliffs, N. J.: Prentice-Hall.

————— (1985). *Organizational Culture and Leadership*. San Francisco: Jossey-Bass.

Schein, Edgar and Warren G. Bennis (1965). *Personal and Organizational Change through Group Methods*. New York: John Wiley and Sons.

Schermer, V. L. (1985). "Beyond Bion: The Basic Assumption States Revisited." In Pines (ed.), *Bion and Group Psychotherapy*. London: Routledge and Kegan Paul.

Schon, D. A. (1979). "Generative Metaphor: A Perspective on Problem-Setting in Social Policy." in Ortony (ed.), *Metaphor and Thought*. Cambridge: Cambridge University Press.

————— (1983). *The Reflective Practitioner*. New York: Basic Books.

Schutz, William C. (1958). *FIRO: A Three-Dimensional Theory of Interpersonal Behavior*. New York: Holt and Rinehart.

————— (1967). *Joy: Expanding Human Awareness*. New York: Grove.

Segal, H. (1964). *Introduction to the Works of Melanie Klein*. New York: Basic Books.

Selvini Palazzoli, M., L. Boscolo, G. Cecchin, and G. Prata (1978). *Paradox and Counterparadox*. New York: Jason Aronson.

Selznick, P. (1957). *Leadership in Administration*. Evanston, Ill.: Row, Peterson.

Sennett, R. (1977). *The Fall of Public Man*. New York: Knopf.

Shadish, W. R. (1984). "Intimate Behavior and the Assessment of Benefits in Clinical Groups." *Small Group Behavior*, vol. 15, pp. 204–221.

Shambaugh, P. (1978). "The Development of the Small Group." *Human Relations*, vol. 31, no. 3, pp. 283–295.

Sherwood, M. (1964). "Bion's Experiences in Groups: A Critical Evaluation." *Human Relations*, vol. 17, pp. 114–130.

Simmons, V. (1985). "Reconstructing an Organization's History: Systematic Distortion in Retrospective Data." In Berg and Smith (eds.), *The Self in Social Inquiry*. Beverly Hills, Cal.: Sage.

Singer, David L., Boris M. Astrachan, Lawrence J. Gould, and Edward B. Klein (1975). "Boundary Management in Psychological Work with Groups." *Journal of Applied Behavioral Science*, vol. 11, pp. 137–176.

Slater, Philip E. (1966). *Microcosm: Structural, Psychological, and Religious Evolution in Groups*. New York: John Wiley and Sons.

Small, Albion (1905). *General Sociology*. Chicago: University of Chicago Press.

Smith, Kenwyn K. (1977). "An Intergroup Perspective on Individual Behavior." In Hackman, Lawler, and Porter (eds.), *Perspective on Behavior in Organizations*. New York: McGraw-Hill.

——— (1982). *Groups in Conflict: Prisons in Disguise*. Dubuque, Iowa: Kendall/Hunt.

——— (1989). "The Movement of Conflict in Organizations: The Joint Dynamics of Splitting and Triangulation." *Administrative Sciences Quarterly*, vol. 34, no. 1.

Smith, Kenwyn, and David N. Berg (1987). *Paradoxes of Group Life: Understanding Conflict, Paralysis, and Movement in Group Dynamics*. San Francisco: Jossey-Bass.

Srivastva, Suresh, and Frank Barrett (1988). "The Transforming Nature of Metaphors in Group Development: A Study in Group Theory." *Human Relations*, vol. 41, no. 1.

Stewart, Wendy (1976). "A Psychosocial Study of the Formation of the Early Adult Life Structure in Women." Unpublished doctoral dissertation, Columbia University.

Stock, Dorothy, and Morton A. Lieberman (1974). "Methodological Issues in the Assessment of Total-Group Phenomena in Group Therapy." In Gibbard, Hartman, and Mann (eds.), *Analysis of Groups*. San Francisco: Jossey-Bass.

Stoltenberg, C. D., and U. Delworth (1987). *Supervising Counselors and Therapists: A Development Approach*. San Francisco: Jossey-Bass.

Sullivan, Harry Stack (1953). *The Interpersonal Theory of Psychiatry*. New York: Norton.

——— (1954). *The Psychiatric Interview*. New York: Norton.

Tarachow, S. (1963). *Introduction to Psychotherapy*. New York: International Universities Press.

Thibaut, J. W., and H. H. Kelly (1959). *The Social Psychology of Groups*. New York: John Wiley and Sons.

Thomas, David (1986). "An Intraorganizational Analysis of Black and White Patterns of Sponsorship and the Dynamics of Cross-Racial Mentoring." Unpublished doctoral dissertation, Yale University School of Organization and Management.

Tillich, Paul (1952). *The Courage To Be*. New Haven, Conn.: Yale University Press.

Trist, E. L. (1985). "Working with Bion in the 1940s: The Group Decade." In Pines (ed.), *Bion and Group Psychotherapy*. London: Routledge and Kegan Paul.

Trist, E. L., and K. W. Bramforth (1951). "Some Social and Psychological Consequences of Goal-Getting." *Human Relations*, vol. 4, pp. 3–38.

Trist, E. L., and C. Stofer (1959). *Explorations in Group Relations*. Leicester, England: Leicester University Press.

Tuckman, Barry W. (1965). "Developmental Sequences in Small Groups." *Psychological Bulletin*, vol. 54, pp. 229–249.

Tuckman, Barry W., and M. Jensen (1977). "Stages of Small Group Development Revisited." *Group and Organizational Studies*, vol. 2.

Turquet, P. M. (1974). "Leadership: The Individual and the Group." In Gibbard, Hartmann, and Mann (eds.), *Analysis of Groups*. San Francisco: Jossey-Bass.

Van Steenberg, Vicki (1988). "Organizational Exits." Unpublished doctoral dissertation, Yale University School of Organization and Management.

Van Steenberg, Vicki, and Jonathon H. Gillette (1984). "Teaching Group Dynamics with a Group-on-Group Design." *Organizational Behavior Teaching Review*, vol. 9, no. 3, pp. 14–29.

Von Glassersfeld, Ernst (1984). "An Introduction to Radical Constructivism." In Watzlawick (ed.) *The Invented Reality*. New York: Norton.

Wade, C., and C. Tavris (1987). *Psychology*. New York: Harper & Row.

Walton, R. E. (1969). *Interpersonal Peacemaking: Confrontation and Third Party Consultation*. Reading, Mass.: Addison-Wesley.

Ware, James (1977). "Managing a Task Force." 478–002, Boston: Harvard Business School.

Webb, Eugene J., Donald T. Campbell, Richard D. Schwartz, and Lee Sechrest (1966). *Unobtrusive Measures: Nonreactive Research in the Social Sciences*. Chicago: Rand McNally.

Webster's Ninth New Collegiate Dictionary (1983). Springfield, Mass.: Merriam.

Weeks, G. R., and L. L'Abate (1982). *Paradoxical Psychotherapy: Theory and Practice with Individuals, Couples, and Families*. New York: Brunner/Mazel.

Weir, J., and S. Weir (1978). Personal communication.

Weiss, A. G. (1987). "Privacy and Intimacy." *Journal of Human Psychology*, vol. 27, no. 1, pp. 118–125.

Wells, L. (1978a). "Assessing the Quality of Student Life: A New Model." Working paper no. 18, Yale University School of Management.

―――― (1978b). "Open System Theory Applied to the Management of Organizations: Special Application to Drug Prevention Programs." In Bauman (ed.), *Prevention: A Course for Local Program Survival—Resource Manual*. Rosslyn, Va.: National Drug Abuse Training Center.

―――― (1978c). "CARS—(Class, Age, Race, and Sex) Study Dynamics of a Microcosm: A Group-Level in Intergroup Laboratory." Working paper, Yale University.

―――― (1980). "Group-as-a-Whole." In Alderfer and Cooper (eds.), *Advances in Experiential Learning, vol 2*. New York: John Wiley and Sons.

Whitaker, Dorothy Stock, and Morton A. Lieberman (1964). *Psychotherapy through the Group Process.* New York: Atherton.

White, R. K. (1959). "Motivation Reconsidered: The Concept of Competence." *Psychological Review,* vol. 66, no. 5, pp. 297–333.

White, Robert W. (1963). "Identification as a Process of Development." In "Ego and Reality in Psychoanalytic Theory: A Proposal Regarding Independent Ego Energies." *Psychological Issues,* vol. 3, pp. 95–119.

Whitman, Roy (1964) "Psychodynamic Principles Underlying T-Group Processes." In Gradford, Gibb, and Benne (eds.), *T-Group Theory and Laboratory Method.* New York: John Wiley and Sons.

Winnicott, D. (1953). "Transitional Objects and Transitional Phenomena." *International Journal of Psycho-Analysis,* vol. 34, part 2.

Winter, S. (1974). "Interracial Dynamics in Self-Analytic Groups." In Gibbard, Hartmann, and Mann (eds.), *Analysis of Groups.* San Francisco: Jossey-Bass.

Yalom, Irvin D. (1970). *The Theory and Practice of Group Psychotherapy.* New York: Basic Books.

Zinner, J. (1976). "Projective Identification in Marital Interaction." In Grunebaum (ed.), *Contemporary Marriage: The Structure and Dynamics of Marriage.* Boston: Little, Brown.

Zinner, J., and R. Shapiro (1972). "Projective Identification as a Mode of Projection and Behavior in Families of Adolescents." *International Journal of Psycho-Analysis,* vol. 53, pp. 523–530.

INDEX

Abstract conceptualization (AC), 165

Active experimentation (AE), 165

Adult development theory applied to group development theory, 243
applied to group dynamics instruction, 237–38, 243

A. K. Rice Institute, experiential learning tradition at, 4, 6, 159, 223

Alderfer, C. A., 103

Alderfer, C. P., 5, 7, 36, 37, 38, 39, 52, 54, 104, 120, 152, 163, 190, 196, 200, 201, 202, 208, 209, 210, 211, 213, 237, 261, 263, 264, 320, 324, 333

Allcorn, S., 41

Altruistic surrender, 61

Ambivalence in group members, 56–57, 59, 68, 173–81
caused by group formation, 40–41
grief/relief at group termination and, 174–78

Analysis in off-line learning context, 25–30

Anger at group termination, 180–81, 182

Anxiety in group members, 56–58
caused by group formation, 40–42
involved in management education, 231–32
paradox of boundaries and, 116–17
rejection of leadership due to, 47
role differentiation and, 70
testing by moving toward, 23–24

Anxiety in leaders
gender dynamics, sexual assault issues, and, 289–93

self-authorization and, 312–13

Application work, 155–70
essential elements of, 162–67
experiential learning theory and, 164–67
group development and, 167–69
organization/human behavior theory and, 162–64
historical roots of, 158–59
introduction to, 156–57
location of, in course designs, 161–62
nature of experiential work and, 160–61

Argyris, Chris, 53, 194, 195, 199, 208, 214, 270

Astrachan, B. M., 39, 52, 53, 54, 194, 237, 296, 297, 303

Authority. *See also* Leader(s) of groups
dynamics of, 267–75
factors shaping roles and, 272–75
leadership style/roles and, 267–72
formal designation in role of, 300–301
formal vs. informal, 299–300
individual's experience of having, 259–62
intimacy and, 97, 102–3
for learning in supervisor development, 322–24

Authorization of leader(s), 295–316
through authorizing group members, 314–15
background discussion of, 297–300
conceptual issues affecting authorization in, 299–300